This card just may

The Princeton Review is giving away a

FREE
SAT, GMAT, GRE, LSAT, or MCAT course
every other month.

We'll choose one lucky winner who will be entitled to a free course. Interested? Simply fill out the card on the right and mail it back to us.

For more information about **Princeton Review** courses and products, call **(800) REVIEW-6.**

Entries must be received by August 15, 1999. You don't need to buy this book to enter. See official rules on reverse side.

W9-AZP-085

Y̶o̶u̶ ... in the drawing for a ~~FREE~~ course.

○ Send me FREE information on the following Princeton Review courses _____

○ Also, please send me FREE information about paying for school (including student loan application/information.)

Name: _____

Address: _____

_____

City: _____ State: _____ Zip: _____

Is this address ○ School ○ Work ○ Home

Phone: _____

E-mail address: _____

School: _____ Graduation Year: _____

Best Business Schools   SABU9

SPECIAL STUDENT RATES!

If you're thinking about returning to school to receive your MBA, Business Week is your complete source for in-depth news and analysis on issues affecting your professional and personal life.

Order now to receive our Best Business School issue coming this Fall! Plus you get Business Week's award-winning news and analysis on:

- **Product marketing**
- **Management trends**
- **International business**
- **World finance**
- **Contemporary economics**
- **Technology**

Please detach and mail the card below.

☐ **YES,** send me a subscription to Business Week at the **SPECIAL STUDENT RATE.** I'll save over 80% off the newsstand price. As a paid subscriber, I will gain **FREE ACCESS** to the Business Week web site, **www.businessweek.com.**

CHECK ONE:
☐ **51 weeks for only $35.00**
☐ **27 weeks for only $19.95**

_____
Name (please print)
Send Business Week to the address below.
☐ home ☐ school

_____
Street

_____
City   State   Zip

_____
University   Graduation Date

_____
Phone

_____
Email Address

☐ **Bill me.** ☐ **Payment enclosed. (If paying by check, please enclose this card in an envelope.)**

Please allow 4-6 weeks for shipment of first issue. Offer good in U.S. only. Prices and terms are subject to change. Local sales tax, if applicable, will be added to your order.

BusinessWeek
Most Read. Best Read. Worldwide.

TPR9855

OFFICIAL RULES:

We will conduct a random drawing on the fifteenth of every other month from all cards we've received between the last drawing and midnight of the day before. We'll hold these drawings through August 15, 1999. The winner of each drawing will receive (at no fee) an SAT, LSAT, GMAT, GRE or MCAT course at any Princeton Review location, each with an approximate value of $695. Your odds of winning depend upon the number of entries received. If you win, you must take your free course within six months of notification; the free course is not transferable except to immediate family members. This promotion is not open to employees of The Princeton Review or Random House and is, of course, void where prohibited by law. All taxes are the sole responsibility of the winners. No purchase is necessary: if the card that's supposed to be attached has already been ripped out, or if you're not buying this book (big mistake), you may enter by sending your own postcard with your name, address, and school to The Princeton Review, 2315 Broadway, New York, NY 10024-4332. You may also write us to get a list of prize winners. By the way, we're not responsible for lost, misdirected, illegible, or mutilated entries.

THE
PRINCETON
REVIEW

Get all the info you need!

Here is the only B-School guide that delivers the latest ratings of the schools by the people who know them best: more than 14,000 recent graduates and corporate recruiters. The new updated edition features:

- Coverage of the top 25 B-schools plus 25 runners-up
- New data on how the best schools compare
- Insider tips on taking the GMAT prep courses and finessing the application process
- Complete E-mail and Web site addresses
- Free application software from Multi-App

Available for $16.95 in bookstores everywhere or by calling 1-800-2MCGRAW.

BusinessWeek
GUIDE TO
SIXTH EDITION
THE BEST BUSINESS SCHOOLS

Includes
Princeton
Review
Application
Software

Ranks the Top 25 Business Schools in the United States

Includes the Top 25 Runners-Up

Tips to Get Into the Best MBA Programs

Rates Application Software Programs

How to Finesse Your Interview

"THE BIBLE FOR PROSPECTIVE STUDENTS."

Sixth Edition

THE PRINCETON REVIEW

THE BEST 75

BUSINESS

SCHOOLS

1999 EDITION

THE PRINCETON REVIEW

THE BEST 75
BUSINESS
SCHOOLS

1999 EDITION

BY NEDDA GILBERT

Random House, Inc.
New York

www.randomhouse.com

Princeton Review Publishing, L.L.C.
2315 Broadway, Second Floor
New York, NY 10024
E-mail: info@review.com

ISSN: 1067-2141
ISBN: 0-375-75200-5

Editor: Gretchen Feder
Production Editor: Amy Bryant and Kristen Azzara
Designer: Meher Khambata
Production Coordinator: Iam Williams

Manufactured in the United States of America on partially recycled paper.

9 8 7 6 5 4 3 2 1

1999 Edition

Table of Contents

PART THREE: THE SCHOOLS

Acknowledgments

This book absolutely would not have been possible without the help of my husband, Paul. With each edition of this guide, his insights and support have been invaluable—this book continues to be as much his as it is mine. That said, I also need to thank my four-year-old daughter, Micaela, and my newest addition, Alexa, for enduring all my time immersed in this project.

The following people were also instrumental in the completion of this book: My father, Dr. Irving Buchen, for his razor's-edge editorial suggestions; David Ro Hall—proofreader; Meher Khambata, who designed this book; Rob Zopf, for his tireless phone interviews with business school administrators; Evan Schnittman, Christine Chung, Tom Meltzer, Amy Bryant, Iam Williams, Karl Engkvist, Jens Stephan, Gretchen Feder, and Jackie Jendras for putting all the pieces together; Alicia Ernst and John Katzman, for giving me the chance to write this book; and to the folks at Random House, who helped this project reach fruition. Special thanks go to all those section-A mates, HBS-92, who lent a hand and provided valuable feedback. Likewise, I'd like to acknowledge Lea Hallert for her insights on technology and business education.

Thanks are also due to the business school folks who went far out of their way to provide essential information:

Robert J. Alig, Director of Admissions—The Wharton School, MBA Program

Will Makris, Director of Admissions—Babson University

David Irons—University of California, Berkeley

John Gould, outgoing Dean, and Allan Friedman, Director of Communications—University of Chicago

Meyer Feldberg, Dean, and Ethan Hanabury, Director of Admissions—Columbia Business School

Skip Horne, Director of Admissions, and Elaine Ruggieri, Director of Public Relations—University of Virginia

Pat Wetherall, Assistant Director of Communications—Dartmouth College

Cathy Cassio and her staff at the News and Publications Office—Stanford University

Preface

In the late 1980s, The Princeton Review began working with *Fortune* 500 companies to provide their employees with on-site preparation classes for the GMAT. In the course of our work, it became clear that most of these prospective business school students were lacking critical information about the business school admissions process on which they were about to embark. Over and over, students asked:

- How many times should I take the GMAT?

- If I take it twice, which score will admissions offices count?

- How high does my score need to be?

- What points do I need to make in my essays?

- What if all I've done is work? I don't have any extracurriculars to write about.

- Should I interview?

- How much do my grades count?

- Who should write my recommendation—an immediate boss who knows me well or a senior V.P. who's a power alum of the school?

- When's the best time to send in the application—early or close to the deadline?

These students were confused, with good reason. Unlike high school students— who can turn to guidance counselors and professional advisors for help navigating the undergraduate admissions process—prospective MBAs have almost nowhere to turn for advice on selecting and applying to the right business school. Even the information that is available—mainly guidebooks and magazine rankings—is obscure and contradictory. What, then, is a b-school applicant to do?

READ THIS BOOK
We surveyed 18,500 students, hundreds of admissions officers, and dozens of recruiters and business school grads to bring you the real scoop on b-school.

Want to know what really happens to the applications you toiled, sweated, and bled over? This book gives you an exclusive inside look at the deliberations of a top admissions committee and shows you what committee members are looking for in an applicant. Ever wonder who actually reads your essays? We not only tell you, we show you what they liked about fifteen essays submitted to twelve top schools. This book tells you what admissions officers are looking for, what your life as a business school student will be like, what to talk about in your interviews, when to apply, and more. But, most importantly, this book gives you essential facts, unique insights, and up-to-the-minute information on the nation's top seventy-five b-schools, so you can make an educated decision about where you should apply.

WHY THESE SEVENTY-FIVE SCHOOLS?

For several years now, two leading magazines have been telling you who's hot and who's not. They've crunched objective data and subjective ratings into a quantified format to create the perception of precise numerical rankings. But the rankings are as imprecise as they are arbitrary. The weighting of different criteria leads to dramatically different interpretations of a program. While the rankings make news and sell a lot of magazines, in real life, prospective students are equally, if not more, interested in those characteristics that distinguish one school from another. What makes a program tops? To find the answers, we took a more holistic approach and gathered input from a variety of sources.

First on our list was student opinion. Mass-interview style, we surveyed more than 18,500 currently matriculated b-school students. We surveyed hundreds of admissions officers and administrators. In addition, we looked at more traditional measures, including a school's acceptance rate, applicants' GPAs and GMAT scores, placement rate, curriculum, learning environment, and caliber of the student body. As we progressed, we learned that many lesser-known schools belonged in this book because of their regional reputation, star faculty, "bang for the buck," or unique course offerings. Finally, we sought to focus on those schools that are accredited by the International Association for Management Education (referred to as the AACSB because of its previous name, the American Assembly of Collegiate Schools of Business, www.aacsb.edu) Of the more than 800 business programs in the nation, 346 are accredited by AACSB. Almost all of the schools included in this book are accredited by the AACSB with the exception of two new schools we've added this year—Pepperdine University (at the time of print Pepperdine was "in the process" of getting AACSB accreditation) and University of Western Onatario (the first Canadian representative). We've included these two non-accredited schools because employers and academics regard them, widely and accurately, as top business schools. We've also added Michigan State University and Baylor University to this new edition.

In a few cases, schools that might have met our criteria for inclusion had to be omitted because they wouldn't allow us to poll their students.

A final note: We've chosen to list schools in our book alphabetically, rather than rank them. We believe our profiles highlight each program's major strengths and weaknesses, as well as capture its distinct personality. The profiles take into account the reputation, prestige, and status of a school without ranking it. The question is, which school is the best for you? We hope this book helps you make the right choice.

GMAT CHANGES

In recent years the GMAT has evolved from a paper-and-pencil exam to a CAT (Computer Adaptive Test). Once entirely multiple-choice, the GMAT now includes two essay questions, collectively known as the AWA (Analytic Writing Assessment). To get the lowdown on the exam, pick up our book *Cracking the GMAT*, which includes both the latest information available on the GMAT CAT and, of course, our techniques and tips on how to beat the test. We'd also be happy to tell you about The Princeton Review's intensive six-week GMAT course. You can reach us at 1-800-REVIEW-6 or by e-mail at info@review.com. Whatever you do, we wish you good luck in b-school and beyond.

Introduction

AT THE TOP B-SCHOOLS, BUSINESS IS BOOMING AND GETTING IN JUST GOT TOUGHER

ONCE UPON A BEAR MARKET

The MBA, often perceived as the golden passport to power and wealth, took some hard knocks in the late 1980s. First, there were all those business scandals in the 1980s that made MBAs look smarmy. Then corporate downsizing shrunk middle management (the destination for grads), and job prospects became bleak. To make matters worse, corporate recruiters became critical of MBA programs, claiming that the business education added no measurable value to the skills of those it was graduating. What was an MBA wannabe to do? Many switched to graduate study in areas in which there was renewed interest—teaching, medicine, and public service. Others decided to forgo the degree. The bottom line? By 1992, the number of individuals taking the Graduate Management Admissions Test (GMAT) had dropped 20 percent from its peak level.

B-schools fell on tough times. Even top-tier programs couldn't count on a bottomless cup of applications, much less a high yield of the applicants they accepted. To fill the spots, schools had to work harder. Applicants were aggressively wooed, provided 800 numbers and Saturday interviews, and treated to personal calls from the dean and faculty. Admission into the top schools was still tough, but under these circumstances, getting in was relatively easier.

THE MBA: GOLDEN AGAIN

But of course, things change. Enter the mid-1990s. A surge in applications, starting salaries, and more job offers and favorable press have made the MBA a winning ticket again. Applications have swung back to levels not seen since the 1980s. At Columbia University, for example admissions officers are reporting application increases of 100 percent over the last five years.

Is the surge in applications limited to the very top schools? No. The Graduate Management Admissions Council reports that in the calendar year of 1996–97, 80 percent of the 100 schools it surveyed saw an increase in applications, the largest increase in their applicant pool in years. In fact, more than a quarter of the programs saw the number of applications surge 20 percent or more.

"Everyone refers to the mid-1980s as the long gone heyday for MBAs," says Ethan Hanabury, the associate director of admissions and administration at Columbia Business School. "But the myth that the MBA is no longer essential has been thoroughly debunked by double-digit increases at the top schools."

Applications at the University of Chicago mirror the trend. "We are seeing an increase in the percentage of applicants who are accepting our offers of admission," comments Donald Martin, director of admissions at the University of Chicago Graduate School of Business. "The increased number of applications combined with the higher matriculation rate indicates a strong interest in business education."

Robert J. Alig, director of admissions and financial aid for the Wharton MBA Program concurs, "The MBA Class of 1998 was another record breaker for the Wharton School, a remarkable feat given that last year's applications were up nearly 20 percent over the previous year. The incredible momentum we've seen over the last several years has continued.... The competition to date has been incredible, with the average GMAT for admitted students being nearly 680. We're also seeing a higher average undergraduate GPA versus last year's class." Nearly 7,500 students applied for the 750 spots available in Wharton's Class of 1998.

Alig also observes that, "As students have witnessed record numbers of applications over the last few years, they've become more savvy consumers. They've started doing a better job of looking at how they might use some of the objective data of the various rankings to clarify the best fit and where they are going to excel. This is a positive for both students and the programs because more candidates are better equipped to contribute both inside and outside the classroom. A student's self-assessment of his or her fit with our school is a critical component of our evaluation."

WHAT'S DRIVING THE DEMAND FOR MBAS?

Gurus point to several factors. First, major curriculum overhauls at the b-schools have helped to produce better-trained, more well-rounded managers. Now that programs are integrating real-life management, leadership, and teamwork projects into class study, business students are graduating with more relevant experiences. Satisfied recruiters say these experiences have expanded the skill set of newly minted MBAs so that they better grasp the complexities of modern, 1990s businesses.

Second, a strong economy has made MBAs, once again, critical to the workforce. After jettisoning layers of middle management during the cost-cutting years of the early 1990s, corporate America now finds it often lacks the management depth to pursue growth initiatives. This is particularly true of industries hit hardest by the cost cutting: health care, telecommunications, and financial services. Further, the economy is widely recognized to be evolving toward a "knowledge-based" economy in which managers must be adept at managing ambiguous environments. These are among the skills b-schools have sought to develop in their re-tooled curriculums. And here's a statistic that should make you a believer: According to the U.S. Bureau of Labor Statistics, managerial employment grew at a 4.7 percent rate during the 2nd quarter of 1996. That's three and a half times faster than the overall employment growth rate.

As corporate America has returned its attention to graduating MBAs, b-schools have transformed their long-neglected placement offices into key components of their programs. From installing state-of-the-art computer data-bases to hiring more career counselors to giving facilities a decorating makeover, b-schools have made recruiting efforts a priority.

Led by the consulting firms and investment banks, industry flagships are rushing b-schools for the best and the brightest. These days, students at the most prestigious schools are finding themselves with multiple job offers, a robust return on their investment.

IS THE MBA A SURE THING AGAIN?

After six years of growth, a booming economy is reassuring to those who will sacrifice a steady paycheck for two years of studying. It's easier to get back into the workforce when the economy is in an upswing. After coming of age during a period of unprecedented corporate restructurings and layoffs, applicants now consider the MBA insulation from future downsizings. Further, with 40 million BAs out there, the opportunity to differentiate oneself with an MBA, particularly from a top-tier school, is still alluring.

But what's the number one reason for the surge in MBA applications? Why would you want to drop out of the workplace for two years and pay up to $51,000 in tuition? Money. And lots of it. Starting compensation packages are booming for MBAs from top schools. The 55 percent of Columbia grads who get scooped up by financial firms earn an average salary of $120,000. Consulting firms are anteing up $119,000 to 20 percent of graduates heading their way. And Columbia is not alone. Four schools achieved median starting salaries of more than $90,000.

GETTING IN JUST GOT TOUGHER

What does all this mean? Basically this: If you plan on applying to the most competitive programs this year, brace yourself. Perhaps you were a sure shot in previous years. But this time around, you'll enter a far more competitive pool. Not only will you be competing against a reinvigorated group of candidates who were always interested in getting the MBA, but against applicants who in years past would have been pursuing legal careers. Scared off by the glut of lawyers, lots of aspiring attorneys have reconsidered their career choices; in recent years, the number of people taking the LSAT has actually dropped.

So getting in is tougher than ever. At some of the most popular b-schools they accept as few as 9 percent of applicants. Of course, in a b-school bull market the payoffs are bigger. But if you want to beat the odds, you'll need to develop a solid application strategy and apply to a diverse portfolio of schools.

Alig advises, "I don't think it's effective to apply to ten or so schools. It compromises a student's ability to critically evaluate each program and do a thorough job on each of the applications by spreading him or herself too thin." His advice: "Apply to four or five. Make one or two a long shot. Make another a solid possibility. And another very safe."

"Over the course of this year we've conducted nearly 6,000 interviews of prospective students, including 3,000 on campus," adds Alig. "One of the reasons we've made the decision to interview as many applicants as we can is to give applicants every opportunity to distinguish themselves from the applicant pool—even if their experiences are quite similar to another candidate's. The interview gives us insights into choices they've made, and that automatically sheds light on their individuality. And this is what our applicants are struggling with—a way to truly distinguish themselves. Just listing the data points on their resume doesn't do that."

Perhaps Alig best sums up the scenario for admissions officers at the top schools: "It's become almost a cliché; most students who apply to this program can handle the workload." But the hurdle for successful applicants is higher: "I'm looking for someone who has left an indelible impression on me that he or she will make the business school community stronger by being here."

PROVEN STRATEGIES FOR WINNING ADMISSION

So now you know. Admission to the top programs will require your absolute best shot. Thousands and thousands of prospective MBA candidates spend loads of time and money making sure they select, and are in turn admitted to, the "best" school. Their time and money go toward working in jobs they think will impress a b-school, studying and preparing for the GMAT, writing essays, interviewing, visiting prospective schools, and buying guides like—but not as good as—this one.

This book is your best bet. It takes you into the secret deliberations of the admissions committees at the top schools. You get a firsthand look at who decides your fate. More important, you learn what criteria are used to evaluate applicants. As we found out, things aren't always the way you'd expect them to be. You also get straight talk from admissions officers—what dooms an application and how to ace the interview.

In addition to getting inside information on the application process, you learn when the best time to apply is, how to answer the most commonly asked essay questions, and the key points to make in your essays. There's also loads of information on what you can do before applying to increase your odds of gaining admission.

We also give you the facts—from the most up-to-date information on major curricula changes and placement rates to demographics of the student body—for the seventy-five best b-schools in the country. And we've included enough information about them—which we gathered from admissions officers, administrators, and students—to help you make a smart decision about where to go.

Good luck!

B-school Admission Goes Electronic

Universities were among the first organizations on the Internet and most MBA programs have a lot of useful information online. B-school web sites typically include detailed information about the program, course offerings, housing options, and campus life. If you are at all interested in a school, checking out its web site is a great way to gather more facts.

PRINCETON REVIEW ONLINE

One of the best places to start your search for b-school information on the Internet is at Princeton Review Online—www.review.com/business. There you can access a variety of services to help you learn more about universities and the b-school admissions process.

Find-O-Rama

Our b-school search engine, Find-O-Rama, is the most sophisticated MBA program search tool available on the Internet and is a great companion to this book. To use Find-O-Rama, you first enter as much (or as little) data as you like about your preferences. You can narrow your search by region, average GMAT scores of admitted applicants, and program size and by using the specialized Quality of Life rating and other b-school characteristics that are in our database. The result of the Find-O-Rama search is a list of all the schools that match your needs and links to those b-schools' web sites.

B-school Admissions Discussion

Visitors to our discussion group post messages describing their experiences as they go through the admissions process and get expert advice from Princeton Review moderators. It's the most popular MBA admissions discussion area anywhere on the Net.

Remind-O-Rama

The b-school admissions process is filled with dates and deadlines. Remind-O-Rama can help you keep on schedule by sending you e-mail reminders about the deadlines for everything from your top choice's application deadline, to the day you need to buy your boss' birthday present.

THE GMAT

As previously mentioned, the GMAT is now offered only in the computer-adaptive (CAT) format. The test begins with two essay questions, called the Analytical Writing Assessment (AWA). In the past, all essay questions that have appeared on the official GMAT have been drawn from a list of about 150 topics that appear in The Official Guide to the GMAT (ETS). Review that list and you'll have a pretty good idea of what to expect from the AWA. By the way, you will be required to type your essay at the computer.

Next comes a 75-minute math section. The math section includes standard problem-solving questions (e.g., "Train A leaves Baltimore at 6:32 a.m....) and data-sufficiency questions; for these questions you must determine whether you have been given enough information to solve a particular math problem. The good news about data sufficiency is that you don't actually have to solve the problem; the bad news is these questions can be very tricky.

The test ends with a 75-minute verbal section. The verbal section tests reading skills (reading comprehension), grammar (sentence correction), and logic (critical reasoning).

For those unfamiliar with CAT exams, here's a brief overview of how they work: on multiple-choice sections, the computer starts by asking a question of medium difficulty. If you answer it correctly, the computer asks you a question that is slightly more difficult than the previous question. If you answer incorrectly, the computer asks a slightly easier question next. The test continues this way until you have answered enough questions that the computer program can assign you an accurate score, at which point the section ends.

APPLYING TO B-SCHOOL VIA ELECTRONIC APPLICATION

Once you've gathered all the information that you need about the schools and have decided where to apply, you may not need to leave your keyboard. Just a handful of years ago, electronic applications were never going to happen. Today, business schools are scrambling to make electronic versions of their applications available.

There is an excellent package for electronic applications, and we've convinced one company to give you a small discount on its software because you bought this book. The software allows you to fill out your applications on-screen, print, and submit directly to the admissions offices. When you use the program, you only have to enter common information once, saving you some time and hassle. The package is called MBA Multi-App. Interested applicants can download a sample multi-app for free and try it out before buying—just go to www.multi-app.com.

In addition to printing out perfect duplicates of the regular applications, multi-app has an easy data-entry mechanism. It is available for Windows, versions 3.1 and above. To order, call MBA MULTI-App at (800) 516-2227 or (610) 544-7197, e-mail them at mcs@multi-app.com, fax them at (610) 544-9877, or write them at MCS MULTI-App, 740 South Chester Road, Suite F, Swarthmore, PA 19081. Visit the MBA MULTI-App web site at www.multi-app.com.

MBA Multi-App is offering a 10 percent discount to anyone who purchases *The Best 75 Business Schools*. (Make sure to mention this book, and don't say we never gave you anything.)

A final note of advice: No matter which form of electronic application you choose, you should still contact the admissions office for an application packet. This guarantees that you will have all the information and materials that you need to put together the strongest candidacy possible. Some, but not all, schools will let you download this information at their web sites; usually, such information is packaged as a .pdf file, which can only be read by a free, downloadable program called Adobe Reader (www.adobe.com/acrobat). Still, despite the increasing online presence of business schools and the convenience of the electronic medium, "snail mail" remains an integral part of the process.

If you have any questions, comments, or suggestions, please e-mail your insights to us at info@review.com. We appreciate your input and want to make our books as useful to you as they can be.

Part One

ALL ABOUT B-SCHOOL

PICKING THE RIGHT BUSINESS SCHOOL FOR YOU

Chapter One

MAKING THE DECISION TO GO

The first step for you may be b-school. Indeed, armed with an MBA you may journey far. But the success of your trip and the direction you take will depend on knowing exactly why you're going to b-school and just what you'll be getting out of it.

The most critical questions you need to ask yourself are the following: Do you really want a career in business? What do you want the MBA to do for you? Are you looking to gain credibility, accelerate your development, or move into a new job or industry? Perhaps you're looking to start your own business, and entrepreneurial study will be important.

Knowing what you want doesn't just affect your decision to go, it also affects your candidacy; admissions committees favor applicants who have clear goals and objectives. Moreover, once at school, students who know what they want make the most of their two years. If you're uncertain about your goals, opportunities for career development—such as networking, mentoring, student clubs, and recruiter events—are squandered.

You also need to find a school that fits your individual needs. Consider the personal and financial costs. This may be the single biggest investment of your life. How much salary will you forego by leaving the workforce? What will the tuition be? How will you pay for it? If you have a family, spouse, or significant other, how will getting your MBA affect them?

If you do have a spouse, you may choose a program that involves partners in campus life. If status is your top priority, you should simply choose the most prestigious school you can get into.

The MBA presents many opportunities, but no guarantees. As with any opportunity, you must make the most of it. Whether you go to a first-tier school or to a part-time program close to home, you'll acquire the skills that can jump start your career. But your success will have more to do with you than with the piece of paper your MBA is printed on.

WHY THE RANKINGS AREN'T A USEFUL GUIDE TO SCHOOL SELECTION

All too many applicants rely on the magazine rankings to decide where to apply. Caught up with winners, losers, and whoever falls in between, their thinking is simply: Can I get into the top five? Top ten? Top fifteen?

But it's a mistake to rely on the rankings. Benjamin Disraeli once said, "There are lies, damn lies, and statistics." Today, he'd probably add b-school rankings. Why? Because statistics rarely show the whole picture. When deciding on the validity of a study, it's wise to consider how the study was conducted and what exactly it was trying to measure.

First, the rankings have made must-read news for several years. Not surprisingly, some of the survey respondents—current b-school students and recent grads—now know there's a game to play. The game is this: Give your own school the highest marks possible. The goal: that coveted number-one spot. Rumor has it that some schools even remind their students of how their responses will affect the stature of their program. This kind of self-interest is known as respondent bias, and the b-school rankings suffer from it in a big way.

The rankings feature easy-to-measure differences such as selectivity, placement success, and proficiency in the basic disciplines. But these rankings don't allow for any intangibles—such as the progressiveness of a program, the school's learning environment, and the happiness of the students.

To create standards by which comparisons can be made, the rankings force an evaluative framework on the programs. But this is like trying to evaluate a collection of paintings—impressionist, modern, classical, and cubist—with the same criteria. Relying on narrow criteria to evaluate subjective components fails to capture the true strengths and weaknesses of each piece.

The statistically measurable differences that the magazines base their ratings on are often so marginal as to be insignificant. In other words, it's too close to call the race. Perhaps in some years two schools should be tied for the number-one spot. What would the tie-breaker look like? A rally cry of "We're number one" with the loudest school winning?

A designation as the number-one, number-five, or number-ten school is almost meaningless when you consider that it changes from year to year—and from magazine to magazine. (At least Olympic medalists enjoy a four-year victory lap.)

JUDGING FOR YOURSELF

Depending on what you're looking for, the rankings may tell you something about the b-schools. But it's wise to use them as approximations rather than the declarations of fact they're made out to be.

The rankings don't factor in your values or all of the criteria you need to consider. Is it selectivity? The highest rate of placement? The best starting salary? Surprise! The number-one school is not number one in all these areas. No school is.

The best way to pick a program is to do your homework and find a match. For example, if you have limited experience with numbers, then a program with a heavy quantitative focus may round out your resume. If you want to stay in your home area, then a local school that's highly regarded by the top regional companies may be best for you. If you know that you want to go into a field typified by cutthroat competition, or a field in which status is all-important . . . well, obviously, keep your eyes on those rankings.

You also need to consider your personal style and comfort zone. Suppose you get into a "top-ranked" school, but the workload is destroying your life, or the mentality is predatory. It won't matter how prestigious the program is if you don't make it through. Do you want an intimate and supportive environment or are you happy to blend in with the masses? Different schools will meet these needs. Lecture versus case study, specialization versus broad-based general management curriculum, and heavy finance versus heavy marketing are other kinds of trade-offs.

One last thing to consider is social atmosphere. What is the spirit of the student body? Do students like each other? Are they indifferent? Perhaps a bit hostile? If you go through graduate school in an atmosphere of camaraderie, you'll never forget those two years. But if you go through school in an atmosphere of enmity . . . okay, you'll still remember those two years. It's up to you to decide how you want to remember them.

Remember when you applied to college? You talked to friends, alumni, and teachers. You visited the campus and sat in on classes (or should have). It's not all that different with b-school. Here are some of the things you should check out:

ACADEMICS

- Academic reputation
- International reputation
- Primary teaching methodology
- Renown and availability of professors
- General or specialized curriculum
- Range of school specialties
- Opportunities for global/foreign study
- Emphasis on teamwork
- Fieldwork/student consulting available
- Student support—extra study sessions, accessible faculty, tutoring
- Academic support—libraries, computer facilities, and expertise
- Grading/probation policy
- Workload/hours per week in class
- Class and section size
- Pressure and competition

CAREER

- Summer and full-time job placement (number of companies recruiting on and off campus)
- Placement rate
- Average starting salaries
- Salaries at five-year mark
- Career support—assistance with career planning, resume preparation, interview skills
- Networking with visiting executives

QUALITY OF LIFE

- Location
- Campus
- Orientation
- Range of student clubs/activities
- Diversity of student body
- Housing
- Social life
- Spouse/partner group
- Recreational facilities

EXPENSE

- Tuition
- Books, computer
- Cost of living
- Financial aid

HOW TO USE THIS BOOK

Each of the business schools listed in this book has its own two-page spread. Each spread has six components: two "sidebars" (the narrow columns on the outside of each page that contain statistics) and four profiles on each school (that contain actual student quotes).

Here's what's in each section.

THE SIDEBARS

The sidebars contain various statistics that we gathered either from the questionnaires we sent to the schools or from our own student surveys. Some schools did not provide us information for all categories, in this case the statistic is left out of the sidebar.

OVERVIEW

■ *Type of School*

Whether the school is public or private.

■ *Affiliation*

Any religion with which the school is affiliated.

■ *Environment*

Whether the campus is located in an urban, suburban, or rural setting.

■ *Academic Calendar*

How the school breaks up its academic year (i.e., semesters, trimesters).

■ *Schedule*

Whether the school offers full-time or part-time schedules.

STUDENTS

■ *Enrollment of Parent Institution/Enrollment of Business School*

Total number of students in the entire institution and MBA program.

■ *Percent Men, Percent Women, Percent Out-of-State, Percent Part-Time, Percent Minorities, Percent International Students, Number of Countries Represented, Average Age at Entry, and Average Years Work Experience at Entry.*

The demographic breakdown of last year's entering class.

ACADEMICS

■ *Student/Faculty Ratio, Percent of Female Faculty, Percent of Minority Faculty, Percent of Part-Time Faculty, and Hours of Study Per Day.*

A breakdown of the faculty and the amount of work they pile on.

■ *Specialties*

This tells you what specialized curriculum options are available to allow students to major in or specialize in one or two areas.

■ *Joint Degrees*

Lists any special graduate degrees offered by the school.

■ *Special Programs/Study Abroad Programs*

Lists any exchange, internship, or job programs.

HITS AND MISSES

Summarizes the results of our survey. The lists show what students felt unusually strong about, both positively and negatively, at their schools. Following are the categories:

- Gym—if this appears under the "hits" list, the students at the school love the gym facilities; if it appears under the "misses" list, the students are dissatisfied with the facilities.

- Helping Other Students—if this appears under the "hits" list, the students feel that students are willing to help each other; if it appears under the "misses" list, the students feel that their classmates aren't willing to help each other.

- Accounting Skills—students rated their improvement in the area of accounting. If this listing appears under the "hits" list, the students were happy with the quality of accounting instruction; if it appears under the "misses" list, they were not satisfied.

- Finance Skills—same as above, only for finance skills.

- Marketing Skills—same, only for marketing skills.

- Quantitative Skills—same as above, mutatis mutandis.

- Placement—a rating of the efficiency of the school's job placement office.

- Ethnic and Racial Diversity—students were asked whether their school is ethnically and racially diverse. If it is, this rating appears in the "hits" list; if not, it appears under "misses."

- Classmates Are Smart/Classmates Are Below Average—reveals students' opinions about the intelligence of their classmates.

- Recruiting—rates students' satisfaction with their school's recruiting efforts.

- Social Life—if students have active social lives, this rating appears in the "hits" list; if not, it appears in the "misses" list.

- Diverse Work Experience—this rating appears in the "hits" list if students said their classmates had come from diverse work backgrounds; if it appears in the "misses" list students came mostly from the same type of company.

- Off-campus Housing—students' rating of the quality of off-campus housing.

- On-campus Housing—students' rating of the quality of on-campus housing.

- Library—a rating of the usefulness of the library.

- Location—this is a rating of whether or not students like the town in which their school is located.

- Cozy Student Community/Don't Like Classmates—students were asked whether they liked to hang out with their classmates. If they did, "Cozy student community" appears in the "hits" list; if not "Don't like classmates" appears in the "misses" list.

- School Clubs—a rating of the breadth and number of extracurricular clubs and organizations on campus.

- Staying in Touch—students were asked whether their classmates were the kind of people they'd want to stay in contact with after business school. If this rating appears in the "hits" list, they did want to stay in touch with their classmates; if it appears in the "misses" list, they felt they wouldn't stay in touch.

PROMINENT ALUMNI

Lists some of the shining MBA stars of the past and what they're doing now.

FINANCIAL FACTS

Gives in-state tuition, out-of-state tuition, tuition per credit, fees, estimated cost of books, costs of on-campus and off-campus housing, the percent of students receiving aid, the percent of first-year students receiving aid, the percent of aid that is merit-based, the percent of students receiving loans, the percent of students receiving paid internships, the percent of students receiving grants, average award package, average grant, and average graduation debt.

ADMISSIONS

Gives the number of applicants, percent of applicants accepted, percent of applicants enrolled for last year's entering class, the average GMAT score, the minimum TOEFL score, average undergrad GPA, the application fee, whether an early decision program is available, the early and regular application deadlines and dates of notification, admission deferment, transfer policy, non-fall admission, and whether the admissions process is need-blind.

APPLICANTS ALSO LOOK AT

Lists other schools applicants also consider.

EMPLOYMENT PROFILE

Placement rate, number of companies recruiting on campus, percent of graduates employed immediately and within six months of graduation, average starting salary, and percent breakdown according to the individual employment fields graduates enter.

THE PROFILES

Academics

This section describes the academic atmosphere of each school, what the professors are like, where the curriculum is headed, and what students think about the education they are receiving.

Placement and Recruiting

One of the most important issues to MBAs is the quality and efficacy of their school's recruiting and placement offices. This section explains the programs each school offers.

Student/Campus Life

From dating to off-campus housing, this section describes the social atmosphere and quality of life at each campus.

Admissions

This section tells you what aspects of applications are most important to the school's admissions officers. We used the admissions officers' responses to our questionnaire, as well as telephone interviews with many admissions officers, to write these sections.

A GLOSSARY OF INSIDER LINGO

You've probably already noticed this, but b-school students, graduates, and professors—like most close-knit, somewhat solipsistic groups—seem to speak their own weird language. With that in mind, here's one last set of tools that will help you on your way through this book and into the business world: a list of MBA jargon (with English translations).

Air Hogs: students who monopolize classroom discussion and who love to hear themselves speak.

Air Time: a precious opportunity—speaking or making comments in class.

Analysis Paralysis: not being able to make a decision because you've gotten lost in the thicket of your own analysis.

Back of the Envelope: an abbreviated analysis of the numbers.

Barriers to Entry: conditions that prevent entry into a particular market.

Beta of a Stock: the inherent volatility of a stock.

Bottleneck: the point in a plant or process that determines or blocks the pace.

Burn Rate: amount of cash a company consumes each day.

Case Cracker: a comment in class that gets to the essence of case.

Case Study Method: popular teaching method that uses real-life business cases for analysis.

Chip Shots: unenlightening comments made during class discussion for the sole purpose of getting credit.

Cold Call: unexpected, often dreaded request by the professor to open a case.

Core Courses: courses in the basic disciplines of business, usually mandatory.

Corner Office: office location that all MBAs aspire to and the exclusive province of partners, managing directors, and senior executives.

Cost-Benefit Analysis: calculating whether something is worth doing on the basis of the real dollar cost versus real dollar benefit. This is often used as a shortcut in analyzing the numbers.

Cycle Time: how fast you can turn something around.

Deliverable: what your end product is.

Finheads: finance heads. See also sharks.

Four Ps: elements of a marketing strategy—Price, Promotion, Place, Product.

Fume Date: date the company will run out of cash reserves.

Functional Areas: the basic disciplines of business.

Globalization: trend of the 1980s and 1990s; expanding the definition of your market to include the challenges of operating in a multicountry, multiconsumer market.

Hard Courses: anything with numbers.

HP12-C: the calculator of choice for number crunching.

I-Bankers: investment banking analysts coming out of the two-year training programs and into b-school.

Incentivize: a bastardized version of the word incentive, used as a verb.

MBA Weenies: students who believe that once they get their MBAs, they'll be masters of the universe.

Net Net: End result.

OOC: out of cash.

Opportunity Costs: the cost of pursuing an opportunity, for example, for b-school, tuition and loss of income for two years.

Out-of-the-Box Thinking: Business strategies that challenge conventional business wisdom.

Poets: students with little quantitative skills or experience (numerically challenged).

Power Naps: quick, intense in-class recharge for the continually sleep deprived.

Power Tool: someone who does all the work and sits in the front row of the class with his or her hand up.

Pre-enrollment Courses: commonly known as MBA summer camp—quantitative courses, generally offered in the summer before the first year to get the numerically challenged up to speed.

Pro Forma: financial presentation of hypothetical events; for example, how much new debt would a company require if it grows 10 percent a year?

Quant Jock: a numerical athlete who is happiest crunching numbers.

Quick and Dirty: an abbreviated analysis, often involving numbers.

Run the Numbers: analyze quantitatively.

Sharks: aggressive students who smell blood and move in for the kill.

Shark Comment: comment meant to gore a fellow student in class discussion.

Soft Courses: touchy-feely courses such as human resources and organizational behavior.

Soft Skills: conflict resolution, teamwork, negotiation, oral and written communication.

Slice and Dice: running all kinds of quantitative analyses on a set of numbers.

The Five Forces: Michael Porter's model for analyzing the strategic attractiveness of an industry.

Three Cs: the primary forces—Customer, Competition, Company.

Total Quality Management: the Edward Demming method of management that caught on with the Japanese and is now "hot" in American business—managing the quality of products, service, work, process, people, and objectives.

Valuation: adds up projected future cash flows into current dollars.

Value-Based Decision Making: values and ethics as part of the practice of business.

## Chapter Two

SUSPENDERS AND POWER BREAKFASTS

What Does an MBA Offer?

NUTS-AND-BOLTS BUSINESS SKILLS

Graduate business schools teach the applied science of business. The best business schools, the ones in this book, combine the latest academic theories with pragmatic concepts, hands-on experience, and real-world solutions.

To equip students with the broad expertise they need to be managers, most business schools start new MBAs off with a set of foundation or "core" courses in what are known as the "functional areas": finance, accounting, management, marketing, operations, and economics. These courses introduce you to the basic vocabulary and concepts of formal business culture. They also develop your practical skills—ones you'll be able to use immediately in your new career.

Your learning occurs on three levels: You become familiar with concepts. For example, in finance you learn that a company's cost of equity is greater than its cost of debt. You acquire tools such as ratio analysis, valuations, and pro formas. Finally, you experience action-based learning by applying your skills and knowledge to case studies, role plays, and business simulations. Over the course of this three-tiered study, you will explore the complete business cycle of many different kinds of organizations.

B-schools also teach the analytical skills used to make complicated business decisions. You learn how to define the critical issues, apply analytical techniques, develop the criteria for decisions, and make decisions after evaluating their impact on other variables.

After two years, you're ready to market a box of cereal. Or prepare a valuation of the cereal company's worth. You'll speak the language of business. You'll know the tools of the trade. Your expertise will extend to many areas and industries. In short, you will have acquired the skills that open doors.

THE FAST TRACK AND BIG BUCKS

Applicants often have big bucks in mind when they decide to go to business school, believing that earning an MBA is equivalent to winning the lottery. At some schools, this is (sort of) the case. The top talent at elite schools are commonly offered salaries in the six-figure range. For example, the median salary for Stanford's 1998 MBAs at graduation was $113,250. Just as impressive is the fact that 99 percent had jobs by graduation day. But this is not an across-the-board experience.

Many factors have an effect on a student's first-job-out-of-school salary. First, there's a correlation between school reputation and average starting salary. The better the school (or the better the current perception of the school), the better the compensation. Second, compensation varies by industry. For example, consulting and investment banking are at the high end of the salary spectrum these days. Some companies in these industries even offer students "sign-on bonuses" and reimbursement of their second-year tuition. By contrast, advertising firms and small businesses offer smaller compensation packages and fewer perks. Third, previous work experience and salary will boost or deflate your perceived value. A clear track record of success before school is likely to secure a bigger package after graduation.

Another common reason for pursuing an MBA is to get on the proverbial "fast track." Many students do find that the degree allows them to leapfrog several notches up the ladder. But the guaranteed fast track is something of an illusion.

B-school students these days are older than they used to be: The average age is twenty-seven, as opposed to twenty-two a couple decades ago. This indicates that students typically spend more time working after college before entering a graduate degree program. Their age, maturity, and previous work experience allow these graduates to move into substantive, responsible positions right after completing their programs. In contrast, twenty years ago a recent MBA's first job out of school was in a management development track, but at a fairly low level in the organization.

All that said, the MBA can lead to accelerated career development. But like your salary, much of this depends on the industry you enter and the program from which you graduated.

ACCESS TO HUNDREDS OF RECRUITERS, ENTRY TO NEW FIELDS

Applicants tend to place great emphasis on "incoming" and "outgoing" statistics. First they ask, "Will I get in?" Then they ask, "Will I get a job?"

If the first is getting tougher to accomplish, then the second is getting easier. MBAs are back in style and hot again, thanks in part to the renewed interest in hiring from consulting firms and investment banks. Students graduating from the classes of 1996 and 1997 are awash with offers. At some schools, students can count up to ten offers, a major change from the early 1990s when grads were lucky to snag two or three. Consulting firms, which traditionally offer generous packages, are making more offers at higher starting salaries than ever before. Investment banks are upping those offers and providing bigger signing bonuses to compete against the consulting firms' appetite for more bodies. Starting salaries are weighing in at the $120,000+ mark, and that doesn't include the approximate $20,000 some newly minted MBAs get as a sign-on bonus. The majority also receive a generous relocation package. Indeed, if you were fortunate enough to have spent the summer in between your first and second year at the consulting company, then you will, in all likelihood, also receive a "rebate" on your tuition. These companies pick up student's second-year tuition bill. The big enchilada, however, goes to those MBA students who worked at the firm before b-school. **These lucky capitalists get their whole tuition paid for.**

A survey of placement offices reveals that salaries are up, ranging from $40,000 to $113,000. At the twenty or so most selective schools, the prime hunting grounds for consultants, 30–40 percent of the graduating classes have heard the siren song of big money and signed on the dotted line with the consulting firms.

What will all these talented MBAs be doing? Many of them will be flying around the country to client companies to help them develop growth strategies, implement new information technologies, and develop closer relationships with key suppliers. To institute these changes, companies often require the help of outside consultants. Because of the breadth of companies and industries that MBAs as consultants are exposed to, consulting is seen as "MBA finishing school." Most new MBA hires will stay for only three years before joining the industry as strategic planners and managers.

Where are the remainder of MBAs headed? Wall Street continues to take a chunk of the remaining students. Investment banking, sales and trading, and venture capital offer packages comparable to consulting. Although the pendulum of Wall Street hires has not swung back to its peak in the mid to late 1980s, nearly 30 percent of Wharton's Class of 1997 headed to the Street. With mergers and acquisitions back in vogue, and a continued boom in the bond and equity markets, Wall Street has its doors wide open to MBAs again.

Mainstream industry also wants its share of MBAs. Like Wall Street, years of downsizing have created the need for fresh hires and talent. For many companies, it's cheaper to hire new MBAs through on-campus recruiting than through other means. MBAs are also attractive because they bring fresh, state-of-the-art ideas, are eager to implement them, can tackle the grittier, more complex problems of the modern business world, and, most important, can make immediate contributions. As an MBA might put it, that's a solid return on one's investment.

GETTING A JOB

For most would-be MBAs, b-school represents a fresh beginning—either in their current profession or in an entirely different industry. Whatever promise the degree holds for you, it's wise to question what the return on your investment will be.

As with average starting salary, several factors affect job placement. School reputation and ties to industries and employers are important. At the top programs, the lists of recruiters read like a "Who's Who" of American companies. These schools not only attract the greatest volume of recruiters, but consistently get the attention of those considered blue chip.

Not to be overlooked are lesser-known, regional schools that often have the strongest relationships with local employers and industries. Some b-schools (many of them state universities) are regarded by both academicians and employers as number one in their respective regions. In other words, as far as the local business community is concerned, these programs offer as much prestige and pull as a nationally ranked program.

Student clubs also play a big part in getting a job, because they extend the recruiting efforts at many schools. They host a variety of events that allow you to meet leading business people, so that you can learn about their industries and their specific companies. Most important, these clubs are very effective at bringing in recruiters and other interested parties that do not recruit through traditional mainstream channels. For example, the high-tech, international, and entertainment student clubs provide career opportunities not available through the front door.

Another important factor is the industry you enter. The place to be in the late 1990s is consulting. The appeal is twofold: First, consulting firms pay the most. Second, they now offer an unbeatable combination of on-the-job training, exposure to strategy (typical for consulting), and more recently, opportunities to be involved in the nitty-gritty of tactical implementation. A hands-on, fix-the-business type of job used to be found only in brand management. But these days, consulting firms are being called on not only to diagnose a client company's ills, but also to administer the medicine as well. Roughly 35–40 percent of top-flight business school grads will go into consulting this year. In fact, at Kellogg, a school renowned for breeding brand managers, 40 percent of its grads will take jobs in consulting, up from 34 percent just a year ago.

Of course, brand management positions in packaged-goods companies such as Procter & Gamble, Church & Dwight (Arm & Hammer), Quaker Oats, and Johnson & Johnson are still appealing; you get to manage a product as though you were a mini-CEO. Also, brand management experience is a real resume builder; becoming a brand manager is the closest thing there is to earning a stripe in the business world. Investment banking, once the place to be, is popular (sky-high salaries are a big draw), but it has been usurped by consulting. An emerging area of demand is for the techno-MBA: people who have information technology skills with more traditional management skills. Companies off the beaten track, such as start-up ventures, offer unique opportunities, but many of them are unknowns. However, numerous schools have developed entrepreneurial programs, so newly credentialed MBAs leave feeling confident that they are better equipped to handle these riskier prospects. Indeed, in the 1990s many more students are interested in these unconventional, high-growth entrepreneurial opportunities.

Your background and experiences also affect your success in securing a position. Important factors are academic specialization (or course of study), academic standing, prior work experience, and intangibles such as your personal fit with the company. These days, what you did before b-school is particularly important; it helps establish credibility and gives you an edge in competing for a position in a specific field. For those using b-school to switch careers to a new industry, it's helpful if something on your resume ties your interest to the new profession. It's smart to secure a summer job in the new area.

Finally, persistence and initiative are critical factors in the job search. Since the beginning of this decade, many fast tracks have been narrowed. Increasingly, even at the best schools, finding a job requires off-campus recruiting efforts and ferreting out the hidden jobs.

RECRUITER SPELLS IT OUT

David Tanzer
Booz-Allen & Hamilton

"It may be kind of self-limiting, but we hire MBAs from the business schools that use the case method. Students trained in this methodology get exposure to a wide variety of business situations. They learn to quickly figure out what's truly important and focus on that. This is an important part of the consulting process.

As a recruiter, when you read a resume, you look for some continuity: that what you're hiring an MBA for is some logical progression of what they've done before. The MBA will allow you to switch careers, but it's still a good idea to build on prior experiences.

In general, the MBA is a screening device. Somebody who got into a good business school has something going for him or her. You find in an MBA the level of maturity you're looking for and the interpersonal skills of someone who has had several years of work experience."

FRIENDS WHO ARE GOING PLACES, ALUMNI WHO ARE ALREADY THERE

Most students say that the best part about b-school is meeting classmates with whom they share common goals and interests. Many students claim that the "single greatest resource is each other." Not surprisingly, with so many bright and ambitious people cocooned in one place, b-school can be the time of your life. It presents numerous professional and social opportunities. It can be where you find future customers, business partners, and mentors. It can also be where you establish lifelong friendships. And after graduation, these classmates form an enduring network of contacts and professional assistance.

Alumni are also an important part of the b-school experience. While professors teach business theory and practice, alumni provide insight into the real business world. When you're ready to interview, they can provide advice on how to get hired by the companies recruiting at your school. In some cases, they help secure the interview and shepherd you through the hiring process.

B-schools love to boast about the influence of their alumni network. To be sure, some are very powerful. But this varies from institution to institution. At the very least, alumni will help you get your foot in the door. A resume sent to an alum at a given company, instead of "Sir or Madam" in the personnel department, has a much better chance of being noticed and acted on.

After you graduate, the network continues to grow. Regional alumni clubs and alumni publications keep you plugged into the network with class notes on who's doing what, where, and with whom.

Throughout your career, an active alumni relations department can give you continued support. Post-MBA executive education series, fund-raising events, and continued job-placement efforts are all resources you can draw on for years to come.

## Chapter Three

WHAT B-SCHOOL IS REALLY LIKE

THE CHANGING FACE OF BUSINESS

In the previous decade, b-schools were regularly taken to task. An article in *The Chronicle of Higher Education* observed, "Hardly a month passes without a new article in the business press lamenting the narrow, overly quantitative focus of graduate business curricula, the irrelevant research done by business schools' faculty members, and the inability of graduates to grapple successfully with the nation's economic problems. Reporters gleefully interview unemployed graduates of business schools and pump corporate executives for unflattering comments about their employees with Master's Degrees in Business Administration."

Things have certainly changed. B-schools are responding to past criticisms by carving out new images for themselves. Many programs, for example, have sprouted social consciences. The 1990s MBA student hardly resembles the Gordon Gekko stereotype (remember that evil arbitrager from the movie Wall Street?) of the 1980s. Gone is the tolerance for avaricious, self-important MBAs. B-schools are recruiting students with broader, more humanitarian outlooks—students interested in contributing as much as in profit-taking. And, importantly, schools are trying to break down the rich-white-male stronghold on the business world by actively recruiting women and minorities.

Schools are also training students differently, both in content and in style. There's a move toward the medical-school model of education—learning by doing. Business "residencies," product "laboratories," and fieldwork augment classroom instruction with real-world experiences. Schools are placing greater emphasis on public service and citizenship. Professional ethics classes are now mandatory in many schools. Outward Bound–style orientations and leadership programs are in vogue. Interpersonal communication skills, such as negotiation, conflict resolution, and team playing, have moved to the forefront. In short, the "bottom line" is no longer the bottom line.

Much has been made in recent years about the rise of a global economy. To make sure MBAs have the skills necessary to be effective in this economy, leading business programs have developed courses on global business operations and international economics. To teach sensitive leadership in an increasingly multicultural work force, they've enhanced offerings on cultural diversity and human resources.

One other change is worth noting. The reason that the average age of the business school student has steadily increased to the current high of twenty-seven is that b-schools have sought older students to satisfy the new demands of the marketplace. Recruiters want graduates with more than a degree; they want the skills that come with maturity, and the maturity that comes with several years of work experience.

AN ACADEMIC PERSPECTIVE

The objective of all MBA programs is to prepare students for a professional career in business. One business school puts it this way:

Graduates should be all of the following:

1. Able to think and reason independently, creatively, and analytically

2. Skilled in the use of quantitative techniques

3. Literate in the use of software applications as management tools

4. Knowledgeable about the world's management issues and problems

5. Willing to work in and successfully cope with conditions of uncertainty, risk, and change

6. Astute decision makers

7. Ethically and socially responsible

Sound like a tall order? Possibly. But this level of expectation is what business school is all about.

Nearly all MBA programs feature a core curriculum that focuses students on the major disciplines of business: finance, management, accounting, marketing, manufacturing, decision sciences, economics, and organizational behavior. Unless your school allows you to place out of them, these courses are mandatory. Core courses provide broad functional knowledge in one discipline.

For example, a core marketing course covers pricing, segmentation, communications, product-line planning, and implementation. Electives provide a narrow focus that deepens the area of study. For example, a marketing elective might be entirely devoted to pricing.

Students sometimes question the need for such a comprehensive core program. But the functional areas of a real business are not parallel lines. All departments of a business affect each other every day. For example, an MBA in a manufacturing job might be asked by a financial controller why the company's product has become unprofitable to produce. Without an understanding of how product costs are accounted for, this MBA wouldn't know how to respond to a critical and legitimate request.

At most schools, the first term or year is devoted to a rigid core curriculum. Some schools allow first-years to take core courses side by side with electives. Still others have come up with an entirely new way of covering the basics, integrating the core courses into one cross-functional learning experience, which may also include sessions on 1990s topics such as globalization, ethics, and managing diversity. Half-year to year-long courses are team-taught by professors who see you through all the disciplines.

TEACHING METHODOLOGY

Business schools employ two basic teaching methods: case study and lecture. Usually, they employ some combination of the two. The most popular is the case study approach. Students are presented with either real or hypothetical business scenarios and are asked to analyze them. This method provides concrete situations (rather than abstractions) that require mastery of a wide range of skills. Students often find case studies exciting because they can engage in spirited discussions about possible solutions to given business problems and because they get an opportunity to apply newly acquired business knowledge.

The other teaching method used by b-schools is lecturing in which—you guessed it—the professor speaks to the class and the class listens. The efficacy of the lecture method depends entirely on the professor. If the professor is compelling, you'll probably get a lot out of the class. If the professor is boring, you probably won't listen. Which isn't necessarily a big deal, since many professors make their class notes available on computer disc or in the library.

THE CLASSROOM EXPERIENCE

Professors teaching case methodology often begin class with a "cold call." A randomly selected student opens the class with an analysis of the case and makes recommendations for solutions. The cold call forces you to be prepared and to think on your feet.

No doubt, a cold call can be intimidating. But unlike law school, b-school professors don't use the Socratic method to torture you, testing your thinking with a pounding cross-examination. They're training managers, not trial lawyers. At worst, particularly if you're unprepared, a professor will abruptly dismiss your contributions.

Alternatively, professors ask for a volunteer to open a case, particularly someone who has had real industry experience with the issues. After the opening, the discussion is broadened to include the whole class. Everyone tries to get in a good comment, particularly if class participation counts heavily toward the grade. "Chip shots"—unenlightened, just-say-anything-to-get-credit comments—are common. So are "air hogs," students who go on and on because they like nothing more than to hear themselves pontificate.

Depending on the school, sometimes class discussions degenerate into wars of ego rather than ideas. But for the most part, debates are kept constructive and civilized. Students are competitive, but not offensively so, and learn to make their points succinctly and persuasively.

YOUR FIRST YEAR

The first six months of b-school can be daunting. You're unfamiliar with the subjects. There's a tremendous amount of work to do. And when you least have the skills to do so, there's pressure to stay with the pack. All of this produces anxiety and a tendency to over prepare. Eventually, students learn shortcuts and settle into a routine, but until then much of the first year is just plain tough. The programs usually pack more learning into the first term than they do into each of the remaining terms. For the schools to teach the core curriculum (which accounts for as much as 70 percent of learning) in a limited time, an intensive pace is considered necessary. Much of the second year will be spent on gaining proficiency in your area of expertise and on searching for a job.

The good news is that the schools recognize how tough the first year can be. During the early part of the program, they anchor students socially by placing them in small sections, sometimes called "cohorts." You take many or all of your classes with your section-mates. Sectioning encourages the formation of personal and working relationships and can help make a large program feel like a school within a school.

Because so much has to be accomplished in so little time, getting an MBA is like living in fast-forward. This is especially true of the job search. No sooner are you in the program than recruiters for summer jobs show up, which tends to divert students from their studies. First-years aggressively pursue summer positions, which are linked with the promise of a permanent job offer if the summer goes well. At some schools the recruiting period begins as early as October, at others in January or February.

IN YOUR SECOND YEAR

Relax, the second year is easier. By now, students know what's important and what's not. Second-years work more efficiently than first-years. Academic anxiety is no longer a factor. Having mastered the broad-based core curriculum, students now enjoy taking electives and developing an area of specialization.

Anxiety in the second year has more to do with the arduous task of finding a job. For some lucky students, a summer position has yielded a full-time offer. But even those students often go through the whole recruiting grind anyway, because they don't want to cut off any opportunities prematurely.

Most MBAs leave school with a full-time offer. Sometimes it's their only offer. Sometimes it's not their dream job. Which may be why most grads change jobs after just two years.

One University of Chicago Business School student summed up the whole two-year academic/recruiting process like this: "The first-year students collapse in the winter quarter because of on-campus recruiting. The second-years collapse academically in the first quarter of their second year because it's so competitive to get a good job. And when a second-year does get a job, he or she forgets about class entirely. That's why pass/fail was invented."

LIFE OUTSIDE OF CLASS

Business school is more than academics and a big-bucks job. A spirited student community provides ample opportunities for social interaction, extracurricular activity, and career development.

Much of campus life revolves around student-run clubs. There are groups

Females at my school were well-represented. But in terms of minority ethnic groups—Black and Hispanic, and that applies to myself—these were underrepresented. I could count on my two hands how many minorities were in that program. This is not an indictment of the school, it's just that as a minority, you have to be comfortable with the numbers.

There's a lot of press out there that says the MBA is not the golden ticket it's cracked up to be. But it does make you more competitive. I remember interviewing for a job in one of the other IBM offices. I had just started the MBA program again, and this manager said, 'It's really good you're doing that. All the other people who work for me have MBAs. Every one of them.' So I can see the degree helping with my short- and long-term career goals.

The MBA gave me credibility. It helped me understand my customers' needs better. Business school changes HOW you think about a problem. And I've made better business decisions because of that."

Female MBA, Graduate School of Business, Claremont College, 1991 Manager, IBM

for just about every career interest and social need—from "MBAs for a Greener America" to the "Small Business Club." There's even a group for significant others on most campuses. The clubs are a great way to meet classmates with similar interests and to get in on the social scene. They might have a reputation for throwing the best black-tie balls, pizza-and-keg events, and professional mixers. During orientation week, these clubs aggressively market themselves to first-years.

Various socially responsible projects are also popular on campus. An emphasis on volunteer work is part of the overall trend toward good citizenship. Perhaps to counter the greed of the 1980s, "giving back" is the b-school style of the moment. There is usually a wide range of options—from tutoring in an inner-city school to working in a soup kitchen to renovating public buildings.

Still another way to get involved is to work on a school committee. Here you might serve on a task force designed to improve student quality of life. Or you might work in the admissions office and interview prospective students.

For those with more creative urges there are always the old standbys: extracurriculars such as the school paper, yearbook, or school play. At some schools, the latter takes the form of the b-school follies and is a highlight of the year. Like the student clubs, these are a great way to get to know your fellow students.

Finally, you can play on intramural sports teams or attend the numerous informal get-togethers, dinner parties, and group trips. There are also plenty of regularly scheduled pub nights, just in case you thought your beer-guzzling days were over.

Most former MBA students say that going to b-school was the best decision they ever made. That's primarily because of non-academic experiences. Make the most of your classes, but take the time to get involved and enjoy yourself.

A DAY IN THE LIFE OF A STUDENT

Male MBA, First Year

Kenan-Flagler Business School,

The University of North Carolina at Chapel Hill

7:00 am: Review notes for my first class.

7:30 am: Eat some high-energy cereal; read *The Wall Street Journal*—professors like to discuss news items that relate to the class topics.

8:00 am: Read review for quantitative methods exam; do practice problems; reread case on control systems for organizational behavior class.

9:00 am: Arrive at school. Go to "reading room" to hang out with everyone. Check student mailbox for invitations to recruiter events.

9:30 am: Integrative Management Class: Guest speaker from case-study discusses how the company approached problems.

10:45 am: Hang out.

11:00 am: Organizational Behavior Class: Get in a couple of good comments; debate the effectiveness of a management decision with another student in class.

12:15 pm: Grab some lunch and sit with friends. Talk about the lousy cafeteria food and who's dating whom.

1:00 pm: Go back to reading room to review for 2:00 class.

2:00 pm: Microeconomics Class: Listen to lecture on monopolistic competition.

3:15 pm: Arrive at home, change into work-out clothes. Go running, lift weights—relax.

6:00 pm: Eat dinner; watch the news. Read the next day's case.

7:30 pm: Head back to campus for study group.

7:45 pm: Discuss cases, help each other with homework problems on interpreting regression statistics; discuss how to account for capital leases versus operating leases.

10:00 pm:	Back at home. Review more cases; read next class assignment in textbook; work on problem set.
Midnight:	Sports on ESPN 'til I fall asleep. Boardroom dreams.

Female MBA, Second Year

The Fuqua School of Business, Duke University

6:45 am:	Get dressed, listen to CNN, and pick up *The Wall Street Journal* on way to school.
8:00 am:	Arrive at school. Bargaining and Negotiations class. Perform role play on conflict resolution.
10:15 am:	Hang out—grab a bagel.
10:30 am:	Intermediate Accounting Class—discussion on cash flow statements—nothing exciting.
12:45 pm:	Arrive at admissions office to review resume of applicant to b-school.
1:00 pm:	Conduct interview of applicant.
1:45 pm:	Write evaluation of candidate. Hand in to admissions secretary.
2:00 pm:	Attend quality advisory board meeting—discuss creation of corporate survey.
3:30 pm:	Competitive Strategy class. Lecture on barriers to entry.
5:45 pm:	Attend recruiter event. Tell the recruiter how interested I am in the industry (I know nothing about it).
7:45 pm:	Over to the health club for aerobics.
8:45 pm:	Drive home, eat dinner, and finally read *The Wall Street Journal*—of course, it's not news by now.
9:30 pm:	Study class notes; prepare next day's case.
11:45 pm:	Quality phone time with my boyfriend.
12:30 am:	Boardroom dreams.

## Chapter Four

MONEY MATTERS

*How to Finance B-School and
Calculate the Return on this Investment*

THE BOTTOM LINE*

Paying for business school is not an expense that most people are prepared to incur without some help. The good news is that getting an MBA takes just two years (and maybe less), after which you can expect your income to increase, perhaps dramatically. The bad news is that there is less in the way of "gift aid," such as scholarships and grants, for business school than there is for law or medical school. You'll likely be forced to take out loans to pay your way. But, after all, what's one more loan? Especially one as valuable as an investment in your future. So relax and get comfortable with debt; it's a concept you'll have to become familiar with when you're running a large corporation. Anyway, it's only money, and you can't take it with you. Figure out what business school will cost you, using the Return on Investment worksheet on page 41, then figure out your rate of return on investment. Feel better? Good.

*Much of this article was reprinted with permission from *Time/The Princeton Review's The Best Graduate School for You*, 1998 edition.

HOW DO I FUND MY MBA?

The vast majority of b-school students finance their education through some combination of the following:

- Federally insured loans. The Perkins loan is available for students who show exceptional "need," as determined by your business school's financial aid office. The Stafford loan is the most popular method of financing an education, and is available to most students. The government makes each of these loans very attractive to students through its subsidy of the programs. (Your tax dollars are working for you, after all!)

- Private lenders. Many lenders (not just banks!) have developed specialized programs for people who want to borrow for b-school. Be careful of guarantee and insurance fees, though, since they can add dramatically to the cost of money.

- Grants and Scholarships. There are fewer of these for business school than for law, medical, or graduate school, so you'll have to dig hard to find one for which you qualify. We've listed some at the end of the chapter, but also consult any organizations you belong to and your business school for more sources.

- Educational Reimbursement from Your Company. Every company will handle this slightly differently, but obviously if you can get your company to pick up part (or all) of the cost of your education, you'll help yourself tremendously. And you may be able to take advantage of this once you complete your MBA as well. In today's heated job market, some companies are even offering newly minted MBA's signing bonuses that cover the previous year's tuition.

- Gifts. If you can get your family or some benefactor to help you out, consider yourself one of the lucky ones.

APPLYING FOR FINANCIAL AID

To become eligible for any financial aid at all, you will need to fill out the Free Application for Federal Student Aid (FAFSA). The application can be submitted any time after January 1 in the year that you will enter graduate school and is typically due shortly thereafter. You can get a copy of the form from a school's financial aid office or download a copy from the U.S. Department of Education (DOE) web site at www.fafsa.ed.gov.

You can also download FAFSA Express software and complete the form electronically. FAFSA Express runs only on a PC with Windows and can be transmitted directly to the Department of Education via modem. An electronic data exchange between your computer and the DOE computers ensures quick receipt of your official Expected Family Contribution. The software also speeds up the application process by automatically checking electronic FAFSA data.

Many schools also require you to fill out their own financial aid forms. Make sure you check with the schools to which you are applying to find out exactly what forms they require and their deadlines for submission. Also, these deadlines may vary by school, so be sure to double check and get the paperwork in on time!

WHAT LOANS ARE AVAILABLE?

Sometime in 1998 Congress is expected to vote to determine the rate students will pay for loans; call 888/888-3469 to get the most up-to-date information on loans. There are several sources of loans for students attending business school. The most common are ones you may be familiar with from your undergraduate years.

Stafford Loans

These are very low-interest loans guaranteed by the federal government. Unfortunately, you can't just decide to take out a Stafford Loan. You must file the FAFSA form to qualify for this loan. The interest rate on Stafford Loans is variable but capped at 8.25%. The current limit for graduate students is $18,500 a year total for both subsidized and unsubsidized Stafford Loans, of which $10,000 must be unsubsidized. The total aggregate amount you can borrow through the Stafford program, including loans from undergraduate school, is $138,500—only $65,500 of which can be subsidized.

If you receive a subsidized Stafford Loan, you pay no interest when you are in school (the government "subsidizes" it) or for the first six months after you graduate, and you can take up to ten years to re-pay the money. For an unsubsidized Stafford Loan, you'll be charged interest while you are in school, but you don't have to start repaying principal until you've been out of school for six months.

All Stafford Loans are subject to an origination fee of up to 4 percent (1 percent of that is usually the guarantee fee). Although the origination fee has to be paid up front, it is deducted from the loan amount and does not come out of pocket. In actual dollars, the amount isn't incredibly onerous: 4 percent of $2,500 is $100. Depending on the school, you either borrow directly from the school or from a bank.

Subsidized Stafford Loans are awarded only as part of the aid packages created by colleges and are based on need; unsubsidized Stafford Loans aren't based on need. For more information on the Stafford and other federal student loan programs, call 888/888-3469 or visit web sites from the DOE (www.ed.gov/prog_info/SFA/StudentGuide) and The Princeton Review (www.review.com).

Perkins Loans

These are loans made by colleges with money provided by the federal government. The interest rate is quite low—currently 5 percent. Students can borrow up to $5,000 each year. As with the Stafford Loans, interest payments are picked up by the government during school, and repayment doesn't begin until after graduation.

Perkins Loans are awarded only as part of an aid package and are based solely on need. Financial aid officers have the only say in deciding which students qualify for these loans. You should never turn down a Perkins Loan.

Grants from Clubs and Organizations

Clubs, alumni groups, and civic organizations provide scholarship money for graduate students, although not as much as for undergraduate students. These awards are usually small, so don't waste a lot of time scouring the countryside for a few hundred dollars but be aware of opportunities in your own backyard. If your local hospital offers scholarship money to former candy stripers and that was your childhood summer job, you may be in luck. You should also be aware that many companies offer scholarships in addition to their tuition reimbursement programs. Although an outside scholarship will help, it won't lower your Expected Family Contribution. You must divulge to the colleges the amount of outside aid you are receiving, and it will be counted against money the college would have given you.

Commercial Loans

Banks and other lenders lend money. That's their job. If you have to go this route, though, you leave the world of below-market interest rates, sometimes paying as much as 19 percent, much higher than the rates offered on federal loans. The terms are also different: in many cases, payment cannot be deferred until after graduation. Before borrowing, check to see if a local lender offers a rate reduction to students who attend a school in its state. See the chart on the next page for a listing of some of the organizations that offer popular loans to business school students:

Each of these loans should be used in addition to either Stafford or Perkins loans or both, whenever possible. Because the loans are unsecured, they generally will charge significant guarantee and insurance fees. Shop aggressively to avoid paying too much.

Lender	Loan Amount Range	Interest Rates	Guarantee and other Fees	Repayment
The Education Resources Institute (TERI) PEP Program www.teri.org	$500 – $15,000 annually on own good credit (up to cost of education)	Prime Rate	10% Guarantee fee on own signature, 6% with creditworthy cosigner	Repayment can begin six months after you leave school. Repayment can be up to 25 years.
The Access Group Business Access Loan 800/282-1550	From $500 up to the cost of education. Maximum total education debt, including all undergraduate and graduate debt, is $120,000.	Based on the 91-day Treasury Bill. Rate equals T-bill +3.25% before repayment and T-bill +3.4% during repayment	At disbursement, a second guarantee fee is charged. At repayment, a second guarantee fee of 2.0% is charged.	Defer interest until repayment begins, which may be 9 months after you leave school. Repayment period can be up to 20 years.
Citibank MBA Assist Loan 800/692-8200	$500 – $15,000 annually.	91-day T-bill +3.40% during school and +4.25% during repayment	At disbursement, a guarantee fee of 8.5% is charged if there is no cosigner or 6% with a cosigner.	Defer interest until repayment begins, which may be 6 months after you leave school. Repayment period can be up to 15 years.
Nellie Mae MBA-Excel Loan 800/9-TUITION	$2,000 – $10,000	Prime Rate +0.5% during the first year and Prime + 1% during subsequent years.	At disbursement, guarantee fee is 9% without a cosigner or 7% with one.	Defer interest until repayment begins, which may be 6 months after you leave school. Repayment period can be up to 20 years.
Sallie Mae MBALOANS 800/239-4211	From $500 up to the cost of education, minus other financial aid. May have to apply for federal student aid before being approved for these loans.	91-day T-bill +3.25% during in-school and T-bill +3.40% during repayment.	At disbursement, guarantee fee of 7.5% is charged. An additional fee of 2.5% is charged at repayment, unless there is a cosigner.	Defer interest until repayment begins, which can be up to 6 months after you leave school. Repayment period can be up to 15 years.

Students and their families may also decide to investigate financing options other than those targeted at the educational market. These can turn into very expensive propositions, so be careful. They include personal lines of credit from your bank, credit cards, loans from your retirement fund or insurance plan, and personal loans from relatives. Personal lines of credit are usually comparable to those charged by credit cards. Another last-resort option is to find a credit card that's trying to attract customers with a low introductory rate and to put your expenses on that. The rates, which can be as low as 6 percent, typically last six months to a year, so pay off as much as you can in that time to save money.

Funding your b-school education may require some fancy financial moves, but it's good preparation for the real world. After all, there's hardly an investment banking, sales, or economics job that doesn't require restructuring debt. Start learning at the company that matters most: You, Inc.

Scholarship	Award	Deadline	Contact	Requirements
Karla Scherer Foundation Scholarship for Women	Varies; renewable	MARCH 1	737 N. Michigan Ave Suite 2330 Chicago, IL 60611 312/943-9191	Female students in finance or economics entering corporate business in the private sector. Need-based.
Donald W. Fogarty International Student Paper	Up to $1,700	MAY 15	APICS 500 W. Annandale Rd. Falls Church, VA 22046-4274 800/444-2742	Business administration and management students. Essay required on topic relevant to resource management.
National Urban League Scholarship Program for Minority Students	$10,000	APRIL 15	6030 Wilshire Blvd., Suite 302 Los Angeles, CA 90036 213/299-9660	Minority students in engineering, sales, marketing, manufacturing, finance, or business administration.
The Consortium for Graduate Study in Management	Full tuition and fees	JAN. 15	200 South Hanley Rd. Suite 1102 St. Louis, MO 63105 314/935-5614	African, Hispanic, and Native American students who are U.S. citizens and have a bachelor's degree.

THE TRUE COSTS AND REWARDS OF BUSINESS SCHOOL

Business school offers the opportunity to improve your current job status or satisfaction level, increase your earning power, or even step into a new career. But the price is high. In dollars and time. The financial price in the beginning is even higher. Will you ever recoup the money? To estimate the financial payoffs of business school, fill out this worksheet created by Jens Stephan, a University of Cincinnati business school professor. "Going to graduate school can be viewed as a classical financial investment decision," says Stephan. "Estimate your return on graduate school, as you would with any investment."

Use Part One to find out what b-school will cost in tuition and lost income. Turn to the profile (A–Z beginning on page 141) for a school you are considering and under Financial Facts you will find the tuition costs for line 2. Part Two will help you figure out how much more—percentage-wise—you will earn in the long run by getting your MBA. Use the Starting Salaries chart to estimate what you may earn your first year out of school. But don't limit yourself to the jobs we list. If you have another job in mind, plug in that starting salary to figure out your return on investment.

Starting Salaries	
consulting	85,000
corporate finance	71,000
investment banking	70,000
marketing/ brand management	69,000

Part One:
INVESTMENT IN GRADUATE EDUCATION

1. Fill in your current salary. If you are not working, estimate what you would earn based on your education and prior work experience. This is your opportunity cost of going to graduate school to earn an MBA degree.

2. Fill in the annual tuition any fees less any aid you will not have to repay.

3. Divide line 2 by .65 to determine the pretax earnings required to pay tuition and fees.

4. Add lines 1 and 3 for your annual investment.

5. Multiply line 4 by the length of the program in years. This represents your total investment in an MBA degree: the opportunity cost (lost earnings) and the out-of-pocket cost (net tuition and fees).

Part Two:
RATE OF RETURN ON INVESTMENT

6. Find the job you expect to obtain after graduation. Enter the starting salary (see starting salaries chart).

7. Subtract line 1 from line 6. This is the expected salary increase resulting form the MBA degree.

8. Find the intersection of your expected salary increase (line 7) and your total investment (line 5) in table A (one-year MBA programs) or Table B (two-year MBA programs). This is an estimate of your annualized percent return on investment in graduate school over a ten-year period measured from the start of your MBA program.

You can also estimate the payback period. Divide your total investment (line 5) by the expected salary increase (line 7), and add the length of the program in years (either one or two). This represents the number of years, from the start of the program, required to recoup your investment in the MBA degree. For example, if your total investment is $100,000 and your expected salary increase is $30,000, then your payback period for a two-year MBA program is 5.33 years ($100,000/$30,000 + 2 years).

TABLE A One-Year MBA Programs

Salary Increase	Total Investment			
	50,000	75,000	100,000	125,000
10,000	9%	–2%	–8%	–13%
20,000	35%	19%	9%	3%
30,000	58%	35%	23%	15%
40,000	79%	50%	35%	25%
50,000	99%	65%	47%	35%

TABLE B Two-Year MBA Programs

Salary Increase	Total Investment						
	50,000	75,000	100,000	125,000	150,000	175,000	200,000
10,000	5%	–5%	–12%	–16%	–19%	–22%	–24%
20,000	27%	13%	5%	–1%	–5%	–9%	–12%
30,000	44%	27%	17%	10%	5%	1%	–3%
40,000	58%	38%	27%	19%	13%	8%	5%
50,000	71%	49%	36%	27%	20%	15%	11%

Part Two

HOW TO GET IN

## Chapter Five

PREPARING TO BE A SUCCESSFUL APPLICANT

GET GOOD GRADES

If you're still in school, work on getting good grades. A high GPA says you've not only got brains, but discipline. It shows the admissions committee you have what you need to make it through the program. If you're applying directly from college or have limited job experience, your grades will matter even more. The admissions committee has little else on which to evaluate you.

It's especially important that you do well in courses such as economics, statistics, and calculus. Success in these courses is more meaningful than your success in classes like "Monday Night at the Movies" film appreciation. Of course, English is also important; b-schools want students who communicate well.

STRENGTHEN MATH SKILLS

Number-crunching is an inescapable part of b-school. Take an accounting or statistics course for credit at a local college or b-school. If you have a liberal arts background, did poorly in math, or got a low GMAT math score, this is especially important. Getting a decent grade will go a long way toward convincing the admissions committee you can manage the quantitative challenges of the program.

WORK FOR A FEW YEARS—BUT NOT TOO MANY

Business schools favor applicants who have worked full-time for several years. There are three primary reasons for this: 1) With experience comes maturity; 2) you're more likely to know what you want out of the program; 3) your experience enables you to bring real-work perspectives to the classroom. Since business school is designed for you to learn from your classmates, each student's contribution is important.

How many years of work experience should you have? From two to five seems to be the preferred amount, although there is no magic number. The rationale is that at two years you've worked enough to be able to make a solid contribution. Beyond four or five, you may be too advanced in your career to appreciate the program fully.

If your grades are weak, consider working at least three years before applying. The more professional success you have, the greater the likelihood the admissions committee will overlook your GPA.

LET YOUR JOB WORK FOR YOU

Many companies encourage employees to go to b-school. Some of these companies have close ties to a favored b-school and produce well-qualified applicants. If their employees are going to the kinds of schools you want to get into, these may be smart places to work.

Other companies, such as investment banks, feature training programs, at the end of which trainees go to b-school or leave the company. These programs hire undergraduates right out of school. They're known for producing solid, highly skilled applicants. Moreover, they're full of well-connected alumni who may write influential letters of recommendation.

Happily, the opposite tactic—working in an industry that generates few applicants—can be equally effective. Admissions officers look for students from underrepresented professions. Applicants from biotechnology, health care, not-for-profit, and even the Peace Corps are viewed favorably.

One way to set yourself apart is to have had two entirely different professional experiences before business school. For example, if you worked in finance, your next job might be in a different field, like marketing. Supplementing quantitative work with qualitative experiences demonstrates versatility.

Finally, what you do on your job is important. Seek out opportunities to distinguish yourself. Even if your responsibilities are limited, exceed the expectations of the position. B-schools are looking for leaders.

MARCH FROM THE MILITARY

A surprising number of b-school students hail from the military (although the armed forces probably had commanders in mind, not CEOs, when they designed their regimen).

Military officers know how to be managers because they've held command positions. And they know how to lead a team under the most difficult of circumstances.

Because most have traveled all over the world, they also know how to work with people from different cultures. As a result, they're ideally suited to learn alongside students with diverse backgrounds and perspectives. B-schools with a global focus are particularly attracted to such experience.

The decision to enlist in the military is a very personal one. However, if you've thought of joining those few good men and women, this may be as effective a means of preparing for b-school as more traditional avenues.

CHECK OUT THOSE ESSAY QUESTIONS NOW

You're worried you don't have interesting stories to tell. Or you just don't know what to write. What do you do?

Ideally, several months before your application is due, you should read the essay questions and begin to think about your answers. Could you describe an ethical dilemma at work? Are you involved in anything outside the office (or classroom)? If not, now is the time to do something about it. While this may seem contrived, it's preferable to sitting down to write the application and finding you have to scrape for or, worse, manufacture situations.

Use the essay questions as a framework for your personal and professional activities. Look back over your business calendar, and see if you can find some meaty experiences for the essays in your work life. Keep your eyes open for a situation that involves questionable ethics. And if all you do is work, work, work, get involved in activities that round out your background. In other words, get a life.

Get involved in community-based activities. Some possibilities are being a big brother/big sister, tutoring in a literacy program, or initiating a recycling project. Demonstrating a concern for others looks good to admissions committees, and hey, it's good for your soul, too.

It's also important to seek out leadership experiences. B-schools are looking for individuals who can manage groups. Volunteer to chair a professional committee or run for an office in a club.

It's a wide-open world; you can pick from any number of activities. The bottom line is this: The extracurriculars you select can show that you are mature, multifaceted, and appealing.

We don't mean to sound cynical. Obviously, the best applications do nothing more than describe your true, heartfelt interests and show off your sparkling personality. We're not suggesting you try to guess which activity will win the hearts of admissions directors and then mold yourself accordingly. Instead, think of projects and activities you care about, that maybe you haven't gotten around to acting on, and act on them now!

PICK YOUR RECOMMENDERS CAREFULLY

By the time you apply to business school, you shouldn't have to scramble for recommendations. Like the material for your essays, sources for recommendations should be considered long before the application is due.

How do you get great recommendations? Obviously, good work is a prerequisite. Whom you ask is equally important. Bosses who know you well will recommend you on both a personal and professional level. They can provide specific examples of your accomplishments, skills, and character. Additionally, they can convey a high level of interest in your candidacy.

There's also the issue of trust. B-school recommendations are made in confidence; you probably won't see what's been written about you. Choose someone you can trust to deliver the kind of recommendation that will push you over the top. A casual acquaintance may fail you by writing an adequate, yet mostly humdrum letter.

Cultivate relationships that yield glowing recommendations. Former and current professors, employers, clients, and managers are all good choices. An equally impressive recommendation can come from someone who has observed you in a worthwhile extracurricular activity.

Left to their own devices, recommenders may create a portrait that leaves out your best features. You need to prep them on what to write. Remind them of those projects or activities in which you achieved some success. You might also discuss the total picture of yourself you're trying to create. The recommendation should reinforce what you're saying about yourself in your essays.

About "Big Shot" recommendations: Don't bother. Getting some professional golfer who's a friend of your dad's to write you a recommendation will do you no good if he doesn't know you very well, even if he is President of the Universe. Don't try to fudge your application—let people who really know you and your work tell the honest, believable, and impressive truth.

PREPARE FOR THE GRADUATE MANAGEMENT ADMISSION TEST (GMAT)

Most b-schools require you to take the GMAT. The GMAT is now a three-and-a-half-hour computer adaptive test (CAT) with multiple-choice math and verbal sections. It also features an analytical writing assessment section, which is comprised of two essays on business-related topics. It's the kind of test you hate to take and schools love to require.

Why is the GMAT required? B-schools believe it measures your verbal and quantitative skills and predicts success in the MBA program. Some think this is a bunch of hooey, but most schools weigh your GMAT scores heavily in the admissions decision. If nothing else, it gives the school a quantitative tool to compare you with other applicants.

Most people feel they have no control over the GMAT. They dread it as the potential bomb in their application. But you have more control than you think. You can take a test-preparation course to review the math and verbal material, learn test-taking strategies, and build your confidence. Test-prep courses can be highly effective. The Princeton Review offers what we think is the best GMAT course available. Another option is to take a look at our book *Cracking the GMAT CAT*, which reviews all the subjects and covers all the tips you would learn in one of our courses.

How many times should you take the GMAT? More than once, if you didn't ace it on the first try. But watch out: Multiple scores that fall in the same range make you look unprepared. Don't take the test more than once if you don't expect a decent increase, and don't even think of taking it the first time without serious preparation. Two tries is best. Three, if there were unusual circumstances or if you really need another shot at it. If you take it more than three times, the admissions committee will think you have an unhealthy obsession with filling in dots. A final note: If you submit more than one score, most schools will take the highest.

If you don't have math courses on your college transcript or numbers-oriented work experience, it's especially important to get a solid score on the quantitative section. There's a lot of math between you and the MBA.

## Chapter Six

ADMISSIONS

HOW THE ADMISSIONS CRITERIA ARE WEIGHTED

Admissions requirements vary from institution to institution. Most rely on the following criteria (not necessarily in this order): GMAT score, college GPA, work experience, essays, letters of recommendation, interviews, and extracurriculars, of which the first four are the most heavily weighted. The more competitive the school, the less room there is for weakness in any one of these areas.

Most applicants suspect that the GMAT score or GPA pushes their application into one of three piles: "yes," "no," or "maybe." But that's not the way it is. Unless one or more of your numbers is so low it forces a rejection, the piles are "looks good," "looks bad," "hmmm, interesting," and all variations of "maybe." In b-school admissions, the whole is greater than the sum of the parts. Each of the numbers has an effect but doesn't provide the total picture.

What's fair about the system is that you can compensate for problem areas. Even if you have a low GMAT score, a high GPA, evidence of quantitative work experience, or the completion of an accounting or statistics course will provide a strong counterbalance.

As we've said, no one single thing counts more than everything else. Your scores, work experience, and essays should give the admissions committee a clear idea of your capabilities, interests, and accomplishments. Any particular weakness can be overcome by a particular strength in another area—so make sure you emphasize whatever strengths you have, and don't take them for granted.

THE GMAT AND GPA

The GMAT score and GPA are used in two ways. First, they're used as "success indicators" for the academic work. In other words, if admitted, will you have the brain power and discipline to make it through the program? Second, they're used to comparing applicants with the larger pool. In particular, the top schools like applicant pools with high scores. They think that having an incoming class with high scores and grade profiles is an indicator of their program's prestige and selectivity.

Some schools look more closely at junior and senior year grades than the overall GPA. Most consider the academic reputation of your college and the difficulty of your curriculum. A transcript loaded with courses like "Environmental Appreciation" and "The Child in You" isn't valued as highly as one with a more substantive agenda.

WORK EXPERIENCE

B-schools play particularly close attention to your work history. It provides tangible evidence of your performance in the business world thus far and hints at your potential. This helps b-schools determine whether you're going to turn out to be the kind of graduate they'll be proud to have as an alum. Your work experience reveals whether you've progressed enough (or too far) to benefit from a b-school education. It is also telling of the industry perspective you'll bring to the program.

Five elements are considered. First, the stature of your company: Does it have a good reputation? Does it produce well-qualified applicants?

Second, diversity of work experience. Have you done something extraordinary like starting your own business or inventing a new software program? Or maybe you've lucked out to work in an industry that is underrepresented at the prospective school?

Third, your advancement: Did you progress steadily to ever more responsible positions, or did you just tread water? Do your salary increases prove that you are a strong performer? Did you put in your time at each job, or just jump from company to company?

Fourth, your professional and interpersonal skills: Did you get along well with others? Work as part of a team? Do your recommenders see you as future manager material?

Fifth (and this is critical), your leadership potential: Did you excel in your positions, go beyond the job descriptions, save the day, lead a team?

THE ESSAYS

Admissions committees consider the essays the clincher, the swing vote on the "admit/deny" issue. Essays offer the most substance about who you really are. The GMAT and GPA reveal little about you, only that you won't crash and burn. Your work history provides a record of performance and justifies your stated desire to study business. But the essays tie all the pieces of the application together and create a summary of your experiences, skills, background, and beliefs.

The essays do more than give answers to questions. They create thumbnail psychological profiles. Depending on how you answer a question or what you present, you reveal yourself in any number of ways—creative, witty, open-minded, articulate, mature—to name a few. Likewise, your essay can reveal a negative side, such as arrogance, sloppiness, or an inability to think and write clearly.

THE RECOMMENDATIONS

Admissions committees expect recommendations to support and reinforce the rest of the application. They act as a sort of reality check. When the information from your recommender doesn't match up with the information you've provided, it looks bad.

Great recommendations are rarely enough to save a weak application from doom. But they might push a borderline case over to the "admit" pile.

Mediocre recommendations are potentially harmful: An application that is strong in all other areas now has an inconsistency that's hard to ignore.

Bad recommendations—meaning that negative information is provided—cast doubt on the picture you've created. In some cases they invalidate your claims. This can mean the end for your application. Again, be careful whom you ask for recommendations.

THE INTERVIEW

Like the recommendations, the interview is used to reinforce the total picture. But it is also used to fill in the blanks, particularly in borderline cases.

Not all b-schools attach equal value to the interview. For some, it's an essential screening tool. For others, it's used to evaluate those hovering in the purgatory between accept and reject. Still others strongly encourage, but do not require, the interview. Some schools make it simply informative. If you can't schedule an on-campus interview, the admissions office may find an alum to meet with you in your hometown.

If an interview is offered, take it. In person, you may be an entirely more compelling candidate. You can further address weaknesses or bring dull essays to life. Most important, you can display the kinds of qualities—enthusiasm, sense of humor, maturity—that often fill in the blanks and sway a decision.

Our strongest advice: act quickly to schedule your interviews. Admissions officers lack the staffing to interview every candidate who walks through their doors. So interview slots go faster than tickets to the Final Four. Grab a slot early by phoning the schools in September. You don't want your application decision delayed by several months (and placed in a more competitive round) because your interview was scheduled late in the filing period. Worse, you don't want to hear that your opportunity for face-to-face selling and convincing is gone, because all time slots are booked.

A great interview can tip the scale in the "admit" direction. How do you know if it was great? You were calm and focused. You expressed yourself and your ideas clearly. Your interviewer invited you to go rock climbing with him next weekend. (Okay, let's just say you developed a solid personal rapport with the interviewer.)

A mediocre interview may not have much impact, unless your application is hanging on by a thread. In such a case, the person you're talking to (harsh as it may seem) is probably looking for a reason not to admit you, rather than a reason to let you in. If you feel your application may be in that hazy, marginal area, try to be extra-inspired in your interview.

Did you greet your interviewer by saying, "Gee, are all admissions officers as pretty as you?" Did you show up wearing a Karl Marx T-shirt? Did you bring your mother with you? If so, it's probably safe to say you had a poor interview. A poor interview can doom even a straight-A, high-GMAT, strong-work-history candidate. Use good taste, refrain from belching, avoid insulting the interviewer's tie, and you'll probably be okay.

B-school interviews with alumni and admissions officers rarely follow a set formula. The focus can range from specific questions about your job responsibilities to broad discussions of life. Approach the interview as an enjoyable conversation, not as a question-and-answer ordeal that you're just trying to get through. You can talk about your hobbies or recent cross-country trip. This doesn't mean that it won't feel like a job interview. It just means you're being sized up as a person and future professional in all your dimensions. Try to be your witty, charming, natural self.

Students, faculty, admissions personnel, and alumni conduct interviews. Don't dismiss students as the lightweights; they follow a tight script and report back to the committee. However, because they're inexperienced beyond the script, their interviews are most likely to be duds. You may have to work harder to get your points across.

Prepare for the interview in several ways: Expect to discuss many things about yourself. Be ready to go into greater depth than you did in your essays (but don't assume the interviewer has read them). Put together two or three points about yourself that you want the interviewer to remember you by. Go in with examples, or even a portfolio of your work, to showcase your achievements. Practice speaking about your accomplishments without a lot of "I did this; I did that." Finally, be prepared to give a strong and convincing answer to the interviewer's inevitable question, "Why here?"

HOW TO BLOW THE INTERVIEW

1. Wear casual clothes.

This is an automatic ding. Wearing anything but professional attire suggests you don't know or don't want to play by the rules of the game.

2. Bring your mom or dad. Or talk about them.

Business schools value maturity. If Mom or Dad takes you to the interview, or your answer to the question "Why an MBA," begins with "Dad always told me . . . ," the interviewer is going to wonder how ready you are for the adult world of b-school.

3. Talk about high school.

Again, they'll question your maturity. Stories about high school, and even college, suggest you haven't moved on to more mature, new experiences.

Exceptions: Explaining a unique situation or a low GPA.

4. Show up late.

This is another automatic ding at some schools. Short of a real catastrophe, you won't be excused.

5. Say something off the wall or inappropriate.

No doubt, the conversation can get casual, and you may start to let your guard down. But certain things are still off-limits: profanity, ethnic jokes, allusions to sex, your romantic life, and anything else that might signal to the interviewer that the cheese fell off your cracker.

6. Forget to write a thank-you note to your interviewer.

Sending a thank-you note means you know how to operate in the business world, and it goes a long way toward convincing the interviewer you belong there.

MAKING THE ROUNDS: WHEN TO APPLY

You worked like a dog on your application—is there anything else you can do to increase your odds of getting accepted? Perhaps. The filing period ranges anywhere from six to eight months. Therefore, the timing of your application can make a difference. Although there are no guarantees, the earlier you apply, the better your chances. Here's why:

First, there's plenty of space available early on. As the application deadline nears, spaces fill up. The majority of applicants don't apply until the later months because of procrastination or unavoidable delays. As the deadline draws close, the greatest number of applicants compete for the fewest number of spaces.

Second, in the beginning, admissions officers have little clue about how selective they can be. They haven't reviewed enough applications to determine the competitiveness of the pool. An early application may be judged more on its own merit than how it stacks up against others. This is in your favor if the pool turns out to be unusually competitive. Above all, admissions officers like to lock their classes in early; they can't be certain they'll get their normal supply of applicants. Admissions decisions may be more generous at this time.

Third, by getting your application in early you're showing a strong interest. The admissions committee is likely to view you as someone keen on going to their school.

To be sure, some admissions officers report that the first batch of applications tend to be from candidates with strong qualifications, confident of acceptance. In this case, you might not be the very first one on line; but closer to the front is still better than lost in the heap of last-minute hopefuls.

Of course, if applications are down that year at all b-schools or—thanks to the latest drop in its ranking—at the one to which you are applying, then filing later means you can benefit from admissions officers desperately filling spaces. But this is risky business, especially since the rankings don't come out until the spring.

Conversely, if the school to which you are applying was recently ranked number one or two, applying early may make only a marginal difference. Swings in the rankings from year to year send school applications soaring and sagging. From beginning to end, a newly crowned number-one or two school will be flooded with applications. Regardless, do not put in your application until you are satisfied that it is the best you can make it. Once a school has passed on your application, it will not reconsider you until the following year.

ROUNDS AND ROLLING ADMISSIONS

Applications are processed in one of two ways: rounds admissions or rolling admissions. With rounds, the filing period is divided into three to four timed cycles. Applications are batched into the round in which they are received and reviewed competitively with others in that grouping. A typical round might go from February 15th to March 15th.

With rolling admissions, applications are reviewed on an ongoing basis as they are received. The response time for a rolling admissions decision is usually quicker than a decision with rounds. And with rolling admissions, when all the spaces are full, admissions stop.

QUOTAS, RECRUITMENT, AND DIVERSITY

B-schools don't have to operate under quotas—governmental or otherwise. However, they probably try harder than most corporations to recruit diverse groups of people. Just as the modern business world has become global and multicultural, so too have b-schools. They must not only teach diversity in the classroom but also make it a reality in their campus population and, if possible, faculty.

Schools that have a diverse student body tend to be proud of it. They tout their success in profiles that demographically slice and dice the previous year's class by sex, race, and geographic and international residency. Prospective students can review this data and compare the diversity of the schools they've applied to.

But such diversity doesn't come naturally from the demographics of the applicant pool. Admissions committees have to work hard at it. While they don't have quotas per se, they do target groups for admission, most notably women and minorities. In some cases, enrollment is encouraged with generous financial aid packages and scholarships.

But those targeted for admission are not limited to women and minorities. The committees seek demographic balance in many areas. Have they admitted enough foreign students, marketing strategists, and liberal arts majors? Are different parts of the country represented?

Only toward the end of the admissions filing period do shortages in different categories emerge. Although you can't predict, women and minorities are almost always on the short list. But here's some good news. According to the Graduate Management Admissions Council, in the 1996–97 academic year, 30 percent of the schools they surveyed said minorities made up 30–39 percent of their applicant pool. Happily, roughly 20 percent of the schools also reported increases in the number of women's applications.

WHO ARE THOSE ADMISSIONS OFFICERS?

ONE SCHOOL'S COMMITTEE REVEALED

Just who are those nameless, faceless people who pore over thousands of applications and determine the future of budding CEOs like you?

Most applicants picture a committee of white male MBAs in blue suits and power ties. But that's not the whole picture. Although many admissions officers do hold MBAs, they represent a wider slice of the demographic spectrum than do the b-school classes they admit. There are more women. More studied liberal arts and worked in fields such as human resources and teaching. In short, they're not necessarily what you'd expect, they're more diverse.

But as diverse as they are in background, they share a certain perspective: They believe that qualities, such as drive and discipline, rather than skills, such as financial analysis, are the true and enduring engines of success. In other words, at least as much value is placed on who you are as on your accomplishments.

Why does knowing this help you? Because in writing your application you need to consider your audience. Admissions officers aren't necessarily the people you thought they were. Moreover, they don't necessarily share your love of business. Their role in the business world is different from yours: They sustain the profession by launching inductees, while you actually practice business. Many officers, even some with MBAs, have limited business experience.

Remember, they're not only admissions officers, they're daughters, sons, mothers, fathers, and grandparents too—in other words, regular people. Would you write the same kind of essay for them that you would for your boss? The essays for b-school should be a combination of the two: strong on substance and heavy on personality.

Here's who reads your application at the Columbia b-school:

THE DIRECTOR OF ADMISSIONS
Gender: Male
Race/Ethnicity: White
Age: Mid-30s
Marital/Family: Single
College Major: Accounting/Economics
Graduate Degree: MBA
First Job out of Graduate School: Brand manager

"Admissions is a real marketing challenge. I enjoy it; I'm out meeting students, helping them identify their goals, and talking about how our school might be right for them. Because I went through this program, I have an understanding of what it takes to be successful in this environment. I can gauge how realistic the applicant's expectations of b-school are."

ADMISSIONS OFFICER
Gender: Female
Race/Ethnicity: African American
Age: Mid-30s
Marital/Family: Married/Mother
College Major: French/Political Science
Graduate Degree: M.A. in French, M.S. in Law and Diplomacy
First Job out of Graduate School: French instructor; developing public policy for higher education

"My previous work in undergraduate admissions gives me a unique point of view in reviewing MBA applications: I expect an applicant to be able to fully articulate why getting the degree is important. If the reasoning isn't clear, it's a problem. I also look for applicants who can bring something special to the student community—really add to the program and yet take advantage of all that we have to offer."

ADMISSIONS OFFICER

Gender: Female
Race/Ethnicity: White
Age: Late 40s
Marital/Family: Married/Grandmother
College Major: English
Graduate Degree: One year in law school—dropped out to be "ski bum";
M.S. in Reading; Candidate for Ph.D. in Philosophy
First Job Out of Graduate School: Teacher in an inner-city high school

"Based on my experiences as a teacher, I can see how some applicants will succeed even with a weak academic history. I err on the side of 'wait—don't reject this student just because the GMAT or academic [cumulative average] isn't high on the charts.' Other things will refocus me on their application: a unique job experience, compliments that people made about the applicant that are very telling, or something that alludes to depth or potential."

ADMISSIONS OFFICER

Gender: Female
Race/Ethnicity: Indian
Age: Late 20s
Marital/Family: Married
College Major: Art History/Asian Studies
Graduate Degree: MBA
First Job out of Graduate School: Strategic planning and financial manager

"As a recent graduate, I try to bring several perspectives to the admissions process: that of an applicant, a matriculate, and a young professional. Because of my international background, I understand the importance of diversity. I look for applicants who show this in both their professional and personal experiences."

ADMISSIONS OFFICER

Gender: Female
Race/Ethnicity: White
Age: Early 30s
Marital/Family: Married
College Major: English
Graduate Degree: M.A. in Writing
First Job out of Graduate School: English teacher for grades 9–12

"Admission to b-school is not the experiment of science nor game of roulette that people often think it is. When I review an applicant's profile, I don't fill in columns and

rows with data. Making a decision is a very difficult, thought-filled, and time-intensive process. I'm always aware that I'm working with the summary of a person's intellect, talent, culture, and aspirations. On Commencement Day, it's a fact that after the students, the admissions officers are the second happiest group in the school. On that day, everyone knows the decision and the relationship was successful!"

ADMISSIONS CONSULTANT
Gender: Female
Race/Ethnicity: White
Age: Mid-30s
Marital/Family: Married
College Major: Stage and Theater
First Job out of School: Actress
Career Prior to Admissions: Stage Director/Administrative Consultant

"I look for clear goals that are realistic and born of experience. When applicants can't articulate why they want the MBA, it's a concern. They don't have to have all the answers, but they should have a sound reason for wanting to be here. I'm also looking for people who have a sense of personal responsibility in the world. It's not a bad thing when a candidate says 'the MBA will help me strengthen the family business.' But I'd like to see somewhere else in the application that their universe is greater than themselves."

WHO DO YOU THINK READS YOUR ESSAYS?

Now that you know who those admissions officers are, here's the next surprise. Many top b-schools farm out the essays to paid readers. Why would the schools use readers instead of trained admissions officers to evaluate the essays? The answer is volume. As the number of applications to top b-schools has soared, it has become cost-effective to hire part-timers to do the most time-intensive work. Admissions officers are then free to make the higher-level admissions decisions.

Most applicants aren't pleased to know that an admissions officer isn't the one reading the essay they worked on for two weeks. But admissions committees couldn't be more pleased. Now instead of an enormous pile of unread essays—some terrific, some not—they have a pile that's been evaluated. Moreover, they point out, the essays are now read in greater depth than before.

But what you need to know is this: How do readers affect the admissions decision?

At most schools readers make general recommendations, then pass them on to other members of the committee for other opinions. They don't have the authority to make a final judgment. They're trained to evaluate essays in the same way admissions officers do—writing style, content, message, etc. More than one staff member usually reads them, often a combination of reader and admissions officer, so a reader's opinion is not the only one. Also, readers don't examine or have input into the evaluation of the applicant's total candidacy.

INSIDE BABSON'S ADMISSIONS DEPARTMENT

WHAT REALLY HAPPENS TO YOUR APPLICATION

Are specific weights or scores assigned to each component of the application?

Do admissions committees get together and read them at one big table—or do they take them home and cover them with coffee stains?

How many people read your essays? How do they decide whether they're good or terrible? Is there is a system for standardizing the reading of the essays? Are they graded? Do they disagree? How are disagreements resolved?

Who are the surprise admits, the surprise rejects? Why are some students put on the wait list? What can be done to pull them off?

These are just a few of the questions surrounding an admissions process that often operates with the concealment strategies of the CIA. But all is not lost. The Babson Graduate School of Business agreed to open its files for our review. And while this is only one school's admissions process, you can certainly draw some interesting conclusions. Here's a flow chart of their process:

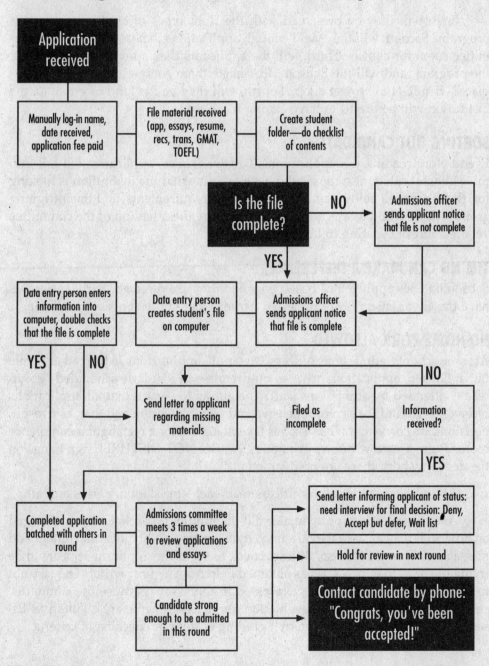

NOW WE CAN TAKE A CLOSER LOOK

THE BABSON ADMISSIONS CHALLENGE

The Babson admissions committee defines its challenge in four ways:

First, will they be presented with the right types of applicants for their program? Second, will they yield enough applications that year to give the committee room for choice? Third, will the applicants they admit make it through the program, and will the Babson MBA make them competitive in the marketplace when it's time to get a job? Fourth, will they be the kind of graduate the institution will be proud to have among its alumni?

SORTING OUT CANDIDATES

Even before reading the applications, Babson expects applicants will fall into three general categories: those who have exactly what the institution is looking for, those who fall below standard admissions requirements, and the intriguing group—those who possess qualities that capture the attention of the committee yet are short of securing initial acceptance.

TIMING CAN MAKE A DIFFERENCE

Babson batches applications based on when they are received. Early applicants have the advantage; they're reviewed earlier when more spots are available.

NO HOMEWORK ALLOWED

At some schools, admissions officers "sign out" applications to be read at home. But at Babson, applications are read on-premises in regularly scheduled "group reads" attended by admissions staff. The aim is to ensure that all applications receive the committee's comprehensive and equal attention and that, as a result, decisions are consistent. The sessions take place in a long rectangular conference room. There are no windows or phones. A "DO NOT DISTURB" sign hangs on the door. In short, there are no distractions.

At least three admissions officers read each application, essays and all.

An officer spends approximately 30–45 minutes on each. Essays are judged on how well they answer the question, style, writing ability, overall content and message, and maturity; also, officers check to see if the applicant appears to be trying too hard to impress or has obtained help from a ghost writer. They try not to form opinions on the views expressed in the essay. Because the committee shares the same standards of evaluation, these assessments are qualitative. Essays are not subjected to an internal grading system or checklist of criteria.

DECISIONS, DECISIONS, DECISIONS

Occasionally there is disagreement about a particular essay. But since the admissions decision is based on the entire package, agreement on one essay is not as important as agreement on the overall candidacy of the applicant. When the committee doesn't agree on this, a lengthy discussion about the applicant takes place. If a consensus isn't reached, one of two steps is taken. Either the application is placed into a pile of "re-reviews" to be read again against each other at a later date (up to two weeks) or, depending on the problem area, the applicant is asked to have an additional interview with a dean or faculty member, do some extra coursework, or retake the GMAT. Applicants in the latter category may be put on conditional admit or wait lists. If they satisfy the additional requirements and a place is available, they're in.

After the "group read" and review session, the three admissions officers are joined by the remaining admissions staff for a presentation of the applicant's candidacy.

CASE STUDIES

Here are the dossiers of four hopeful applicants to Babson, and the admissions committee's evaluation:

> **Applicant I** is an undergraduate finance major from the University of Connecticut. She has a B grade point average and scored in the high 500s on the GMAT. Her work experience is substantive: five years, including two spent in the Peace Corps. The essays are descriptive and full of enthusiasm for her Peace Corps experience. The admissions committee learned she was up against major odds trying to secure loans from various funding sources for native African business people.

The committee used the interview with this applicant to obtain further insight into why she chose to go into the Peace Corps rather than pursue her original career. A small but important point the applicant had overlooked—what had motivated her decision? In the interview, the admissions officer found her poised, well prepared, and able to articulate why she wanted the MBA. Her clarification of her job experience helped the committee better understand why she made the career decision she made.

Decision: *Admit*

Applicant II is a pharmaceutical salesman for a major international firm. His GMAT score is borderline, his GPA from a small liberal arts school in Maine is a low B. In reviewing his file, however, the committee found that he played a star position on his college's varsity hockey team and held a leadership position in student government. This helped explain and balance his marginal grades.

This applicant requested an interview early in the admissions process (this showed initiative even though interviews are required). He communicated clear expectations of the degree and what he wanted to accomplish. His essays also reflected a concise and persuasive presentation of his ideas. The letters of recommendation strongly supported his candidacy. His successes at work (many of them involving quantitative skill) also gave weight to his future business potential.

Decision: *Admit*

Applicant III is an art major from the Art Institute in Chicago. In addition to her current position as a marketing assistant at a special-events planning company, she has been recognized as one of the most creative students in the school and won the opportunity to present her work in the gallery at the museum. The committee felt a gallery show in such a prominent institute is a great accomplishment, particularly for a recent undergraduate.

This applicant took a "risky" approach to the essays, disclosing very personal information about emotional challenges she faced as a young adult. The essays were forthright, strong, and well structured. Most compelling was that her art exhibit was a pictorial essay of young women experiencing the same emotional challenges. The committee saw this as evidence that she had moved beyond the limitations of her emotional issues.

The greatest concern for this applicant was whether she would be able to manage the quantitative demands of the program. She has performed poorly on the math section of the GMAT. Her undergraduate coursework and limited work history provide no evidence of quantitative experience. For her benefit and the benefit of her classmates, she needs to bolster her skills before she can begin.

Decision: *Denied. Needs to retake the GMAT, take quantitative courses, and reapply.*

Applicant IV is a Venezuelan banker, one of many applying to the school because of its program's ties to Latin America.

This applicant was visiting Boston on a business trip and thought she would use the opportunity to come in for an interview before she applied. She was outstanding interpersonally. Her application later revealed an undergraduate GPA of a B+, eight years of work experience, and a mid-400 GMAT score. She has progressed in her job from being an economist with a bank to a senior loan officer—a nice progression. But her low GMATs blocked a clear "accept." Moreover, the committee needed to balance the number of students so there was not a predominant presence in any class from any one country.

Decision: *Hold her application for review in the next round and within the Latin American pool of candidates; ask her to retake the GMAT.*

## Chapter Seven

THE RIGHT STUFF

CREATING PERFECTION TAKES TIME

No one ever said it was going to be easy. Depending on where you're applying and how prolific a writer you are, a b-school application will take anywhere from 50 to 100 hours to complete. Sound excessive? Go ahead and try it. You'll probably scrap and rewrite an essay many times over. It takes time for thoughts to gestate. Indeed, it might feel like a fine wine ages faster than it takes you to write an essay.

This chapter should speed the process along. It deciphers some of the most commonly asked essay questions. It also provides you a list of mistakes applicants most often make.

COMMON ESSAY QUESTIONS

WHAT THEY'RE REALLY ASKING

Each school has its own set of essay questions. Although posed differently, all search for the same insights. Here's a list of commonly asked questions and what's behind them.

1. Theme: Career Goals and the MBA

Describe your specific career aspirations. How will your goals be furthered by an MBA degree and by our MBA program in particular?

How do you feel the X school MBA degree can help you attain your specific career and personal goals for the five years after you graduate?

Discuss your career progression to date. What factors have influenced your decision to seek a general management education? Based on what you know about yourself at this time, how do you envision your career progressing after receiving the MBA degree? Please state your professional goals, and describe your plan to achieve them.

Translation:

What do I want to be when I grow up, and how will the MBA get me there?

This may be the most important essay question. It lays out the reasons why you should be given one of the cherished spots in the program. Even if your post-MBA future is tough to envision, this question must be answered.

A good way to frame this essay is to discuss how the MBA makes sense in light of your background, skills, and achievements to date. Why do you need this degree? Why now? One common reason is being stymied in your work by a lack of skills that can be gained in their program. Or you may want to use the MBA as a bridge to the next step. For example, an actress wants an MBA to prepare for a career in theater management. The more specific, the better.

It may be easier to provide specifics by breaking your plans into short-term and long-term objectives.

Don't be afraid to present modest goals. If you're in accounting and want to stay there, say so. Deepening your expertise and broadening your perspective are solid reasons for pursuing the degree. On the other hand, feel free to indicate you'll use the MBA to change careers; 70 percent of all students at b-school are there to do just that.

If you aspire to lofty goals, like becoming a CEO or starting your own company, be especially careful that you detail a sensible, pragmatic plan. You need to show you're realistic. No one zooms to the top. Break your progress into steps.

Finally, this essay question asks how a particular program supports your goals. Admissions committees want to know why you've selected their school. That means you not only have to know, but also show, what's special about their program and how that relates specifically to your career aspirations.

(Hint: Many admissions officers say they can tell how much someone wants to go to their school by how well their essays are tailored to the offerings in their program.)

2. Theme: Extracurriculars and Social Interaction: Our Nonwork Side

What do you do for fun?

What are your principal interests outside of your job or school?

What leisure and/or community activities do you particularly enjoy? Please describe their importance in your life.

Translation:

Would we like to have you over for dinner? Do you know how to make friends? What are your special talents—the b-school Follies needs help. Are you well balanced, or are you going to freak out when you get here?

B-school is not just about business, case studies, and careers. The best programs buzz with the energy of a student body that is talented and creative and that has personality. You won't be spending all your time in the library.

Are you interesting? Would you contribute to the school's vitality? Are you the kind of person other MBAs would be happy to meet? Describe activities you're involved in that might add something to the b-school community.

Are you sociable? B-school is a very social experience. Much of the work is done in groups. Weekends are full of social gatherings. Will you participate? Initiate? Get along with others? Communicate that people, not just your job, are an important part of your life.

Can you perform at a high level without being a nerd?

B-school can be tough. It's important to know when to walk away and find some fun. Do you know how to play as hard as you work?

How well rounded are you? Business leaders have wide-angle perspectives; they take in the whole picture. How deep or broad are your interests?

(A warning: Don't just list what you've done. Explain how what you've done has made you unique.)

3. Theme: The Personal Statement

Does this application provide the opportunity to present the real you?

The admissions committee would welcome any additional comments you may wish to provide in support of your application.

What question should we have asked you?

Translation:

What did we miss? Appeal to us in any way you want; this is your last chance. Be real.

If you have an experience or personal cause that says something interesting about you, and it hasn't found a place in any other essay, this is the time to stick it in. Keep in mind that you are hoping to present yourself as unique—so show some passion!

4. Theme: Whom You Most Admire

If you were able to choose one person from the business world, past or present, to be your personal professor throughout the MBA program, who would this person be and why?

Describe the characteristics of an exceptional manager, using an example of someone whom you have observed or with whom you have worked. Illustrate how his or her management style has influenced you.

Translation:

What are your values? What character traits do you admire?

This is the curve-ball question. The committee isn't looking to evaluate your judgment in selecting some famous, powerful person in your firm or in the world. What they're really after, which you reveal in your selection of the person, is the qualities, attributes, and strengths you value in others, as well as in yourself. Some important qualities to address: Drive, discipline, vision, ethics, and leadership. As always, provide specific examples, and avoid choosing anyone too obvious.

Since the person you select is not as important as what you say about him or her, your choices can be more humble. You might write about a current boss, business associate, or friend. Bad choices are your mother or father.

If you like, it's perfectly fine to go for a famous figure. Indeed, there may be someone whose career and style you're passionate about. Make sure your essay explains why you find this person so compelling.

5. Theme: Ethics

Describe an ethical dilemma you have experienced and discuss how you handled the situation.

Can ethics be taught? How would you teach it?

Translation:

Do you know what an ethical dilemma looks like? Are you a sleazebag? What kinds of decisions and judgments might you make in your future practices as a business professional?

The last decade brought great attention to the ethics of the business world. In the aftermath of the BCCI, savings and loan, and insider-trading scandals, b-schools don't want to turn out graduates who are fast into their suspenders, fast into a deal, and fast to swindle their clients and partners.

Although the above two questions are not identical, they get at the same issues: your judgment and integrity. In the first question, it's important to present a real ethical dilemma. Applicants often write about the dilemma of obeying or not obeying a supervisor's orders because they knew a better way. But this is not an ethics problem (unless the order was improper or illegal). This is a management problem. Also, it doesn't showcase your sense of honor and conduct, which is what the essay is about.

Write about an ethical dilemma in which there was no easy course—one that entailed costs either way. For example, you sold a product to a client and later discovered the product was faulty; your employer wants you to keep mum. You've built your sales relationships on trust and personal attention, so you want to be forthcoming. What did you do?

The second question requires some imagination. Ethics is indeed tough to teach. And if you teach it, is it enough?

Like the essay above, this essay should communicate your sense of values. A lesson in ethics might include an exploration of the reasons behind business principles and practices. It might also include role plays and simulations to tease out different perceptions of what's right and wrong.

MUST-FOLLOW CHECKLIST FOR THE ESSAYS

- Communicate that you're a proactive, can-do sort of person. Leaders take initiative and aren't thwarted by roadblocks.

- Put yourself on ego alert; stress what makes you unique, not what makes you great. You want admissions officers to respect and like you.

- Position yourself as a stand-out from the crowd; emphasize your distinctiveness.

- Make sure your leadership qualities really come through. Admissions officers want to hear about skills that enabled you to rally folks around your solution.

- Communicate specific reasons why you're a "fit" for a school (but avoid pompous, fluff statements such as "I am the ideal or perfect candidate for your program.").

- Use your gender, ethnicity, minority, or foreign background—but only if it has affected your outlook or experiences.

- Bring passion to your writing—admissions officers want to know what you're really excited about.

- Avoid too many sentences that begin with "I." Use examples and anecdotes instead.

- Play up an unorthodox path to b-school. Admissions officers appreciate risk-takers. But be convincing about your ability to handle the program, especially quantitative skills that schools can take for granted in applicants in finance.

STRAIGHT TALK FROM ADMISSIONS OFFICERS:
FIFTEEN SURE-FIRE WAYS TO TORPEDO YOUR APPLICATION

1. Write about the high school glory days.

Unless you're right out of college, or you've got a great story to tell, resist using your high-school experiences for the essays. What does it say about your maturity if all you can talk about is being editor of the yearbook or captain of the varsity team?

2. Submit essays that don't answer the questions.

An essay that does no more than restate your resume frustrates the admissions committees. After reading 5,000 applications, they get irritated to see another long-winded evasive one.

Don't lose focus. Make sure your stories answer the question.

3. Fill essays with industry jargon and detail.

Many essays are burdened by business-speak and unnecessary detail. This clutters your story. Construct your essays with only enough detail about your job to frame your story and make your point. After that, put the emphasis on yourself—what you've accomplished and why you were successful.

4. Write about a failure that's too personal or inconsequential.

Refrain from using breakups, divorces, and other romantic calamities as examples of failures. What may work on a confessional talk show is too personal for a b-school essay.

Also, don't relate a "failure" like getting one "C" in college (out of an otherwise straight "A" average). It calls your perspective into question. Talk about a failure that matured your judgment or changed your outlook.

5. Reveal half-baked reasons for wanting the MBA.

Admissions officers favor applicants who have well-defined goals. Because the school's reputation is tied to the performance of its graduates, those who know what they want are a safer investment.

If b-school is just a pit stop on the great journey of life, admissions committees would prefer you make it elsewhere. However unsure you are about your future, it's critical that you demonstrate that you have a plan.

6. Exceed the recommended word limits.

Poundage is not the measure of value here. Exceeding the recommended word limit suggests you don't know how to follow directions, operate within constraints, organize your thoughts, or all of the above.

Get to the crux of your story and make your points. You'll find the word limits adequate.

7. Submit an application full of typos and grammatical errors.

How you present yourself on the application is as important as what you present. Although typos don't necessarily knock you out of the running, they suggest a sloppy attitude. Poor grammar is also a problem. It distracts from the clean lines of your story and advertises poor writing skills.

Present your application professionally—neatly typed and proofed for typos and grammar. And forget gimmicks like a videotape. This isn't "America's Funniest Home Videos."

8. Send one school an essay intended for another—or forget to change the school name when using the same essay for several applications.

Double check before you send anything out. Admissions committees are (understandably) insulted when they see another school's name or forms.

9. Make whiny excuses for everything.

Admissions committees have heard it all—illness, marital difficulties, learning disabilities, test anxiety, bad grades, pink slips, putting oneself through school—anything and everything that has ever happened to anybody. Admissions officers have lived through these things, too. No one expects you to sail through life unscathed. What they do expect is that you own up to your shortcomings.

Avoid trite, predictable explanations. If your undergraduate experience was one long party, be honest. Discuss who you were then, and who you've become today. Write confidently about your weaknesses and mistakes. Whatever the problem, it's important you show you can recover and move on.

10. Make the wrong choice of recommenders.

A top-notch application can be doomed by second-rate recommendations. This can happen because you misjudged the recommendors' estimation of you or you failed to give them direction and focus.

As we've said, recommendations from political figures, your uncle's CEO golfing buddy, and others with lifestyles of the rich and famous don't impress (and sometimes annoy) admissions folk—unless such recommenders really know you or built the school's library.

11. Let the recommender miss the deadline.

Make sure you give the person writing your recommendation plenty of lead time to write and send in their recommendation. Even with advance notice, a well-meaning but forgetful person can drop the ball.

It's your job to remind them of the deadlines. Do what you have to do to make sure they get there on time.

12. Be impersonal in the personal statement.

Each school has its own version of the "Use this space to tell us anything else about yourself" personal statement question. Yet many applicants avoid the word "personal" like the plague. Instead of talking about how putting themselves through school lowered their GPA, they talk about the rising cost of tuition in America.

The personal statement is your chance to make yourself different from the other applicants, further show a personal side, or explain a problem. Take a chance and be genuine; admissions officers prefer sincerity to a song and dance.

13. Make too many generalizations.

Many applicants approach the essays as though they were writing a newspaper editorial. They make policy statements and deliver platitudes about life without giving any supporting examples from their own experiences.

Granted, these may be the kind of hot-air essays that the application appears to ask for, and probably deserves. But admissions officers dislike essays that don't say anything. An essay full of generalizations is a giveaway that you don't have anything to say, don't know what to say, or just don't know how to say whatever it is you want to say.

14. Neglect to communicate that you've researched the program and that you belong there.

B-schools take enormous pride in their programs. The rankings make them even more conscious of their academic turf and differences. While all promise an MBA, they don't all deliver it the same way. The schools have unique offerings and specialties.

Applicants need to convince the committee that the school's programs meet their needs. It's not good enough to declare prestige as the primary reason for selecting a school (even though this is the basis for many applicants' choice).

15. Fail to be courteous to employees in the admissions office.

No doubt, many admissions offices operate with the efficiency of sludge. But no matter what the problem, you need to keep your frustration in check.

If you become a pest or complainer, this may become part of your applicant profile. An offended office worker may share his or her ill feelings about you with the boss—that admissions officer you've been trying so hard to impress.

## Chapter Eight

ESSAYS THAT WORK

Writing Your Way into Business School

CASE EXAMPLES:
ADMISSIONS OFFICERS CRITIQUE WINNING ESSAYS

To show you how some applicants have answered the essay questions, we asked the b-schools for samples of "winning" essays. To show you what worked, we also asked the admissions officers to provide a critique.

As you read through the essays, keep in mind that each was but one of several submitted by an applicant for admission. Moreover, they were part of a package that included other important components. One essay alone did not "win" admission.

One other reminder. The purpose of including essays in this book is to give you a nudge in the right direction, not to provide you with a script or template for your own work. It would be a mistake to use them this way.

Obviously, this collection is by no means all-encompassing. There are thousands of winning essays out there; we just couldn't include them all.

A final note: Because Harvard features a whopping ten-essay application, we especially wanted it in this section. Harvard declined our request. So to access what apparently is guarded as closely as FBI files, we contacted the students and grads directly. To our delight, everyone was eager to supply an essay. We selected those we believe the admissions officers would also have considered "winning."

BOSTON UNIVERSITY

Essay #1:

Imagine a straight line of infinite length, stretching out of sight in two directions. Assuming the line represents time, one can stand at any present moment and simultaneously look back at past experience and project one's sight into the future.

The time line is an assumption that makes planning possible. Though it may someday be proven a false, or at least incomplete, model, it can be useful for both personal and professional planning. For this essay, I'll limit myself to the latter.

Where I Stand

Looking back at what I've done and ahead to what I'd like to do, I can find great sense in beginning a graduate management program.

I have: a foundation of experience in the administration of educational and cultural institutes. Past jobs have ranged from directing a college admissions office to promoting an opera company, to managing a modern dance company, to running a day care center, to editing a weekly newspaper.

I have: an understanding of how groups function, what makes an organization healthy, and various ways people can organize to accomplish a goal. This has come from work experience as well as graduate study in organization theory and design at Harvard and at M.I.T.

I have: dreams and plans for a range of jobs and enterprises that extend ahead through my life.

From Here to There

Among many goals, I would like to direct a major cultural institution. I would also like to head a major educational institution, run a major foundation, and start and run my own cultural or educational organization—not necessarily all at the same time.

To achieve the above, there are skills and arenas of knowledge and experience that I'd like to have in my grasp. Some of these are presently out of reach, others are at my fingertips, but none are firmly in hand.

Financial management is, for me, perhaps the largest arena of knowledge in which I want, but do not have, agility. A course of study that refreshes my quantitative skills and teaches me principles of economics, fiscal planning, and other financial management skills would be very useful.

Another such arena includes management information systems and computer programming. I presently work on word processing equipment with comfort and joy. I hope, with time and guidance, to do the same with other systems at an even deeper level.

I would also like more personal contact with professional peers, particularly in the Boston and New England region. The public management program appears to offer that.

Some of my more obvious strengths and weaknesses should be evident from the above. I have confidence in myself. I have a great deal of curiosity. I generate ideas and develop interests, and can usually turn these into realistic, well-organized, and flexible plans. These I consider my strengths.

I can also stretch myself too thin, which can be a problem. Though I realize taking on the new demands some letting go of the old, I also believe experience increases capacity. There seems to me a need for more trained generalists to protect against overspecialization and fragmentation.

One great tool for that kind of protection is humor. My own sense of the comic can be quite dry and subtle, or broad and bizarre. Regardless of the form in which it spills out, it provides me perspective, balance, and spontaneity.

Cooperation, too, is a central motivation for me, and I am glad to see it stressed in the public management literature.

Arrivals

To accept two accomplishments and to label these significant runs counter to my way of assessing substance. I try to resist measuring my achievement by individual moments of arrival. Still, when pressed, I can come up with a few.

Performing professional theater at the age of 17 is an accomplishment that seems more significant now than it did at the time. Being appointed a college admissions director at 23 seems similarly significant. Both provided a sense of competence at a young age, and both provided peer experience with people older and more experienced than myself.

Doing well in a graduate program at Harvard feels notable in that the school was an environment very different from any in which I had worked before. The program became a test of adaptability as well as intellect. Other accomplishments might include a few backpacking ventures taken in severe conditions, some of which became life threatening. These provided dramatic tests of my reserves, and gave me confidence in my capacity for survival.

Less dramatic, and not quite finished, is a quilting project that I have worked on for more than six years. I have just completed the top sheet, a mutipieced pattern in fabric. Still ahead is the quilting process itself, stitching the top sheet to a sturdy backing, with a layer of batting between the two. When done, the quilt takes on an identity far greater than the sum of its many parts.

The work on this piece has been a teacher of patience and harmony. The quilt, with its assortment of shapes and fabric, can serve as a model for the organization for one's life and the people and activities in it.

Now, imagine a fine thread of infinite length weaving in and out of all those pieces.

Critique: Admissions officers review several hundreds or thousands of applications each year. Due to this high volume, any given applicant should formulate a creative approach in composing the essay to attract attention to its quality and content. Unfortunately, many applicants write essays that are similar to a detailed resume or a cover letter. This not only discourages a thorough review but also eliminates the opportunity for the individual to express his or her own uniqueness. The admissions officers are also usually interested in how an applicant responds to a specific question, rather than a general statement.

This essay creatively suggests the applicant's general outlook on his life, what he hopes to achieve, and how he will do it. He does not go into great detail about any of these issues but allows what he does say to have a powerful impact. Reading this essay gives the evaluator the opportunity to get to know the values as well as interests and accomplishments the candidate has. This is particularly helpful when applying to a school that does not have evaluative interviews as part of the application process.

The essay is also brief and concise and makes an effort to link all the topics mentioned in the essay to create a well-defined image. The use of subtitles introduces the outline and scope of the essay.

BRIGHAM YOUNG UNIVERSITY

Essay #1

Donald J. Buehner

MBA Admissions Committee
640 TNRB
Brigham Young University
Provo, UT 84602

Dear Members of the BYU MBA Admissions Committee:

In response to your request, I am writing to inform you of my intentions for this coming year as well as to describe my employment experience acquired during the past year.

I plan to attend the MBA program commencing in September 1991. You should have already received my Bishops Form.

During the past year I have had extensive international and national work experience. In February of 1990 I was promoted by Franklin International Institute Inc. to assist in opening a European Distribution Center in England. My specific assignment was to establish and manage the order entry and customer service departments as well as to hire and train British employees in the various operational functions. Inclusive with this training assignment was to implement the corporate values, philosophies, and quality, and to install in our employees the high standards of excellence and consumer satisfaction for which the Franklin International Institute strives. During my six-month assignment, I worked under pressured time constraints.

The international exposure in Europe during historic times as Britain and the other eleven continental countries prepare for the economic union in 1992 was extremely beneficial for me. Combined with my work experience in Japan and my mission to South Africa, as well as my ability to speak Japanese, Dutch, and Afrikaans, working in the British Isles increased my confidence and desire to pursue a career in international business.

My next promotion came in September last year, which was to help open and manage the first Franklin Day Planner Retail center to be situated in a mall. This opportunity is providing me with more valuable experience in hiring, training, and management skills, as well as useful retail understanding including sales, stock control, and profit and loss flows. Working with the extremely qualified and professional upper management of Franklin International has been valuable in shaping my career goals.

Regarding my decision to defer attendance at Brigham Young for one year, I believe Dr. Peter Clarke's counsel that additional exposure in the workforce would only enhance my graduate experience was wise advice. I feel better prepared to both learn from and be a progressive participant in the Master of Business Administration program at Brigham Young University. I request admittance for the fall of 1991.

Essay #2

Dean of Business School
Brigham Young University
Provo, UT 84601

Dear Sir:

In preparation for a career as an International Businessman, I am seeking entrance into the graduate program at Brigham Young University. This letter will provide the requested information regarding my wish to study at BYU.

My family experience has significantly influenced my preparation for a career in business administration. As the youngest of six children I have shared family responsibilities of managing our 48-acre farm. Because my father worked full-time, my brothers and I learned at a young age to operate a farm. At fourteen, being the only son left at home, I learned to creatively utilize my resources and to seek expert advice from local farmers in managing the farm. I learned other important business principles, such as hard work, commitment, and honesty. I also learned frugality by saving a portion of my earnings in order to attend University and in addition, support myself for two years as a voluntary missionary in South Africa.

I have actively sought for balance by being involved in school plays, learning to play the trumpet and guitar, and to sing. I have sought excellence in athletics: baseball, football, track and field, and swimming. I was actively involved in scouting and obtained the Eagle Scout award and the Order of the Arrow, an award earned through leadership, service, and courage. Such activities taught me self-discipline and team unity.

At sixteen, I was selected to go for one year as a High School Rotary International Exchange student to South Africa. My responsibility was to represent America while there, and then upon returning home, to be an ambassador for South Africa to enhance world peace and understanding. In this effort, I made presentations about America to business clubs, high schools, and social groups. I also became immersed in South African culture by learning to speak Afrikaans, play their sports, enjoy their food, and listen carefully to their interesting and unique perspectives. From this experience in such a diverse land, I learned to respect foreign cultures, and I feel I developed a special talent to communicate with a relate to a wide variety of people.

As a missionary to South Africa, I served as a district and Zone leader, and Assistant to the President. As an Assistant, I became responsible for the mission's 52-car fleet, the supply and distribution of mission products, and the transportation arrangements for more than 130 missionaries. Working both in an intimate and business level in a foreign country was exciting and challenging. On my mission I decided I could best serve my fellow men as an international businessman. This decision was based on my passion for South Africa and my ability to relate with and influence a variety of people for good.

During the summer of my sophomore year at Brigham University, I decided to enhance my international marketability by going to Japan and learning Japanese. After arriving in Japan, I negotiated to establish and to teach an English program to an expanding Japanese company. Through this experience, I became excited and confident in my ability to learn languages, and to conduct business in foreign cultures by being understanding and alert to their traditions and values.

One of my major accomplishments has been financing and completing a college education. In this pursuit, I demonstrated creativity in my capacity to see business opportunities and make them profitable. For example, I installed security door-viewers in apartment complexes in exchange for rent by discovering existing trends of vacancy of various apartments, as well as installing door-viewers in a cost-effective manner. While working ten to thirty hours a week, I maintained an average of fifteen credit hours, I achieved an overall 3.61 GPA with a 3.74 GPA in my major. I feel this reflects my commitment to achieving excellence under challenging situations.

In addition to the university curriculum I have had a valuable experience in the work field. As a salesman for an insulation company in San Francisco, I succeeded at and learned to love honest sales by being competent in my service and by discovering the true needs of the people. My marketing experience as a sales rotator for Karl Lagerfeld products in Utah included direct selling as well as overseeing advertising displays in department stores such as Nordstrom's.

As a full-time employee of Franklin International, I have demonstrated total commitment. I have also sought creative ways to better the company through my organizational behavior training at BYU. Recently, I helped restructure the leadership responsibilities in my department in order for more on-going training and less busywork. As a result of the confidence of my superiors, I have been offered positions of trust and leadership. In March until August, I will be establishing the customer service/order entry department for our company in England. My responsibilities will include hiring, training, and managing a British team of fifteen employees.

I am extremely enthusiastic about the future of international business administration. I believe there are major breakthroughs yet to be made in the filed. After completing an MBA, I hope to gain practical experience and exposure with a major international business firm. Eventually, I intend to establish resorts, clinics, and camps in which to motivate and train people of all cultures. To incorporate values and thought patterns conducive to healthier, happier, and more productive lifestyles. Such training would include a physical appreciation of body and environment, as well as a spiritual appreciation of fundamental values such as honesty and integrity. I envision training focused at salvaging youth from drug abuse and inspiring them to become producers. I believe this personal passion can best be accomplished as a professional and competent businessman.

I want to attend the graduate program at BYU for many reasons. I understand the working relationship between local corporations and the business school is conducive to consistent business exposure and experience combined with serious academic study. I desire a top-quality accredited program that incorporates high moral values as part of the curriculum. I am also impressed with the close working association with professors and students at the Business School. I look forward to a challenging and stimulating relationship with professors and peers and feel my unique exposure to business in South Africa, Japan, England, and America will allow me to contribute interesting insight and comparisons.

Thank you for your consideration.

Critique: Don's letter of intent gives us a picture of a well-rounded human being. He talks about his preparation in terms of his work experience as a youth as well as an adult, his high school activities in music, sports, and travel, his community experience in scouting and service to his church, as well as his academic preparation.

International Experience: Since 85 percent of our students speak second languages and 35 percent speak a third, we are interested in international experiences that enrich the class. Don mentions four experiences of significance.

The first was his high school exchange student experience in South Africa. He not only explains how he presented information about America to business clubs and social groups, he also talks about what he has learned individually in playing South African sports, learning Afrikaans, and relating to people of different cultures.

The second experience was Don's voluntary mission for the Church of the Jesus Christ of Latter-Day Saints to South Africa. The admissions committee is well aware of the growth and maturity that occurs on a mission, but Don chose to elaborate by explaining his specific responsibilities as a leader and manager for the mission's fleet of cars.

The third was a choice Don made as a college student to learn Japanese and Japanese ways. He explains his work with a Japanese company in helping to expand their English program.

The fourth experience was Don's assignment in England to open a new branch of the Franklin International (now Franklin Quest) office.

Work Experience: Don shows valuable work experience from his youth. He supports his assertion that he learned how to work early with specifics about being in charge of a farm at fourteen because his brothers had grown up, looking to neighboring farmers for advice, and saving his earnings for his own future plans.

Don financed his own college education. He mentions creative part-time work—installing door-viewers.

After college Don gained marketing and sales experience with some well-known companies before he joined Franklin International and was promoted to management positions.

Leadership: Evidence of Don's leadership skills is shown in his experience as district and Zone leader and eventually Assistant to the President on his church mission in South Africa.

Future Plans: Don has some definite ideas about what he would like to do in international business administration. He presents his plan to establish resorts and camps to train people. This information gives the admissions committee some idea about whether our program can contribute to what he has in mind.

Good Writing Skills: Don's writing indicates an ability to express himself well and reflect on his undergraduate preparation. He frames his letter in the first paragraph by telling us what the letter is about and he concludes in the final paragraph by pulling together the reasons the Marriot School of Management is attractive to him. This indicates he has done his homework to find out what our program is about. Within the framing are clear paragraphs explaining Don's experiences that make him a viable candidate.

What the Student Brings to the Class: Don shows he has something to contribute to his peers. He shows diversity in his experiences, a teachableness, some definite goals, and an ability to work hard. His international experiences show an ability to cooperate and get along with people and demonstrate good problem-solving skills.

This area is very important. The Admissions Committee works at building a class with diversity in backgrounds and educational experiences that will enrich and contribute to the whole class.

UNIVERSITY OF CALIFORNIA–BERKELEY

Question #1: *What seminal influences, broadly defined, have especially contributed to your personal development? What correlation, if any, has your personal development to your professional goals? In your response to this question, please do not discuss the influence of members of your immediate family, athletic endeavors, or professional experiences.*

Essay #1:

Bangkok, Vientiane, Malaysia, Singapore, Tokyo, Washington D.C., Manhattan, Boston, Camden, and San Francisco are the places where I have grown up. My father was a diplomat, my mother a teacher, and I am the youngest of four children. Together, my family moved every two or three years to a new city. Growing up was an adventure: as children, my brothers, sister, and I did not choose to move so frequently, but we became accustomed to it. We learned to assimilate quickly, make new friends, adjust to unfamiliar customs, even speak foreign languages.

The diverse cultural experiences that are part of my childhood have shaped the way I think about the world and my purpose in it. Living abroad cultivated my curiosity in politics and international relations, and moving frequently developed my interpersonal skills and created a strong personal motivation to make the best of a new situation.

Living abroad and moving frequently influenced who I am today, yet they are facts about my life that I have had little control over. When I think about who I am today, I focus on the choices I have made, the actions I have taken, and the guidance I have received from relatives and friends through various struggles. One choice I made stands out as an important influence because it resulted in challenges that stretched me in new directions and dramatically changed my perspective.

*   *   *   *

Following High School graduation, I worked as a roustabout out on an offshore oil rig in the Gulf of Mexico, 125 miles off the coast of Louisiana. For graduation, my family had pitched in for a round-trip plane ticket to Europe. I had been preparing for a trip across the continent when my oldest brother called about a job opportunity on an oil rig. I opted for the job because it was both an adventure and an opportunity to earn a lot of money for college (my savings amounted to one year at Harvard).

Within a week I was on a helicopter heading for Block 352, an oil field leased from the government by Chevron. I had several lasting impressions of the experience. The first is primarily sensory as I recall the physical conditions under which we lived and worked. The incessant noise of power generators and welding machines hummed in our ears day and night. Every species of dirt and grime thrived on the rig. The platform was characterized by its oppressive heat, magnified by the flames from the acetylene torches and welding rods and by the exhaust from the welding machines. The only activity we looked forward to was mealtime in an air-conditioned bunkhouse.

The work was dangerous, and if it were not for luck and the other hands who kept a close eye on me, I certainly would have been injured. That summer seven people died on Block 352, four in a helicopter accident, two in a crane accident; the seventh was a close friend of mine. At twenty-one, Eric was the closest person to my age. When I first started, he and I worked closely together and he explained everything he knew about work on the rig. Eric was related in one way or another to many of the people in our crew, and as Eric's friend, I became one of the clan. Most of the elder clans looked out for me as they did for Eric.

One day Eric was hurrying around a corner when he tripped on the extra slack of his torch line and he fell through a hole he had just cut in the deck. He fell 200 plus feet, hit the structure before landing, and drowned, taken swiftly under either by the current or the barracuda that circle below waiting for kitchen trash.

The lawyers and the search party came and went, and work began as usual the next morning. I was struck by two reactions to Eric's death. The first was the other hands barely spoke of it. It was as though the danger of the job was something they had all accepted and put behind them so they could carry on. I will never know if I could have helped Eric if I were there, but I still wonder why it wasn't me. The other response was an unusual step taken by the foreman that morning: someone still needed to descend through the hole that Eric had fallen through and climb out to the very end of the structure to attach a cable. Without a word, our foreman joined us, climbed through the hole, attached the cable, and was back before we realized the spell was broken. His action made me realize that to earn respect as a leader, never ask another person to attempt what you might not try yourself.

Another lasting impression I have of work on the rig, in direct contrast to the harsh conditions, is the strong personal relationships that made the experience memorable. The men I worked with from 5:00 a.m. to 10:00 p.m. were an extraordinary crew, all Cajuns from southern Louisiana, all hard working, all part of a team. On my first day, one of the hands later told me, they thought I was an engineer because I came dressed with new Chevron hard-hat, clean Levi's, and a clean T-shirt. Far from an engineer, I was worse than a 'worm' (someone new on the rig) because I had no training. As a young kid from Maine who did not know how to cut, weld, fit, grind, or stack steel pipe, I had a lot of ground cover. The interests that had been a strong part of my identity in high school: student athlete, leader, etc. were suddenly irrelevant. Where I had come from and where I was going at the end of the summer had no bearing in the context of working offshore. All that mattered was what I could accomplish that summer. The way to join this crew was straightforward: work hard, learn quickly, and interact during mealtime.

Initially I was a "rigger," someone who supports welders by hauling steel and creating safe, makeshift platforms for welders to stand on as they weld. Early in the summer I asked our foreman, Henry Calais, if I could learn to weld. I did not know about the months of training it takes to become a certified pipe welder, but Henry was kind and offered instead to have me work with Charlie Reitenger as his assistant. Charlie was the crew's "fitter" and, after Henry, was the most experienced person on the platform. A fitter measures and cuts pipe to length so that when the ends of two sections meet, they are adjacent, plumb, and square.

Charlie never wore a shirt, just a jeans jacket with cut-off sleeves. Charlie was an intense man with a subtle sense of humor; on the morning of our first day working together, immediately after a healthy breakfast (at an unhealthy 5:00 a.m.) Charlie opened his first can of Skoal Long cut, pinched a lip full of tobacco, and then offered me a can. We were hanging mid-air, about 200 feet above the water, and descending rapidly toward the workboat below as the crane operator lowered us. I smiled declining: "Thanks, no, maybe after a second cup of coffee." This exchange became a morning routine with us.

Charlie and I did not start off with a lot in common. I was not sure how to create a common ground between us, but I began by showing interest in what he had to teach me. For the first week I hauled steel all over the platform for Charlie to measure and cut. Over time Charlie taught me everything there is to know about cutting and fitting pipe, and I, in turn, taught him some of the basic concepts of trigonometry. I was less successful with physics. One day I was trying to calculate how high we were above the water by dropping a welding rod and counting how many seconds it took to hit the water. For a moment Charlie thought I was an idiot. He argued that my methodology was flawed because a heavier object would fall faster.

I tried to explain that gravity exerts the same force on all objects, but as our discussion progressed other hands took an interest, and Charlie prevailed by the sheer weight of popular opinion. Galileo would have been empathetic; we eventually conducted an experiment from the heliport, which is the highest level on the rig. We dropped several objects of varying mass before the debate was finally resolved and a basic law of physics restored. It was quite a revelation, and I was surprised by how it consumed the conversation that evening, interrupting the usual ribald dinner talk.

The summer spent offshore was unique preparation for college and for life. I still have not taken a summer off to travel in Europe, but I have never regretted passing up that opportunity to work on the oil rig. The experience exposed me to the human drama of a working class that I had not had contact with. The extreme working conditions and contact with a much older group of peers accelerated a period of growth and maturity for me. Working on the rig gave me an opportunity to reexamine what I wanted to accomplish in college and who I wanted to become. When the summer was over I felt like a completely changed person. In the helicopter heading back to Morgan City, Louisiana, I realized how fortunate I was to have the opportunity to go to college.

Critique: In reviewing Haas MBA application essays, the admissions committee places considerable weight on intellectual performance and potential; a sense of purposiveness; evidence of ethical character; and skill in the development, organization, and presentation of thoughts and ideas. We seek candidates who demonstrated initiative, creativity, thoughtfulness, receptiveness, and resourcefulness in the conduct of their personal and professional lives. We look for individuals who can provide a satisfactory account of who they are, what they have accomplished in the context of their own experiences and opportunities, and what they intend to accomplish during graduate school and beyond. Most compelling are those candidates whose reflections on their experiences and on their record of accomplishments, however defined, suggest an adaptability to make significant contributions to their class and to the Haas School.

The previous essay ostensibly describes a summer job following graduation from high school. Although the nature of the job may be unusual by MBA-application standards, it is not merely the novelty or drama of the situation that makes this essay successful. Its principle strengths are the degree of thought and writing skill the author exhibits in this composition. The essay is compelling because the author imparts a deep insight, wry humor, and a seemly modest ability to work successfully with people of widely different backgrounds, education, and cultures to the mutual benefit of all concerned. It is exceptional because while the author suggests that he was the principal beneficiary of that summer job on the oil rig in the Gulf, it is clear that his account is as instructive to the reader as his participation was to his colleagues.

CASE WESTERN RESERVE UNIVERSITY

Question #1: *Describe the most difficult personal or professional challenge that you have faced in the past five years. What did you learn from that experience?*

Essay #1:

In 1990, I formed my own company, Asian Profiles, Inc., to conduct research on the automotive industry, focusing primarily on East Asian markets. The compiled research is stored in a computer database system which allows me to analyze the data and forecast future automotive trends. Through the evaluation of automotive markets, I am able to construct "profiles" of East Asian nations and determine their relative potential as manufacturing sites and/or consumer markets for American automobile manufacturers and suppliers. My position as a research consultant and president of the company has given me the opportunity to test my professional and personal strengths as well as verify my leadership abilities.

Asian Profiles, Inc., has created a multitude of professional challenges for me. Running a small business of any kind requires a great deal of resourcefulness and ingenuity. When I started my business, my company had a database system with zero information. Four of the major management decisions I was confronted with at the time were: assessing the type of information my clients required, determining the availability of such information, selecting appropriate sources for the information, and choosing the methods for retrieving such information. I take pleasure in the fact that my company now has an extensive operating database. However, I am still faced with the above management decisions in addition to the daily challenge of determining the speed at which I need to retrieve information, and the price I am willing to pay for it. I have to constantly ask myself, "Is there a better, quicker, more cost-effective way to find this information?" Often the answer is yes, and I have found that local resources can offer more practical means of information retrieval than other sophisticated sources such as computer network systems and expensive publications. Ultimately, though, I have come to realize that people are the most valuable resource in the business. Since incorporating my company, I have carefully developed useful contacts whom I can call upon for professional advice. (To date) my company has enjoyed great success primarily because I have learned when to seek advice, when to give it, and when to solve a problem on my own. During this period I have learned that networking is an important part of any successful business career.

Being self-employed is a true test of one's personal character. When I first made the decision to go into business for myself, many questions ran through my mind. I wondered where I was going to find reliable data, how I was going to compile it, and when I would find time to learn new computer programs. One thing I never questioned, though, was whether I was capable of attaining my goals. From the outset I understood that being self-employed would require incredible self-discipline and emotional maturity. Because I did not have the years of work experience behind me, I have had to learn to rely on my own judgment. For example, soon after incorporating Asian Profiles, Inc., I was faced with the challenge of negotiating business contracts, setting up the company's finances, and deciding which computer system to purchase. With advise from experts and personal research, I found that lack of experience did not have to be a stumbling block to success but, rather, was a challenge to overcome. As company president, I have had to become my own supervisor and supporter, which has been the most challenging aspect of the position. Employing a healthy level of self-judgment has allowed me to improve my job performance by acknowledging and working with my strengths and weaknesses.

In addition to the professional challenges Asian Profiles, Inc., has created for me, it has also given me the opportunity to test my leadership abilities. Although I perform all the research and manage the company myself, I am fortunate to have the support of two secretaries. Being a manager has been a novel and rewarding experience for me. I have learned that in any working relationship, being a good manager is more about leading people and less about being a boss. I have worked hard to establish a consistent and professional management style for dealing with my clients and employees. With the personal and professional responsibilities required of a small business manager, I have had the opportunity to realistically assess my leadership capabilities. I am confident that I do possess leadership potential, but I recognize the need for expanded experience and new challenges, Asian Profiles, Inc., has fostered in me a tremendous amount of self-reliance and business know-how which I will continue to draw upon in my future endeavors.

Critique: We gave this essay high marks on the following dimensions:

Style: Well-constructed essay; gave succinct but sufficient background information about the experience, then described the challenge, how she met the challenge, and what she learned. Tone of the essay was honest and eminently readable.

Content: Situation was unique and interesting to the reader. Descriptions provided specifics, which made the challenge more believable. Cause and effect between the situation and the learning process were made clear.

Reader would have liked to have seen reference to any measurable success resulting from meeting the challenge and learning from the experience.

DARTMOUTH

Question #1: *Discuss your career progression to date. What factors have influenced your decision to seek a general management education? Based on what you know about yourself at this time, how do you envision your career progressing after receiving the MBA degree? Please state your professional goals, and describe your plans to achieve them.*

Essay #1:

As a senior, my initial goal was to gain a thorough education in finance, which I could then apply in a field related to my personal interest in the outdoors. The most efficient way to achieve this education was as an analyst at a major investment bank. Most of the available positions were in New York. Although I was offered an analyst position there, I realized that I was unwilling to sacrifice my personal interest in order to move into the city. Instead I headed West and dedicated a year of fulfillment of these interests before beginning my professional career.

I spent the summer and fall as a professional river guide on the Snake River in Wyoming. Guiding more than 2,000 people in class IV white water rafting and fly-fishing trips taught me to interact comfortably with clients and to effectively promote myself and my abilities. I often draw upon these marketing skills in my current career when soliciting new clients. I then spent the following winter and spring in California managing a cross-country ski touring center. In this position, I gained valuable experience managing people and an appreciation for the numerous responsibilities of running a business, regardless of its size and purpose. More importantly, both experiences instilled within me an appreciation for our natural environment and an obligation to help preserve it.

Shortly thereafter, I began my professional career at Drexel Burnham Lambert in San Francisco. I was one of the first junior members to join its innovative debt restructuring group. The culture was highly entrepreneurial. Since we were the first group on Wall Street to enter the debt restructuring field, we had no standard operating procedures to rely on and therefore created our own. Our success has been a function of our creativity in developing innovative restructuring techniques as well as our cooperative group dynamics. All members of the team are encouraged to contribute to the creative process, regardless of their position. I performed well in this environment and was rewarded with a promotion from analyst to associate, a position usually reserved for MBA graduates. As the business flourished and the group expanded, I had the opportunity to train and manage several second- and third-year associates who were new to the group and therefore junior to me in experience. When Drexel entered bankruptcy, I was the only one out of ten junior members invited to join the senior group in their move to another investment bank, Smith Barney. Our group's continued success at Smith Barney has allowed me to further expand my responsibilities. We recently closed the largest public debt restructuring ever completed, which resulted in the sale of one of America's oldest and largest publishing companies. In this transaction I led our team of associates and analysts from Smith Barney and two other investment banks representing the buyer in a comprehensive financial review and valuation of our client. In collaborating with senior team members, I presented these analyses to our client's Board of Directors, who relied upon them in determining the viability of the offer.

In the last four and a half years, I have gained a solid background in finance, experience in line management, and strong negotiating skills by executing numerous transactions in a wide variety of industries. Clearly, I have surpassed the original goal I set out as a senior in college. I now plan to pursue other professional goals that I have developed during my tenure at Drexel and Smith Barney.

My next professional goal is to combine my desire to run my own business with my passion for mountaineering, as a manufacturer of outdoor recreational equipment. Mountaineering has advanced at such a rapid pace that athletes in several technique disciplines have exceeded the limits of the equipment available to them. Modern technologies have only been applied to improve the equipment in such recently popular areas as technical rock climbing where sufficient demand has justified the cost of implementation. My focus would be on product development through technology-based innovation in other areas of mountaineering that are gaining popularity, such as back-country skiing. I believe that the increased costs of such technology can be offset by more efficient production management. For example, back-country ski boots are still made of leather, which freezes when wet and must be hand-stitched. A lightweight plastic boot with a removable synthetic liner, however, would not only improve performance but reduce production costs as well through automation of the manufacturing process. I plan to enter the outdoor recreational equipment market with lines through a) additional technological innovations, b) joint ventures with or acquisitions of other specialty manufacturers, and c) leveraging my brand recognition to promote related clothing and accessories which typically yield a higher profit margin.

Clearly, my goal is not to run a Fortune 500 company. I believe the future of American manufacturing lies in small, highly specialized companies that can not only quickly respond to technological change but also help direct the public's shifting values regarding our natural environment. To create this type of enterprise, I plan to assemble a small team of individuals with diverse skills but common interests. The structure of this enterprise will combine the many positive organizational aspects of my current organization. I will create a "meritocracy" in which personal and professional growth will be rewarded with increased responsibility. All members of the team will be encouraged to contribute to the creative process regardless of their position. Compensation will be based strictly on performance rather than tenure, so that all members who share the responsibilities may also share the profits. Personal profit, however, will not be the sole motivation. The team will also be motivated by a common interest in environmental protection.

My mentor in the outdoor is Yvon Chouinard, founder of Patagonia, a leading manufacturer of outdoor equipment and clothing. Through product innovation he has advanced the sport of mountaineering and achieved a position at the forefront of the outdoor industry. As an industry leader, he has become a vocal proponent of "sustainable development," which encourages managers to balance economic growth with environmental concerns. I agree with his thesis that our country's current business practices are generally not sustainable. In the past several years, I have witnessed the effects of irresponsible growth at Drexel and many of its clients' that I helped restructure. Currently we are all witnessing the effects of irresponsible growth on our natural environment. Through the success of my own company, I could fulfill the obligation to the environment I developed years ago as a river guide. As an industry leader, I would be in a position to promote responsible and sustainable growth at all levels—by example within my own organization and industry, by communication with other industry leaders, and by volunteering my time and skills to increase public awareness of the need to protect the wilderness areas on which my industry and interests depend.

I understand that, in order to pursue my entrepreneurial interest in manufacturing, I will need the skills to manage across an entire organization, from finance and production to sales and marketing. I have developed strong financial skills and gained experience in line management in my current career. An MBA education is clearly not a perfect substitute for experience, but I believe it will provide me with the framework necessary for effective decision-making in these areas. An MBA program would also allow me to further research my business ideas through the experience of my peers, independent study, and related summer employment. Education and experience may not change my goals, but they may well change the means by which I achieve them. Finally, since I will not be able to create this organization alone, I look forward to the opportunity to meet other individuals who share my interests in entrepreneurship, manufacturing, and sustainable development.

Critique: The admissions essay is a critical component in an application to the Amos Tuck School's MBA program. Throughout the process of reviewing an application, which includes careful reading of essays, the admissions committee will seek compelling reasons to admit the applicant. Although writing an excellent essay will not guarantee an applicant admission into Tuck, submitting a poorly organized or badly written essay as part of an otherwise good application will significantly reduce his or her chances for acceptance.

In addition to meeting our more immediate and obvious expectations of a well-organized, articulate presentation of his candidacy, the applicant who wrote our example essay offers (1) compelling reasons for the admissions committee to accept him and (2) convincing evidence that he would both thrive in, and contribute to, the academic and social environment at Tuck. In evaluating any essay, however, keep in mind that we judge neither the experiences nor the goals an applicant presents. Instead, we judge (1) how well the applicant presents these experiences and goals, (2) how well the applicant's accomplishments support his long-term goals, and (3) how the applicant's rationale for wanting an MBA fits into his or her overall career plan.

There are a number of indicators throughout the example essay that the writer possesses attributes that Tuck seeks: (1) the types of experiences and interests that demonstrate sufficient intellectual preparation for a rigorous curriculum of professional study, (2) a high motivational level for achievement, (3) a creative approach to problem solving, (4) a blend of leadership skills to successfully manage multiple aspects of an organization, (5) the interpersonal skills needed to work successfully with diverse groups of people, and (6) an appreciation of a need to balance one's professional and personal lives.

The applicant demonstrates these attributes in describing his career progress, relating each stage to long-term goals. He explains why general management training, central to Tuck's educational mission, is essential for implementing the next stage of his plan toward reaching those goals. The applicant knows what he wants—skills to manage an R&D-based manufacturing operation in close proximity to the great outdoors—and has a clear-cut idea of how to get it. In his essay, he indicates that he made a steady progression of conscious choices that supported his long-term goals by strategically identifying: (1) Where to live and work (on a river in Wyoming, near a ski area in California, then in a major financial center in California), (2) What types of industries were most valuable to gain experience in for his personal and professional interests (an outdoor excursion outfit, a customer-service oriented sports operation, an investment banking firm), (3) What roles would prove useful for the future (leader of white-water rafting trips, general management of a cross-country ski touring center, a member of a team in an investment bank's new debt-restructuring group), and (4) What issues to monitor (the environmental consequences of commercial land development, growth pattern of technological innovations in the sports-equipment industry, how manufacturing factors into the overall national economy).

The applicant asserts that he is management material and backs up this assertion in describing how his superiors at Drexel Burnham Lambert promoted him to a level of responsibility normally reserved for MBAs. He also demonstrates familiarity with current consequences of a slow economy by showing successful adjustment to a new position in another company after his own employer went bankrupt. This flexibility, along with his varied experiences, will enable him to offer an interesting perspective in class discussions.

In conclusion, this particular applicant's attitude, experience, goals, and interests all provided a close match with what Tuck seeks in prospective MBAs. The admissions committee was confident that his interests and abilities provided a close fit with our requirements and that he would be happy in the type of environment that Tuck offers: a rural, residential lifestyle; small classes emphasizing cooperative, highly interactive group learning; a close-knit and cohesive community that welcomes people from diverse backgrounds; and the ability to take full advantage of the career placement services and connections one would expect from an Ivy League business school.

HARVARD

Question #1: *Discuss a change you would make in your work environment and how you would implement that change.*

Essay #1:

The Gillette Personal Care Division is in financial difficulty having severely missed its profit objectives in the last half of 1989. The Division responded to its profitability problems by giving the sales force a more aggressive sales quota. To control escalating costs, the corporate Controller took over P&L responsibility from the divisional marketing department.

I feel the above divisional and corporate responses to raising profitability were ill-considered and create new problems. First, the way in which a Sales Representative will respond to an aggressive new sales quota can, ironically, exacerbate the profitability problem. To achieve the aggressive new sales quota, the sales force will push high-volume brands (i.e. White Rain) that contribute little to profit. This short-term volume increase comes at the expense of the field's promoting and building smaller, high margin brands.

Second, the Controller cut out advertising and field discretionary funds, showing his insensitivity to market considerations and trade issues; an immediate spike in profits comes at the expense of future consumer pickup.

The change I propose to make is to make the field more responsible for Divisional profitability. This can be done by giving the Sales Reps new Business Development Funds and more profit "accountability." With the funds, the Reps would be better able to respond to opportunities to develop and build the brands.

However, "accountability" would present implementation problems. How do you define and enforce accountability? The field cannot control many of the variables that impact on profitability: production costs, advertising commitments, price increases, and the size of trade allowances. Nor can the field break out different regions on a P&L basis. Because developing and maintaining some accounts will be more expensive than others. It might cost more to develop more promising markets where P&G, for example, is also trying to make inroads.

The best solution for field profit accountability is a dual quota system: by sales and by brand. A brand quota would force the Rep to promote a more profitable mix of product regardless of whether he understood the profitability concerns. With the Business Development Fund, he would be able to build the profitable brands emphasized in the new brand quota.

These funds would encourage the Rep to be much more entrepreneurial. The rep could design trade push and consumer pull programs that best suit his territory. Sales Planning would represent the interests of the sales force in determining fair brand quotas with the marketing department. Ultimately, this change would help balance Divisional and corporate needs. With the Business Development funds, Reps would better be able to respond to local opportunities. With brand quotas, Corporate could better control product profit mix.

The downside is that the trade will come to expect these additional allowances and give little incremental promotional support. Further, career Reps might not adapt well to the new entrepreneurial demands and may develop ineffective programs. While the immediate solution would be to give the Business Development funds to the Reps who could use the funds most effectively, this would create resentment. The longer-term solution is to recruit and build a sales force of entrepreneurial Reps who could run their own "franchises."

Question #2: *Describe your avocations and hobbies.*

Essay #2:

My most passionate nonacademic pursuit is athletics. I have learned invaluable lessons through playing on the Harvard Varsity Water-polo and Squash teams. As goalie in the Water-polo team, I learned the importance of teamwork. During a fast-paced game, a goalie must be able to quickly identify potential problems and solve them in an effective manner. Collective responsibility is integral to teamwork. One cannot lay the blame on another player without jeopardizing team unity.

Squash taught me that progress can only be achieved through diligence and patience. Hitting a small black ball thousands of times for hundreds of hours in a small room can be perceived as a meaningless pursuit—or a disciplined process of developing precision and control. There are no shortcuts to improvement in the game of squash.

I have found these valuable lessons of teamwork and discipline to be easily transferable to other areas. Working with others in a competitive and tense environment can only be successfully achieved through proper teamwork. The discipline that I developed on the squash court has (similarly) enabled me to focus in other pursuits with equal determination.

Question #3: *Describe your most substantial accomplishments, and explain why you view them as such.*

Essay #3

1) Last spring I exported nearly $100,000 worth of exercise equipment to Japan. This shipment saved my company more than $250,000, due to the price discrepancies between the United States and Japan. I was solely responsible for selecting the equipment, negotiating the price, arranging the insurance, and packing and shipping the equipment to Japan. The first step of the process of selecting the equipment and the company involved inspecting manufacturing facilities based in California, Maryland, Texas, Vermont, and Colorado. I researched the legitimacy of the companies by calling their previous clients, checking credit records, and calling the Better Business Bureau. After exporting the equipment to Japan, I flew to Japan to facilitate the import process. This involved meeting with Japanese customs, as well as assisting in the domestic transportation and installation of the equipment.

I consider this a major accomplishment for three reasons. Firstly, I was solely responsible for the entire project. Secondly, it was a complicated process that involved many unrelated details. Finally, and not least of all, the fact that it was successful also contributes to my sense of pride.

2) When the Japanese company opened its third health club in Japan in July, 1988, it was a great sense of personal satisfaction. Two summers ago, I participated in the planning and design of this club. I saw many of my substantive recommendations implemented, including the installation of a racquetball court system that has movable glass walls to allow squash, racquetball, basketball, and volleyball to be played on the same court. My idea more effectively utilizes very limited and costly space and also provides greater recreational variety for the users. I have previously discussed my export deal that provided more than half of the equipment for the club, which was another source of personal satisfaction. In addition to helping design the club, I was actively involved in sales and marketing. I also conducted club tours for prospective members, and designed a new marketing strategy targeting foreigners living in the area. My combined efforts resulted in more than 150 new members.

These accomplishments demonstrate my ability to work successfully in a large group setting as well as in an entirely different language and culture. In addition to the satisfaction of seeing my design recommendations actually implemented, I also enjoyed the challenges of sales and marketing.

3) I am currently co-teaching a Harvard college freshman seminar focusing on the economic development of Japan with Professor X. As a teacher, I had to design a reading list that would provide sufficient information without overwhelming the freshmen who have had no background on the topic. A reading list has to have an overall argument with weekly topics to provide specific examples. Teaching in a seminar format presents a tremendous intellectual challenge of stimulating and guiding discussion. I try to give only directive or stimulative comments rather than to lecture. In this manner students will ask questions and I will try to steer the discussion so that the student is able to answer his or her own question.

Teaching the seminar represents the cumulative total of my academic career. My studies have largely revolved around Japanese economics and Japanese history. In addition, my practical experience of working in a Japanese company in Japan complements my academic understanding and has further enhanced my abilities as a teacher.

UNIVERSITY OF MARYLAND

Essay #1:

My multi-page application answered the question, "Who am I?" Now it is the time to answer another one—"Why am I here, in the pool of applicants to the Maryland MBA program?" That's a question many people have asked me.

My friends' confusion is understandable. Why would a graduate student who enjoys doing research and teaching, with an expertise in a politically important part of the world and who allegedly would be able to get full funding in any school if he chose to go all the way to the Ph.D. in political science, want to change his career to take an unknown road in business? Quite a legitimate question. Let me explain why I chose to apply to the Maryland MBA Program and not to do something else; first revisit my life history.

In 1990 I joined the analytical division of a trading firm in Moscow—International Secondary Resources Exchange. I discovered consulting as a career and developed an interest in assessment of market potential, including a degree of political risk. At the time, Russia and other former communist countries were opening their markets and it was fascinating, but also very important to try to predict how promising the Russian market was. So I decided to get my masters in political science in order to be able to competently assess such important categories for estimating market potential as government capacity, public administration competence, political risk (legal and other obstacles to foreign investment), entrepreneurial culture, and economic training of the population.

Still working on projects with the exchange, I started a graduate program with concentration in international relations, comparative politics (Europe), and economics. It has been an important part of my education, given the importance of the political situation and, therefore, political forecasting for the business future of the former communist world.

My education now has to enter its most critical stage—actual study of business. This would let me have a deep understanding, as I hope, of financial and other market structures, competitiveness, and other factors that a consultant needs to take into account when recommending whether to conduct business in a foreign country.

Taking advantage of my bi-cultural background, long study of international relations and foreign languages, and business experience, I plan to pursue a career as an international business consultant. The

UMCP certainly has a focus on global business. I am attracted by the Center for International Business Education and Research—I work for CIBER at the University of Utah and my colleagues spoke highly of the Maryland Program. At the same time the School offers a strong general management program—something I need, coming from a country with no free market traditions.

These are the "career" reasons to apply to Maryland. But there is also a "character" reason. It is critically important for me to be challenged. Only when sufficiently challenged, can I work at full capacity and deliver results. Without doubt, Maryland provides enough challenge, without mentioning that an application process itself is very stimulating.

Business schools' quality criteria are no secret. From these I pay special attention to location. The Washington-Baltimore metropolitan area is a perfect location for somebody interested in an international business career. It is also the place to be for a person, who, coming from Utah, is just hungry for student body diversity and culture attractions. I visited the area on two occasions during my first year in this country and just fell in love with the place.

Add to these advantages a critical one for me—generous financial aid options. Unfortunately, without financial aid, I will not be able to attend school.

The Program's diverse environment is of special importance for me. I appreciate diversity and I think I could add something myself to the already culturally rich Maryland MBA Program—after two years in the United States I am a walking example of cultural interaction. I picked up a lot of American practices, keeping at the same time some of my old ones. I do not protest anymore when my friends take me out to dinner around my birthday, but on my birthday itself, I, as the Russian tradition goes, have them over for dinner. I try not to go with the flow and never say "how are you?" when I do not care and "nice to meet you" when I do not mean it, but sometimes I am supposed to say these meaningless phrases. I still pass with my face, rather than my back, to people sitting in a theater. I use Kleenex tissues, but still have a handkerchief in my pocket just in case. I kept my main dining habit—never putting down a knife when having salad and a main course. I changed, on the other hand the way I approach desert [sic], when I dine by myself; I still eat it with a spoon, as the Russians do. And I drink both hot tea and coke.

From my Russian background I keep moral integrity, industriousness, strong attachment to my family, self-reliance, cooperative spirit, sense of humor, strong interest in spending time with children, and my three other hobbies—movies, soccer, and travel. My American present made me friendly, punctual, conscientious, self-disciplined, law-abiding, determined to help people who are less lucky than I am (first of all, my fellow Russians), and two more past-times—basketball and hiking. I hope that a person combined with two cultures will be a good edition to the School's environment.

I believe that the Maryland MBA Program will provide me with a training I need and enough challenges to launch me into a new intellectual orbit. And, also, it would just be nice to be back East.

Critique: One important way MBA programs strengthen their international focus is by attracting talented students from different parts of the world. Indeed, a priority of the Maryland Business School is actively to recruit such students, because they increase both the breadth and depth of the school's international perspective.

In addition to fulfilling the basic requirement of every application's essay section—i.e., answer the questions asked (a surprising number of people fail to do this)—"Andrei's" statement also provided the admissions director with a vivid glimpse into his personality. And though English is obviously not his first language, his command of "Americanisms" is impressive and his sense of humor engaging. He comes across as a bright, self-motivated, high-energy individual. Just the type for Maryland.

He also did his homework. For instance, he mentions Maryland's Center for International Business Education and Research and the fact that the university is located in the culturally rich Washington D.C. area. To the admissions director, this means he is serious about his application to the program; that he is not using the shotgun approach in applying to graduate school.

Had he wanted to make an even stronger impression, however, "Andrei" should have asked a native English speaker to read over his essay. One or two native speakers, for that matter. They would have helped him smooth over some of his sentences with proper punctuation and usage. For though his message is clear to the reader, his occasional lapses into fractured English somewhat detract from his many fine qualities.

UNIVERSITY OF MICHIGAN

Question #1: During your years of study in the Michigan MBA program, you will be part of a diverse multicultural, multi-ethnic community within both the Business School and the larger University. What rewards and challenges do you anticipate in this campus environment, and how do you expect this experience to prepare you for a culturally diverse business world?

Essay #1:

High return on investment...

One quality I have always admired is independent thinking. I always strive to be different and befriend those who share the same goal. I see conformity as a moral deficiency. "Group think" is the enemy of creativity and innovation. In contrast, diversity in thought is the key to any successful endeavor. I want to be a part of creative concepts proposed from a wide array of sources. These creative concepts can only be reached by assembling individuals with discordant views and from varying backgrounds. For this reason, I find the growing diversity of Michigan's student body to be one of its greatest selling points. I feel that understanding a wide range of views, opinions, and judgments on a variety of subject matter broadens the base of experience from which effective solutions maybe derived. Therefore, learning, sharing, and growing within the context of diverse individuals is an avenue for developing a successful manager.

While there will be rewards from this melting pot, there is always the potential for difficulty when assembling people with divergent views and from different cultures. As a member of an international exchange program, in both training and travel, I was able to witness the glaring problems of cultural bias, prejudice, and close-mindedness. One thing I learned through this experience is that nobody is above prejudice of some kind, myself included. Everyone has some innate sense that they are superior to other individuals in some manner. When people feel superior because of their intellect, we call them arrogant. When people feel superior because of their nationality or culture, we call them elitists. And when people feel superior because of their race, we call them racists. The first step in understanding each other is to better understand ourselves and develop an understanding of our own prejudices. This will be the challenge facing every student in the melting pot. For some this challenge will be great and for some it may be overcome easily, but in either case I feel that the rewards from integration of people and ideas provide a great return on the time and energy invested to make it so.

Beyond the hallowed halls...

I expect my time at Michigan to enhance my understanding and appreciation of the benefits of mixing ideas and opinions among people from different backgrounds. The business community I will enter is a global-, multinational-, multicultural-based body. Any business manager willing to shun certain peoples or ideas because they are foreign will be injuring his company. And yet, I have every reason to believe that I will inevitably encounter these types of individuals.

While universities are taking the lead in cultural and ethnic diversification, the business world is somewhat behind. The reasons for this are twofold: those people who are fearful of new ideas tend to fight diversity, while those individuals in favor of diversity often find developing it a daunting task. For this reason, many companies concede to the status quo, to the old way of doing business. Yet there are firms willing to shift paradigms of current thinking. These are the companies that will prosper in the future. The company that takes the initiative to broaden its personnel base will find that any short-term expenses it may incur in this diversification process are easily offset by the long-term benefits of having a dynamic, progressive, and enterprising staff. This is the type of firm I would like to associate with. Just as I expect to do at Michigan, I hope in the business company to be an active part of the melting pot of ideas, developing creative concepts, and forcing new paths by engaging divergent viewpoints.

Critique: Originality, insight, and graceful writing immediately capture the reader of this essay. Tackling the topic directly and substantively, the author effectively relates the subject to past personal experiences and future career aspirations. The writer avoids the platitudes that slide all too easily into application essays. With admirable honesty, he acknowledges the challenges posed by a multicultural environment, admits the prejudices he has felt, and identifies the personal rewards of being part of the Michigan community.

The essay goes beyond any superficial treatment of the issue and reveals how the author thinks. Indeed, the independent thinking admired by the writer emerges from the piece. The reader finds clear evidence of the analytical reasoning skills so critical to success and leadership in management. Finally, the writing style, characterized by flowing, balanced prose and apt word choice, is eloquent. The essay convinces the reader that this is someone whose thinking and ability to convey thoughts will enrich the learning process in and out of the classroom.

UNIVERSITY OF NOTRE DAME

Question #1: *As a Notre Dame student, what contributions would you make to the life of the program, both inside and outside the classroom? How will an MBA from Notre Dame help you achieve your short-term career goals and long-term professional aspirations?*

Essay #1

As a Notre Dame M.B.A. student there are many contributions I will make to enhance the excellence of the program. These contributions include attributes such as professional insight, an inquisitive mind, and innovative ideas along with a high moral and ethical standards.

My two years' experience with Sikorsky Aircraft has given me a good understanding of multifunctional disciplines within American aerospace firms. I have grown from these experiences, and I will bring them to the classroom in the form of anecdotes. My job has helped me to gain a good perception of some of the best and worst ways to run a business. These experiences are ones you could never pick up from a textbook, but they will enhance the lessons found in one.

To the classroom I also bring an inquisitive mind. I am never satisfied with the statements of "that's the way it is" or "if it's not broke don't fix it." I feel that if you do not ask why or try to completely appreciate a theory or technique, you may never truly understand it. There is always an alternative to any method or theory, and questioning is a way of developing new understandings.

Outside the classroom I bring innovation. I enjoy adding to the competitiveness of the organization of which I am a part, and I am always willing to try new things. For example, while at Michigan State, I assisted in developing the first annual Materials and Logistics student/faculty retreat. This retreat is now an event supported by both the University and the professional world. In the same respect, as an intern at Sikorsky Aircraft, I worked in our Overhaul and Repair facility (O&R). One of my first observations was that O&R had no definitive way of tracking our suppliers' performance. Every individual department had a different tracking system. I combined the best attributes of each system to form a consolidated tracking run which is now used throughout the entire 600-person facility.

Two other contributions I will bring to Notre Dame cannot be labeled either inside or outside of the classroom because they pertain to both. Number one, I am a good team player. I have a good disposition, which helps me not only get along with many different types of people but to enjoy working with them. Number two, through my business trips and experience of serving on MSU's Anti-Discrimination Judicial Board I have developed a unique appreciation of others' cultures and beliefs. I enjoy learning about other people and what makes them tick.

A Notre Dame M.B.A. will help me obtain my short-term and long-term goals by providing a solid foundation and setting a direction from which I can build. Before choosing the M.B.A. programs to which I would apply, I sat down with a former professor to obtain his insight into this decision. He told me that when choosing an M.B.A. program, I am choosing a label to carry with me throughout my career. This label aligns me with beliefs and practices of my M.B.A. institution. I chose to apply to Notre Dame because of the school's strong stand on ethics and the international market. At Notre Dame I will be exposed to people not only from the Midwest but from around the world. This will further help me to broaden my horizons and understanding of people.

My long-term professional aspiration is to enter into a field of management consulting. An M.B.A. from Notre Dame in Interdisciplinary Studies will enhance my understanding of all aspects of business. This will contribute significantly to becoming effective in the consulting profession.

In conclusion, as a Notre Dame M.B.A. candidate I will bring a sincere attitude to succeed in the classroom, high ethical standards, and the willingness to go the extra mile. Upon graduation from Notre Dame, I will represent the university as a sign of excellence a Notre Dame M.B.A. portrays in the professional world.

Critique: We chose Ed's essay because it was clearly and concisely written, using examples from college and career to make his points. For example, he used his experience in O&R at his current employment to highlight his technical and analytical abilities with the establishment of a tracking system now used throughout the facility. He backed up his claim for being innovative by citing his assistance in developing the first faculty and student retreat in his college department.

He dealt with both the short-term and long-term orientation of the program. In seeking advice from his professor, he showed seriousness about making his choice of schools. He wanted an international thrust to his studies and chose Notre Dame because of its reputation in that area as well as its commitment to ethics in business. That fit in nicely with what he learned from his experience on the Anti-Discrimination Judicial Board of his university. And his choice of Interdisciplinary Studies reinforces Notre Dame's focus on preparing students for General Management. Finally, his choice of consulting for a career flows naturally from his prior experiences and his curricular choices.

We like Ed's essay because it was to the point, responded to the essay question, and in a subtle but concrete way "sold" the candidate to the admissions committee. Ed managed to weave in accomplishments on the job with commitments he planned to make to the Notre Dame program. He demonstrated college leadership in a large, public, "anonymous" kind of school in which students often get lost. Based on his experience, his career goals and aspirations appear to be realistic. While he has high ideals, they do not seem to be "pie in the sky" notions, and he displayed a certain kind of maturity and sensitivity that we liked.

STANFORD UNIVERSITY

Question #1: *Tell us about those influences that have significantly shaped who you are today.*

Essay #1:

I am a descendant of a long line of Quaker business people. My family, the ..., have been Quaker since 1630. The common punch line about this group, at gathering of Friends, is that Quaker business people set out to do good and ended up doing very well. I am just beginning to emerge as a Quaker in business.

Relating to background about my quaker heritage should help to illustrate how values of the Religious Society of Friends (the official name of "Quakers") have shaped my sense of who I am. Quakers have particular ethics that I try to develop in myself and live out. Quakers believe that there is a God in every person—they often call it the "Inner Light"—and that all people, regardless of rank and position, should be treated with dignity and integrity. This vision has helped me to see the potential in other people, even those who may be difficult to work with. It has also helped me to relate comfortably to people of every rank; in my current job, I enjoy friendships with everyone from secretaries to the president. In addition, a belief in my own Inner Light helped my self-confidence, especially in those situations where intuition must complement facts and objective measures in making decisions.

This faith in the Inner Light has many other implications, of course, but two of the most important ones involve how group decisions should be made, and the equality of women.

As a way of doing business, Quakers believe in consensus decision-making; in fact, they don't believe in hiring or paying ministers. All administration for Quaker Meeting is done by voluntary committees. From participating in consensus decision-making, I have learned to work with diverse groups of people, to negotiate between individual agendas, and to build effective teamwork between people. Consensus decision-making gives everyone a chance to contribute, and helps all members of the group to understand and articulate both the problem and the solution.

Because of the Quaker belief that all people possess an Inner Light, they have traditionally believed in the full equality of men and women. In fact, Quakers held separate business meetings for men and women until about 50 years ago, because it was felt that otherwise women would be overshadowed by the men. This separation allowed Quaker women to develop leadership skills in speaking and administration.

Strong Quaker women like Lucretia Mott, a leader in the movement to abolish slavery, and Elizabeth Cady Stanton, a leader among the suffragettes, were products of this culture.

Several other characteristic Quaker beliefs are placing a high value on simplicity, and on speaking and living the truth. For example, Quakers refuse to swear to anything, even at a trial or for a marriage license, because it implies that at other times one might not tell the truth. Being practical and "grounded" are Quaker values that discourage otherwordly or naive thinking. As a general rule, Quakers don't proselytize or even talk very much about their religion. They believe that their lives should speak of their convictions.

Quaker values can interact with business priorities in many ways, mostly positive, but some potentially negative as well. For example, because Quakers didn't limit their business contacts to the highest social echelon, they found opportunities for more customers and a wider circle of business associates. As Quaker women developed leadership skills, their ingenuity contributed to the success of Quaker businesses. Quaker businesses put a high value on providing products that truly add value for consumers, rather than devising ways to trick them into buying something. In the days before *Consumer Reports*, people saw many advantages to doing business with Quakers, because it was widely known that they wouldn't cheat you. Since Quakers were known to try to seek the truth regardless of the cost to themselves or whether the news was welcome, their word was trusted. Of course, being honest didn't prevent Quakers from being shrewd business people.

But although Quakers tend to be highly ethical, they can also be somewhat naive. Consensus decision-making can be far too slow and unwieldy for some decisions, and it runs a risk that people will feel coerced by the group into settling for less than they want. Rather than making everyone responsible, it can end up making no one responsible. Even people with an Inner Light can behave badly. "Speaking truth to power," to use the common catch-phrase for Quakers, can either increase long-run credibility or can be a cover for venting harsh feelings at inappropriate times.

My mother has told me that she married my father partially because he had been raised Quaker and was comfortable with strong, independent women. During my senior year at college, I was disheartened to find that many men of my own age found me intimidating. It was also a time when my mother was diagnosed with serious and potentially life-threatening breast cancer. Now I'm happily married, and my mother has at least survived the chemotherapy, but I still keep and reread a letter I received from my father that year about the strong women in my family. Here's an excerpt.

"Let's start with this generalization: Highly articulate, handsome, intelligent women are not terribly rare. No doubt you yourself have many friends that would easily fit such categorization. But if you add two further adjectival phrases, then such women are rare indeed. Namely, passionate commitment and courageous. (I'm willing to concede that these may even be redundant... they, in your case, certainly go together.) Obviously these same characteristics are very rare in men too.

"The problem arises primarily for women. These characteristics scare the bejabbers out of others...they may be admired by some, vilified by others, and wholly misunderstood by the majority. But even those that admire them generally want to do it at a safe distance. Let's face it—sparks are given off by such people. The prudent man usually decides that the warmth and excitement isn't worth the high risk of being consumed in a conflagration set off by so many sparks.

"You are the fourth in line of such women."

I am enclosing a photocopy of this letter with application (Attachment I) because it illuminates the way Quakers like my father can support and encourage women in leadership. Also, it provides some insight into my family.

Another important influence is my new husband, Timothy. We were married July 6 of this year. Tim is the managing editor of the *Journal of Economic Perspectives*, which is based at Stanford. My husband's background in economics informs and counterbalances my perspectives.

My career has forced me to balance the idealistic qualities of Quakerism with real-life experience, where the rubber meets the road. My first job out of college was as editor and then executive director for a nonprofit foundation called Fellowship in Prayer (FIP), whose purpose was to "encourage the practice of prayer or meditation among people of all faiths." This nonprofit was a rare one; it actually had an endowment that grew from $2.7 to $3.5 million during my three-year tenure. My job was to organize the programs and facilities from complete chaos to something more effective and methodical. I managed the budgets so that operating expenditures came only from the interest on the endowment, not from the capitol. I also learned some lessons that went well beyond business. I was sexually harassed by two members of the Board of Trustees, and had to face the problem of other Board members stealing from the endowment.

Perhaps my biggest lesson from Fellowship in Prayer was that systems—the way information is transferred, decisions are made and reporting relationships defined—largely determine the effectiveness of the organization. When I started working there, the organization had no functioning systems in place, and no objectives or strategies beyond the general mission statement quoted a moment ago. I had previously looked on things like standard operating procedures and methods of reporting and accountability as necessary evils. But I found that it's not nearly enough to have an operating budget and some staff. An organization also needs some definite goals, strategies for achieving them, and ways of measuring success. While working at FIP, I came to understand that structure is enabling: without it, people spend too much time wondering what they are supposed to be doing or reinventing the wheel. Now I appreciate the need to organize structures, and the significance when such systems work well.

My position as executive director at FIP forced me to learn a wide range of business skills and responsibilities. I wrote the annual budget and the annual report and oversaw expenditures. I bought a $300,000 property for headquarters of the foundation (previously, it had rented space), arranged for $20,000 of structural repairs and another $20,000 for redecorating and furnishing, and moved the office. I edited the bimonthly magazine for nine months, until I became executive director. I supervised other staff. I tried to create a counterbalance to the power of the Board of Trustees, some of who had been stealing from the foundation, by recruiting a lawyer with financial expertise to the Board. I also formed an advisory board composed of Christians, Jews, Baha'is, Buddhists, a Mohawk Chief, and others to improve the programs and create a balance of power with the Board of Trustees. Also, this group helped in generating ideas for programs, like lectures and retreats.

I also worked on developing my own speaking and writing skills; I gave lectures, workshops, and retreats myself. I have continued to pursue my interest in designing programs and giving talks that help people deepen their spirituality and fulfill their potential. During the past few years, for example, I have led retreats at the Quaker center in Ben Lomond, California, and for Faith at Work, a national ecumenical group with which I continue to do volunteer work. With my application, I have enclosed some flyers publicizing these retreats (attachment II). I wrote the ones for Quaker Center.

Critique: General Guidelines—The strongest essays give us a real sense of who the applicant is. Because we do not offer interviews, this is the applicant's only opportunity to provide insight into who they are; in a way, it is like an interview on paper. But it should be more personal and less résumé-like. Ideally, after reading the essay, we should have a good idea of what this person would like to discuss if we (hypothetically) met over coffee. We're looking for who someone is rather than what he or she has done. This is the fundamental distinction we make: we want to get to know the person behind the grades, scores, and job accomplishments— what are his or her passions, values, interests, and goals? We expect applicants to get beyond the standard "I did this; I did that" model to share with us what they care about and what has shaped them. We look for an honest and natural tone, hoping to find essays that are engaging and immediate rather than dry and distant—ideally, a conversation on paper.

For this student, being Quaker has been the most significant influence in her life. She does a good job of focusing deeply on that single influence, extracting specific insight from its effects on her. She ties it in to her values (simplicity, truthful living, living one's convictions), her social/emotional experiences (dating, equality of women), and even her philosophy of business (consensus decision-making, honesty). For her, being Quaker is more than a religious faith; it is a life choice, and by explaining its influences on her she provides insight into who she is and why she developed that way.

This essay is honest and immediate; she opens up about personal matters in a way that allows us to get to know the real her; for example, she shares a personal and emotional letter her father sent her during a difficult time for her family. She has analyzed the positives and negatives that her Quaker upbringing has fostered, further showing intelligent self-analysis and thoughtfulness. Overall, she presents a picture of a smart, committed woman who has thought hard about who she is and is able (and willing) to communicate what she cares about and why.

Toward the end of the essay she shifts from the personal to the professional (from the "who" to the "what"), but does so relatively effectively. We learn how she puts her passions into action, as well as some key lessons she has learned from her initial work experiences. There is a bit too much "I did this; I did that" at the end of the essay; it would have been stronger had she let her resume tell us her accomplishments, focusing here only on personal introspection. However, as a whole the essay is strong because some of that introspection is present, and even the "what" section tells us something about her.

TULANE UNIVERSITY–A.B. FREEMAN SCHOOL OF BUSINESS

Question 31: *Why are you seeking a Tulane MBA at this time? In your answer, please include critical academic and professional experiences that led to your decision, a self-assessment of your suitability for graduate management school, your career goals, and your specific interest in the Freeman School.*

Essay #1:

I am seeking a Tulane MBA because the curriculum and international programs offered by the A.B. Freeman School of Business at Tulane University will expand my knowledge of core business concepts while allowing me to focus on the area in which I plan to make my career: international business. As the national accounts officer at ABC Bank, I serve as the account handling officer for the bank's national and multinational corporate customers, such as General Motors Acceptance Corporation, Anheuser-Busch, and Westinghouse Electric. In working with these firms, both now as an officer and previously as a credit card analyst, I have observed that many of them plan to increase their international presence, especially in Mexico and Europe. My career objective is to work for a multinational firm for several years to gain the experience needed to ultimately establish my own international service-related firm. The knowledge needed and experience offered by the programs at the Freeman School will help me achieve this goal.

After working at ABC Bank for three years, I have decided that I need more academic training in order to pursue a more challenging career. The will and drive to succeed has characterized my tenure at ABC Bank. I attribute my success to two of my personal strengths that will be equally important in future careers: persistence and interpersonal skills.

After graduating from the University of XYZ in August of 1986, my goal was to secure a credit analyst position with ABC Bank. I believed the analyst position would help me build a foundation for making credit decisions as a lender, as well as allow me to study the operations of many industries. Upon applying for the position, however, I was told that no analyst positions were available and that the bank preferred to hire internally for such jobs. With this guideline in mind, I asked for any available job at the bank. I was offered a commercial-vault teller position and accepted it. Although the work of processing commercial deposits for eight hours a day was monotonous, I kept my strategy in mind: perform my teller duties well, be persistent with credit management, and thereby earn the credit analyst job. After nine months in the vault, my determination was rewarded; the credit manager offered me the position that I sought. As an analyst, I was responsible for writing detailed analyses of a firm's operations to assist the commercial lenders with credit decisions. After working only eleven months in the credit area (the normal tenure is eighteen to twenty-four months), I was elected national accounts officer, thus becoming the bank's youngest officer. Although I wrote very good credit reviews, I was not promoted for this reason; there were several other analysts who also wrote good reviews. I was promoted largely because of my strong interpersonal and communications skills, since the National Accounts position requires an officer who can work well with both current and prospective customers. The National Accounts position entails handling the lending and cash management needs of the bank's national customers.

At ABC Bank, I have moved from a teller to an officer position in a short time. I have used my intelligence, persistence, and interpersonal skills to move up rapidly, and now I wish to pursue a more challenging career. I am ready to use my past experience, combined with my strengths that I have discussed above, to obtain a graduate management degree and then excel in the area of international business.

Goal: Career in International Business

I want to build on my three years of banking experience and my travels, literally around the world, in preparation for an international management position either within the United States or abroad. My travels to Australia, Latin America, and South Africa on behalf of my family's cattle ranch first stimulated my interest in international business and trade. This interest has subsequently evolved during my three years in the banking business.

While I was a credit analyst, I learned much more about the international direction in which many firms are increasingly moving. Some of the firms that I reviewed are aggressively pursuing opportunities in Mexico because of their proximity to the border, the probable free trade agreement between the United States and Mexico, and the burgeoning maquiladora industry along the international border. The common denominator among these firms is a desire to take advantage of Mexico's abundance of labor and natural resources. I believe these two resources, coupled with Mexico's progressive government and an increasing interest in Mexico by U.S. business, will provide great opportunity in this emerging area of trade.

In addition, the National Accounts position has afforded me the opportunity to travel nationwide to call on my customers' home offices, and, in the course of conducting the bank's affairs, inquire about each firm's international operations. Although noting the obstacles, political and economic, many customers have eagerly outlined their plans to expand into Latin America, Eastern Europe, and China. They made it clear to me that trends such as the movement toward common markets and the increasing capability of long-distance communication via satellite will further encourage foreign trade. Furthermore, most noted their company's need to employ more personnel in the international area; the general consensus among my contacts is that there will be an increasing demand for international managers in the next decade.

At present, I am undecided as to which path I will choose in international business. Some possibilities that I have considered are finance-related and should capitalize on my lending and cash management experience with a multinational bank. Another option I am considering is to establish a firm that provides translation services to companies wishing to conduct business abroad. As more firms enter the international market, the language barrier could be an obstacle to many U.S. businesses. A translation service would overcome this problem and innovations such as video teleconferencing make this idea quite feasible.

Why a Tulane MBA?

Clearly, there are a number of options available to someone pursuing a career in international business in order to be an effective manager. The Freeman School's curriculum provides the opportunity for me to obtain this knowledge.

The program's first year of required core courses, such as Financial Accounting and Marketing Management, followed by a flexible course scheduled in the second year appeals to my desire to expand my knowledge in the areas of finance and accounting, and then focus on international topics. I also hope to take advantage of the school's international internship program or the study abroad program. It is important that I take advantage of one of these programs, since I believe one should have a sense of culture and economic climate of a region if she or he hopes to conduct business in that area.

Since I will spend almost two years in a Masters program and the school I choose could well determine my career options, I have treated the selection of schools to which I will apply with great care. I am quite aware of the Freeman School's outstanding reputation for international studies. Furthermore, since New Orleans is one of the nation's largest ports, I will have the opportunity to obtain first-hand knowledge about international commerce. Finally, several of the school's alumni have highly recommended the Freeman School to me due to its significant global focus.

In summary, the combination of my three years of banking experience, international travels, and completion of the MBA program at

Tulane should prepare me quite well to succeed as an international manager. As you can see, I have demonstrated both motivation and initiative during my tenure at ABC Bank. I realize that my grade point average is below the published median 3.1 for a recently entering class. I attribute my relatively low GPA to lack of career focus and immaturity during my undergraduate years. I want to assert my belief, however, that I have as much character, determination, and will to succeed as any student in the MBA program. I might note that there are several credit analysts who obtained their jobs before I did mainly due to higher GPA's; most of these analysts are still in the credit department writing reviews while I travel nationwide representing the bank. I can successfully complete the MBA program at Tulane and would certainly like the opportunity to do so.

Critique: Our admissions committee felt that this was an extremely strong essay. Many applications have the tendency to treat this as an open-ended "Tell us about yourself" kind of question and write very general essays that elaborate on their backgrounds without providing adequate rationale regarding their suitability for MBA studies, an outline of their of their goals, or how a Freeman MBA can help them attain these goals. Although often cleverly written, such essays do not help the committee in making an admissions decision.

This essay is well structured, well written, and gives us a clear picture of the applicant as an individual who is both motivated and focused. The description of his rapid progression at ABC Bank from commercial vault teller to credit analyst (his initial goal) to national accounts officer clearly shows that the applicant is able to assess his options, set goals and successfully develop and execute a strategy to reach them. These are characteristics we seek in our MBA students. The essay also shows that the applicant has gained important knowledge and insights along the way which have helped him formulate his goals for the future. These goals include a Freeman MBA and a career in international business.

Although this applicant confesses that he is still weighing two options in the area of international business (rather refreshing, since many of the very specific career goals we read about are obviously contrived or not well supported in the essay), he makes a convincing case for his interest in the field. He also explains his interest in the Freeman School well, citing our global focus, locations in one of the nation's largest port cities, and some of our specific international programs. The applicant shows a strong interest in the Freeman MBA program. He has researched the program and has clearly taken the time to speak with alumni.

Finally, the applicant acknowledges a weakness (his GPA), and, without making excuses, emphasizes the characteristics he has which he believes will make him a strong candidate for our program. These characteristics were amply demonstrated throughout the essay, but he does a nice job of summarizing them and "closing the sale" at the end.

UNIVERSITY OF VIRGINIA

Question #1: *What is the most difficult ethical dilemma you have faced in your professional life? Articulate the nature of the difficulty. Upon present reflection, would you have resolved this dilemma in a different manner?*

Essay #1:

Upon graduation from college, my sense of adventure and quest for learning continued when I accepted a nontraditional position with the Bank of Credit and Commerce International (BCCI). I accepted a position with BCCI with the understanding that overseas placements were the requirement, given the bank's limited US presence. BCCI was founded in 1972 by Pakistani financier Agha Hasan Abedi, whose goal was to create the first multinational bank for the Third World. Its shareholders were rich Middle Eastern oil sheiks. Healthy growth fueled by increasing international trade helped BCCI expand to $20 billion in assets that circled the globe in a 70-country branch network.

After completing BCCI's international trade finance training program with distinction at Pace University in New York, I received my first placement in London, England, working as a trainee in bank branch operations and special country-analysis projects. After quickly completing my London assignment in three months, BCCI management promoted me to a marketing role at their main offices in the United Arab Emirates (UAE). The ruling sheiks of each of the emirates were BCCI's major stockholders and had enormous international political and economic clout.

By quickly absorbing the local culture and the basics of the Arabic language, I earned the respect of my peers at the bank and in the local business community. Through my efforts, I marketed and received commitments for trade financing and investing from many multinational businesses operating in the UAE.

It was right after my third month working in the UAE that I was faced with a major ethical dilemma. During my search for new business, I learned from a contact at the government ministry of trade that a European sportswear manufacturer had applied for permission to start up a business in the UAE. (An application to do business is required of all foreigners along with the requirement to find a local partner.) I immediately informed bank management of the prospect and began my research into the company. After an initial meeting with the company in the UAE a few weeks later, I learned that the firm required a $30 million line facility. I requested the necessary financial information from the company and began my analysis of the company to assess its creditworthiness. My recommendation to bank management was not to proceed any further with the company, given its losses over the past three years and very high leverage. The risks posed by the company's profiles were too great.

My manager, who had always valued my credit skills, mysteriously ignored my recommendation and ordered me to negotiate a loan facility with the company. I was puzzled by my manager's actions, especially since he offered no explanation. I structured a smaller facility at a premium interest rate with adequate primary and secondary fallback collateral to protect the bank from any credit risks. After presenting the new proposal to my bank manager, he dismissed it without comment and made the necessary arrangements to grant the company a $30 million unsecured line of credit at an interest rate reserved for the bank's highest creditworthy clients. A new provision was added, though. A finder's fee of one percent of the loan ($300,000) was due. Even though the fee was paid, there existed no mention of it in the loan documents. Through a search of the bank's accounting records, I learned that the fee was transferred out of the UAE to my manager's personal account abroad. I was naive to think that the manager did not have his contacts in the bank who would report my inquiring.

My manager explained that the fee was not to be considered extorted funds, rather it was his finder's fee. Further, he explained that this was a customary practice. In fact, to show good will, he offered to share his fee with me and suggested $50,000. The only stipulation was that I had to keep the matter quiet from "jealous" employees.

My dilemma was whether to accept part of my manager's illegally obtained funds and keep quiet or to report the matter to a higher level of bank management. Being only 23 years of age and in a foreign country 8,000 miles away from home, I was scared. If this was a customary practice and the branch was covering up for him, then my reporting this incident would put my job in jeopardy as well as my life. I was always taught by my family to practice high ethical and moral standards and to obey the law. This was my guiding principle in refusing the illegal funds and notifying the bank's London headquarters of this serious matter. Immediately, I was transferred back to London within 48 hours, and no mention of the incident was ever made to me either in the UAE or in London. My newly assigned job in London was nonmarketing related and consisted of counting checks in a windowless basement room. Even though it felt like BCCI management was punishing me for good ethical conduct, I still believed that my decision was right. I resigned from the bank one month later and returned to the United States, where I obtained a banking job with an organization that, I feel proud to say, has never presented me with a choice of compromising my ethics and moral standards.

If, in the future, I am unfortunately presented with an ethical dilemma of any degree, I feel confident in holding my ethical and moral standards as priority.

Critique: What makes an application to the Darden School stand out from among the thousands received each year? One important key is well-written essays. As with many business school applications, the essay portion in the applicant's chance to showcase his or her writing talents while at the same time communicating a lot of explicit (and sometimes implicit) information to the admissions committee.

Many b-schools offer the first-year student traditional courses in such functional areas as accounting, marketing, and operations, but Darden was one of the first to include required, graded courses in both communications and ethics. Nowhere at Darden do these two disciplines dovetail more perfectly than in Essay #4 of Darden's application, which asks: "What is the most difficult ethical dilemma you have faced in your professional life? Articulate the nature of the difficulty. Upon present reflection, would you have resolved this dilemma in a different manner?"

While this essay question often prompts the most reflection and introspection on the part of the applicant, it is also often the least understood. The admissions committee is looking not necessarily to judge the nature of the dilemma but rather the candidate's ability to articulate an often personal and complex decision-making process. The key to an effective Essay #4 is in dissecting the term ethical and dilemma. Too often, themes reflected in this essay are of a legal nature: Should I disagree with my boss? Should I turn a co-worker in who's stealing office supplies? Should I break the law? And many situations do not accurately present a true dilemma in which there is no clear right or wrong answer but two or more possible solutions, none of which are necessarily better than another.

The essay above serves as an outstanding example by setting the scene, explaining clearly the nature of the dilemma and summing up the candidate's experience in a concise and well-written essay. The admissions committee was particularly impressed by the author's honest approach and engaging writing style. The firm does not have to be well-known, in this case BCCI, nor must the dilemma involve large sums of money or shady characters. Rather, the essay should reflect the candidate's personal and professional commitment to ethics, a commitment that also underlies the foundation of the Darden School.

Part Three

THE SCHOOLS

## Chapter Nine

Schools Rated by Category

ABOUT THESE "RANKINGS"

Now before you say, "Hey, wait a minute! I thought this book wasn't going to rank schools," let us explain. Surveying 18,500 business school students is no easy task. In fact, it practically killed several staff members. But among the fruits of our labors—a reward that made our task seem worthwhile—was the fascinating numbers we came up with. We wanted to present those numbers to you in an informative and slightly less-than-serious way. The following rankings cannot and must not be considered objective. These lists are based entirely upon student opinion. So when our list rates a campus location, for example, we didn't use any scientific formula based on cost of living, climate, crime rate, etc. We simply listed the schools at which students raved about the location most, or complained about it most. So focus on the categories that are important to you, and make of these opinions what you will.

And remember, every one of the schools profiled in this book is a top-notch institution.

ACADEMICS

STUDENTS DEVELOP STRONG GENERAL MANAGEMENT SKILLS

University of Virginia
Harvard University
Dartmouth College
Georgetown University
Yale University
University of North Carolina at Chapel Hill
University of Michigan
Stanford University
University of Southern California
Wake Forest University

WEAK GENERAL MANAGEMENT SKILLS

CUNY Baruch College
University of Texas at Arlington
University of Wisconsin—Madison
University of Chicago
University of Florida
Syracuse University
University of Washington
Pepperdine University
University of Pittsburgh
University of Massachusetts at Amherst

QUANT JOCKS
(students develop strong quantitative skills)

Carnegie Mellon University
University of Rochester
University of Chicago
Massachusetts Institute of Technology
Purdue University
Yale University
University of Pennsylvania
Columbia University
University of Maryland
College of William and Mary

POETS
(weak quantitative skills)

Harvard University
CUNY Baruch College
University of Western Ontario
Syracuse University
University of Texas at Arlington
Claremont Graduate University
Northeastern University
University of Kansas
Northwestern University
University of Minnesota

STUDENTS DEVELOP STRONG INTERPERSONAL SKILLS

Dartmouth College
Penn State University
Southern Methodist University
University of Southern California
University of Tennessee at Knoxville
Case Western Reserve University
Georgetown University
Texas Christian University
Michigan State University
University of Maryland

WEAK INTERPERSONAL SKILLS

CUNY Baruch College
University of Texas at Arlington
University of Western Ontario
University of Kentucky
Syracuse University
University of Kansas
University of Wyoming
Harvard University
Northeastern University
University of Massachusetts at Amherst

STUDENTS DEVELOP STRONG PRESENTATION SKILLS

Penn State University
Southern Methodist University
Dartmouth College
University of Tennessee at Knoxville
University of Arizona
Texas Christian University
Tulane University
Vanderbilt University
University of Maryland
University of Notre Dame

WEAK PRESENTATION SKILLS

CUNY Baruch College
University of Massachusetts at Amherst
Harvard University
University of Kentucky
University of Texas at Arlington
Washington University
University of Kansas
University of Pittsburgh
Columbia University
University of Wyoming

STUDENTS DEVELOP STRONG TEAMWORK SKILLS

Dartmouth College
Georgetown University
Wake Forest University
University of Southern California
Yale University
Case Western Reserve University
University of California—Los Angeles
University of Tennessee at Knoxville
Vanderbilt University
Babson College

NOT MUCH TEAMWORK

Harvard University
CUNY Baruch College
University of Texas at Arlington
University of Wyoming
University of Kentucky
University of Kansas
Syracuse University
University of Chicago
Northeastern University
Pepperdine University

STUDENTS DEVELOP STRONG OPERATIONS SKILLS

Carnegie Mellon University
Washington University
College of William and Mary
Georgia Institute of Technology
Rensselaer Polytechnic Institute
Vanderbilt University
University of Southern California
Wake Forest University
Georgetown University
University of Western Ontario

OPERATIONS NOT A STRONG POINT

University of Chicago
University of Wisconsin—Madison
University of Texas at Arlington
CUNY Baruch College
University of Georgia
Syracuse University
Texas Christian University
University of Massachusetts at Amherst
Michigan State University
Dartmouth College

STUDENTS DEVELOP STRONG ACCOUNTING SKILLS

Cornell University
University of Chicago
University of Rochester
Southern Methodist University
University of Texas at Austin
Dartmouth College
Wake Forest University
University of Southern California
University of Alabama
University of Michigan

WHAT'S A SPREAD SHEET

Duke University
Syracuse University
University of Texas at Arlington
University of Wisconsin—Madison
Harvard University
University of Western Ontario
Michigan State University
University of Colorado at Boulder
University of Kansas
Loyola University

FINANCE WHIZZES
(students develop strong finance skills)

University of Rochester
University of Pennsylvania
New York University
University of Chicago
Yale University
Columbia University
Massachusetts Institute of Technology
University of Southern California
Vanderbilt University
Wake Forest University
Have Trouble Making Correct Change

HAVE TROUBLE MAKING CORRECT CHANGE
(weak finance skills)

Syracuse University
University of Massachusetts at Amherst
University of Kentucky
University of Georgia
University of Washington
University of Texas at Arlington
University of Wisconsin—Madison
University of Alabama
CUNY Baruch College
Duke University

STUDENTS DEVELOP STRONG MARKETING SKILLS

College of William and Mary
Northwestern University
Vanderbilt University
University of Southern California
Georgetown University
University of Tennessee at Knoxville
Penn State University
Hofstra University
University of Michigan
Dartmouth College

WEAK MARKETING SKILLS

Southern Methodist University
Tulane University
University of Kentucky
University of Texas at Arlington
University of Georgia
Massachusetts Institute of Technology
University of Denver
University of Wyoming
Harvard University
University of Alabama

COMPUTER GENIUSES
(students comfortable with computers and managing data)

Carnegie Mellon University
Wake Forest University
Purdue University
University of Iowa
Massachusetts Institute of Technology
University of California—Los Angeles
Rensselaer Polytechnic Institute
Duke University
Dartmouth College
University of Rochester

HOW DO I TURN THIS THING ON?
(students uncomfortable with computers)

Harvard University
CUNY Baruch College
University of Texas at Arlington
University of Massachusetts at Amherst
University of North Carolina at Chapel Hill
University of Western Ontario
Claremont Graduate University
Syracuse University
Yale University
Georgetown University

PRESSURE

OVERALL MELLOW
Stanford University
University of California—Berkeley
Yale University
Arizona State University
University of Massachusetts at Amherst
University of Colorado at Boulder
University of Kentucky
University of Texas at Arlington
University of California—Los Angeles
Duke University

OVERALL TENSE
University of Virginia
Carnegie Mellon University
University of Western Ontario
Rice University
Purdue University
University of Chicago
College of William and Mary
University of Southern California
University of Pittsburgh
Michigan State University

GOOD SAMARITANS
(non-competitive students)
Yale University
Stanford University
Northwestern University
University of California—Berkeley
University of Massachusetts at Amherst
Wake Forest University
University of California—Los Angeles
Dartmouth College
Georgetown University
University of Virginia

BACK-STABBERS
(competitive students)
University of Western Ontario
University of Alabama
Baylor University
University of Chicago
Texas A & M University
Brigham Young University
University of Tennessee at Knoxville
Michigan State University
Texas Christian University
Columbia University

UP ALL NIGHT
(heavy work load)
Carnegie Mellon University
University of Virginia
College of William and Mary
Georgetown University
Rice University
Purdue University
Dartmouth College
University of Southern California
Indiana University
Babson College

LIGHT WORK LOAD
University of Texas at Arlington
University of Kentucky
Stanford University
CUNY Baruch College
Loyola University
Arizona State University
University of Georgia
Northwestern University
Texas Christian University
University of Wyoming

SOCIAL LIFE & FELLOW STUDENTS

"SHINY, HAPPY MBAS"
(best quality of life)
Dartmouth College
Vanderbilt University
Southern Methodist University
Yale University
Case Western Reserve University
Cornell University
Duke University
University of North Carolina at Chapel Hill
Georgetown University
University of Texas at AustinBusiness

DON'T BOTHER ME
(students aren't very friendly)
CUNY Baruch College
University of Texas at Arlington
Northeastern University
Harvard University
Syracuse University
University of Connecticut
Hofstra University
University of Chicago
University of Kansas
University of Kentucky

SCHOOL OF THE LIVING DEAD
(worst quality of life)
Northeastern University
University of Connecticut
CUNY Baruch College
Indiana University
University of Michigan
University of Kansas
University of Texas at Arlington
Syracuse University
University of Minnesota
Stanford University

SOCIAL BUTTERFLIES
(active social lives)
University of California—Los Angeles
Dartmouth College
Stanford University
University of California—Berkeley
University of Colorado at Boulder
Thunderbird
University of Notre Dame
University of North Carolina at Chapel Hill
Arizona State University
University of Southern California

TOP OF THE MORNING TO YOU
(students are very friendly)
Dartmouth College
University of California—Los Angeles
Georgetown University
Yale University
University of California—Berkeley
College of William and Mary
University of Southern California
Vanderbilt University
Wake Forest University
University of Colorado at Boulder

THE HEART IS A LONELY BROKER
(moribund social lives)
CUNY Baruch College
University of Texas at Arlington
Carnegie Mellon University
University of Rochester
University of Kentucky
University of Kansas
Northeastern University
Hofstra University
University of Virginia
Rice University

HERE'S MY CARD
(students will keep in touch)
Dartmouth College
University of California—Los Angeles
University of California—Berkeley
Stanford University
Southern Methodist University
University of Maryland
Georgetown University
University of Southern California
Massachusetts Institute of Technology
University of Notre Dame

WHAT'S NETWORKING?
(students won't stay in touch)
CUNY Baruch College
University of Texas at Arlington
Northeastern University
Syracuse University
University of Connecticut
Hofstra University
University of Kansas
University of Kentucky
University of Wyoming
University of Pittsburgh

MULTICULTURAL SMORGASBORD
(ethnic & racial diversity)
University of Rochester
Case Western Reserve University
Thunderbird
Massachusetts Institute of Technology
University of Michigan
University of Maryland
Tulane University
Penn State University
Carnegie Mellon University
University of Illinois at Urbana—Champaign

WHITE BREAD
(ethnic & racial homogenity)
Brigham Young University
University of Alabama
University of Colorado at Boulder
Dartmouth College
College of William and Mary
Wake Forest University
Baylor University
Rice University
University of Wyoming
University of Virginia

STUDENTS ARE EAGER TO HELP OTHERS
Dartmouth College
Yale University
University of California—Los Angeles
University of California—Berkeley
Georgetown University
University of Virginia
Vanderbilt University
Wake Forest University
Cornell University
Carnegie Mellon University

ONLY IF YOU ASK
CUNY Baruch College
University of Texas at Arlington
Northeastern University
University of Connecticut
Harvard University
University of Kansas
Syracuse University
Loyola University
University of Western Ontario
University of Kentucky

GENIUS FOLK
(students say classmates are smart)

Yale University
Stanford University
Dartmouth College
Carnegie Mellon University
Massachusetts Institute of Technology
Georgetown University
University of Maryland
University of California—Los Angeles
University of California—Berkeley
University of Pennsylvania

NOT SO BRIGHT
(students say classmates are not smart)

CUNY Baruch College
Northeastern University
Syracuse University
University of Texas at Arlington
University of Kansas
University of Wyoming
University of Connecticut
University of Denver
University of Kentucky
Texas Christian University

"BEEN THERE, DONE THAT"
(students have diverse work experience)

Yale University
University of California—Berkeley
Georgetown University
University of California—Los Angeles
Cornell University
University of Maryland
Northwestern University
Duke University
Babson College
University of Michigan

DO YOU WANT FRIES WITH THAT?
(students' work experience NOT diverse)

Baylor University
University of Kansas
University of Alabama
Brigham Young University
Texas Christian University
Texas A & M University
Syracuse University
University of Wyoming
University of Kentucky
CUNY Baruch College

FACILITIES

ON-CAMPUS HOUSING GOOD
Dartmouth College
Harvard University
University of Western Ontario
University of Notre Dame
Rensselaer Polytechnic Institute
University of Michigan
Purdue University
Indiana University
Brigham Young University
University of Illinois at Urbana—Champaign

LOUSY
Carnegie Mellon University
University of Pennsylvania
Arizona State University
CUNY Baruch College
Duke University
University of North Carolina at Chapel Hill
University of Chicago
Wake Forest University
Texas Christian University
Case Western Reserve University

MAXIMUM PUMPITUDE
(gym facilities excellent)
Harvard University
Vanderbilt University
Tulane University
University of Illinois at Urbana—Champaign
Arizona State University
University of Texas at Austin
University of Alabama
Purdue University
University of Arizona
Texas A & M University

"WIMPY, WIMPY, WIMPY"
(like, maybe a jump rope or something)
CUNY Baruch College
Massachusetts Institute of Technology
University of Pennsylvania
Claremont Graduate University
Stanford University
Duke University
Thunderbird
University of Chicago
University of Texas at Arlington
Texas Christian University

SCHOOL TOWN IS PARADISE
University of Washington
Columbia University
University of Texas at Austin
University of North Carolina at Chapel Hill
Georgetown University
Dartmouth College
Michigan State University
Southern Methodist University
University of Georgia
University of Wisconsin—Madison

SCHOOL TOWN A PIT
Rensselaer Polytechnic Institute
Thunderbird
University of Connecticut
Yale University
University of Pennsylvania
Hofstra University
University of Notre Dame
Indiana University
Purdue University
Baylor University

SO MUCH TO DO
(lots of school clubs & activities)
Harvard University
University of Pennsylvania
Duke University
University of Texas at Austin
Vanderbilt University
Columbia University
Cornell University
Dartmouth College
Case Western Reserve University
University of Western Ontario

BOOOOOORING
(not many school activities)
CUNY Baruch College
Northeastern University
Loyola University
University of Texas at Arlington
University of Connecticut
Claremont Graduate University
Michigan State University
University of Kentucky
University of Kansas
University of Wyoming

A FIVE-STAR LIBRARY
Vanderbilt University
University of Alabama
University of California—Los Angeles
University of Western Ontario
University of California—Berkeley
University of Michigan
Wake Forest University
University of Illinois at Urbana—Champaign
University of Notre Dame
Harvard University

SOMEONE LOST THE BOOK
Georgia Institute of Technology
University of Kentucky
Ohio State University
University of Denver
Michigan State University
New York University
Columbia University
University of Kansas
College of William and Mary
University of Wyoming

PLACEMENT & RECRUITING

RECRUITING
(quality, range, & number of comparnies recruiting on-campus)

University of Pennsylvania
Columbia University
Northwestern University
Stanford University
Massachusetts Institute of Technology
University of California—Los Angeles
Dartmouth College
University of Chicago
Duke University
Purdue University

RECRUITING
(not satisfactory)

University of Wyoming
CUNY Baruch College
Northeastern University
University of Texas at Arlington
University of Kentucky
Hofstra University
University of Massachusetts at Amherst
Boston University
Babson College
University of Denver

WE GOT JOBS
(placement office very effective)

University of California—Los Angeles
Duke University
Stanford University
Purdue University
University of Pennsylvania
Dartmouth College
Carnegie Mellon University
Vanderbilt University
Washington University
Pepperdine University

ARE YOU HIRING?
(placement office not so great)

University of Wyoming
CUNY Baruch College
University of Massachusetts at Amherst
University of Kentucky
Northeastern University
University of Georgia
Hofstra University
University of Texas at Arlington
Baylor University
Yale University

## Chapter Ten

SCHOOL PROFILES

UNIVERSITY OF ALABAMA
Manderson Graduate School of Business

OVERVIEW

Type of school	public
Affiliation	none
Environment	metropolis
Academic calendar	other
Schedule	full-time only

STUDENTS

Enrollment of parent institution	19,000
Enrollment of business school	114
% male/female	73/27
% out-of-state	32
% minorities	8
% international (# countries represented)	11(5)
Average age at entry	26
Average years work experience at entry	2

ACADEMICS

% female faculty	12
% minority faculty	7
Hours of study per day	4.17

SPECIALTIES

Systems Consulting, Strategic Planning and Implementaion, Strategic Business Management, Marketing.

JOINT DEGREES

3/2 MBA, 3 years; MBA/JD, 4 years; 3/2 MBA + Undergrad, 5 years.

SPECIAL PROGRAMS

The Three/Two Program, Executive MBA Program, Dual Degree with Esc Toulouse.

STUDY ABROAD PROGRAMS

France — Esc Toulouse

SURVEY SAYS...

HITS
Library
Getting into courses a breeze
Gym

MISSES
Social life
General management
School clubs

PROMINENT ALUMNI

Thomas Cross, Managing Partner, Price Waterhouse; Samuel A. DiPiazza, Vice Chairman, Coopers & Lybrand; Ron Stewart, Senior Partner, Andersen Consulting

ACADEMICS

If you've postponed or avoided getting an MBA because of the high tuition, the University of Alabama offers one of the least expensive, most sought-after MBAs.

But this doesn't come at the cost of academics. One student raved, "The MBA program of the University of Alabama is the best kept secret in America. A simply outstanding education, it deserves serious consideration as one of the best MBA programs in the nation." First-year students take core courses in a "lockstep" sequence; that is, all sixty students take the courses together in a preset order. Praised one MBA, "The school is very flexible in what electives you can take. I could take an advertising class in the Communications School to go with my marketing concentration." Second-year students select a concentration in one of the following: systems consulting, strategic planning and implementation, finance/accounting, marketing, banking and financial services, or production/operations management. Raved one student, "Best strategy professors anywhere!" Several students lobbied for an expanded coursework in the MIS area. Beyond the basic curriculum, students are enrolled in a year-long professional development program that could easily pass for a finishing school.

Students we surveyed gave their professors above-average marks for their teaching and after-class accessibility. Students are equally pleased with the administration. "The new President is very committed to academics," reported one MBA. Indeed, Alabama is among only a dozen or so schools where students are satisfied with the way the school is run. Alabama has tried hard to win its students' respect. Chief among it's efforts is the high-tech b-school building. The students seem to be responding well. "U of A has excellent facilities with top-of-the-line multimedia rooms and computer labs," wrote one. The head of the systems consulting concentration, Dr. Shane Sharpe, received both the university-wide outstanding commitment to teaching award and the Morris Mayer award for selfless dedication to the students and the university. U of A scores well on the basics, too: Students say it's a cinch to get into popular courses.

As one might expect, the overwhelming majority of students say this program is well worth the investment. They hope its national reputation becomes as good as the experience they feel they're getting.

PLACEMENT AND RECRUITING

In response to past complaints, the Alabama Placement Office has worked to improve service to its small MBA student body. Previously, Manderson relied on the university-wide placement office, but last year it added an MBA-specific, full-time Placement Manager to the b-school staff. This move has not only increased recruitment opportunities but also freed up staff to provide more of such services as career counseling and personal coaching for interviews and resume writing. Professors are also helpful in this regard; the placement office reports that "faculty are available and are very involved with students to assist in making the all-important 'foot in the door' introduction relative to career

Martha Carroll, Director
P.O. Box 870223, Tuscaloosa, AL 35487
Admissions: 205-348-6517 • Fax: 205-348-4504
Email: mba@alston.cba.ua.edu
Internet: www.cba.ua.edu

University of Alabama

opportunities." As a result of these efforts, on-campus recruiting increased 19 percent during the 1996–1997 academic year and is on track to increase another 15 percent for the 1998 graduating class. During the summer of 1997, 100 percent of students seeking internships obtained them.

STUDENT/CAMPUS LIFE

The workload at Alabama is at its heaviest during the first-year. The majority of students report spending an average of fifteen to twenty-five hours a week preparing for class, although this is light by top b-school standards. Everyone works in a study group. By the second year, students have a better understanding of teamwork and performance requirements; therefore, they are a bit more relaxed.

Students are very competitive, but also cooperative. "It's sort of like a family," wrote one MBA, "we all want to see each other do well." Most students claim their closest friends are found within the b-school. "I know everyone's names, undergraduate institute/major, and interests," claims one student. Some people pan the cozy environment as "conforming" and "small town", however. Although they would like to see more racial and geographic diversity, students are impressed by the depth and range of professional experiences that their peers bring to the program. They're even more impressed by their classmates' smarts, which they describe as "sharp."

The majority of students live off-campus in nearby apartments. Parking isn't great. Consider living within walking distance or bringing a bike. Back on campus, students work out in a fully equipped, high-tech gym. They also enjoy Alabama's top-ranked athletic teams; football is a big social focus as is the nationally ranked gymnastics team. Griped one MBA, "There's nothing to do in Tuscaloosa if you don't like football and beer." Another gushed, "Lots of students follow the team on the road. Tuscaloosa is quite possibly the road trip capital of the world!" For those who want to do more than watch football, the MBA Association sponsors a wide range of professional and social events, including MBA Week, which features an intramural sporting competition, a community service activity, a variety of panel discussions and other keynote speakers, and a golf tournament with both MBAs and local business leaders as players.

ADMISSIONS

The admissions office evaluates, with equal weight, the following categories: GMAT scores, work or other experience, essays, letters of recommendation, extracurricular activities, and a personal interview.

According to the school, "We evaluate applications in a holistic manner. We evaluate applicants' abilities, capabilities, and goals based on all required elements of the application. Each category provides us with various information relative to academic abilities, writing skills, communication skills, and team work skills." Decisions are made on a rolling admissions basis. Applicants are notified of a decision within four to six weeks after the application has been received. Wait-listed applicants are notified by June 15th. Admitted applicants may defer admission for up to one year.

FINANCIAL FACTS

Tuition (in/out-state)	$2,594/$6,808
Cost of books	$600
Room & Board (on/off-campus)	$4,000/$4,000
% of students receiving aid	41
% first-year students receiving aid	22
% aid that is merit-based	100
% of students receiving paid internships	30
% of students receiving grants	30
Average award package	$6,000
Average grant	$6,000

ADMISSIONS

# of applications received	168
% applicants accepted	47
% acceptees attending	70
Average GMAT (range)	601 (560–640)
Average GPA (range)	3.30 (3.00–3.60)

Application fee (in/out-state)	$25/$25
Early decision program available	Yes
Regular application deadline	May 15
Regular notification	Rolling
Admission may be deferred?	Yes
Maximum length of deferment	1 year
Transfer students accepted?	Yes
Non-fall admission available?	No
Admissions process need-blind?	Yes

APPLICANTS ALSO LOOK AT

Vanderbilt University, University of Florida, University of Georgia, Emory University, University of Texas at Austin, University of Tennessee at Knoxville, Tulane University, Wake Forest University

EMPLOYMENT PROFILE

Placement rate (%)	100
# of companies recruiting on-campus	165
% grads employed immediately	98
% grads employed within six months	100
Average starting salary	$46,800

Grads employed by field (avg. salary):

Accounting	15% (NR)
Consulting	20% ($46,800)
Finance	37% ($38,300)
Human Resources	10% (NR)
Marketing	9% ($42,000)
MIS	16% ($53,300)
Operations	9% ($51,000)
Strategic Planning	5% (NR)
Other	2% ($39,200)

UNIVERSITY OF ARIZONA
Karl Eller Graduate School of Management

OVERVIEW
Type of school	public
Affiliation	none
Environment	metropolis
Academic calendar	semester
Schedule	full-time only

STUDENTS
Enrollment of parent institution	21,511
Enrollment of business school	214
% male/female	69/31
% minorities	15
% international (# countries represented)	11 (NR)
Average age at entry	27

ACADEMICS
Hours of study per day	3.93

SPECIALTIES
Marketing, MIS, Entrepreneurship, Finance

JOINT DEGREES
JD/MBA; MBA/MIM; MS MIS/MIM

SPECIAL PROGRAMS
Accelerated Three/Two program with the College of Arts and Sciences

SURVEY SAYS...
HITS
Presentation skills
Gym
Getting into courses a breeze

MISSES
General management
Quantitative skills
MIS/operations

ACADEMICS

Where can you find a first-rate Management Information Systems Department, a resort-like campus, gorgeous weather, and bargain-basement tuition? At the University of Arizona (U of A), which not only boasts a nationally renowned information technology department but is also consistently supported by large grants from some of America's premier technology companies, including IBM, Apple Computer, and Hewlett Packard. Interested in the development of new business ventures? Then U of A is also a natural choice. Students can study in the Berger Entrepreneurship Program in the Eller Center for the Study of the Private Market Economy, which was cited as a model program by the U.S. Association for Small Business in 1989. Here students get hands-on experience in workshops and two-person projects presented in a Business Plans Competition judged by local Arizonans. Other strong departments include marketing, finance, and operations.

The U of A offers a basic MBA with a heavy quantitative slant. To balance out the emphasis on quantitative analysis, students also receive special training in communication and presentation skills. New at Eller is the Management Experience, a computer-simulation game student teams begin in the third week of their first semester and tell us is "excellent!" According to the school, "Students make weekly decisions regarding market opportunities, product development, production planning, and strategic positioning. They receive weekly feedback in the form of sales results, market-share data, and bottom-line profits." Even in the virtual world of bits and bytes, the takeover spirit runs high. Second-years recruit their own teams to take over the first-years' companies.

Overall, students are in accord—the U of A MBA is worth the investment of time and money. "The tuition is dirt cheap, and scholarship money is easy to come by," wrote one student. "As a future entrepreneur, why would I spend $20k a year in tuition when that can be my seed capital?" MBAs praised the cohesiveness of the program, but a few critics complained that the program was "over-hyped" and there was too much "work for work's sake." Another mentioned that "The MIS department is the focus and other departments tend to be after-thoughts." Other criticisms were leveled at the "non-responsive administration," and students asked for "a better open-door policy with faculty." Most agreed, however, that Eller offers a "country-club lifestyle and a good quality MBA."

PLACEMENT AND RECRUITING

Eller MBAs were more satisfied this year than last year with the quality and diversity of companies recruiting on-campus. In 1994, 90 percent of Eller grads had jobs within three months of graduation. The average starting salary was $43,000. Twenty-five percent of students went into finance; 22 percent each into strategic planning and marketing. However, a few lamented that "recruitment for true marketing positions is low." Top employers: Hewlett-Packard, Tektronix, Ford Motor Company, American Management Systems, Andersen Consulting, IBM, Dial Intet, Ernst and Young, General Motors.

Christopher P. Puto, Associate Dean
College of Business and Public Administration, Tucson, AZ 85721
Admissions: 520-621-6227
Internet: www.bpa.arizona.edu

STUDENT/CAMPUS LIFE

Most U of A students agree that classmates are professionally diverse. But one MBA moaned, "Students lack business perspective, are too grade oriented." Racial minorities are scarce, but content. One MBA writes, "As an African-American student it's been great. I had a few reservations initially, but the eight of us think it's great." Some MBAs report being very competitive, while others say "competition is evident only as part of teams." Cooperation abounds. One student wrote about his classmates, "If you have a problem with a particular marketing case . . . they will help you out. You have an extra case of beer . . . they will help you out."

Students here study an average of twenty-five to thirty-five hours a week, and report an intense first-year workload. By the second year, both the workload and pressure lighten up. Still, like other b-school students, many U of A MBAs say they do assignments selectively—skimming and skipping—to manage it all. Bonus points go to the school for actively preparing students for the demands of the program in two ways: Quantexcel learning sessions and a four-week summer prep session offered to all first-years. Classes are small and held Monday through Thursday. Classless Fridays are reserved for activities such as on-site business visits and the quantexcel workshops.

Social and professional activities are organized by the student-run Master of Business Administration Student Association. Students get most pumped about the gym, which is reportedly amazing. The majority of students live off-campus in surrounding neighborhoods. The U of A campus is beautiful, and outdoor activities are abundant. "There's so much to do," wrote one MBA. " Golf, tennis, hiking are all popular pastimes. The study breaks on my mountain bike are quite excellent." Everyone seems to like Tucson, although it's hardly a hopping metropolis. A few hours' drive away are Phoenix, the Grand Canyon, or even a Mexican beach.

ADMISSIONS

The admissions department considers work experience most important, followed by undergraduate coursework, undergraduate GPA, GMAT scores, essays, and recommendations. The admissions office notes, "In general, we look at the 'whole person' and not just isolated components of individual performance such as GMAT or GPA."

FINANCIAL FACTS

Tuition (in/out-state)	$2,010/$8,378
Room & Board (on/off-campus)	$2,700/NR
% of students receiving aid	25

ADMISSIONS

# of applications received	542
% applicants accepted	37
% acceptees attending	35
Application fee (in/out-state)	$35
Regular application deadline	April 15
Regular notification	Rolling
Admission may be deferred?	Yes
Maximum length of deferment	1 year
Admissions process need-blind?	NR

APPLICANTS ALSO LOOK AT

University of Texas at Austin, Arizona State University, University of California—Los Angeles, Thunderbird, University of California—Berkeley, Texas A & M University, University of Minnesota, Stanford University

EMPLOYMENT PROFILE

Average starting salary	$40,700

ARIZONA STATE UNIVERSITY
College of Business

OVERVIEW

Type of school	public
Affiliation	none
Environment	metropolis
Academic calendar	trimester
Schedule	Full-time/part-time/evening

STUDENTS

Enrollment of parent institution	44,500
Enrollment of business school	874
% male/female	71/29
% part-time	63
% minorities	16
% international (# countries represented)	11(19)
Average age at entry	28
Average years work experience at entry	5

ACADEMICS

Student/faculty ratio	25:1
% female faculty	15
% minority faculty	11
Hours of study per day	3.99

SPECIALTIES
Service Marketing and Management, Supply Chain Mgmt, Information Mgmt, Financial Management and Markets, Health Administration.

JOINT DEGREES
MB/M Econ; MBA/MIM; MBA/M ACC; MBA/MSIM; MBA/M Tax; MBA/MHSA, 2 years; MBA/JD and MBA/M Arch, 3 to 4 years

SPECIAL PROGRAMS
PepsiCo Minority Scholarship Program

STUDY ABROAD PROGRAMS
Groups Esc Toulouse—Toulouse, France; Universidad Carlos III—Madrid, Spain; Instituto Technologico Autonomo DE Mexico—Mexico City, Mexico; Instituto Technologico y De Estudios Superiores De Monterrey—Mexico City, Mexico

SURVEY SAYS...
HITS
Off-campus housing
Gym
Getting into courses a breeze

MISSES
On-campus housing
Profs not great teachers
Quantitative skills

PROMINENT ALUMNI
Gary Tooker, President, Motorola; Tom Evans, *US News and World Report*

ACADEMICS

Arizona State University understands the virtues of niche marketing. Rather than try to be all things to all MBAs, ASU focuses on creating graduates who excel in a few specific areas. Thus the choices for second-year students, who elsewhere would be free to pursue numerous electives, are limited. As one second-year puts it: "This program is very specialized. There are five tracks: services marketing, finance, supply chain management, and information technology. This program is great if you are looking for in-depth expertise in one of these areas." Students tell us that they like the fact that "the lockstep program focuses students and faculty on specific disciplines." Of the five tracks, students agree that the one offered by the fewest top MBA programs—the supply chain track—is the best. By offering the supply chain major in cooperation with the National Association of Purchasing Management (NAPM), ASU guarantees that its students receive plenty of hands-on experience and graduate with numerous contacts.

Because the ASU College of Business is just one part of a huge university system, MBAs here have ample opportunities to pursue dual degrees. The school offers an MBA/MIM (International Management) degree in conjunction with Thunderbird, an MBA/MS-Information Management degree, an MBA/MS in Economics, and a combined MBA/Juris Doctor (law degree). Students may also concurrently complete their MBA with master's degrees in Health Sciences Administration, Architecture, or Accountancy. As at most b-schools, first-year at ASU is crammed with core requirements. The school's brochure warns that students "must maintain minimum nonacademic obligations while in the first-year, as the schedule...leaves little opportunity for other activities." Students concur, but quickly note that second year isn't nearly as intense.

Professors here receive below-average grades from students, who tell us that "as with all academic institutions, there are great and marginal instructors." Another explains that "some of the faculty for the core courses need improvement. In the school's defense, they realize this and are attempting to correct this." Students are generally more sanguine about the administration, which they describe as "considerate of our feelings and very concerned with the MBA program image, and so take our comments and suggestions seriously." Students also appreciate the "excellent, up-to-date multimedia equipment in all classrooms and computer labs for student and professor use." Although our survey shows that the program does not entirely meet students' academic expectations, it also shows that most consider an ASU MBA a worthwhile degree. Their explanation: "The value of this degree is extremely high given the price. Students leave here well-equipped to work with top-level executives as well as loading dock or field representatives."

PLACEMENT AND RECRUITING

ASU students have mixed feelings about the Career Management Office (CMO). Several are very pleased with its work, calling the program "strong." One student reports that "An enormous number of companies recruit here. It has opened many doors of opportunity I never imagined existed." Yet students' overall grades for the office are merely average. The most common complaint is that the CMO is less effective in assisting with placements outside of ASU's

Judith K. Heilala, Director of Recruiting and Admissions
P.O. Box 874906, Tempe, AZ 85287
Admissions: 602-965-7635 • Fax: 602-965-8569
Email: judith.heilala@asu.edu
Internet: www.cob.asu.edu/mba

**Arizona State
University**

perceived areas of strength. "Placement for non-supply and information-systems majors needs improvement," writes one student.

Students report a high level of satisfaction with the quality of companies recruiting on-campus, although many feel that not enough of them come to ASU and that companies from outside the Southwestern region are particularly underrepresented. Students who contact alumni when searching for jobs find them to be helpful. In 1997 the demand in the national and international job market for ASU MBAs increased. While maintaining a diverse employer base of technology, consulting, and financial organizations, a significant increase in hiring by computer/electronics manufacturers and consumer products/services firms is particularly noteworthy. Recent top hirers include IBM, Hewlett-Packard, Intel, Honeywell, Frito-Lay, Qualcomm, Deloitte & Touche LLP, Exxon, Lucent Technologies, Pillsbury, and Televerde.

STUDENT/CAMPUS LIFE

Arizona's trimester academic calendar is "very quick," making life for ASU MBAs a little more hectic than it might otherwise be. Still, students report that "stress levels are low" because "most people are very willing to help you" in this "great teamwork atmosphere." Most students are only mildly competitive, "mature, older, often married, and here to learn." Many students "participate in volunteer or sports activities both on- and off-campus. Although when approached for help most students offer it, the class is divided into regular and somewhat closed social cliques." Although the student body is "very geographically and ethnically diverse," those unaccustomed to the Southwest should be forewarned: as one Easterner remarks, "the students and the general social atmosphere are more conservative than to what I'm accustomed."

First-year students find that their schedule is pretty well defined, as in, "Sleep-class-study but at least one day per week is yours." Free time opens up for second-year students, who enjoy the campus, the city, and the surrounding area. "Very diverse area," comments one student. "You can play golf one day and go skiing the next." Another agrees: "So many things to do within a two-hour drive! Hiking, skiing, pro sports—you name it and Arizona has it!" On-campus facilities—from the computer labs and library to the gym—are universally considered "great." No wonder students tell us that "living in Phoenix is great; it's like going to school in paradise. The campus and the town are basically resorts."

ADMISSIONS

According to the admissions department, your work experience/resume and GMAT score are weighted most heavily. Then, in descending order, your college GPA, "a personal statement reflecting on maturity, strength of purpose, academic potential, and ability to communicate clearly"; letters of recommendation; extracurricular activities; and the interview. Applications are reviewed in rounds. The deadlines for each round are December 15, March 1, and May 1. It is advisable to apply in round one or two. Joint degree programs include: MBA/MIM with Thunderbird and MBA/JD. Scholarships and assistantships are available, including the PepsiCo Minority Scholarship Program.

FINANCIAL FACTS

Tuition (in/out-state)	$3,988/$10,640
Fees (in-state/out-of-state)	$70/$70
Cost of books	$2,100
Room & Board (on/off-campus)	NR/NR
% of students receiving aid	95
% of students receiving loans	21
% of students receiving paid internships	78
% of students receiving grants	39
Average award package	$11,335
Average grant	$2,254

ADMISSIONS

# of applications received	1,360
% applicants accepted	41
% acceptees attending	49
Average GMAT (range)	609 (500–750)
Minimum TOEFL	580
Average GPA (range)	3.30 (2.20–4.00)
Application fee (in/out-state)	$45/$45
Early decision program available	Yes
Early decision deadline	March 1
Early decision notification	February 15
Regular application deadline	May 1
Regular notification	Rolling
Admission may be deferred?	Yes
Maximum length of deferment	once
Transfer students accepted?	No
Non-fall admission available?	No
Admissions process need-blind?	Yes

APPLICANTS ALSO LOOK AT

University of Texas at Austin, University of Arizona, University of California—Los Angeles, Thunderbird, University of California—Berkeley, Stanford University, University of Washington, University of Colorado at Boulder

EMPLOYMENT PROFILE

Placement rate (%)	98
# of companies recruiting on-campus	179
% grads employed immediately	83
% grads employed within six months	100
Average starting salary	$62,500

Grads employed by field (avg. salary):

Accounting	1% ($52,000)
Consulting	13% ($64,864)
Finance	15% ($63,770)
Marketing	26% ($67,329)
MIS	15% ($62,189)
Operations	26% ($61,174)
Other	4% ($68,500)

BABSON COLLEGE
F. W. Olin Graduate School of Business

OVERVIEW

Type of school	private
Affiliation	none
Environment	suburban
Academic calendar	semester
Schedule	Full-time/part-time/evening

STUDENTS

Enrollment of parent institution	3,340
Enrollment of business school	1,644
% male/female	66/34
% out-of-state	22
% part-time	76
% minorities	5
% international (# countries represented)	9(37)
Average age at entry	29
Average years work experience at entry	6

ACADEMICS

Student/faculty ratio	14:1
% female faculty	28
% minority faculty	9
% part-time faculty	35
Hours of study per day	4.88

SPECIALTIES

Strengths of faculty and curriculum in entrepreneurship, marketing, finance, international focus, a fully-integrated, modular first-year curriculum, field-based programs, mentor program, international internships, management consulting programs.

SPECIAL PROGRAMS

International Management Internship Program (IMIP), Management Consulting Field Experience (MCFE), International Study Programs, Business Mentor Program

STUDY ABROAD PROGRAMS

France, Spain, Czech Republic, Russia, China

SURVEY SAYS...

HITS
Diversity of work experience
Teamwork skills
Profs are great teachers

MISSES
School clubs
Quantitative skills
Gym

PROMINENT ALUMNI

Neil F. Finnegan, President and CEO, U.S. Trust; Akio Toyoda, Assistant Manager, Domestic Marketing, Toyota Motor Corp.; Junichi Murata, President, Murata Machinery, Ltd.

ACADEMICS

Although it offers a wide variety of academic options, Babson's MBA program is primarily associated with entrepreneurial studies, a discipline that Babson was among the first in the nation to offer. The school stresses its strength in entrepreneurship in its promotional materials; its slogan is "Entrepreneurial Leadership in a Changing Global Environment," and Babson boasts that the program was ranked number one in the country by both *US News and World Report* and *Success* magazines in 1996. Students agree that the program is top-notch: more than 80 percent of respondents give the entrepreneurship program our highest rating. "Outstanding," is how one student puts it. Students are enthusiastic about course offerings, opportunities for "in-the-field" learning, and the "entrepreneurial incubator space" provided in the newly built Olin Hall, which makes subsidized office space available to student entrepreneurs as well as to recent graduates.

Babson's other strengths lie in management and international business—both areas in which our survey shows not only high satisfaction levels but also improvement in recent years. Students are less satisfied with finance and accounting studies. Students in all departments are pleased with the quality of instruction. Writes one, "Faculty are fabulous. They are tough, fun, and fully committed to students and the program. It really helps the process because they're behind you." Professors are "extremely accessible" and "have extensive professional experience (CEOs, entrepreneurs, etc.). Research is very important, but teaching is tops."

All two-year MBA students (Babson also offers a one-year program and a part-time, evening program) participate in interdisciplinary studies, called "modules," during their first-year. Modules, which are team-taught, cover such subjects as Creative Management in Dynamic Organizations and Designing and Managing the Delivery System. Students respond enthusiastically. Writes one, "First-year integrated curriculum is unbelievable, three professors teaching one class is common and dynamic." One-year MBAs complete modules during a summer session; evening students take traditional courses in lieu of modules. The first-year program also includes a Business Mentor Program, which allows students to work as consultants for companies in the Boston area. The mentor program requires students to assess their assigned company's competitive position in the market and then to work with company executives to evaluate one aspect of the business. A student reports that "the mentor team experience during the first-year is a terrific way to integrate the coursework and learn a lot about teamwork." The new Olin Building houses "mentor rooms allocated to teams that are so useful, with phone, voice-mail, computers, etc."

Babson "strongly encourages" students to complete an international concentration, which combines a concentration in finance or marketing with courses in international studies. Students who choose this option must demonstrate proficiency in a second language by graduation.

PLACEMENT AND RECRUITING

All Babson students are required to complete the MBA Career Education curriculum. The curriculum includes a fifteen-hour first-year program called Career Management, which covers the basic skills of self-assessment and presentation. Babson considers its mentor and internship programs to be important

Rita Edmunds, Director of Admissions
Babson Park, MA 02157-0310
Admissions: 781-239-4317 • Fax: 617-239-4194
Email: mbaadmission@grad_sch@babson.edu
Internet: www.babson.edu/mba/index.html

Babson College

components of its P&R program. As students near graduation they take advantage of Career Search, a computerized database of more than 800,000 employers nationwide, and ACE, an alumni database. Companies that have recruited on campus in the past include SAP, Kellogg, EMC Corporation, Oracle Corporation, Fleet Financial Group, Johnson & Johnson, and A.T. Kearney.

Babson students are very satisfied with their access to internships and mentoring. They are generally pleased with the help they receive from Babson alumni in their job searches. Their satisfaction with the job placement office and with on-campus recruiting is around the national average.

STUDENT/CAMPUS LIFE

Babson MBAs form a close-knit group who think highly of each other. "We're a diverse group of young people with very high aspirations and entrepreneurial goals," writes one student. Another notes that "many are from liberal arts backgrounds; from interesting and diverse backgrounds." Mandatory teamwork forces students to spend a lot of time together, which fortunately they don't mind. In fact, they're very likely to spend their spare time in each other's company. Students report that the on-campus hot spot for group gatherings is "Roger's Pub on Thursday nights. It's lots of fun; a great place to have some beer and blow off some steam." About the only complaint students raise about each other is that "students are primarily from the Northeast or are non-USA. We could use a more diverse mix of American students to match the diversity among the international experience."

Babson's campus is a beautiful 450-acre wooded expanse, "complete with live deer!" Students are very enthusiastic about the "outstanding new building, Olin Hall, that brings all MBA functions within four walls and sits on a beautiful campus. Life is sweet!" Located in the college town of Wellesley, Babson offers students serene surroundings. Because Boston is only 15 miles away, Babson students also have easy access to the business and cultural advantages of a big city. Still, social life takes a distant back seat to school work at Babson. Says one student, "Babson life is busy—class, class, lunch, class, study group, drinks, sleep. Not much more to say." Explains another, "The workload is very heavy when you include school activities, internships, and job search."

ADMISSIONS

The Babson admissions office ranks your work experience as most important, and then, in descending order, the interview (required), GMAT scores, college GPA, essays, letters of recommendation, and extracurricular activities. According to the school, though, "The ranking of these criteria will vary by candidate."

The school writes: "At Babson, we consider each candidate as an individual and look at the entire package, not simply at test scores and GPAs. Accordingly, we require an interview. This personal approach provides both Babson and our candidates an opportunity to determine whether there is a "fit" within the Babson community. We look for goal-oriented individuals with an entrepreneurial spirit, a global mindset, and an ability to grapple with the ambiguities of managing change in a dynamic business world. For the one-year program, applicants must have an undergraduate degree in business administration. Babson batches applications by rounds. There are three rounds for the two-year program and two rounds for the one-year program. Students may defer admission for up to one year."

FINANCIAL FACTS

Tuition	$21,940
Tuition per credit	$682
Fees	$660
Cost of books	$1,300
Room & Board (on/off-campus)	$9,810/$9,810
% of students receiving aid	53
% first-year students receiving aid	55
% aid that is merit-based	15
% of students receiving loans	43
% of students receiving grants	3
Average award package	$14,300
Average grant	$15,400
Average graduation debt	$40,335

ADMISSIONS

# of applications received	1,459
% applicants accepted	58
% acceptees attending	52
Average GMAT (range)	608 (570–640)
Minimum TOEFL	600
Average GPA (range)	3.15 (2.82–3.39)
Application fee (in/out-state)	$50/$50
Early decision program available	Yes
Early decision deadline	January 15
Early decision notification	March 15
Regular application deadline	March 1
Regular notification	May 15
Admission may be deferred?	Yes
Maximum length of deferment	1 year
Transfer students accepted?	Yes
Non-fall admission available?	Yes
Admissions process need-blind?	Yes

APPLICANTS ALSO LOOK AT

Harvard University, Boston University, Dartmouth College, Northwestern University, Massachusetts Institute of Technology, New York University, Georgetown University, University of Pennsylvania

EMPLOYMENT PROFILE

# of companies recruiting on-campus	243
% grads employed within six months	94
Average starting salary	$59,670

Grads employed by field (avg. salary):

Consulting	19% ($62,725)
Entrepreneurship	17% ($68,000)
Finance	29% ($61,400)
General Management	10% ($53,000)
Marketing	18% ($49,900)
MIS	4% ($56,500)
Venture Capital	1% (NR)
Other	2% (NR)

BAYLOR UNIVERSITY
Hankamer School of Business

OVERVIEW

Type of school	private
Affiliation	Baptist
Environment	NR
Academic calendar	NR

STUDENTS

Enrollment of parent institution	NR
Enrollment of business school	52
% male/female	60/40
% minorities	5
% international (# countries represented)	10(3)
Average age at entry	24

ACADEMICS

Student/faculty ratio	15:1
% female faculty	40
Hours of study per day	3.65

SPECIALTIES

Each semester, one publicly held company volunteers to serve as the MBA's "Focus Firm." Its core issues become the center piece of the MBA curriculum. The focus-firm approach to learning provides you real-time delivery of theoretical applications, technological advances, global awareness, functional intergration, and team-centered learning.

JOINT DEGREES

JD/MBA 3 years; MBA/IM 15 months

SPECIAL PROGRAMS

The Intergrated Management Seminar is a unique one-semester seminar that satisfies all business prerequisites. It is offered for students without previous business training.

STUDY ABROAD PROGRAMS

Mexico, France, Australia, China , Japan, Korea, Thailand, England

SURVEY SAYS...

HITS
Small classes
Off-campus housing
Computer skills

MISSES
MIS/operations
School clubs
Social life

ACADEMICS

MBAs across the country rarely mention "Christian environment" when listing the assets of their programs, but then again few MBAs attend schools as closely aligned with a church as is the Hankamer School of Business at Baylor University. Baylor guarantees that its Baptist traditions endure, in part by maintaining continuity in its academic community. Not only does the school welcome returning undergraduates but, as one student explains, "Most professors are Baylor alumni. They are dedicated to students and the school."

The Hanmaker School reaches out to students who might be passed over by other programs, an aspect appreciated by many who attend the school. The "relatively easy entry requirements" initially attracted one MBA to the school, while another notes that Hanmaker is "the only good one-year program I found that did not require work experience." To bring such students up to speed, Hanmaker requires a semester-long Integrated Management Seminar (IMS). Non-business degree undergraduates begin their tenure at Hanmaker with this intensive review of macroeconomics, microeconomics, accounting, marketing, management, finance, statistics, and information systems. Hanmaker nurtures its students, leading one to report that "the school's greatest strength is the close-knit atmosphere and helpful environment. It's a small-school environment. This aids not only in the educational process but in job searches as well."

Those who successfully complete IMS join entering students with undergraduate business degrees in Lockstep One, a semester of required courses in basic business subjects. The following semester, Lockstep Two involves two required courses, one 'restricted elective' (students may choose from among three quantitative courses), and one elective. The Hanmaker program concludes with Lockstep Three, during which students may pursue a field of concentration (although they are not required to do so). Lockstep Three also includes a final core course called "Strategic Management and Business Policy."

The students we surveyed tell us that the "greatest strengths of Baylor are its emphasis on team projects, presentation skills, and applicability of coursework to the real world." The faculty "is great. Their availability and openness to one-on-one work helps students. They spend more time with students because this is not a research school." Standout departments include accounting, finance, and management. Marketing, operations, and international business studies receive subpar grades from students. The workload here is described as "moderate." One student tells us, "I study less in graduate school than I did as an undergraduate, and I get out more. My grades are not affected." Classrooms are excellent, other facilities less so, although "a new graduate center and computer lab will be added in the fall [1998], improving crowded facilities."

PLACEMENT AND RECRUITING

Hanmaker students give their placement office below-average marks, although they also note that "the school is currently overhauling the placement office, so that it is an area that is improving." Currently, business grads share placement services not only with business undergraduates but also with the rest of Baylor's large undergraduate population. Students give high marks to the quality of companies that recruit on-campus, although they would like to see a wider

Laurie Wilson, Director of Graduate Business Admissions
P.O. Box 98001, Waco, TX 76798-8001
Admissions: 254-710-3718 • Fax: 817-755-1066
Internet: hsb.baylor.edu/mba

Baylor University

assortment of potential employers represented. Those who responded to our survey are less enthusiastic about Baylor's alumni network; of those who contacted alums during their job searches, more than one-third found them to be of no help.

STUDENT/CAMPUS LIFE

Hanmaker graduate students are typically young and eager. Writes one student, "Many are in their early twenties. Very ambitious, talented, and ready to learn." Adds another, "Many students are driven and are hard workers. They force others to go beyond 'normal' levels of performance." Some students, however, complain that "We need to recruit more diverse students, and students with more work experience." Most would agree that the school is "not very ethnically or culturally diverse," although it does attract a sizable international contingent. Nor is it particularly tolerant of eccentricity. One student who doesn't comfortably fit into the 'Baylor bubble' warns: "Baylor attempts to assimilate students and force them to fit the Baylor image. I have experienced a great deal of hostility and resentment due to the fact that I have long hair, wear tie-dyes, and am liberal." For those comfortable within its confines, though, the Baylor community offers "an interesting group of individuals who have high standards. On the whole, an impressive group."

Life at Baylor is "well balanced. The week is spent studying hard, and the weekends are spent relaxing with friends." The atmosphere "is very relaxed, and students and faculty are always helpful and outgoing." Business-related and religious club meetings are augmented by "many outside social activities when students to get to know each other beyond schoolwork." Students also report that "International events are plentiful. Activities, special speakers, and interesting speeches are always available." Although students give the town of Waco middling grades, they do enjoy the fact that they are "close to river, lake, and parks" and live in a "great climate." Many head for Dallas, Houston, or Austin whenever they can make the time.

ADMISSIONS

The admissions office at the Hankamer School of Business MBA program considers applicants' previous academic achievements, GMAT scores, and relevant work experiences. Applicants must have achieved a minimum GPA of 2.7 in undergraduate and, if applicable, postgraduate study. Baylor ignores certain types of courses when determining applicants' GPAs; check with the admissions office for further details. Their academic records should also demonstrate "a scholarly and professional interest considerably above the average." Baylor's promotional material also notes that "Managerial experience, leadership, and other practical experiences are among criteria used in evaluating an applicant's potential for success." International applicants must meet additional language proficiency requirements; applicants to the joint MBA-JD program must take the LSAT as well as the GMAT. Applicants to the accelerated "Lockstep Program" must have received a "B" or better in college-level courses in accounting, economics, finance, statistics, information systems, production management, and marketing. Those failing to meet this requirement must take the one-semester Integrated Management Seminar.

FINANCIAL FACTS
Tuition	$11,088
Tuition per credit	$308
Fees	$500
Cost of books	$1,000
Room & Board (on/off-campus)	$4,800/$4,800
% aid that is merit-based	70

ADMISSIONS
# of applications received	212
% applicants accepted	73
% acceptees attending	47
Average GMAT (range)	581 (440–680)
Minimum TOEFL	600
Average GPA	3.25
Application fee (in/out-state)	$25/$25
Early decision program available	No
Regular application deadline	July 1
Regular notification	
Admission may be deferred?	Yes
Maximum length of deferment	1 year
Transfer students accepted?	Yes
Non-fall admission available?	Yes
Admissions process need-blind?	Yes

APPLICANTS ALSO LOOK AT
Texas A & M University, University of Texas at Austin, Southern Methodist University, University of Texas at Arlington, Rice University, Texas Christian University, Thunderbird, Cornell University

EMPLOYMENT PROFILE
Placement rate (%)	90
# of companies recruiting on-campus	50
% grads employed immediately	90
% grads employed within six months	95
Average starting salary	$42,800

Grads employed by field (avg. salary):
Accounting	40% ($45,000)
Finance	26% ($50,000)
General Management	13% ($30,000)
MIS	13% ($50,000)
Other	6% ($55,000)

BOSTON UNIVERSITY
School of Management

ACADEMICS

Boston University's commitment to upgrading its MBA program—best exemplified by a state-of-the-art facility opened in January 1997—has students cheering that "the school is on a very positive path." The "shiny new building puts all business services in one place and provides good high-tech resources." But BU has revamped more than its physical appearance: In the past several years, the school has switched over to a more deeply integrated curriculum, emphasizing "total quality management." Writes one student, "The program is beautifully organized; an almost flawless cross-functional pedagogical approach."

BU structures its MBA program to "concentrate on process instead of function," teaching management as "a system—a horizontal continuum of interdependent departments or functions." The idea is to create students who are "cross-trained" in accounting, finance, marketing, and operations, and who know how to borrow from one discipline to supplement another. This structure stresses teamwork and team teaching over individual achievement, and practical, hands-on education over theory. Professors even assist this approach because the "vast majority of [them] came to BU to teach, not just to conduct research." By and large, professors are "extremely helpful, open for discussion, [and] enthusiastic," although a few were singled out as "arrogant." As for the administration, students note that "it does its best to meet student needs," but warn that "it takes time to navigate the rigid administration structure. To get something done, you need to campaign and sell it."

The third-largest private university in the United States and one of the country's largest MBA programs, Boston University has the resources to offer a wide variety of specialties and dual degrees. Students single out dual degree offerings in both Health Care Management and Public and Non-Profit Management as prime reasons for choosing BU. The Finance Department, the Entrepreneurship Program, and the dual offering of a MS/Management of Information Systems also receive their plaudits. But students here also have their complaints. They give mediocre marks to their instruction in marketing, operations, and computer skills. Also, despite the new building and its expanded resources, students continue to tell us that "we need more computers!" and that the "library facilities need to be expanded."

PLACEMENT AND RECRUITING

BU recently created a new placement facility dedicated exclusively to MBAs in an effort to upgrade its career services. So far, student assessments of the Feld Career Center are only middling: nearly half our respondents rate the career center "okay" or worse (however, 9 percent give it an "excellent" grade). Students concede that "the Career Center has come a long way but," they add, "still needs more work." The main focus of the center is its interactive software recruiting program, called "1st Place!". The Feld Center collects resumes of all students, then uses "1st Place!" to match students with prospective employers. A full-time staff of ten also helps students scout potential internships and jobs, compose resumes, and prepare for interviews.

Peter Kelly, Director
595 Commonwealth Avenue, Boston, MA 02215
Admissions: 617-353-2670 • Fax: 617-353-7368
Email: mba@bu.edu
Internet: management.bu.edu

The greatest number of student complaints about the Feld Center concern the number and quality of on-campus recruiters. "The school needs to attract the more exclusive companies to campus," writes one second-year student. "Alumni make it easy to interview with top firms, but I would like to see more on campus." According to the school, during the 1997–98 recruiting season, they achieved a 37 percent increase of on-campus recruiting visits, and means salries were up by nearly 10 percent.

STUDENT/CAMPUS LIFE

BU attempts to make its large MBA student body feel a little smaller by breaking its incoming classes into cohorts of roughly fifty students. Each cohort stays intact throughout first semester, completing core courses together. The system works: students report that their classmates are friendly, helpful, and strongly motivated but not "cut-throat." Says one student, "The first-year cohort program gives us a group of peers that not only are our competitors but our friends." Another agrees: "There is a very supportive atmosphere among the student community, where students share information and take the time with others who may be falling behind." Students regard their groups as diverse, primarily because of the pronounced presence of international students. Warns an African-American student, "There are lots of international students, but few African-Americans."

Students at BU work hard, although most students report that the workload here is manageable. Writes one first-year student, "It's hard work but very fun. My cohort (fifty strong) is extremely close. We spend a lot of time with each other outside of class." Adds another student, "The intense workload is broken up by numerous opportunities to recreate and be social." Those opportunities include student-managed clubs and events ("Students are active in creating extracurricular activity. The Council is active in social activities"), as well as frequent forays away from the campus, which is adjacent to Boston's historic Back Bay district. Fenway Park is just a stone's throw away, the symphony hall isn't much further, and the rest of this "great city" is easily accessible by car or public transportation. Students stay on campus to enjoy the BU Pub (where they can often share a drink with professors), a new MBA-only lounge named, creatively enough, "The Lounge," and intramural sports. Golf and tennis are very popular, as are volleyball matches against nearby MIT and b-school rival Wharton.

ADMISSIONS

The admissions selection process places equal importance on all credentials: essays, college GPA, GMAT score, work experience, letters of recommendation. Interviews are encouraged, but not required. Advises the school, "Work experience is strongly preferred. BU is interested in attracting a high level of diversity in the classroom in work experience, ethnicity, nationality, and gender." Decisions are made on a rolling basis beginning in January for the September cycle (full- and part-time). Applicants are advised to apply early and are notified of a decision within four to six weeks of receipt of the completed application. Students may defer admission up to one year. Scholarships are awarded on the basis of academic merit.

FINANCIAL FACTS

Tuition	$22,830
Tuition per credit	$713
Fees	$268
Cost of books	$1,142
Room & Board (on/off-campus)	NR/$9,130
% of students receiving aid	60
% first-year students receiving aid	60
% aid that is merit-based	100
% of students receiving loans	50
% of students receiving grants	48
Average award package	$29,900
Average grant	$11,400
Average graduation debt	$37,000

ADMISSIONS

# of applications received	1,368
% applicants accepted	47
% acceptees attending	57
Average GMAT (range)	608 (580–640)
Minimum TOEFL	600
Average GPA (range)	3.20 (2.90–3.40)
Application fee (in/out-state)	$50/$50
Early decision program available	No
Regular application deadline	April 15
Regular notification	Rolling
Admission may be deferred?	Yes
Maximum length of deferment	1 year
Transfer students accepted?	Yes
Non-fall admission available?	Yes
Admissions process need-blind?	Yes

APPLICANTS ALSO LOOK AT

Babson College, New York University, Harvard University, Northeastern University, Columbia University, Georgetown University, Massachusetts Institute of Technology, Northwestern University

EMPLOYMENT PROFILE

Placement rate (%)	81
# of companies recruiting on-campus	191
% grads employed immediately	81
% grads employed within six months	96
Average starting salary	$63,115

Grads employed by field (avg. salary):

Accounting	6% ($6,233)
Consulting	28% ($62,476)
Finance	16% ($61,318)
General Management	15% ($48,778)
Human Resources	1% ($41,000)
Marketing	15% ($62,723)
MIS	3% ($59,633)
Operations	4% ($58,125)
Strategic Planning	1% (NR)
Other	11% ($48,933)

BRIGHAM YOUNG UNIVERSITY
Marriott School of Management

ACADEMICS

Brigham Young University is the official school of the Church of Latter-day Saints. Two slogans greet BYU visitors as they enter the campus: "Enter to Learn; Go Forth to Serve" and "The World Is Our Campus." This sets the tone for what is easily one of the most ethics-oriented and spiritual b-schools in the nation. There's a dress code. Students are expected to abstain from drugs, alcohol, and tobacco. In the classroom, ethics and the moral responsibilities of leadership are emphasized. Says one MBA, "The university and b-school are remarkably strong in moral responsibility and honor code. This is where the competitive advantage of the school is." A by-product of the Latter-day Saints affiliation is that many members of the church serve as missionaries in foreign countries. A large majority of the student body has had one to two years of foreign work experience; most speak a second language, or even a third. The high level of cross-cultural knowledge enhances the study of international business.

BYU features a progressive curriculum. In almost all of the core courses, several professors share the podium, team-teaching cases from a cross-functional perspective. This approach doesn't please everyone, however, as one student griped, "Overemphasis on case method. I feel I'm not getting the practical skills that will be valuable in the short-term."

There are only 120 or so students in each entering MBA class, and during the first-year, students take roughly ten core courses in the functional areas. MBA students at BYU no longer share these core courses with the Master of Accountancy Program as they did in the past. However, MBA students will continue to share the core courses with students from the Master of Organizational Behavior, Master of Public Administration, and Master of Information Systems programs. The school lumps all the first-year business masters students together and then divides them into more manageable smaller sections.

In the second year, there are three required courses: Ethics, Business Policy, and a management seminar. After that, students have twelve electives, enabling them to specialize in any of eleven areas. A popular offering is Management Consulting and Projects, in which Utah businesses pay students to consult in their organization.

Overall, students say BYU is meeting their academic expectations. Students judged their teamwork, presentation, general management, and finance skills as strong. But students felt they had weak spots in marketing, operations, quantitative methods, accounting, and computers. The most common criticism is that the range of students goes from "very prepared" to "what are they doing here." Also, in the complaint box, "there are too many free-riders."

PLACEMENT AND RECRUITING

Students at the Marriott School have access both to the MBA program's Career Services office and to the larger university's placement center. The CS office also maintains a graduate resume book and a web-based job and application bulletin board. The Marriott School participates in the West Coast MBA Consortium.

Given the close-knit Mormon community worldwide, it should come as no surprise that placement opportunities here are greatly enhanced by alumni relations. A required alumni-student mentoring program guarantees students

Merlene Reeder, Program Administrator
640 TNRB, Provo, UT 84602
Admissions: 801-378-3701 • Fax: 801-378-4808
Email: msmonline@byu.edu
Internet: msm.byu.edu/program/grad/mba

will make connections with former Marriott School students. Although students report mixed feelings about the effectiveness of the Career Services office, they have nothing but good to say about the benefits of their alumni contacts.

STUDENT/CAMPUS LIFE

Students report a heavy workload. They crack the books an average of twenty to thirty hours a week. Not surprisingly, they say it's important to do all the required reading. Teamwork is heavily promoted, which results in what students report as "a strong camaraderie among the MBA students." Students say they're competitive, but—you know the answer here—most are eager to help a fellow classmate out. They do draw a line with camaraderie. In particular, they dislike "competing with undergrads for computer lab time and printing facilities."

Life at a Latter-day Saints school can be interesting for a single person. At what is known as "Breed-em Young" University, dating (especially among undergrads) is often geared toward finding a mate. Indeed, several b-school students told us they chose BYU to do just this. (Not that we want to get in the personals business, but each was looking for a wife.) The school honor code doesn't permit drinking or smoking on or off campus, so social events do not include either of these activities. Extracurriculars here are devoted to church, family life, informal get-togethers, and outdoor activities in the nearby mountains. The MBA Association sponsors many events, including community service projects such as reading to the blind and helping foreign students with English. There's even a vice-President for community service.

The Latter-day Saints community is divided into "wards" of 100 or so families who meet for worship services and plan social activities. Non-church members are welcome to attend. There's also an active "Spouse Association" that organizes dinners and outings. According to one student, "Single housing is great." In prior surveys married housing got the thumbs down from students, but the school has just added 426 new apartments dedicated soley to married housing. The majority of students opt to live in suburban-style garden apartments off-campus in the foothills of the Wasatch Mountains.

As for diversity: forget it. The majority of students here are Latter-day Saints. They're conservative. They're white. Of the student body, 70 percent are married and many of them have two or more children. Non-Latter-day Saints do attend school here. But the only part of the honor code they're exempted from is mandatory church attendance.

ADMISSIONS

According to the admissions office, your GMAT score is considered most important. After that, in descending order, your college GPA, letter of intent, letters of recommendation, language spoken, work experience, and leadership activities are considered. Writes the school, "Though we look carefully at GMAT and GPA qualifications, we also look at the person behind the numbers. The letter of intent and letters of recommendation are valuable resources in getting acquainted with the person. Because of the international emphasis in our MBA program, we look favorably at applicants who speak a second and third language. As a result we encourage any undergraduate major except business, and we also encourage some work experience."

FINANCIAL FACTS

Tuition	$5,120
Tuition per credit	$285
Cost of books	$700
Room & Board (on/off-campus)	$4,600/$4,600
% of students receiving aid	90
% of students receiving loans	72
% of students receiving grants	34
Average grant	$2,200

ADMISSIONS

# of applications received	475
% applicants accepted	48
% acceptees attending	60
Average GMAT (range)	620 (580–650)
Minimum TOEFL	570
Average GPA (range)	3.50 (3.36–3.68)
Application fee (in/out-state)	$30/$30
Early decision program available	Yes
Early decision deadline	January 15
Early decision notification	February 28
Regular application deadline	March 1
Regular notification	Rolling
Admission may be deferred?	Yes
Maximum length of deferment	2 years
Transfer students accepted?	Yes
Non-fall admission available?	No
Admissions process need-blind?	No

APPLICANTS ALSO LOOK AT

University of California—Los Angeles, Arizona State University, University of California—Berkeley, University of Virginia, University of Washington, University of Texas at Austin, Dartmouth College, Harvard University

EMPLOYMENT PROFILE

Placement rate (%)	80
# of companies recruiting on-campus	221
% grads employed immediately	71
% grads employed within six months	87
Average starting salary	$57,616

Grads employed by field (avg. salary):

Consulting	10% ($53,143)
Finance	30% ($55,750)
General Management	8% ($53,500)
Human Resources	1% ($55,000)
Marketing	19% ($49,663)
MIS	8% ($55,867)
Operations	16% ($49,677)
Other	8% ($59,250)

UNIVERSITY OF CALIFORNIA—BERKELEY
Haas School of Business

no anhc — need to call to reirdage

OVERVIEW

Type of school	public
Affiliation	none
Environment	metropolis
Academic calendar	semester
Schedule	Full-time and evening (part-time)

STUDENTS

Enrollment of parent institution	29,000
Enrollment of business school	480
% male/female	68/32
% out-of-state	70
% minorities	22
% international (# countries represented)	31 (40)
Average age at entry	28
Average years work experience at entry	5

ACADEMICS

Student/faculty ratio	5:1
% female faculty	14
% minority faculty	10
% part-time faculty	50
Hours of study per day	4.14

SPECIALTIES
Entrepreneurship, International Business, Management of Technology, Finance, Marketing, Real Estate, Health Care Management, Organizational Behavior, Corporate Strategy

JOINT DEGREES
Concurrent degree programs in Law, Public Health, Asian Studies, and International and Area Studies, JD/MBA, MBA/MA in Asian Studies, MBA/MPH, MBA/MIAS.

SPECIAL PROGRAMS
Entrepreneurship, International Management, Management of Technology, and Health Care.

STUDY ABROAD PROGRAMS
12 countries in Europe, Asia, Latin America, United Kingdom, Netherlands, Belgium, France, Italy, Spain, Austria Switzerland, Brazil, Mexico, Hong Kong, Japan.

SURVEY SAYS...

HITS
Diversity of work experience
Can't wait to network
Library

MISSES
Safety
On-campus housing
MIS/operations

PROMINENT ALUMNI
Alex Mandl, CEO and President, AT&T Communications Services; Paul Hazen, Chairman and CEO, Wells Fargo Bank; Robert A. Lutz, President, Chrysler Motors

ACADEMICS

Haas students appreciate the diversity their MBA program provides. When asked to name the field of study that attracted them to Berkeley, students reel off a virtual laundry list of subjects. Some come for the nationally renowned Real Estate Development program, administered in conjunction with the Department of City and Regional Planning and the Fisher Center for Real Estate and Urban Politics. Others cite the certificate program in technology offered by Haas and Berkeley's School of Engineering. Still others appreciate the availability of numerous courses in public and non-profit management. Haas' entrepreneurship program is also well regarded. For those willing to exert the herculean effort necessary, Haas also offers a joint JD/MBA, an MBA/MA in Asian Studies, a combined MBA/Masters in Public Health Services Management, and an MBA/MIAS (International Studies).

Such diversity is one of the benefits a program at a large university can provide. Typically at large schools the downside is that students feel lost in the enormity of their program, ignored by professors, administrators, and even fellow classmates. Not so at Haas, however. Professors here receive high marks for being "very accessible and helpful. They use a lot of cross-referencing to integrate concepts taught in other disciplines (i.e., finance will refer to an economic theory)." One student notes, "I knew the professors at Berkeley would be top-notch, but I didn't realize how personable they would be. I talk to my professors outside of class all the time." Administrators are "extremely responsive" and "put a lot of energy into protecting us from the UC bureaucracy."

Like most b-schools, Haas fills its first-year with requirements, allowing students only a single elective. Students appreciate the integrated core: "Some of the top faculty teach the core, which dramatically impacts the quality of the first-year experience. Core courses are very well integrated, ensuring one receives each component as part of the big picture." Courses are "challenging and demanding without being too high pressure. Emphasis is on learning, not grades." One respondent concludes, "My only complaint is that the outside world does not know the quality of education and students at Haas."

PLACEMENT AND RECRUITING

Berkeley MBAs give the school high marks for attracting top-notch recruiters to campus. In fact, the career center boasts that they offer "strong recruiting opportunities in a full range of career options, from investment banking and management consulting to high tech and entertainment start-ups, and everything in between." Students are also enthusiastic about the number and quality of opportunities for off-campus projects and internships. However, they give the Chetkovich Career Center only average grades for overall effectiveness. It should be noted, though, that our survey shows an upward trend at Haas; this year's respondents gave career services higher marks than did students in our previous surveys.

Haas reports that the top recruiters of recent MBAs are A.T. Kearney, Andersen Consulting, Charles Schwab, Citibank, Hewlett-Packard, Intel, McKinsey and Company, Mitchell Madison Group, Price Waterhouse, Silicon Graphics, and Sun Microsystems.

Laurie Stewart, Director of Admissions
500 Forbes Avenue, Pittsburgh, PA 15213
Admissions: 412-268-2272 • Fax: 412-268-7094
Email: gsia-admissions+@andrew.cmu.edu
Internet: www.gsia.cmu.edu

Carnegie Mellon University

STUDENT/CAMPUS LIFE

First-year students report a killer workload, which is "murderous on non-math, non-engineering students. Many barely get by." The pressure is compounded by the acceleration of the mini-semester schedule and up-all-night, number-crunching assignments. Fortunately, many courses are structured around team projects. Most students rely on help from their study groups. MBAs at GSIA get to know each other quickly. A total student body of approximately 500 full timers fosters a "close-knit group of people." "With the workload they throw at us, we bond together in misery" wrote one MBA. Begged one student, "Ease up on the homework. I'd like to cook or do laundry before the year is over." Still, this is not an unhappy bunch. The majority report a high quality of life and say taking the time off to pursue their MSIA at Carnegie Mellon is well worth it.

The volunteer GSIA social committee organizes many school events: picnics, holiday parties, boat cruises, and talent shows are all regular events. The socially responsible can "give back" to the community through the I Have A Dream tutor program. Though there are frequent, casual get-togethers, students say their social lives are hindered by the ultra-heavy workload. MBAs agree that their classmates are ethnically and racially diverse, though a few survey respondents griped there were "not enough women." As for types, one student told us there are "a lot of conservative geeks." But you know the saying—it takes one to know one.

Carnegie Mellon's campus is located in the Oakland section of Pittsburgh, a relaxed, safe, "college town" area. The immediate neighborhood is tree-lined and residential. Students describe the campus as "petite but elegant." New additions recently doubled the physical size of the b-school. MBAs told us the "new building and facilities are super" though the library is still sub-par. Because on-campus housing is not available, many students live in the nearby communities of Shadyside, Oakland, and Squirrel Hill, which are among Pittsburgh's trendiest. As for the city of Pittsburgh, well, it's better than you think. Consistently rated one of America's most livable cities, it's clean, modern, and teeming with cultural events.

ADMISSIONS

According to the admissions office, the following criteria are equally weighed: essays, college GPA, letters of recommendation, extracurricular activities, work experience, interview (required), and GMAT score. Notes the school, "When we evaluate an application, we try to understand that person as an individual. For example, we examine the entire academic record: grade trends, the major, the school extracurriculars, and part-time work, if any." Applications are batched in rounds. The admissions office suggests applying in round two.

FINANCIAL FACTS

Tuition	$24,000
Tuition per credit	$250
Fees	$100
Cost of books	$3,000
Room & Board (on/off-campus)	NR/$9,400
% of students receiving aid	94
% first-year students receiving aid	94
% aid that is merit-based	10
% of students receiving loans	46
Average award package	$17,900
Average grant	$6,800
Average graduation debt	$22,000

ADMISSIONS

# of applications received	1,341
% applicants accepted	30
% acceptees attending	64
Average GMAT	640
Average GPA	3.20
Application fee (in/out-state)	$50/$50
Early decision program available	Yes
Early decision deadline	November 15
Early decision notification	December 15
Regular application deadline	March 15
Regular notification	April 15
Admission may be deferred?	Yes
Maximum length of deferment	2 years
Non-fall admission available?	No
Admissions process need-blind?	NR

APPLICANTS ALSO LOOK AT

Massachusetts Institute of Technology, University of Pennsylvania, Northwestern University, University of Michigan Business School, University of Chicago, New York University, Stanford University, Duke University

EMPLOYMENT PROFILE

Placement rate (%)	97
# of companies recruiting on-campus	183
% grads employed immediately	85
% grads employed within six months	97
Average starting salary	$71,545

Grads employed by field (avg. salary):

Accounting	2% ($68,833)
Consulting	29% ($77,422)
Finance	29% ($67,249)
General Management	5% ($64,667)
Marketing	10% ($70,110)
MIS	4% ($72,100)
Operations	11% ($69,882)
Strategic Planning	7% ($72,458)
Other	1% ($60,000)

CASE WESTERN RESERVE UNIVERSITY
Weatherhead School of Management

OVERVIEW

Type of school	private
Affiliation	None
Environment	metropolis
Academic calendar	semester
Schedule	Full-time/part-time/evening

STUDENTS

Enrollment of parent institution	9,757
Enrollment of business school	1,083
% male/female	67/33
% out-of-state	15
% part-time	61
% minorities	9
% international (# countries represented)	40(48)
Average age at entry	29
Average years work experience at entry	4

ACADEMICS

Student/faculty ratio	14:1
% female faculty	15
% minority faculty	1
% part-time faculty	26
Hours of study per day	4.54

SPECIALTIES
Marketing, Finance, MIS, Entrepreneurship, Nonprofit, Management, Health Care Management, Operations Management, Organizational Behavior

JOINT DEGREES
MBA/JD; MD/MBA; MSN/MBA; MSMS/MBA; MNO/JD; MNO/MA; MNO/MSSA; MBA/MIM

SPECIAL PROGRAMS
The Weatherhead Mentor Program, International Exchange Programs, the 48 Credit-Hour Accelerated Curriculum, 11-month program for students with undergrad business degrees

STUDY ABROAD PROGRAMS
Hungary, England, Ireland, Russia, Poland, Czech Republic, Ukraine, Netherlands, Denmark, Norway, Germany, Israel, Mexico, and Australia.

SURVEY SAYS...
HITS
Ethnic and racial diversity
Off-campus housing
Students are happy

MISSES
On-campus housing
Computer skills
Quantitative skills

PROMINENT ALUMNI
John G. Breen, Chairman & CEO, Sherwin-Williams Co.; Michael B. McCaskey, President, Chicago Bears Football Club; Robert W. Gillespie, Jr., Chairman, President & CEO, KeyCorp

ACADEMICS

The Weatherhead School of Management seeks to separate itself from the MBA pack through its openness to innovation. As one student puts it, "The outstanding aspect of this school is its flexibility. Staff and faculty are open to new course ideas and curriculum enhancements." Since entirely revamping its MBA program in 1990, Weatherhead has continually sought to upgrade, integrate, and expand its program on a regular basis.

The Weatherhead curriculum, designed to impose continuity on the two-year MBA program, uses several required programs to achieve this goal. First is the Management Assessment and Development (MAD) program, a two-year strand that forces students to assess their strengths and weaknesses, then design curricula that will bolster their marketability. The program, which is overseen by mentors, faculty advisors, and "facilitators," requires MAD groups to meet periodically throughout their Weatherhead tenure to assess their progress and reconsider career goals. Students approve of the program. One explains that "the management assessment/competency program, required of all students, is a great idea." The school also encourages students to consider choosing their electives in thematically linked clusters, such as The Global Manager, Leadership and Ethics in Management, and Technology Issues and the Manager.

The first-year courseload at Weatherhead is dictated entirely by core requirements. Eight core courses and the Strategic Issues and Applications (SIA) program, which spans the entire year, are integrated to create the first-year curriculum. SIA places students in management teams, then—as a group—they must walk through their paces with a series of increasingly difficult case studies that ultimately culminates in a class-wide competition. "Classes for first-years are very team-oriented. We work in groups of four to eight people on class projects. The students are constantly on the move from classes to meetings to studying to sleep." Writes one student, "You'll be up to your ears in group projects with students from many other countries. Very challenging, but rewarding."

Weatherhead students report that they are generally satisfied with the faculty. As one explains, "The quality of professors is quite variable. Most are good but some are bad. The problem is that in core courses you cannot select the professor you want." Profs receive high marks for being "Totally accessible. They give us their home phone numbers and invite us to call until midnight." Our survey shows a high level of satisfaction with "small class sizes" and the "innovative" administration. Students are particularly approving of finance, accounting, and management courses, and several single out the availability of a specialized degree in non-profit management as their reason for choosing Weatherhead.

PLACEMENT AND RECRUITING

In 1998, students had the oppurtunity to meet with ninety companies who recruited Weatherhead MBAs. Eighty-three percent of the class of 1998 had jobs at graduation, 33 percent in finance and another 37 percent headed into consulting. Major recruiters included: Ernst & Young, A.T. Kearney, Citibank, General Electric, SAP America and Oracle. The average starting salary was $63,000. Students can participate in the career day and several national and international consortiums, as well as meeting companies coming on campus.

Linda Gaston, Director of Marketing and Admissions
10900 Euclid Avenue, Cleveland, OH 44106
Admissions: 216-368-2030 • Fax: 216-368-5548
Email: wsommba@pyrite.edu
Internet: weatherhead.cwru.edu

**Case Western Reserve
University**

STUDENT/CAMPUS LIFE

The Weatherhead student body boasts a large international contingent. One student writes approvingly that, "because of the high number of international students, our diversity makes for an interesting learning and recreational environment." Students think highly of their classmates, giving them good marks for in-class contributions, cooperation in team projects, and overall friendliness. One respondent is pleased that "Unlike undergrad, where you choose to define yourself by your friends, Weatherhead students seek to surround themselves with people who may be different and challenging to them." Students are deeply involved in clubs, on-campus activities, and community service. Writes one student: "Very strong student association, very strong office of student life. Lots of multicultural activities, lots of clubs. If you have an interest that isn't covered by a club, you can simply start one up. Too much choice, really. Too many options, too little time." Students are happy at Weatherhead.

Case's campus is a hotbed of extracurricular activity. One student reports that there are "Lots of outside activities like Casino Night and the softball tournament with the faculty. Every week there's something going on, from an International Festival for a whole week to a Speaker's Corner. Students congregate at one of two "meeting places, the atrium and the computer lab" to plan study groups and the evening's social events. Students have mixed feelings about Cleveland. Although some feel the city has "a lot to offer," others say, "Cleveland is not the best city in the world," but add, "that's good because people concentrate more on studying rather than on other activities."

ADMISSIONS

According to the admissions office, your work experience is most important and then, in descending order, college GPA, the interview, GMAT scores, essays, letters of recommendation, and extracurricular activities. Personal interviews are recommended for admission. Students are notified of a decision four weeks after filing an application. Decisions are made on a rolling admissions basis. Students may defer admission for up to one year.

FINANCIAL FACTS

Tuition	$20,100
Tuition per credit	$838
Cost of books	$730
Room & Board (on/off-campus)	$5,800/$9,970
% of students receiving aid	70
% first-year students receiving aid	72
% aid that is merit-based	26
% of students receiving loans	85
% of students receiving paid internships	5
% of students receiving grants	27
Average award package	$22,000
Average grant	$12,000
Average graduation debt	$18,500

ADMISSIONS

# of applications received	717
% applicants accepted	73
% acceptees attending	48
Average GMAT (range)	605 (520–620)
Minimum TOEFL	590
Average GPA (range)	3.20 (2.67–3.37)
Application fee (in/out-state)	$50/$50
Early decision program available	Yes
Early decision deadline	March 15
Early decision notification	April 15
Regular application deadline	April 10
Regular notification	Rolling
Admission may be deferred?	Yes
Maximum length of deferment	1 year
Transfer students accepted?	Yes
Non-fall admission available?	Yes
Admissions process need-blind?	Yes

APPLICANTS ALSO LOOK AT

Northwestern University, University of Michigan Business School, Ohio State University, New York University, University of Chicago, Duke University, University of Pennsylvania, Georgetown University

EMPLOYMENT PROFILE

Placement rate (%)	98
# of companies recruiting on-campus	140
% grads employed immediately	83
% grads employed within six months	98
Average starting salary	$63,000

Grads employed by field (avg. salary):

Consulting	37% ($57,379)
Finance	33% ($55,552)
General Management	7% ($59,840)
Human Resources	1% ($55,000)
Marketing	11% ($54,302)
MIS	9% ($50,250)
Operations	9% ($50,250)

UNIVERSITY OF CHICAGO
Graduate School of Business

OVERVIEW

Type of school	private
Affiliation	none
Environment	metropolis
Academic calendar	quarter
Schedule	Full-time/part-time/evening

STUDENTS

Enrollment of parent institution	12,236
Enrollment of business school	2,762
% male/female	76/24
% part-time	60
% minorities	16
% international (# countries represented)	12(39)
Average age at entry	28
Average years work experience at entry	4

ACADEMICS

Student/faculty ratio	16:1
% female faculty	14
% part-time faculty	30
Hours of study per day	4.13

SPECIALTIES

Finance, Marketing, General Management, Int'l Business, Accounting, Managerial Decision Making and Strategy

JOINT DEGREES

MBA/MA Area Studies and Business; MBA/MA International Relations and Business; JD/MBA Law and Business; MD/MBA Medicine and Business; MBA/MS Physical Sciences and Business; Public Policy Studies and Business; MBA/MA Social Service Administration and Business

SPECIAL PROGRAMS

IMBA(International MBA Program)

STUDY ABROAD PROGRAMS

Australia, Hong Kong, France, Spain, Netherlands, Brazil, Mexico, Israel, United Kingdom, Chile, Sweden, Austria, Belgium, Japan, China, Italy, South Korea, Switzerland

SURVEY SAYS...

HITS
Accounting
Quantitative skills
Finance

MISSES
MIS/operations
Safety
General management

PROMINENT ALUMNI

Charles Harper, Chairman, RJR Nabisco; John A. Edwardson, Jr., President, United Airlines, Inc.; Jon Corzine, Chairman, Goldman Sachs & Co.

ACADEMICS

The University of Chicago has a lot to boast about. For starters, it's the first b-school whose faculty has included five Nobel laureates. Merton Miller, winner of the 1990 Nobel Prize in Economics, and Robert Fogel, winner of the same in 1993, currently teach in Chicago's MBA program. It's also the first to publish a scholarly business journal and to initiate a Ph.D. program. But the nation's second-oldest b-school hasn't chosen to rest on its laurels. As one student put it, "This school is continuously trying to improve itself. There are so many innovative opportunities here." Chief among them is LEAD, a mandatory leadership program that students—not faculty—run each year. Another first for Chicago: Among b-schools, LEAD pioneered the emphasis on leadership, interpersonal and multicultural programs, and learning by doing. Unsurprisingly, Chicago students give themselves high marks for their interpersonal skills (unique to a "quant" school) and tell us minorities and women are more than comfortable here. Students declare the curriculum "the single most flexible around." Beyond the required LEAD program, students can pick and choose from a variety of courses to satisfy Chicago's core requirements, and students aren't required to repeat work they have mastered elsewhere. "There's no hand holding here, and there's a lot of freedom," commented one student, "which is great for students who know what they want." The newest addition to Chicago is the International MBA, which, according to the school, "builds truly global management skills by giving people substantial knowledge of the culture and language of a foreign country." Students can also participate in Chicago's Laboratory in New Product and Strategy Development, acting as consultants to major corporations.

Chicago is best known for its economics and finance departments and is considered "numbers-heavy." But a majority of Chicago MBAs told us "it's much more than a quant school." Though students rate their quant and finance skills as excellent, they also consider themselves to have strong accounting, teamwork, and communication skills. "The excellent academics at Chicago have given me all the tools I need for the business world," wrote one MBA. They also feel terrific about Chicago's faculty, whom they consider passionate, accessible teachers. "Where else can you take classes with Nobel Prize winners both current and future!" exclaimed one student. Another MBA declared, "I would pit my instructors against any other faculty in the nation, bar none." Chicago administration has responded to some prior student complaints about facilities and administration. They recently completed an extensive renovation on classrooms and student areas and have announced plans to construct a new student building. The MBA program recently added some new administrative positions to provide a higher level of service to students. One complaint we did here from students is about the inordinate focus on the job search. "It begins on Day Number 1," griped one student, "classes just come second."

PLACEMENT AND RECRUITING

Chicago MBAs say that they are satisfied with their career placement office, though several agreed "more West Coast contacts" would be nice. In 1997, nearly 300 companies recruited on campus for both summer internships and full-time positions. Ninety-seven percent of the second-year class had a job by graduation. Top employers of Chicago MBAs are McKinsey and Co., Andersen Consulting, Goldman Sachs, Lehman Brothers, Deloitte & Touche Consulting, and A.T. Kearney.

Don Martin, Director of Admissions and Financial Aid
1101 East 58th Street, Chicago, IL 60637
Admissions: 773-702-7369 • Fax: 773-702-9085
Email: admissions@gsb.uchicago.edu
Internet: gsbwww.uchicago.edu

University of Chicago

STUDENT/CAMPUS LIFE

Students ranked their workload at Chicago as substantial. As one student put it, "If you want to party your way to an MBA, forget it." Much of the pressure results from trying to juggle a job search with academics. Classes tend to be large, and the majority of students work in study groups. MBAs described their classmates as "involved students who expect great work from each other." One student wrote, "Anality is rampant, but we're smart, successful, and on the cutting edge!" Another MBA boldly predicted, "We will be the CEOs, CFOs, partners, and managing directors of the future!" Though the student body is professionally diverse, a few students complained about their narrow focus. One MBA wrote, "The students here are not intellectually diverse; they do not explore and utilize the other facilities here. As a result, an MBA degree becomes shamefully one-dimensional, as does one's conversation. It's business, business, business!"

The school sits on a beautiful campus in the Hyde Park section of Chicago. Known as the "South Side," it's not centrally located, so many students live on the North Side and commute. Some lament the lack of a sense of "community," but students tell us there is a "great transportation system" which provides "easy access to the Chicago downtown and the fantastic lakefront." Hyde Park used to have a reputation for being dangerous, but we were told that "school buses run until one in the morning around Hyde Park areas, which are heavily patrolled. Emergency phones are almost everywhere." As for the social scene, it's teeming with activity. There are plenty of planned activities, both professional and social. And students report that "there are surprising amounts of weekly social events that are low-key and cool to hang at." Although students report active social lives, this doesn't include dating. But the group thing works. Chicago MBAs say they'll be buddies with their classmates long after they graduate.

ADMISSIONS

According to the admissions office, your GMAT scores, work experience, essays, college GPA, letters of recommendation, and extracurricular activities are all considered equally. The interview is strongly recommended, but not required. Notes the school, "All of the above are considered equally. We have no cutoffs on GPA or GMAT scores." Applicants are notified of a decision following each of three rounds: December 1, January 16, and March 20.

FINANCIAL FACTS

Tuition	$24,904
Tuition per credit	$2,490
Fees	$351
Cost of books	$1,300
Room & Board (on/off-campus)	$10,210/$10,210
% of students receiving aid	65
% first-year students receiving aid	63
% aid that is merit-based	100
% of students receiving loans	65
% of students receiving paid internships	98
% of students receiving grants	9
Average award package	$42,670
Average grant	$9,000
Average graduation debt	$60,000

ADMISSIONS

# of applications received	3,432
% applicants accepted	26
% acceptees attending	53
Average GMAT (range)	676 (610– 730)
Minimum TOEFL	600
Average GPA (range)	3.42 (2.91–3.85)
Application fee (in/out-state)	$125/$125
Early decision program available	No
Regular application deadline	March 1
Regular notification	March 1
Admission may be deferred?	Yes
Maximum length of deferment	1 year
Transfer students accepted?	No
Non-fall admission available?	Yes
Admissions process need-blind?	Yes

APPLICANTS ALSO LOOK AT

Northwestern University, University of Pennsylvania, Stanford University, Harvard University, Columbia University, University of Michigan Business School, Dartmouth College, University of California—Los Angeles

EMPLOYMENT PROFILE

Placement rate (%)	99
# of companies recruiting on-campus	437
% grads employed immediately	97
% grads employed within six months	99
Average starting salary	$89,400

Grads employed by field (avg. salary):

Accounting	1% ($84,000)
Consulting	32% ($125,000)
Entrepreneurship	4% (NR)
Finance	47% ($120,000)
General Management	15% ($89,000)
Marketing	9% ($81,000)
Operations	1% ($100,000)
Strategic Planning	1% ($87,000)
Other	2% ($95,000)

CLAREMONT GRADUATE UNIVERSITY
The Peter F. Drucker Graduate School of Management

http://cgshy.enbord.com/desktop.asp

OVERVIEW

Type of school	private
Affiliation	none
Environment	suburban
Academic calendar	semester
Schedule	Full-time/part-time/evening

STUDENTS

Enrollment of parent institution	2,177
Enrollment of business school	200
% male/female	60/40
% out-of-state	47
% part-time	56
% minorities	23
% international (# countries represented)	20(26)
Average age at entry	28

ACADEMICS

Student/faculty ratio	6:1
% female faculty	29
% minority faculty	5
Hours of study per day	3.88

SPECIALTIES

Strengths of faculty and curriculum in Strategic Management, Leadership/Ethics, Cost Management, Marketing.

JOINT DEGREES

Dual-degree programs in Economics, Education, Information Science, Psychology, and Public Policy, and by special arrangement in other disciplines.

SPECIAL PROGRAMS

Strategic Management; International Fellows Certificate Program in Advanced English and Cultural Proficiency for Management

SURVEY SAYS...

HITS
Small classes
Profs are great teachers
General management

MISSES

Quantitative skills
School clubs

PROMINENT ALUMNI

Dr. Robin Cooper, Consultant and Professor of Cost Management; Peter F. Drucker, Author and Teacher; Dr. Peter Farquhar, Consultant and Professor of Marketing.

ACADEMICS

The primary drawing card of the Peter F. Drucker Graduate Management Center at Claremont Graduate University is the school's namesake, Peter Drucker. At no other school have so many students named a single professor as the reason for choosing the MBA program. Drucker, for those who don't know, literally wrote the book on modern management practices. The *Practice of Management* was the first book to recognize management as a distinct and important business skill. Drucker has since written numerous other books on management, entrepreneurship, economic history, and Japanese painting (!). Drucker was also a columnist for *The Wall Street Journal* for more than twenty years. Students happily report that Drucker, born in 1909, still teaches well and often. Writes one, "Professor Drucker is very accessible and enjoys spending time socially and academically with us. A family atmosphere is fostered here."

Drucker, however, is not the only "name" professor here. Students also drop the names Robin Cooper, an originator of activity-based accounting, and Jim Meyers, both of whom "consult extensively and bring real-world knowledge into the classroom." Writes a student, "If you plan carefully, you can assemble a schedule of world-class professors. This is unusual in a school with part-time students." Students tell us that teachers are not only famous but capable as well: "The teaching style is the school's greatest strength. Super-high emphasis on hands-on learning." Another student adds, "Teachers are enthusiastic and concerned with ensuring students understand subject matter." Small classes and numerous opportunities "to build dual-degree combinations" enhance the learning experience here even further.

The Drucker school offers both a traditional MBA, which they call the "Early Career MBA," and an Executive Management Program geared toward mid- and senior-level executives. The coexistence of these programs allows for numerous mentoring opportunities, a definite plus for those pursuing the early career option. Both programs stress "leadership and strategy training," with an emphasis on management technique. Students praise the school for its instruction in marketing and international business, and also report "dramatic improvements in operations." In all areas, students appreciate a "progressive style of education" that "encourages us to do 'out of the box' thinking and support it," as well as a "good balance between business skills and ethics." Students are also pleased that "the new administration is significantly improving the program." Among those improvements are new, state-of-the-art classroom and computer lab facilities for the Drucker School.

PLACEMENT AND RECRUITING

Drucker MBAs currently share career services with students from CGU's five other graduate departments. The Office of Career Services and Corporate Relations (OCSCR) provides one-on-one counseling, resume assistance, electronic and hard-copy job postings, a career resources library, and a number of workshops in career skills management. The office also coordinates on- and off-campus recruiting and alumni relations. Among the top companies recruiting recent Drucker grads are Avery Dennison, FHP, Andersen Consulting, Deloitte & Touche LLP, and PepsiCo.

John Noonan,
1021 North Dartmouth Avenue, Claremont, CA 91711
Admissions: 909-607-7811; 800-944-4312 • Fax: 909-607-9104
Email: drucker@cgu.edu
Internet: www.cgu.edu/drucker

The task of OCSCR is made somewhat easier by the fact that a substantial number of Drucker MBAs are part-timers holding jobs they wish to keep. Even so, students give the service only average grades, telling us that there is a "need for a greater number of recruiters and/or opportunities for best jobs." One student reports hopefully that "Career Services needs improvement. This will improve soon, as the majority of students become full time."

STUDENT/CAMPUS LIFE

Although the balance is shifting from part-time to full-time students, Drucker's student body still consists of a large part-time contingent. Students consider their group a "diverse mix that includes a former Navy pilot who flew in the Antarctic, a Northwestern grad trying to break into singing, and a Bank of China investment banker who managed bond issues." There is a large contingent of foreign nationals at Drucker. The American minority population here, however, is slight. Students "vary greatly in experience, level of social interaction, and ability to contribute to class," but the best among them are "collaborative, intelligent, and team-oriented . . . very motivated and always coming out with initiatives that contribute to the well-being of the academic community and the local community." One student tells us that his "classmates are likely to pose useful challenges in the classroom."

As at most schools with large part-time populations, Drucker's extracurricular world is subdued. Students don't mind much, explaining that "Life here is very peaceful, but if you want excitement, you can take a short drive to downtown, the beach, or Santa Monica. The atmosphere is very conducive to learning." Another student notes that "In the two years I have been here, the social life has improved dramatically, as has student involvement." All students join the Graduate Management Association, which sponsors both career-related events (such as corporate speakers), and social events like the annual spring formal and the occasional barbecue. Claremont's setting, not far from the picturesque San Gabriel Mountains, is breathtaking, and the southern California climate is conducive to all sorts of outdoor activities. About the only gripe students voice about life here is that the "gym facilities and on-campus housing could stand some improvement."

ADMISSIONS

According to the admissions office, college GPA and work experience are considered most important. Then, in descending order of importance, GMAT score, letters of recommendation and essays, interview, and extracurricular activities. Adds the school, "Extracurriculars and work experience are not required, but are considered. Interviews are recommended." Admissions decisions are made on a rolling basis. Students may defer admission for up to one year.

FINANCIAL FACTS

Tuition	$19,500
Fees	$130
Cost of books	$1,008
Room & Board (on/off-campus)	NR/NR
% of students receiving aid	52
% of students receiving loans	28
% of students receiving grants	24

ADMISSIONS

# of applications received	301
% applicants accepted	54
% acceptees attending	31
Average GMAT	573
Average GPA	3.13
Application fee (in/out-state)	$40
Early decision program available	No
Regular application deadline	Rolling
Regular notification	Rolling
Admission may be deferred?	Yes
Maximum length of deferment	1 year
Transfer students accepted?	Yes
Admissions process need-blind?	Yes

APPLICANTS ALSO LOOK AT

University of California—Los Angeles, University of Southern California, Stanford University, University of California—Berkeley, Dartmouth College, Boston University, New York University, University of Texas at Austin

EMPLOYMENT PROFILE

% grads employed immediately	74
% grads employed within six months	94
Average starting salary	$57,593

Grads employed by field (avg. salary):

Consulting	25% (NR)
Finance	40% (NR)
Marketing	30% (NR)
Operations	5% (NR)
Other	

UNIVERSITY OF COLORADO AT BOULDER
Graduate School of Business Administration

OVERVIEW

Type of school	public
Affiliation	none
Environment	city
Academic calendar	semester
Schedule	Full-time/part-time

STUDENTS

Enrollment of parent institution	25,000
Enrollment of business school	265
% male/female	71/29
% out-of-state	44
% part-time	43
% minorities	11
% international (# countries represented)	8(1)
Average age at entry	27
Average years work experience at entry	5

ACADEMICS

Student/faculty ratio	25:1
% female faculty	19
% minority faculty	9
% part-time faculty	4
Hours of study per day	4.34

SPECIALTIES

Strengths of faculty and curriculum in Technology/Innovation Management, Finance, Marketing, Entrepreneurship.

JOINT DEGREES

JD/MBA, 4 years full time; MBA/MS in Telecommunications, 5–6 semesters full time

SURVEY SAYS...

HITS
Social life
Cozy student community
Boulder

MISSES
Profs not great teachers
MIS/operations
School clubs

PROMINENT ALUMNI

G. Chris Andersen, Paine Webber, Inc.; Marcia Pryde, A.T. Kearney, Inc.; William W. Reynolds, Owner and President, W.W. Reynolds Companies; Jerry McMorris, CEO, Nations Way Transport Services and President, Colorado Rockies; Richard F. Fuld, Jr., Chairman and CEO, Lehman Brothers.

ACADEMICS

The Graduate School of Business Administration at Boulder boasts a surprising number of strong offerings for a program of its size. More intriguing still, Colorado's strengths lie in such off-the-beaten-path disciplines as entrepreneurship, telecommunications, and real estate. And although a Boulder MBA is expensive for out-of-state students, native Coloradans can enjoy this unexpected bounty at a bargain-basement price.

Our survey shows a number of Colorado students reporting that "our entrepreneurship is the best in the nation." Offered jointly with the College of Engineering, Boulder's Center for Entrepreneurship emphasizes internships, field projects, and mentoring in its efforts to create tomorrow's venture capitalists. A joint MBA/MS in Telecommunications, also offered in conjunction with the engineering school, benefits from the fact that major telecommunications companies US West and TCI are located in the region. Similarly, Technology and Innovation Management majors profit from "one of the largest clusters of technology firms in the United States" located right in Colorado. Students praise the Real Estate Center for "the fabulous support they give. Great for networking and internships, as well as mentors." Students are less upbeat about Colorado's Accounting, Operations, and Marketing departments, giving all below average marks.

Colorado professors "are a mixed bag." When it comes to teaching skills, "approximately half are excellent, the other half are subpar." Students agree that professors try hard to make themselves accessible to students; writes one, "Professors are willing to go out of their way to help students achieve their academic and career goals." The administration "is great-both administration and faculty have an open-door policy and are willing to listen to students' issues/concerns." First-year foundation classes, organized in a "lockstep system," are "great and let you know right off the bat that this program is very well run." On the downside, students complain that "the library could stand to be updated a little" and also feel that "a dedicated MBA computer lab would be useful. The current labs, while technologically excellent, are commonly overrun with undergrads."

PLACEMENT AND RECRUITING

University of Colorado at Boulder established an MBA Career Placement Office (CPO) recently; previously the MBA program had relied on a career services office serving the entire university community. Colorado's CPO offers "a variety of services to MBA students including career management workshops, professional development seminars, and job-development outreach and hosts a variety of networking opportunities with top regional employers throughout the year." Just fewer than one hundred companies recruited on campus in the last year, and many more participated in an on-campus career fair. CU also participates in the Rocky Mountain MBA Consortium. The CPO reports, "Strong ties with the host of emerging and dynamic growth companies in the Boulder/Denver area also help to promote a supply of high-quality internships and job opportunities."

Dina Maestas, Admissions Coordinator
Campus Box 419, Boulder, CO 80309
Admissions: 303-492-1831 • Fax: 303-492-1727
Email: busgrad@colorado.edu
Internet: www-bus.colorado.edu

*University of Colorado
at Boulder*

Students have mixed feelings about the Colorado CPO. On one hand, respondents give it only average grades. On the other hand, the current survey shows considerable improvement from previous year's results. Furthermore, some students are extremely enthusiastic about the service. One writes, "The MBA-specific career placement office works its butt off to match students with desirable companies. The Center for Entrepreneurship is able to find internships in Denver/Boulder because of its strong ties to the community."

STUDENT/CAMPUS LIFE

With small minority and international populations, Colorado's students tend toward a certain sameness. The vast majority of students here are white males from reasonably affluent backgrounds. Sums up one first-year, "students here are like anywhere else: good and bad. Most are intelligent, many are shallow and cliquish. Most are materialistic and a bit spoiled. Some are egotistical and antagonistic. Others are very nice people, supportive and respectful." Warns another, "some are lacking in social skills. Almost none lack in business skills, however, and the majority of students are great, friendly, and knowledgeable." The mountain setting attracts a "few token shiny-happy skiers," writes one student, "but the vast majority are dedicated and intelligent."

"If you enjoy balancing social life with a solid academic life," notes one student, "Boulder offers the perfect mix." Our survey shows that most MBAs at Boulder spend a manageable 25 hours a week studying. Participation in campus clubs and organizations is also high, and the university's many high-profile intercollegiate sporting events are popular among MBAs. Colorado students "value sports and leisure time. Most are athletic and love sports. People appreciate the quality of life here," which includes "many opportunities for socializing" and a "relaxed, friendly atmosphere." Boulder is "beautiful and fun" but also a "fast-growing city that's much too expensive." One student writes, approvingly, "being in a small city gives you the advantage of concentrating on your work," while many others laud the accessibility of "fabulous snow skiing." Denver is less than an hour's drive from campus, and students make the trip whenever they yearn for big-city amenities.

ADMISSIONS

According to the admissions office, the entire application is evaluated with special consideration given to GMAT score, work experience, and college GPA. Essays, letters of recommendation, and extracurricular activities are also reviewed. The MBA program has three rounds of admission for its full-time program. Applicants are encouraged to apply early.

FINANCIAL FACTS
Tuition (in/out-state)	$3,710/$14,670
Fees (in-state/out-of-state)	$327/$327
Cost of books	$625
Room & Board (on/off-campus)	$4,131/$10,000
% of students receiving aid	80
% first-year students receiving aid	80
% aid that is merit-based	10
% of students receiving loans	65
% of students receiving paid internships	90
% of students receiving grants	10
Average award package	$12,000
Average grant	$1,810
Average graduation debt	$20,000

ADMISSIONS
# of applications received	435
% applicants accepted	51
% acceptees attending	58
Average GMAT (range)	615 (550–690)
Minimum TOEFL	500
Average GPA (range)	3.12 (2.50–3.68)
Application fee (in/out-state)	$40
Early decision program available	Yes
Early decision deadline	January 15
Early decision notification	March 15
Regular application deadline	March 15
Regular notification	May 15
Admission may be deferred?	Yes
Maximum length of deferment	1 year
Transfer students accepted?	No
Non-fall admission available?	No
Admissions process need-blind?	Yes

APPLICANTS ALSO LOOK AT
University of Texas at Austin, University of Denver, University of Washington, University of Arizona, University of California—Berkeley, Arizona State University, University of Michigan Business School, Northwestern University

EMPLOYMENT PROFILE
Placement rate (%)	84
# of companies recruiting on-campus	94
% grads employed immediately	50
% grads employed within six months	100
Average starting salary	$49,756

Grads employed by field (avg. salary):
Consulting	14% ($54,400)
Entrepreneurship	7% ($47,500)
Finance	31% ($55,792)
General Management	10% ($44,210)
Marketing	31% ($44,210)
Strategic Planning	3% ($42,000)
Venture Capital	13% ($97,500)
Other	7% ($40,000)

Segs and decision at 21, reserved slot 8/15 deadline 4/20/00

COLUMBIA UNIVERSITY
Columbia Business School

10-12 wks after receive app

8/15-10/15 - 8-10 wks early decision
must submit nonrefundable deposit of $2500 within 3 wks
of receiving acceptance

OVERVIEW

Type of school	private
Affiliation	none
Environment	metropolis
Academic calendar	semester
Schedule	full-time only

STUDENTS

Enrollment of parent institution	19,018
Enrollment of business school	1,394
% male/female	63/37
% minorities	23
% international (# countries represented)	28(52)
Average age at entry	27
Average years work experience at entry	4

ACADEMICS

Student/faculty ratio	7:1
% female faculty	16
% part-time faculty	45
Hours of study per day	4.24

SPECIALTIES

Integrate the core disciplines of accounting, finance, management, marketing and operations, as well as: globalization, ethics, total quality and human resource management.

JOINT DEGREES

MBA/MS Industrial Engineering; MBA/MS Social Work; MBA/MS Urban Planning; MBA/EdD Education Administration; MBA/MS Journalism; MBA/MS Mining Engineering; MBA/MS Nursing; MBA/MS Operations Research; MBA/EdD Higher Education; MBA/Master of Public Health; MBA/Master of International Affairs; MBA/Juris Doctor; MBA/BA or BS General Studies

SPECIAL PROGRAMS

The Executive MBA and Summer MBA programs.

STUDY ABROAD PROGRAMS

Australia, Austria, Belgium, Brazil, China, Finland, France, Germany, Hong Kong, Italy, Netherlands, Phillipines, Spain, Sweden, Switzerland, United Kingdom, Singapore, and Israel.

SURVEY SAYS...

HITS
New York
Quality of recruiting
Finance

MISSES
Library
Gym
MIS/operations

PROMINENT ALUMNI

Warren Buffett, Chairman, Berkshire Hathaway Inc.; Henry Kravis, Founding Partner, Kohlberg Kravis Roberts & Company

ACADEMICS

A cornerstone to the Columbia Business School experience is a balance between theoretic foundation and testing of ideas. Columbia's New York advantage and ties to the global business community provide the opportunity for students to learn from world-renowned faculty and practitioners. Students agree that finance is the outstanding department here, but one MBA notes, "I think it's a shame that marketing can't recruit as well as finance, because it makes the school too one-dimensional." However, other students relate: "Resources and programs at the school are very strong for those interested in international careers." Columbia has a math requirement that can be satisfied by previous coursework, passing an exemption exam, or attending the popular summer "math camp." To bolster skills in school, review sessions are held for all quantitative core courses and some upper-level electives on class-free Fridays. According to our survey, Columbia MBAs are "exceptionally computer literate due to the initiative requiring each person to own a laptop and use course material provided on the computer network." Unique to Columbia's program is the fact that students can begin school in any one of three terms starting in September, January, or May.

According to the students in our survey, Columbia is a school whose candle continues to burn brighter and brighter. One student says, "Considering the fact that I have been taught by some truly outstanding professors, not to mention several of the 'big guns' from Wall Street, who serve as adjunct faculty for many second-year courses, and that Dean Feldberg stands alone as one of the greatest deans in the nation for any course of study, I would say that my degree from CBS will understandably be well-respected." To promote camaraderie, Columbia's administration implemented "clusters," which section first-year students into "homeroom" groups of roughly sixty each. Students take all ten first-year core classes with their cluster. MBAs say this school is sizzling. Get your application in early. A surge in applications has made Columbia extremely difficult to get into.

PLACEMENT AND RECRUITING

Columbia Business School maintains one of the strongest worldwide recruiting programs, consistently ranking among the top five favorite hunting grounds of corporate recruiters and, increasingly, for entrepreneurial start-ups. The Business School's location and relationships with global firms and industry leaders create unique opportunities for students. Explains one student, "Due to the fact that so many class projects involve major companies and respected CEOs, quality interaction is a given. Access to high-powered, successful business people is not a problem."

Many students take advantage of networking opportunities through Columbia's strong base of more than 90 international alumni clubs, as well as the over 10,000 alumni who live in and around New York. Writes one student, "There are so many alums on the Street. They are very receptive to phone calls asking for advice or for finding potential connections. Networking is so easy due to the attention given Columbia education and the location of the school."

More than 390 companies recruited on-campus in 1997, and more than 190 companies made presentations.

Ded transcripts
enclose in stamped bones envelope

code for GMAT reg# 2174
Username: PhippsK02 Password: Xg2LL3

Linda B. Meehan, Assistant Dean and Executive Director of Admission and Financial Aid
105 Uris Hall, 3022 Broadway, New York, NY 10027
Admissions: 212-854-1961 • Fax: 212-662-5754
Email: gohermes@claven.gsb.columbia.edu
Internet: www.columbia.edu/cu/business/default.html

Columbia University

STUDENT/CAMPUS LIFE

Columbia is by no means a cookie-cutter institution—the school purposely admits students who add different perspectives to the learning experience. The majority of first-year students describe an up-all-night workload and hit the books on the average of thirty hours per week outside of class. This is due, in part, to a shorter academic year than many schools (about six weeks shorter compared to other b-schools around the country). Unsurprisingly, students say it's important to do all or most of the work, and most form study groups to get through it. Explains one second-year student, "The first semester—the first-year, in fact—is a living hell, because everyone's trying to outdo one another. Then the work seems to level off and everyone becomes the average, everyday, work-til-you-drop New Yorker."

Indeed, Columbia seems to be encouraging its students to become less cutthroat and more supportive of the collective pursuit. Writes one MBA, "The redesigned courses here had a positive effect on stressing effective group work (while still being able to differentiate yourself through exams)." Another student agrees, "Students are more friendly and interested in helping other students than CBS is generally given credit for." Students seem to enjoy each other's company, too, with many of them stating that they'll continue their friendships beyond graduation. Even so, some sharp elbows remain. Several students mention that "especially around exam time, people tend to keep to themselves and offer little in the way of help." But as at least one student explains, "Hey, this is New York. You like friendly? Beat it!"

Columbia students agree that being located in the financial capital of the world is quite an advantage, and its location allows the school to get a lion's share of visiting luminaries, from Henry Kravis to Warren Buffett. Confirms one student, "The Distinguished Leader Lecture Series brings so many heavy hitters to campus; I have learned more, I think, about the real world through these speakers than I have in the classroom." And speaking of classrooms, the long-awaited and much-needed replacement for the "one-room schoolhouse" will be unveiled in January 1999. The planned facilities boast state-of-the-art classrooms, space for group and team study, and reception and event rooms.

ADMISSIONS

Applicants are evaluated in three categories: professional promise, personal characteristics, and academic credentials. The Admissions Committee looks for well-rounded people from diverse economic, social, ethnic, geographic, and professional backgrounds. Ideal applicants have demonstrated leadership, have the ability to work as members of teams, are active in the community, and can contribute to the academic experience of their peers. Requirements include: minimum two years' work experience, GMAT, bachelor's degree, essays, letters of recommendation, and TOEFL for international students whose native language is not English.

FINANCIAL FACTS

Tuition	$25,140
Fees	$1,040
Cost of books	$1,014
Room & Board (on/off-campus)	$9,648/$9,648
% of students receiving aid	70
% aid that is merit-based	61
% of students receiving loans	65
% of students receiving grants	35
Average award package	$39,000
Average grant	$4,900

ADMISSIONS

# of applications received	5,257
% applicants accepted	13
% acceptees attending	71
Average GMAT (range)	670 (610–720)
Minimum TOEFL	610
Average GPA (range)	3.45 (3.00–3.80)
Application fee (in/out-state)	$125/$125
Early decision program available	Yes
Early decision deadline	October 15
Early decision notification	Rolling
Regular application deadline	April 20 (fall)
Regular notification	Rolling
Admission may be deferred?	Yes
Transfer students accepted?	No
Non-fall admission available?	Yes
Admissions process need-blind?	Yes

APPLICANTS ALSO LOOK AT

Harvard University, New York University, University of Pennsylvania, Stanford University, Northwestern University, University of Chicago, Dartmouth College, Duke University

EMPLOYMENT PROFILE

Placement rate (%)	98
# of companies recruiting on-campus	393
% grads employed within six months	98
Average starting salary	$102,930

Grads employed by field (avg. salary):

Accounting	1% ($95,000)
Communications	4% ($80,000)
Consulting	20% ($119,000)
Entrepreneurship	1% (NR)
Finance	55% ($120,000)
General Management	3% ($95,000)
Human Resources	1% ($77,500)
Marketing	8% ($81,000)
MIS	2% ($110,000)
Operations	1% ($70,000)
Strategic Planning	2% ($110,000)
Venture Capital	1% ($107,000)
Other	1% (NR)

UNIVERSITY OF CONNECTICUT
School of Business Administration

ACADEMICS

According to students, the best things about the University of Connecticut are the low-cost/high-value education, the Accounting and Finance department, the Center for Real Estate Studies, and the international diversity of its students. An added benefit is the school's strong ties with the local business community. Students have frequent contact with visiting business professionals from the region. Notes one, "The consulting project that we do in the second year with the Connecticut Small Business Association is very important. We help small Connecticut companies achieve growth." MBAs say academics at UConn are both challenging and rigorous. They also say that "the majority of coursework deals with applying business theory to real-life situations." MBAs take six electives to concentrate in one of nine areas. Although more than one student suggests, "there needs to be more flexibility in allowing students to take what they want to take!" Once again, tons of students praise UConn for being a "very global program." Reports one, "Many foreign students are in the program. Gives you an excellent overview of management throughout the world." Shares another, "I participated in one group that had one person from Uganda, three people from Taiwan, and one from India." All students must take an international studies course. Collaboration is heavily emphasized. Reports one, "Teamwork and group activities, as well as presentation skills, are promoted throughout the program and in all classes." A few loners tell us that the enforced "teamwork is too much." As for the professors, 77 percent rate them good or better. They feel about the same when it comes to their after-class accessibility. Still, the comments we received about professors were mixed. While one MBA enthuses, "Our professors make us LEARN," another says, "Sometimes it seems as if professors do not communicate with each other at all, piling the work up in two to three week periods with tests and reports." Students rate themselves strong in finance, accounting, and general management—all UConn power subjects. Ninety percent of students say their presentation skills are tops, and teamwork skills are not far behind. Academic weak spots: marketing and operations. All in all, students say this program is well worth the investment of time and money. Seventy-two percent are absolutely convinced this program is exceeding their academic expectations. But this MBA went straight to the bottom line, "In-state tuition is probably one of the lowest in the country. Great value!"

PLACEMENT AND RECRUITING

UConn does particularly well with placement in accounting and finance. This year, the majority of students tell us it has done well in attracting more companies to the school. When students were disappointed, it was with the range of companies. Still, students say there has been improvement. As one MBA points out, "UConn is highly regarded in the local area. This is very important given the number of headquarters in the area." In 1998, 38 companies recruited on-campus. Sixty percent of 1998 UConn MBAs had been placed by graduation in May. In 1997, 94 percent were placed within three months of graduation. Employers grabbing the most MBAs: G.E., "Big 6" Accounting Firms, CIGNA, IBM, Andersen Consulting, American Management Systems, and United Technologies. The average starting salaries of grads were $48,000.

David D. Palmer, Executive Director of MBA Programs
368 Fairfield Road, U-41 MBA, Storrs, CT 06269
Admissions: 860-486-2872 • Fax: 860-486-5222
Email: mbagen@sbaserv.sba.uconn.edu
Internet: sba.uconn.edu

**University of
Connecticut**

STUDENT/CAMPUS LIFE

UConn MBAs report an average of twenty-five to thirty-five hours of study a week. The majority warn it's important to do all or most of the assigned reading. Study groups help students synthesize their ideas, but 57 percent say there's still a lot of pressure. This may be caused by school policy: first-year students must maintain a 3.0 GPA to continue in the program. Reports this MBA, "Everyone needs to maintain a B average. But this brings only serious players to the table."

As one student put it, "This is a good combination of a large-university campus with the small, intimate environment of only 260 students. The small size gives UConn a sense of 'family.'" Students are competitive, but not into one-upmanship. They help each other academically and also enjoy hanging out together. "MBAs at UConn are diligent and down-to-earth," declares this MBA, "without having the 'fluff' of an A-school." According to our survey, 84 percent of students say their classmates "are not only very bright, but have diverse work experiences." But one MBA was harsh in his criticism of classmates' abilities: "Students for the MBA program should be admitted with a minimum of three-years work experience. Currently, the atmosphere is almost like a baby-sitting arrangement." Twenty percent of students agree with this MBA: "Diversity is weak. It needs improvement."

The be-all and end-all extracurricular group is the student-run Graduate Business Association (GBA), which UConn MBAs rave about. Says one, "The GBA provides opportunities for networking with business professionals as well as socializing with fellow students." Some of the most popular GBA social activities are held at favorite watering holes Ted's and Husky's. Of the students, 60 percent live off campus, but housing can be pricey. Also, you'll need a car. UConn is located in Storrs, a rural area about a one-and-a-half-hour train ride from New York City and forty-five minutes from Hartford. A final note: a new business school building is planned for the near future. Also, UConn's computer facilities were recently upgraded.

ADMISSIONS

According to the admissions office, the following three criteria are considered most important and are weighted equally: your GMAT score, work experience, and college GPA. Then come your essays, letters of recommendation, and extracurriculars. Writes the school, "We do not use cutoffs for GMAT scores or GPA. Evidence of high promise in one area can offset average accomplishment in another." Admissions decisions are made on a rolling basis throughout the year. There are no deadlines until the class has filled up. Students typically receive a decision within one month of completion of their file. They may defer admission for up to one year, depending on the circumstances.

FINANCIAL FACTS

Tuition (in/out-state)	$6,230/$14,654
Tuition per credit (in/out-state)	$388/$388
Fees	$920
Cost of books	$450
Room & Board (on/off-campus)	$6,600/$6,600
% of students receiving paid internships	70

ADMISSIONS

# of applications received	349
% applicants accepted	44
% acceptees attending	39
Average GMAT (range)	562 (520–620)
Minimum TOEFL	550
Average GPA (range)	3.20 (3.00–3.60)
Application fee (in/out-state)	$40/$45
Early decision program available	No
Regular application deadline	Rolling
Regular notification	Rolling
Admission may be deferred?	Yes
Maximum length of deferment	1 year
Transfer students accepted?	Yes
Non-fall admission available?	No
Admissions process need-blind?	Yes

APPLICANTS ALSO LOOK AT

New York University, Boston University, University of Massachusetts, University of Maryland, Penn State University, University of Texas at Austin, Yale University, Columbia University

EMPLOYMENT PROFILE

Placement rate (%)	98
# of companies recruiting on-campus	38
% grads employed immediately	63
% grads employed within six months	90
Average starting salary	$48,000

Grads employed by field (avg. salary):

Accounting	11% ($46,800)
Consulting	32% ($48,200)
Entrepreneurship	5% (NR)
Finance	30% ($46,800)
Human Resources	2% ($43,000)
Marketing	8% ($45,000)
MIS	5% ($56,000)
Operations	5% ($58,000)
Other	6% ($45,000)

CORNELL UNIVERSITY
Johnson Graduate School of Management

OVERVIEW

Type of school	private
Affiliation	none
Environment	city
Academic calendar	semester
Schedule	full-time only

STUDENTS

Enrollment of parent institution	20,000
Enrollment of business school	531
% male/female	67/33
% minorities	11
% international (# countries represented)	21(40)
Average age at entry	27
Average years work experience at entry	4

ACADEMICS

Student/faculty ratio	12:1
Hours of study per day	4.71

SPECIALTIES

Strengths of faculty and curriculum in the flexibility of the core program, access to the rich resources of Cornell U, collaborative community with easy access to faculty members.

JOINT DEGREES

MILR/MBA; MBA/MEng, 5 semesters; MBA/MA Asian Studies, 6–7 semesters; JD/MBA, 4 years

SPECIAL PROGRAMS

Semester in Manufacturing, Twelve-Month Option for scientists and engineers, Park Leadership Fellows Program, International Business, Asian and European Business Studies, Finance

STUDY ABROAD PROGRAMS

16 institutions with which the school partners.

SURVEY SAYS...

HITS
Accounting
Safety
Profs are great teachers

MISSES
Gym
Computer skills
Quantitative skills

PROMINENT ALUMNI

Kenneth Derr, CEO, Chevron; Lou Noto, CEO, Mobil; Charles Knight, Chairman and CEO, Emerson Electric.

ACADEMICS

Cornell offers a strong general management education supplemented by innovative, interdisciplinary programs that allow students to tailor their education to their individual career goals and to develop specialized skills. There are four joint-degree programs: MBA/Master of Industrial and Labor Relations, MBA/JD, MBA/Master of Engineering, and a joint MBA/MA in Asian studies. Cornell also offers a specialized program called FALCON (Full-year Asian Language Concentration) designed for students who want to develop proficiency in a foreign language. Now an essential component of the first-year curriculum, the Immersion Learning Programs are one of the school's most distinguishing factors. Students can "immerse" themselves in marketing, manufacturing, investment banking, or finance—the school plans to expand this program in upcoming years.

One offering for the potential Cornell MBA is the Twelve-Month Option. This program allows students with advanced scientific or technical degrees and relevant industrial work experience to earn an MBA in half the time. Students spend the summer in one intensive course that replaces the six core courses that usually are taken in the first-year of the two-year MBA program. Then, in the fall, they continue in the regular program.

A distinguishing factor at the Johnson School is the flexibility students have in taking electives at other university schools. In fact, according to the school, about 15 percent of Johnson MBAs pursue a joint degree with some of the other departments at Cornell. "Selecting classes every semester is like attending a mile-long buffet table," said one happy student.

A noteworthy new attraction at Cornell is the Park Leadership Fellows program. In 1997 the school started to offer thirty full-tuition, two-year fellowships to entering students who are U.S. citizens and who have a high level of academic achievement, have demonstrated exceptional leadership skills, strong professional accomplishments, and a commitment to community service.

Instruction at Cornell got high marks. "There hasn't been teaching this good since Socrates!" raved one MBA. Another enthused, "The pace of instruction is phenomenal. There is so much to cover . . . it's thrilling. Kind of like a roller coaster ride without the seatbelt." Previous years' complaints about the MBA school's facilities will now be quelled with the opening of the newly renovated Sage Hall. This nineteenth-century landmark has been brought up to twenty-first-century standards with the help of $38.2 million. The new facility ("management education environment") boasts 1400 network ports, real-time data feeds, videoconferencing, advanced visualization capabilities, multimedia production facilities, and technolgoy-enhanced classrooms.

PLACEMENT AND RECRUITING

Cornell's Career Services Office (CSO) has received mixed reviews from students in the past, but by all accounts the service is improving. "Many new companies are recruiting on campus," writes one student. CSO reports that CS First Boston, Microsoft, and Schroder & Co. are among the new companies included in "a 32 percent increase in on-campus recruiting for the fall semester" of 1997. CSO adds that this increase "encompasses a greater variety of firms,

Daphne E. Atkinson, Director of Admissions
Malott Hall, Ithaca, NY 14853
Admissions: 607-255-4526 • Fax: 607-255-0065
Email: mba@johnson.cornell.edu
Internet: www.gsm.cornell.edu

Cornell University

including technology and strategy consulting" and that these companies come from a wider geographical range. The school also believes that the recent addition of the Parker Center for Investment Research to the Johnson School will improve graduates' prospects in the world of finance. A number of student-run activities supplement the CSO's efforts: "The Consulting Symposium, Week on Wall Street, and the Marketing Symposium are all great recruiting events," according to one student.

STUDENT/CAMPUS LIFE

Cornell's reputation for collaboration is well earned, according to students. "If you need help, open your mouth and people start helping," said one student. "We're like a big family outside of class," reported another. An MBA told us this story: "One student missed two weeks of class due to a family crisis and a fellow student took it upon himself to videotape all the classes and mail them to her so she wouldn't fall too far behind. This is typical of the close-knit, caring atmosphere." Married students report being happy too. Said one MBA, "The Joint Ventures Club (for spouses and significant others) is a life-saver. It gives my wife and kids a support system and alleviates any guilt I feel when I put in long hours at the library. I think they are having more fun at Cornell than I am."

As for the campus itself, it's beautiful. Students agreed, "Ithaca is a great place to live in." They praised the "clusters of bars and diverse ethnic restaurants." According to our survey, both on- and off-campus housing is considered excellent. Parking, unfortunately, is "expensive and difficult to find." Extracurricular activities abound. "Golf and hockey are the big sports—about fifty men and fifty women are involved in the school's three hockey teams." An unusual attraction is the Frozen Assets Hockey Team, an all female group of MBAs who compete against Dartmouth's Tuck School in an annual tournament.

Students at the Johnson School report regular interaction with the rest of Cornell, which enhances their social lives as well as their learning experiences. Reported one MBA, "There are many learning opportunities through frequent guest speakers." There are also a large number of out-of-class experiences: the "Johnson Outdoor Experience," which takes place over one weekend in September and is a retreat for first-years led by second-years, winter-break trips to Venezuela, India, and China, and week-long Outward Bound-like summer leadership programs in rugged locales like the Hurricane Islands, the Adirondacks, and the Rockies.

ADMISSIONS

The admissions office considers, in no particular order, the type of undergrad institution attended, your GMAT scores, work experience, essays, college GPA, letters of recommendation, and extracurricular activities. A minimum of two years work experience is required; four-to-five years is average. Adds the school, "As we put together a diverse class—one in which students can expect to learn as much from their peers as from the faculty—we look for strong leadership skills, the maturity and initiative to use the resources of the Johnson School and Cornell, solid academic ability, and the potential for career success." The school has four decision deadlines; notification occurs within six to eight weeks of receipt of the completed file. Deferrals are granted to students on a case-by-case basis.

FINANCIAL FACTS

Tuition	$23,460
Cost of books	$890
Room & Board (on/off-campus)	$7,300/$7,300
% of students receiving aid	90
% aid that is merit-based	23
% of students receiving loans	90
% of students receiving grants	18
Average award package	$25,113
Average grant	$10,389
Average graduation debt	$40,300

ADMISSIONS

# of applications received	2,561
% applicants accepted	25
% acceptees attending	41
Average GMAT	636
Minimum TOEFL	600
Average GPA	3.30
Application fee (in/out-state)	$90/$120
Early decision program available	No
Regular application deadline	April 15
Regular notification	approx. 6–8 weeks after deadline
Admission may be deferred?	Yes
Maximum length of deferment	1 year
Transfer students accepted?	No
Admissions process need-blind?	Yes

APPLICANTS ALSO LOOK AT

University of Pennsylvania, Dartmouth College, New York University, Duke University, Northwestern University, Stanford University, Columbia University, University of Chicago

EMPLOYMENT PROFILE

Placement rate (%)	83
# of companies recruiting on-campus	138
% grads employed immediately	83
% grads employed within six months	95
Average starting salary	$65,000

Grads employed by field (avg. salary):

Accounting	5% ($58,500)
Consulting	15% ($73,800)
Finance	35% ($57,900)
General Management	12% ($62,200)
Human Resources	1% ($58,300)
Marketing	20% ($63,000)
MIS	1% ($67,500)
Operations	3% ($58,300)
Strategic Planning	2% ($77,500)
Venture Capital	5% ($65,000)

CUNY BARUCH COLLEGE
Zicklin School of Business

ACADEMICS

The Baruch School of Business has recently changed its name to the Zicklin School of Business. Larry Zicklin, a 1957 graduate, donated $18 million to the school in May of 1998—one of the ten largest gfts ever to a business school. The contribution is earmarked for transforming Baruch from a predominantly part-time MBA program (many of its students work, taking classes at night) into a world-class, full-time program. According to Dean Sidney Lirtzman, the gift "comes at a critical moment in our history, as the faculty restructures the school to create a great national full-time MBA program of such excellence that it will establish our ranking within the top twenty-five business schools in the United States." What the future holds for Baruch/Zicklin, then, is a question to be answered gradually over the next several years, as the City University of New York administration determines exactly how this money will be spent.

In the immediate future, Baruch should continue to serve a majority of part-timers in search of an affordable MBA. Cost, in fact, is the reason most respondents give for choosing Baruch. The accounting department, generally considered Baruch's strongest, runs a close second. Writes one student, "Baruch is THE place to get your CPA in New York." Students also give the finance classes high marks, but are less sanguine about marketing, operations, and communications courses. In most departments, professors are "great, very dedicated, but a few rotten apples are always present." As at many government-controlled schools, the administration at Baruch is mired in red tape. "A bureaucratic nightmare," is how one student puts it. Another simply states, "I can't believe how inefficient the administrative staff here is. They are horrible!" A former undergraduate and current MBA, while not exactly contradicting his colleagues, notes hopefully that the administration "has improved a lot since I graduated from undergraduate six years ago." Chief among students' complaints is the difficulty of enrolling in popular courses. Many students report that "building facilities are currently poor," but add, "that will change with the new fourteen-story building that is under construction." The facility is slated to open in 2000.

Core courses constitute the first half of a Baruch MBA; the second half entails coursework covering students' chosen area of specialization. A select group of full-time MBAs participate in the Jack Nash Honors program. The Nash program places students in their own cohort of Baruch MBAs for coursework and gives them access to program-specific research projects (that include a $5,000 stipend). Nash students have their own faculty advisor, their own meeting area (the MBA Honors Center), and study in new multimedia classrooms. Participants regard the program as one of Baruch's major drawing points.

PLACEMENT AND RECRUITING

Baruch recently opened an Office of Graduate Career Services (GCS), dedicated exclusively to the placing of MBA and MS students. The GCS office offers both students and corporate clients individualized attention by identifying and helping to clarify needs, and matching student prospects to hiring criteria. So far, however, students have not noticed an improvement over the old career services office, which served both the graduate and undergraduate populations. More than half of Baruch's MBAs give the service average or below-average

Michael Wynne, Director of Graduate Admissions
17 Lexington Avenue, New York, NY 10010
Admissions: 212-802-3000 • Fax: 212-802-2335
Email: graduate_admissions@baruch.cuny.edu
Internet: bus.baruch.cuny.edu

CUNY Baruch College

grades. Satisfaction levels with both the placement office and with on-campus recruiting here are among the lowest in our survey.

Among those hiring Baruch MBAs in recent history have been: Deloitte & Touch, Andersen Consulting, Coopers & Lybrand, Republic National Bank, Smith Barney, Reuters, Toys 'R US, and KPMG Peat Marwick.

STUDENT/CAMPUS LIFE

The Baruch MBA enrollment is one of the largest in the country. The size of the program and the school's location combine to create a student body that is "diverse and interesting," and one that provides valuable insights to class discussion. Students "run the gamut from a cellular biologist to an actor, twenty-one to thirty-nine-years-old. A great group for any class discussion." Notes another student, "we are a potpourri of different cultures, but we all get along very well." Class unity is diminished by the size of the student body, however, since students are less likely to see the same faces in each class than they would be at a smaller school. Also, many students continue to work while attending Baruch. Explains one student, "The location of Baruch in New York City and the convenience it offers working students is probably the reason there is less camaraderie." As a result, Baruch students are less likely to become involved in school clubs and activities than are their counterparts in other MBA programs. This lack of class unity doesn't bother most Baruch students. As one puts it, "Baruch . . . doesn't strive to be anything else because the city can provide the rest of the equation." Students appreciate the school's excellent new library.

By far the biggest quality-of-life issue at Baruch is New York City itself. The effect of Baruch's urban setting is magnified by the fact that "there really is no campus. It's eight buildings scattered across the East Side." The city has its advocates among students. As one puts it, "New York is the greatest city in the U.S. Lots to do. The financial heart of the world." Another agrees that "New York City is the place to be if you're a b-school student. I can literally walk to Wall Street every day to get a whiff of the financial goings-on." The city also has its downsides, of course: the dearth of affordable housing, the noise, the occasional rudeness of its residents, and a public transportation system that is efficient but intimidating to many out-of-towners. Baruch is located near a beautiful park, but don't get your hopes up: Gramercy Park is the last private park in New York City. Only those who live on its perimeter are given the key necessary to enter it.

ADMISSIONS

According to the admissions board, your college GPA and GMAT scores are considered most important. After that the board considers, in descending order, your essays, letters of recommendation, and work experience. TOEFL and TWE are required for students with degrees from non-English speaking countries. Students may defer admission for up to two years.

FINANCIAL FACTS

Tuition (in/out-state)	$4,350/$7,600
Tuition per credit (in/out-state)	$185$320
Fees (in-state/out-of-state)	$33/$33
Cost of books	$550
Room & Board (on/off-campus)	$0/$5,678
% of students receiving aid	20
% first-year students receiving aid	20
% aid that is merit-based	30
% of students receiving loans	43
% of students receiving paid internships	10
Average grant	$10,000
Average graduation debt	$10,500

ADMISSIONS

# of applications received	1,483
% applicants accepted	56
% acceptees attending	51
Average GMAT	570
Minimum TOEFL	570
Average GPA	3.20
Application fee (in/out-state)	$40/$40
Early decision program available	No
Early decision deadline	N
Early decision notification	N
Regular application deadline	June 15
Regular notification	Jan 1
Admission may be deferred?	Yes
Maximum length of deferment	2 years
Transfer students accepted?	Yes
Non-fall admission available?	Yes
Admissions process need-blind?	Yes

APPLICANTS ALSO LOOK AT

New York University, Columbia University, Hofstra University, Syracuse University, University of Maryland, Boston University, University of California—Los Angeles, Penn State University

EMPLOYMENT PROFILE

Average starting salary	$50,000

Grads employed by field (avg. salary):

Accounting	17% ($44,668)
Consulting	4% ($56,000)
Finance	46% ($49,043)
Marketing	13% ($43,150)
MIS	7% ($42,731)
Other	11% ($65,200)

DARTMOUTH COLLEGE
The Amos Tuck School of Business Administration

ACADEMICS

Founded in 1900, Tuck was the first graduate school of management in the world and the only top U.S. business school that offers only the MBA degree. This means Tuck focuses all of its resources on its MBA students. Tuck has a reputation for developing talented general managers through rigorous, quantitatively demanding academics. By any standards, the workload is heavy and the curriculum very structured. Reports one student, "Tuck stretches you beyond your nightmares, but there is nowhere I could have learned more!"

Tuck students live and die by teamwork. Students experience an Outward Bound-type of orientation similar to that offered at other b-schools, and group projects continue to dominate classwork well into the second year. In terms of the basics, first-years take thirteen required core courses. Second-years choose from over fifty electives to specialize or build breadth. The emphasis at Tuck is on a general management education. Most students claim the integration of the curriculum is one of the great strengths of the school. The curriculum at Tuck stresses a "theory into practice" understanding of business. Students and grads alike remain enthusiastic about Tuck's first-year, four-day business simulation game, TYCOON. Student teams start with assets of $25 million with which to purchase and then manage a company. Professors impose "surprise" conditions and disasters on different companies—from floods to labor strikes—to test students' managerial abilities. The result is best summarized by this student: "At work I realized that I was much more adept at blending strategy with practical details and organizational behavior than my colleagues from other schools." Students also raved about the Executive-in-Residence Program.

Tuck features a learning environment that is personal and intimate. An unusually low student/faculty ratio of ten to one means Tuck professors are accessible to students. Moreover, the emphasis is on teaching, not research, and students feel the professors are committed to seeing them succeed. According to students, they're also off-the-Richter-scale terrific teachers, and there's "no such thing as not getting into a class." More cooperative than competitive, Tuckies are an all-for-one and one-for-all bunch. Wrote a typical booster, "This is the most supportive academic environment I've ever been in." But one realist countered, "The workload has been humbling. This place is no picnic."

PLACEMENT AND RECRUITING

"Employment opportunities at Tuck are equal to or better than any other school," wrote one happy MBA, and the statistics bear out the assertion. During the 1997–98 academic year, more than 170 firms recruited on campus. Tuck's strengths are in the worlds of financing and consulting, as evidenced by the fact that 80 percent of graduates place into those fields. This satisfies most students. As one put it, "Everyone goes to Wall Street or consulting, but that's why people come here—to get those jobs." The Career Services (CS) office is quick to point out, however, that finance and consulting businesses represent only 35 percent of the companies that recruit on campus. CS also notes that "students had an average of fifteen on-campus interviews each." And in case you might otherwise forget, CS wants us to remind you that, "At Tuck, students can ski to school in the morning and interview with Morgan Stanley and McKinsey in the afternoon," reports CS. "Tuckies have choices, they have access, they are sought after by the market, and they can bring their dogs to school."

Sally O. Jaeger, Director of Admissions
100 Tuck Hall, Hanover, NH 03755
Admissions: 603-646-1100 • Fax: 603-646-1441
Email: Tuck.Admissions@dartmouth.edu
Internet: www.dartmouth.edu/tuck

STUDENT/CAMPUS LIFE

Tuckies, as they like to call themselves, give their school the highest quality-of-life ratings. One student told us he chose Tuck because "everyone was smiling when I visited." Whether they were married with children or single, in their mid-thirties or a few years out of college, dozens of students wrote, "I LOVE TUCK!" In fact, the survey results suggest a veritable lovefest! Tuckies are extremely happy. Many raved, "Best two years of my life" and "I've made friends that will last a lifetime." Almost all first-year students live in Tuck dorms, a very cozy, residential experience, and most of them are on a first-name basis. (Married students and their spouses can live in nearby Sachem Village.) It appears to be an intense experience overall; another student wrote "I've never felt happier, more frustrated, self-confident, humbled, energized, exhausted, relaxed, or insane. . . and all at the same time."

Many describe the campus as "beautiful" and the rural, outdoorsy setting as "perfect." Tuck is located in the quaint town of Hanover, right next to the Connecticut River, Vermont, and the Appalachian Trail, so students have access to many outdoor activities. Students can stay fit hiking, canoeing, and biking. Skiing is available at Killington, Stowe, and Dartmouth's Skiway. And each year Tuck hosts Winter Carnival, an invitational slalom race, complete with serious apres-ski partying. Tuckies also enjoy an active social life in which spouses and partners are gladly included in the "partying, dancing, and late nights." Intramural sporting events are common, as are student club activities. But Tuck is also family oriented; the campus is crawling with babies and puppies. Though many agree with the student who declared "coming to Tuck is the best decision I ever made," there are a few voices outside the work hard/play hard family who feel less enthusiastic. One student wrote, "There is a singular, monolithic culture here, and I'd caution minorities to think twice about coming. The so-called 'Tuck experience' does not extend to all students." Many expressed a wish for a more diverse community, both ethnically and geographically. In response, Tuck has taken steps to create a global environment in rural New Hampshire: Tuck's Global Alliance connects the school to international programs and to the world in a way it never was before. The goal being, graduates who are prepared to be future global business leaders. A final note: Whereas alumni-fund agents at most schools are happy to achieve 20 percent participation in annual giving from recent grads, Tuck alumni have an astounding 62 percent participation rate, proving that this tight-knit group stays close long after graduation.

ADMISSIONS

The admissions office reports that "although the GMAT, GPA, and work experience are very important, we look for well-roundedness in our candidates; a formula is not used to determine admission. Tuck looks for applicants who exhibit leadership, creativity, and a strong foundation of business skills." Strong letters of recommendation are important.

An interview is also strongly recommended. Tuck admits students by "rounds". It is advisable to apply "within the first three" since the applicant pool is so competitive. Only 12 percent of applications are accepted.

FINANCIAL FACTS

Tuition	$24,900
Fees	$1,000
Cost of books	$1,800
Room & Board (on/off-campus)	$12,300/$12,300
% of students receiving aid	70
% first-year students receiving aid	72
% aid that is merit-based	0
% of students receiving paid internships	0
Average award package	$29,173
Average graduation debt	$49,004

ADMISSIONS

# of applications received	3,194
% applicants accepted	12
% acceptees attending	51
Average GMAT (range)	667 (610–730)
Minimum TOEFL	600
Average GPA (range)	3.40 (3.00–3.80)

Application fee (in/out-state)	$100/$100
Early decision program available	No
Regular application deadline	April 22
Regular notification	May 18
Admission may be deferred?	Yes
Maximum length of deferment	1 year
Transfer students accepted?	No
Non-fall admission available?	No
Admissions process need-blind?	Yes

APPLICANTS ALSO LOOK AT

Northwestern University, Stanford University, Harvard University, University of Pennsylvania, Duke University, University of Virginia, University of Michigan Business School, University of Chicago

EMPLOYMENT PROFILE

Placement rate (%)	100
# of companies recruiting on-campus	145
% grads employed immediately	99
% grads employed within six months	100
Average starting salary	$75,000

Grads employed by field (avg. salary):

Consulting	43% ($90,000)
Finance	33% ($75,000)
General Management	9% ($75,000)
Marketing	8% ($70,000)
Operations	3% ($75,000)
Other	4% ($67,500)

UNIVERSITY OF DENVER
Daniels College of Business

OVERVIEW

Type of school	private
Affiliation	none
Environment	metropolis
Academic calendar	quarter
Schedule	full-time/part-time/evening

STUDENTS

Enrollment of parent institution	8,800
Enrollment of business school	376
% male/female	64/36
% out-of-state	42
% part-time	39
% minorities	11
% international (# countries represented)	25(30)
Average age at entry	27
Average years work experience at entry	5

ACADEMICS

Student/faculty ratio	13:1
% female faculty	10
% minority faculty	1
% part-time faculty	5
Hours of study per day	4.14

SPECIALTIES

Accounting, Finance, MIS, Marketing, Real Estate and Construction Management, Finance Real Estate, Entrepreneurship, International Business, Information Technology, Electronic Commerce

JOINT DEGREES

JD/MBA; JD/MIM; MSM/Engineering

SPECIAL PROGRAMS

Master of Accountancy, Master of Science in Finance, Master of Science in Tourism/Resort Management, Master of Real Estate and Construction Management, Master of Science in Management, Master of International Management

STUDY ABROAD PROGRAMS

Varies

SURVEY SAYS...

HITS
Small classes
Denver
Star faculty

MISSES
Library
MIS/operations
School clubs

PROMINENT ALUMNI

James Unruh, CEO, Unisys Corp.; Peter Coors, CEO, Coors Brewing Company; June Travis, Executive Vice President, National Cable TV Association

ACADEMICS

The Daniels College of Business offers a wide array of degree options to incoming students. Although many opt for a traditional MBA, Daniels also offers the internationally minded an MBA-like degree called a Masters in International Management (MIM). In designing this degree, Daniels took advantage of its university setting by incorporating classes at the College of Law and the Graduate School of International Studies to the curriculum. Students widely praise the MIM program, which is chiefly responsible for the school's large international student body. Daniels also offers many subject-specific master's degrees in fields such as accountancy, taxation, finance, real estate, and hotel management. The program encourages MBA and MIM candidates to pursue elective options in these disciplines and even to seek a concurrent master's degree in one.

Students here praise the core curriculum, an integrated and interdisciplinary program. Instead of offering distinct courses in accounting, finance, marketing, and statistics, Daniels offers seven fundamentals courses with names like Foundations of Business Decisions and High Performance Management. These courses require students to take a comprehensive approach to business problem solving by applying diverse analytical skills. Second-year students design their own areas of specialization; writes one student, "Excellent opportunities for specialization. There is something for everybody." Another praised the "flexible" scheduling that allows him to "concentrate on areas that I feel are most important." According to students, the best specializations here are in finance, management, and accounting. Marketing and operations, on the other hand, earn low grades from our respondents.

"Most professors" at Daniels "are excellent. A couple seem to do just the minimum." Most students agree that "the majority of teachers are well-prepared and always helpful in students' pursuit of academic endeavors," although a few might also add that "some profs are great researchers but lack the ability to teach." Our respondents appreciate Daniels' small class sizes, reporting that "classes have ten to fifteen students, sometimes less." The administration, on the other hand, receives much lower marks for being "way too bureaucratic" and "generally unfriendly." A new b-school building, currently under construction, should remedy current students' dissatisfaction with facilities.

PLACEMENT AND RECRUITING

According to the Daniels Career Placement Center (CPC): "From your first week in orientation, you will interact with the Career Placement Center staff and begin to integrate your academic and career objectives. The creation of the Rocky Mountain MBA Consortium in the fall of 1996 has contributed significantly to the increased number and diversity of companies actively recruiting DCB graduates. The staff of the Career Placement Center aggressively target employers with site visits to promote the Daniels College of Business programs and to identify job and internship opportunities within large and mid-sized companies as well as within Denver's booming entrepreneurial community. Approximately 85 percent of graduates find employment in the Denver area."

Jan Johnson, Executive Director
2020 South Race #122, Denver, CO 80208
Admissions: 303-871-3416 • Fax: 303-871-4466
Email: dcb@du.edu
Internet: www.dcb.du.edu

Despite these efforts students in our survey still want more, particularly when it comes to the quality and diversity of companies that recruit on campus. Daniels CPC receives overall average marks from surveyed students. A large portion of our respondents, one-quarter, report that the opportunity to work with mentors is "poor" here.

STUDENT/CAMPUS LIFE

Daniels students describe their program's student body as "very ethnically diverse. There are some language barriers in my work group!" In fact, our survey revealed an unusual amount of tension between Americans and the large international contingent here, with a surprising number of respondents complaining about difficulties communicating with classmates. Still others felt strongly that professors apply a double standard when grading the two groups. These hard feelings are no doubt amplified by the fact that students here are "very competitive. Everyone is out for themselves." Several respondents also complain that "too many students are admitted directly from undergrad." Not surprisingly, our survey shows that students are relatively less happy with their classmates here than are MBAs in other programs. It should also be noted that some of those surveyed characterize their fellow students as "friendly" and "easy to get along with" but that a substantial minority of respondents give their classmates excellent marks for helpfulness and ability to contribute to class discussions.

Students' feelings about the school's location are less ambivalent. In fact, many choose Daniels precisely because it is in Denver. One student sums up: "It's all about location, location, location. Great city, great mountains, great outdoor life." On-campus clubs and activities are not overwhelmingly popular. Students here prefer to use their spare time to explore the city or to take advantage of the great skiing and outdoor activities available in the outlying areas. Explains one: "There are plenty of activities to participate in. Thursday night at the bars, weekend skiing." Most Daniels students are aware of the great temptation that Denver and the mountains offer, and compensate (some would say overcompensate) by burying themselves in their studies. One student explains that his classmates "like to ski and have fun, but still study too much. Most become bookworms on weekends." Academic pressure here is heightened by the quarter system, which many consider "intense. It means students are pressured to perform in the 10-week period." One student simply scribbles: "Too hectic. The quarter system must go!"

ADMISSIONS

Undergraduate academic performance, GMAT results, and work experience are considered most important in the selection process. Writes the school, "Essay responses, letters of recommendation, gender, international background, and ethnic background round out application elements that are converted to a cumulative point system, thereby taking into account the full applicant profile."

FINANCIAL FACTS

Tuition	$18,216
Tuition per credit	$506
Fees	$695
Cost of books	$1,500
Room & Board (on/off-campus)	$8,100/$8,100
% first-year students receiving aid	70
Average grant	$11,508

ADMISSIONS

# of applications received	711
% applicants accepted	74
% acceptees attending	48
Average GMAT (range)	500 (470–740)
Minimum TOEFL	550
Average GPA (range)	3.20 (2.50–3.70)
Application fee (in/out-state)	$50/$50
Early decision program available	Yes
Early decision deadline	Rolling
Early decision notification	Rolling
Regular application deadline	May 1
Regular notification	Rolling
Admission may be deferred?	Yes
Maximum length of deferment	1 year
Transfer students accepted?	Yes
Non-fall admission available?	Yes
Admissions process need-blind?	No

APPLICANTS ALSO LOOK AT

University of Colorado at Boulder, Arizona University, Indiana University, Stanford University, Arizona State University, Colorado State University, University of California—Berkeley, Thunderbird University

EMPLOYMENT PROFILE

Placement rate (%)	85
# of companies recruiting on-campus	86
% grads employed immediately	85
% grads employed within six months	95
Average starting salary	$45,186

Grads employed by field (avg. salary):

Accounting	15% ($35,430)
Consulting	20% ($46,140)
Finance	22% ($45,000)
General Management	13% ($47,000)
Marketing	22% ($44,000)
MIS	10% ($44,300)
Operations	5% ($44,000)
Other	3% ($42,000)

DUKE UNIVERSITY
The Fuqua School of Business

OVERVIEW

Type of school	private
Affiliation	Methodist
Environment	metropolis
Academic calendar	semester
Schedule	full-time only

STUDENTS

Enrollment of parent institution	10,000
Enrollment of business school	680
% male/female	69/31
% minorities	26
% international (# countries represented)	30(40)
Average age at entry	27
Average years work experience at entry	5

ACADEMICS

Student/faculty ratio	10:1
% female faculty	19
% part-time faculty	18
Hours of study per day	4.37

SPECIALTIES

Fuqua's MBA Program is based on an integrative, general management curriculum, which emphasizes cross-functional, strategic & global perspectives. The Program is widely recognized for particular strength in the area of; Finance, Marketing Decision Science, Operations

JOINT DEGREES

MBA/JD, 4 years; MBA/Master of Public Policy, 2–3 years; MBA/Master of Forestry, 2–3 years; MBA/Master of Environmental Management, 3 years; MBA/MS Engineering, 2–3 years; MBA/MD, 5 years

SPECIAL PROGRAMS

International exchange programs, overseas study tour courses, the MBA Enterprise Corps, GATE programs

SURVEY SAYS...

HITS
Placement
School clubs
Campus is attractive

MISSES
On-campus housing
Gym
Profs not great teachers

PROMINENT ALUMNI

J. Derek Penn, Senior Vice President, Head Trader, International Equity Trading, Shearson Lehman Bros., Inc.; Robert Derek Bandeen, Managing Director, Morgan Stanley Co. Incorporated; Thomas B. Roller, President & CEO, Wolverine Tube Inc.

ACADEMICS

From marketing to finance, from quant skills to teamwork, Fuqua's departments are solid across the board. Distinct to the school since the fall of 1992 is an experiential program called Integrative Learning Experiences (ILE). Four week-long seminars embrace the trendy topics of the '90s, such as diversity, internationalization, etc., and provide students an opportunity to learn by doing. Each ILE precedes a semester of traditional classroom instruction. Over the two-year program, students take four ILEs: Team Building and Leadership Development, Competitive Business Strategy, Competitive Advantage Through People and Processes, and Emerging Trends in Management. The last two are the "capstone" experiences in that they involve business-simulation games and team competitions. Raved one student, "Fuqua's updated curriculum is on top of market trends."

First-years squeeze in fourteen core courses and have room for two electives. As one student put it, "The pace is very fast since we only have six-week terms." A prereq for the program is a working knowledge of calculus. Advised one student, "Liberal arts majors with no experience in business courses should be prepared to hit the ground running." Second-year students take a minimum of eleven electives, one or two of which must satisfy the international field requirement. Four of these electives may be taken in other schools or departments at Duke University. As for the faculty, one student wrote, "Profs all have open-door policies. They know your name."

The teaching at Duke got mixed reviews. One student wrote, "Contrary to published reports, the core instruction is outstanding!" But others said that "the academic experience is disappointing" and "research professors should stick to research." Ratings fell this year for most academic departments, including finance and entrepreneurial studies. Students wished for more general academic resources; they continually voiced the need for more computers, more team study rooms, and more space overall. However, students rated their fellow students and future job opportunities higher this year.

PLACEMENT AND RECRUITING

Referring to the relatively short time that Fuqua has been in existence (the school was founded in 1970), one student noted, "Our greatest weakness is our youth; we have a smaller pool of alumni than other schools." The Career Services and Placement Office (CSO) at Fuqua works hard to overcome this handicap, however, evidenced by the fact that 350 companies recruited on campus in 1997. The increase in the number of recruiting visits, according to CSO, represents "one of the fastest growth rates of any leading school." In response to previous student complaints, CSO has more actively sought international placement opportunities for Fuqua grads, as well as more "opportunities with small and mid-sized companies."

STUDENT/CAMPUS LIFE

At 330 students per entering class, Fuqua is at its max and students feel the pinch. "We're tighter than Superman's tights!" exclaimed one student. The modern b-school complex, which was completed in 1983, boasts state-of-the-art facilities, but obviously not enough space. Expansion is on the horizon, how-

Robert L. Williams, *Director of Admissions*
One Towerview Road, Durham, NC 27708
Admissions: 919-660-7705 • Fax: 919-681-8026
Email: fuqua-admissions@mail.duke.edu
Internet: www.fuqua.duke.edu

ever, and facilities will more than double in size with the addition o[f]
buildings over the next five years. Fuqua plans to build a new fa[c]
building, an expansive student life commons building, and an additi[on]
room building.

Duke's campus is one of the nation's most beautiful, complete with ne[w]
architecture and sweeping lawns. A mile of woodlands divides the ca[mpus in]
two. Fuqua is perched on the edge of Duke Forest on Duke's West C[ampus.]
Most students opt to live off campus in small groups in nearby apartme[nt]
plexes. Students agree North Carolina's Research Triangle area is a grea[t place]
in which to live. Housing, both on and off campus, is spacious and qui[te eco-]
nomical. Most students bring a car, but at peak times parking can be [near]
impossible.

There are many extracurricular activities to provide a break from the [daily]
grind. There's a FuquaVision show every other month (like a "Saturday Night
Live" video), and a Winter Gala Black Tie party. Intramural sports are big. And
if you like to golf, students say the university course is terrific. Student clubs
play a big part in campus life as well. The Black MBA Organization hosts a Wall
Street panel. The Entrepreneurship Club hosts a two-day seminar. The annual
Fuqua MBA Games, which bring together MBA students from across the nation,
have raised more than $610,000 for North Carolina Special Olympics in the past
decade, including a record $152,000 in 1998. Although students report an above-
average social life, dating, for some reason, barely figures into the picture. But
that doesn't dampen anyone's enthusiasm for the school. One student exclaimed, "I have never been involved with a more intelligent and fun group of
people! Students have a genuine concern for each other's performance." However, some we surveyed feel that "students are more grade-conscious than they
should be."

ADMISSIONS

The admissions office does not require interviews, but encourages them as "an
important part of the application process." Other key components are the
GMAT score, your college GPA, essays, work experience, letters of recommendation, and participation in extracurricular activities. Decisions are made on a
rolling admissions basis. Applicants are notified of a decision six to eight weeks
after the admissions office has received a completed application. Accepted applicants may defer admission for up to one year for health issues or special job
opportunities. Fuqua may also offer college seniors a two-year deferred admission with the expectation that there will be substantive work experience in the
interim.

EMORY UNIVERSITY
Goizueta Business Sc[hool]

OVERVIEW

Type of school
Affiliation
Environment
Academic calendar
Schedule

ADMISSIONS

# of applications received	3,045
% applicants accepted	19
% acceptees attending	58
Average GMAT (range)	663 (580-750)
Average GPA (range)	3.33 (2.80-3.80)
Application fee (in/out-state)	$115/$115
Early decision program available	No
Regular application deadline	March 28
Regular notification	6 weeks after file is complete
Admission may be deferred?	Yes
Maximum length of deferment	1 year
Transfer students accepted?	Yes
Non-fall admission available?	No
Admissions process need-blind?	Yes

APPLICANTS ALSO LOOK AT

Northwestern University, University of North Carolina
at Chapel Hill, University of Pennsylvania, University
of Virginia, Stanford University, University of
Michigan Business School, Dartmouth College,
Harvard University

EMPLOYMENT PROFILE

Placement rate (%)	99
# of companies recruiting on-campus	330
% grads employed immediately	96
% grads employed within six months	99
Average starting salary	$71,250

Grads employed by field (avg. salary):

Consulting	25% ($82,658)
Entrepreneurship	1% (NR)
Finance	32% ($71,192)
General Management	9% ($62,287)
Marketing	25% ($65,729)
Operations	3% ($68,000)
Strategic Planning	4% ($70,036)
Other	1% ($70,000)

private
Methodist
metropolis
semester
full-time only

STUDENTS

Enrollment of parent institution	10,000
Enrollment of business school	455
% male/female	72/28
% out-of-state	87
% part-time	39
% minorities	11
% international (# countries represented)	25(30)
Average age at entry	27
Average years work experience at entry	5

ACADEMICS

Student/faculty ratio	6:1
% female faculty	21
% minority faculty	3
% part-time faculty	15
Hours of study per day	4.64

SPECIALTIES

Academic specialties of faculty include Relationship Marketing, Leadership Decision Analysis, Organization/Management, Accounting, Finance.

JOINT DEGREES

JD/MBA, 4 years; MBA/Div, 4 years; MBA/MPH, 2+ years; MBA/MN, 2 years

SPECIAL PROGRAMS

Customer Business Development Track, International Exchange Programs, The Center for Leadership and Career Studies, Area Studies Tracks

STUDY ABROAD PROGRAMS

Italy, Spain, France, Finland, Venezuela, Costa Rica, Mexico, Austria, England, Singapore, Germany

SURVEY SAYS...

HITS
Star faculty
Marketing
Atlanta

MISSES
On-campus housing
Quantitative skills
MIS/operations

PROMINENT ALUMNI

Michael Golden, vice President, New York Times Company; Ely Callaway, chairman, Callaway Golf; Jonathan Pond, President, Financial Planning Information, Inc.; Andy Conway, Beverage Analyst, Morgan Stanley.

Ask students at Goizueta to identify the best aspect of their school and nearly all will mention its rising status in the business world. "There is a sense of excitement at the school that the school is improving immensely," writes one; adds another, "I love the 'up-and-coming' aspect of the school." This excitement is due in no small part to an "exceptional" new facility. The "brand new and state-of-the-art business center" was built with a grant from Roberto Goizueta, CEO of Coca-Cola and namesake of Emory's business school.

International business and marketing are among Goizueta's strong suits (not surprising considering that these are also among the Coca-Cola Company's greatest strengths). Students also speak highly of the management department, but have major complaints about finance "Finance capacity of the faculty and curriculum severely lacking," is how one typical respondent puts it. On the general availability of second-year electives, students feel that "we need a wider diversity of course offerings." Students are quite voluble about the faculty, to whom they give average marks for teaching ability but high grades for accessibility and willingness to provide extra help when necessary. Several students note that teaching quality consistently improves throughout the program. One says, "Early on in the program, the faculty are less impressive. Those in the later classes are excellent," while another adds, "Core courses in accounting, economics, and especially marketing are weak." Some complain of the "high turnover rate among the faculty. Lots of new faces each semester."

Goizueta allows some choice to first-year students through its Flex/Core program, which helps students develop a specialization they might exploit when searching for summer internships. Still, first-year courses are largely prescribed-as they are at most MBA programs—although Goizueta allows students to place out of core requirements provided they pass a departmental exam. Exploiting one of its greatest assets, Goizueta includes an international business component in its core, a tack not taken by many other leading business schools. Each semester at Goizueta starts with a "lead week" activity; either a game-situation competition or a "focus module" to give students the chance to study a subject in depth. Students with an undergraduate business degree might wish to consider the intensive one-year accelerated MBA. No matter which option they choose, students usually leave Goizueta feeling like this student, who had an "excellent experience, very intellectually stimulating. This has prepared me extensively for real-world complex problems."

PLACEMENT AND RECRUITING

Our survey shows that students have mixed feelings about the Career Services Office at Goizueta; half give the service middling or worse marks. The main concern among our respondents is in the area of recruitment by companies from beyond the Atlanta region. Students feel the school should be doing more to attract farther-flung companies to the campus; several report that the problem is particularly acute "in relation to students who spend a semester abroad." Yet half also express satisfaction with the service, which offers numerous self-assessment, one-on-one counseling, and mock-interview programs for first-year students—all in a new resource center. The office also administers the Goizueta

Julie Barefoot, Assistant Dean of Admissions and Student Services
1300 Clifton Road, Atlanta, GA 30322
Admissions: 404-727-6311 • Fax: 404-727-4612
Email: Admissions@bus.emory.edu
Internet: www.cc.emory.edu/BUS

Business School Mentor Program, and a number of off-campus projects and year-long seminars with Atlanta-based companies that continue into the summer as internships, all of which get high marks from students.

Goizueta participates in a "number of off-campus events that expand the number of interviewing opportunities available to students," including MBA consortia, a trip to Wall Street, and a West Coast trip to visit "high-tech firms, consulting firms, and investment banks." The companies hiring the most Goizueta grads recently are IBM, Deloitte & Touche, KPMG Peat Marwick, Ernst & Young, BellSouth, Hewlett-Packard, The Coca-Cola Company, and Intel.

STUDENT/CAMPUS LIFE

The Goizueta student body is "a small community, very close-knit." Students keep to themselves within the university system by necessity, since there is "no time to mingle with students from other schools in the university." Fortunately for them they think highly of each other, regarding classmates as "well-rounded, energetic, insightful, and fun to be around. There is something to learn from each of them." Several remarked that the "exceptional international students" here are "a great asset." Sums up one student: "Although very busy, my life here is great. Not only do we study together, we socialize together on weekends. Emory has made us a very tight and cohesive group."

As if studies didn't keep them busy enough, students here "have high involvement into ALL aspects of running the school." The Graduate Business Association, to which all students belong, either manages or funds many subject-specific and minority clubs, sponsors parties on a regular basis, organizes intramural sports, and holds a weekly "coffee and doughnuts" breakfast for students and faculty. Furthermore, students form various student advisory groups consult with faculty and administration in such areas as admissions, career services, and marketing the Goizueta MBA program to the rest of the nation. Students love the Emory campus, located in a residential neighborhood just 15 minutes from downtown Atlanta, praising it for its "very collegiate environment" and "Southern feeling." Those so inclined will find "almost a party every weekend," although many prefer to use their sparse spare time to take advantage of all that the South's largest city has to offer: sports, culture, fine dining, and an excellent nightlife.

ADMISSIONS

According to the admissions office, your work experience is considered most important. After that, in descending order, your GMAT scores, interview, essays, college GPA, extracurricular activities, and letters of recommendation are considered. Notes the school, "Interviews are strongly encouraged. Candidates are also encouraged to visit a class with one of our current students." Emory requires that applicants have completed one semester of college calculus and be computer literate. Decisions are made on a rolling admissions basis. The school may allow applicants to defer admission for up to two years; this is decided on a case-by-case basis.

FINANCIAL FACTS
Tuition	$22,600
Tuition per credit	$885
Fees	$200
Cost of books	$890
Room & Board (on/off-campus)	NR/$8,400
% first-year students receiving aid	50
% aid that is merit-based	46
% of students receiving loans	44
Average grant	$7,800
Average graduation debt	$30,000

ADMISSIONS
# of applications received	918
% applicants accepted	35
% acceptees attending	37
Average GMAT (range)	626 (560-710)
Minimum TOEFL	600
Average GPA (range)	3.30 (2.10-4.00)
Application fee (in/out-state)	$45
Early decision program available	Yes
Early decision deadline	December 31
Early decision notification	January 31
Regular application deadline	April 15
Regular notification	Rolling
Admission may be deferred?	Yes
Maximum length of deferment	2 years
Transfer students accepted?	Yes
Non-fall admission available?	No
Admissions process need-blind?	Yes

APPLICANTS ALSO LOOK AT
Duke University, University of North Carolina at Chapel Hill, University of Virginia, Vanderbilt University, University of Pennsylvania, New York University, Northwestern University, Georgetown University

EMPLOYMENT PROFILE
Placement rate (%)	92
# of companies recruiting on-campus	87
% grads employed immediately	92
% grads employed within six months	98
Average starting salary	$61,086

Grads employed by field (avg. salary):
Consulting	30% ($65,215)
Finance	21% ($56,399)
General Management	14% ($65,611)
Marketing	29% ($65,327)
Venture Capital	6% ($60,000)
Other	Academics

UNIVERSITY OF FLORIDA
Florida MBA Programs

ACADEMICS

Diverse offerings in a paradise-like atmosphere are what draw most MBAs to the University of Florida Graduate School of Business. Students here rave about the Entrepreneurship program, the finance department, and the numerous dual- and joint-degree offerings, among which is a popular international business program administered in conjunction with Thunderbird.

In an effort to add flexibility to its list of assets, the Florida MBA recently revamped its schedule, dividing the fall and spring semesters into two seven-and-a-half week modules. The module system is intended to give students greater access to popular courses and allow for more independence in designing their academic programs. Students appreciate the school's efforts, reporting that "the module system gives students the opportunity to be exposed to a greater number of courses, which provides a stronger concentration background and better preparation to meet the needs of corporate America." Several, however, warn, "the module system is yet to be perfected."

Each set of modules is accompanied by a required Professional Development Program (PDP), which—according to the school—is designed "to significantly enhance the MBA experience...by providing opportunities for professional growth outside of the class room through an integrated framework of MBA co-curricular and extracurricular programs." Such activities as a distinguished speaker series, management seminars, technology tutorials, and courses to improve writing and presentation skills are included in the PDP program. One student approves of the entire package, "Our program has really improved student services since I arrived. The electives have been great, giving us lots of opportunity to choose a variety of courses, while the core provides a solid foundation."

Most students agree that "professors are generally very good teachers. They communicate well," although several warn that, "a few are terrible." The administration, which students describe as "reactive and detached in relation to students," gets lower marks.

Finally, Florida offers four unique programs for working professionals seeking an MBA. According to the school's promotional literature, the aptly named Flexible MBA program "combines leading-edge interactive technology, a week-long international trip, and only eight campus visits over twenty months to provide a high caliber MBA degree via the Internet." In addition, the Executive MBA (meets Friday-Sunday, once a month for twenty months); the Manager's MBA (meets Friday-Sunday, once a month for twelve months); and the Weekend MBA (meets Saturday and Sunday, once a month for thirty months) are all creative programs that use work experience as entrance determiners and that target working professionals.

PLACEMENT AND RECRUITING

The Florida MBA Program Career Services Office (CSO) reports that it "has experienced a major improvement in the last two years." Our survey bears out this assertion: student ratings of the CSO have improved with our recent survey. However, our survey also confirms that most students still agree that "the career services office needs improvement."

Todd D. Reale, Director of Admissions and Marketing
134 Bryan Hall, P.O. Box 117152, Gainesville, FL 32611-7152
Admissions: 352-392-7992 • Fax: 352-392-8791
Email: ufmba@dale.cba.ufl.edu
Internet: www.cba.ufl.edu/mba

In its efforts to upgrade services, Florida has added two full-time professional and one administrative staff member and developed a "unique Professional Development Program [to offer] seminars in career search skills including interviewing, presentation, and business communications techniques." The school also notes that "The Class of 1997 was the best ever for placement, setting records for mean average salaries and diversity in placement across the U.S. Approximately 50 percent of the class accepted job offers outside the state of Florida." Top employers for Florida MBAs include CSX, EDS, Ernst & Young, Fannie Mae, G.E. Capital, Harris Corporation, IBM, and Tech Data.

STUDENT/CAMPUS LIFE

Florida students see their classmates as very practical-minded about their education. "Ends-oriented real learning takes a back seat to grades and a 'where will this get me?' attitude," is how one student puts it. However, students also regard themselves as "very intelligent, motivated, and, most importantly, very cooperative." The word "friendly" pops up frequently in students' descriptions of each other, and many agree with the student who writes that "the strong ties among students make a lot of the work seem almost fun." Diversity is not the strong suit of this student body, however. Several students complain that the population is "not very geographically diverse. They're mainly from Florida and the Southeast." One student does note, however, "A good mix of international students adds to the enjoyment of earning a Florida MBA." Not surprisingly, as one of the best undergrad public business programs in the country, "many students have undergraduate degrees from the University and Florida." The school has recently changed is requirements for work experience; on average, for the fall 1998 entering class, the students have five years' work experience. This should alleviate some student complaints about the diversity and real-world knowledge of their classmates.

As for campus life, one student summarizes it this way: "Quite simply, the Florida MBA program is a bargain financially, has excellent students, and is probably unparalleled socially." Students are active in such clubs as the MBA Association, the Consulting Club, and Graduate Women in Business. Many respondents are quick to point out that "the MBA program is a small part of a large university. There's a lot of diverse activities outside of the MBA program for students to take advantage of." Among those are "a beautiful campus, including a lake, open lawns, and many trees" and "superb athletic programs that provide a feeling of unity and allegiance to the school." One student notes that "most of our activities revolve around drinking beer" but this caused neither him nor anyone else in our survey to complain. Students report that "Gainesville has everything you need but is still a small town. People used to larger cities may find the adjustment difficult." They also note that "the town is geared around the students. If you need a quiet place to study, you can find it. If you need a place to have fun, you can find it."

ADMISSIONS

Florida's admissions office requires an interview, explaining that it "allows applicants to elaborate on strengths and weaknesses that may impact their applications. The admissions committee looks for well-rounded candidates with excellent academic ability, significant work experience, active community involvement, and strong personal character."

FINANCIAL FACTS

Tuition (in/out-state)	$3,096/$10,426
Tuition per credit (in/out-state)	$129/$434
Cost of books	$670
Room & Board (on/off-campus)	NR/$8,130
% of students receiving aid	70
% first-year students receiving aid	70
% aid that is merit-based	0
% of students receiving paid internships	70
Average award package	$11,000

ADMISSIONS

# of applications received	507
% applicants accepted	39
% acceptees attending	61
Average GMAT (range)	600·(520–670)
Minimum TOEFL	600
Average GPA (range)	3.21 (2.73–3.70)
Application fee (in/out-state)	$20/$20
Early decision program available	Yes
Early decision deadline	February 1(Fall), August 15(Spring), Jan 1(Summer)
Early decision notification	March 15(Fall), October 1(Spring), Feb 15(Summer)
Regular application deadline	May 1
Regular notification	June 15
Admission may be deferred?	Yes
Maximum length of deferment	1 year
Transfer students accepted?	Yes
Non-fall admission available?	Yes
Admissions process need-blind?	Yes

APPLICANTS ALSO LOOK AT

University of North Carolina at Chapel Hill, Duke University, University of Virginia, University of Texas at Austin, Emory University, University of Georgia, Vanderbilt University, University of Pennsylvania

EMPLOYMENT PROFILE

Placement rate (%)	95
# of companies recruiting on-campus	176
% grads employed immediately	78
% grads employed within six months	98
Average starting salary	$53,517

Grads employed by field (avg. salary):

Accounting	10% ($50,518)
Consulting	19% ($56,521)
Finance	20% ($50,518)
General Management	16% ($46,525)
Human Resources	5% ($50,500)
Marketing	16% ($52,001)
MIS	6% ($59,500)
Operations	5% ($69,667)
Other	3% ($72,250)

GEORGETOWN UNIVERSITY
School of Business

OVERVIEW

Type of school	private
Affiliation	Roman Catholic
Environment	metropolis
Academic calendar	semester
Schedule	full-time only

STUDENTS

Enrollment of parent institution	11,000
Enrollment of business school	431
% male/female	65/35
% minorities	16
% international (# countries represented)	23(49)
Average age at entry	27
Average years work experience at entry	4

ACADEMICS

% female faculty	22
% minority faculty	7
Hours of study per day	5.20

SPECIALTIES

Curriculum emphasizes international business, business government relations, ethics and management communications.

JOINT DEGREES

MBA/MSFS Foreign Service, 3 years; MBA/JD, 4 years; MBA/MPP Public Policy, 3 years; MD/MBA, 5 years

SPECIAL PROGRAMS

The International Business Diplomacy Certificate, Area Studies Certificate, Summer Study Abroad Opportunities, International Exchange Opportunities, Summer Pre-Enrollment "Prep" Workshops

STUDY ABROAD PROGRAMS

Spain, France, Australia, Germany, Sweden, Mexico, Belgium, England, Japan, Czech Republic, Hong Kong

SURVEY SAYS...

HITS
Teamwork skills
Diversity of work experience
Cozy student community

MISSES
Computer skills
On-campus housing
Quantitative skills

PROMINENT ALUMNI

Rick Torres, Director, Food Business Development for Latin America, Philip Morris; Maximo Blandon, Vice President, Morgan Stanley; Ivy Cohen, President, "Just Say No" International

ACADEMICS

At Georgetown, academics are rigorous, and coursework is relevant to what's going on in the real world. One student told us it "forces you to do the impossible. But you'll love it." Beginning in the fall of 1998, Georgetown adopted a new curriculum of six-week modules that focus on business fundamentals and week-long intensive integrative courses. All required courses are now in the first-year with the exception of two "selectives" (required courses in which students have a choice) in the second year. The two selective course areas are decision support and the global experience. If you pick the global experience, you will be required to travel to a particular region of the world to apply your skills to help solve one company's specific business problem.

Georgetown's forte is the focus on international business, which students praised. "The international flavor is strong: nearly a quarter of students are foreign and almost everyone else has lived or worked abroad and speaks a second language." Most students agree, "DC is the absolute best place to study international business with access to anyone and anything." Students may take electives at the School of Foreign Service or other graduate schools, and because Georgetown is part of the University Consortium System in the DC area, they can also take courses at consortium schools. Finally, to further pursue an interest in global business, students can get elective credit for courses taken in Area Studies Programs and may also apply to receive an Area Studies Certificate. This involves choosing a geographic area of the world to study, taking all six electives in that area, and demonstrating proficiency in the native language. Area Studies options are African, Arab, Asian, Latin American, Russian, and German. One student noted, "Although Georgetown is a very international school, it has a more European and South American focus, not so much Asian."

Across the board, students reported that Georgetown provides excellent training in general management, marketing, accounting, quantitative skills, operations management, and interpersonal/presentation skills. "The academic experience is as deep as anywhere, without the stress," writes one student. The MBAs are also happy with the quality of teaching. "The faculty is why I came Georgetown," writes one student. "They are unbelievably dedicated." Students say the school's only major weaknesses are due to its youth, which results in a lack of a national reputation and a small library collection. However, the overwhelming majority of MBAs feel they're getting an incredible return on their investment. Fired-up Georgetown students say, "In ten years we will be tops!"

PLACEMENT AND RECRUITING

Georgetown's office of MBA Career Management (MBACM) reported an increase in on-campus recruiting of 20 percent in 1998, with more than 100 organizations visiting campus. The school also touts the MBA Consortium, of which Georgetown is a founding member, as a major recruiting event for its students. The Consortium sponsors national recruitment meetings in Atlanta and New York. Georgetown also participates in the International MBA Consortium Employment Conference, a three-day 'interviewing event' featuring more than seventy multinational corporations, and boasts that "11 percent of the class [of 1997] reported accepting a job outside their home country of origin." MBACM works with students throughout the program to develop and update resumes,

Nancy D. Moncrief, Assistant Dean
105 Old North Building, Box 571148, Washington, DC 20057-1148
Admissions: 202-687-4200 • Fax: 202-687-7809
Email: mba@gunet.georgetown.edu
Internet: www.gsb.georgetown.edu

Georgetown University

which the school collects and publicizes, both in print and via the Internet. Top employers of the class of 1997 include Coopers & Lybrand, Price Waterhouse, Continental Airlines, IBM, Chase Manhattan Bank, and Procter & Gamble.

STUDENT/CAMPUS LIFE

Georgetown offers an intimate, cooperative learning environment students enjoy. Group work defines the learning experience—all courses require it. "Classes are small, and students develop close relationships with each other, the faculty, and administration." Almost everyone works in a study group. Not surprisingly, students are extremely friendly and supportive. Students say any competition at Georgetown is healthy, and there is a strong spirit of cooperation. "The wide diversity of future career interests diffuse the head-to-head competitive atmosphere at other programs I visited," wrote one student. Georgetown MBAs rate their classmates smart, proactive, and hardworking, the type of people they expect to stay in touch with long after graduation. This atmosphere of camaraderie extends into an active social life. Students say, "We play hard after we've worked hard. It's a huge plus that we all get along so well outside the classroom." Student clubs that compete for their time: Graduate Women in Business, Alliance for Cultural Awareness, MBA Volunteers, and Students for Eastern European Development.

B-school students share an undergrad campus that comprises 104 acres and sixty buildings—many of them historic landmarks—though students feel the school is rapidly outgrowing the space. "Our facilities have character," writes one student, "but the MBA program needs more room to continue its development." The athletic fields are what you'd expect of a sports powerhouse, and students applaud their first-rate gym. On-campus housing, we were told, is also terrific. As for the semi-urban setting, don't worry about it—students say the campus is ultrasafe. About the DC location, one student wrote, "Living in the capital is great. Not sequestering oneself in a small, varsity town keeps you up-to-date and fresh." What really impressed us, however, was the students' high regard for their classmates: "The school attracts a unique group of people who are truly interested in making a difference in the business world."

ADMISSIONS

According to the admissions office, your work experience, college GPA, and GMAT score are considered most important. Then come your essays, interview, letters of recommendation, and extracurricular activities. Writes the school, "The admissions committee generally numbers twelve individuals, and includes both first- and second-year MBA students, faculty, and administrators. Each applicant's file is reviewed and discussed by the committee. General considerations are professional experience, academic performance and potential, and personal interests, qualities, and skills. International experience and community involvement are of particular interest to the admissions committee, as are positions of leadership held in academic, professional, or community organizations." Decisions are made on a rolling admissions basis. Applicants are notified of a decision four to six weeks after the completed application has been received.

FINANCIAL FACTS

Tuition	$23,800
Fees	$180
Cost of books	$930
Room & Board (on/off-campus)	NR/$8,034
% of students receiving paid internships	90
% of students receiving grants	22
Average grant	$10,568
Average graduation debt	$41,941

ADMISSIONS

# of applications received	2,063
% applicants accepted	30
% acceptees attending	37
Average GMAT (range)	634 (560–710)
Minimum TOEFL	600
Average GPA (range)	3.26 (2.78–3.73)

Application fee (in/out-state)	$65/$65
Early decision program available	No
Regular application deadline	April 15
Regular notification	Rolling
Admission may be deferred?	Yes
Maximum length of deferment	1 year
Transfer students accepted?	Yes
Non-fall admission available?	No
Admissions process need-blind?	Yes

APPLICANTS ALSO LOOK AT

University of Pennsylvania, Harvard University, Columbia University, University of Virginia, Duke University, New York University, Northwestern University, Dartmouth College

EMPLOYMENT PROFILE

Placement rate (%)	97
# of companies recruiting on-campus	59
% grads employed immediately	84
% grads employed within six months	97
Average starting salary	$60,300

Grads employed by field (avg. salary):

Communications	13% ($55,250)
Consulting	30% ($65,200)
Entrepreneurship	3% (NR)
Finance	22% ($62,670)
General Management	4% ($52,500)
Human Resources	1% ($47,800)
Marketing	18% ($52,675)
MIS	6% ($55,500)
Operations	5% ($51,770)
Strategic Planning	9% ($63,350)
Other	7% ($58,500)

UNIVERSITY OF GEORGIA
Terry College of Business, Graduate School of Business Administration

OVERVIEW

Type of school	public
Affiliation	none
Environment	metropolis
Academic calendar	semester
Schedule	full-time only

STUDENTS

Enrollment of parent institution	29,693
Enrollment of business school	163
% male/female	72/28
% out-of-state	46
% minorities	9
% international (# countries represented)	20(11)
Average age at entry	26
Average years work experience at entry	4

ACADEMICS

% female faculty	16
% minority faculty	4
Hours of study per day	4.06

SPECIALTIES

One of the program's greatest strengths is the opportunity to specialize in many areas, including Entrepreneurship, Real Estate, Risk Management., MIS, Corporate Finance, Investments Marketing, Qualitative Analysis, Production Operations, Accounting, Economics, Organizational Consultation, Legal Studies & International Business.

JOINT DEGREES

JD/MBA, 4 years; 5-year MACC

SPECIAL PROGRAMS

Progressive Partners Program (minority initiative)

STUDY ABROAD PROGRAMS

Netherlands, Nijenrode University

SURVEY SAYS...

HITS
Athens
Campus is attractive
Getting into courses a breeze

MISSES
Finance
MIS/operations
Profs not great teachers

PROMINENT ALUMNI

Alice Lusk, Vice President, NCR; Doug Ivester, CEO. Coca-Cola; Phil Gramm, U.S. Senator

ACADEMICS

The University of Georgia in Athens offers students either a one-year accelerated MBA or a two-year program. The one-year MBA is designed for students with an undergrad degree in business. The required coursework is designed to supplement the individual student's background. In the regular two-year program, second-year students choose two "sequences" from among twenty to develop a specialization. Sequences are unique to UGA—pre-selected courses are packaged to guarantee expertise in an area. Some of the most popular are corporate finance, MIS, entrepreneurship, and strategic marketing. The most interesting component of the program is the year-long professional development series, called the MBA PLUS program, which focuses on teamwork, leadership, and presentation skills. A highlight of the series is Fabulous Friday, in which corporate heavyweights conduct workshops on hot topics.

Though professors are considered accessible and there is a low student/teacher ratio, students report the instruction is "very average." This may be because professors have to do double-duty. Faculty serve all students in the College of Business, both undergrad and grad. Not surprisingly, we heard complaints about the sharing situation. "It's not what I had hoped to experience," griped one MBA, "I'm just not 100-percent challenged." Another student wrote, "I learn on my own. It's almost as if class time is a waste." The administration was described as a "bureaucracy slowly strangling the school," though MBAs were pleased that "the program director meets regularly with students."

Students say the "first-year courses do a good job of providing a class personality" but they recommended cutting first-year class size, evening out the workload, and recruiting students with more work experience. Technology could also be improved, according to MBAs. "The computer labs are always full or disabled by viruses," wrote one student. "Triple the Internet connection," recommended another. On the plus side: Students reported a large number of merit-based assistantships.

PLACEMENT AND RECRUITING

The UGA Career Services office offers assistance with resume preparation, interviewing skills, mock interviews, a resume referral program, job search strategies, and a photo and resume profile book, which is distributed to Fortune 500 firms and smaller regional firms in the Southeast. It also conducts the distinctive Executive Breakfast Club, at which students visit with senior management of Fortune 500 companies over breakfast. Off campus, UGA markets its MBAs at four Consortium events: the National MBA Consortium at Chicago, the Capital Consortium in Washington, D.C., the Southeastern MBA Consortium in Atlanta, and the International Consortium in Orlando.

Students in our survey expressed disappointment with the Career Services office, although, given the successful placement rate of graduates (see sidebar), this may have more to do with students' general dissatisfaction with the MBA program (see 'Academics,' above). UGA MBAs most frequently find work with FedEx, Fannie Mae, International Paper, Delta Airlines, Intel, Andersen Consulting, and Arthur Andersen & Co.

Donald R. Perry, Jr., Director, MBA Admissions
346 Brooks Hall, Athens, GA 30602-6264
Admissions: 706-542-5671 • Fax: 706-542-5351
Email: ugamba@cba.uga.edu
Internet: www.cba.uga.edu

University of Georgia

STUDENT/CAMPUS LIFE

First-year UGA students report a heavy workload and spend an average of twenty to thirty hours a week prepping for class. Much of the pressure is created by the quarterly academic schedule, which leaves the workload "uneven" and "like a roller coaster." The majority of UGA MBAs use study groups and divvy up the load. By the second year, things lighten up considerably. UGA MBAs are competitive, but not overly so. Students describe their classmates as "a mix of motivated 'gunners' and disinterested 'slackers.'" Students are interested in lending a hand, a by-product of the emphasis on teamwork. The small class size fosters a close-knit atmosphere. One student told us, "We click as a group." But a dissenting MBA thought the group was just cliques ("The majority of my class thinks socializing is standing around a keg of beer") and that "Married people stick together." Another agreed: "Many students are naive or immature, attempting to pick up where undergrad left off."

UGA is located in Athens, a small city with a college-town feel. "Athens epitomizes what a college town should be! There is a broad spectrum of individuals and culture present downtown," raved one MBA. For road trips, Atlanta is just seventy miles away. Students agreed the campus was safe, though most opt for off-campus living in apartments. For fun, the Graduate Business Association sponsors social, professional, and athletic activities. Especially popular are intramural sports teams of all types. "Almost half the class escapes from the stress of the work week on intramural basketball teams," writes one student. Weekly happy hours provide relief from a diet of regression analysis.

ADMISSIONS

UGA weighs your GMAT score, work experience, and college GPA most heavily. After that, they weigh your letters of recommendation, extracurricular activities, and essays equally. Writes the school, "We are interested in being as service oriented to our applicants as we are to those candidates we admit. We are open to questions and try to respond in a timely manner to requests for information." The school recommends that students complete undergraduate coursework in financial accounting, statistics, and microcomputers (spreadsheet applications) prior to applying. UGA uses a three-round admissions process and offers an early decision program. The school permits students to defer admission for up to one year.

FINANCIAL FACTS

Tuition (in/out-state)	$3,069/$9,630
Fees (in-state/out-of-state)	$597/$597
Cost of books	$825
Room & Board (on/off-campus)	$4,470/$6,150
% of students receiving aid	80
% first-year students receiving aid	80
% aid that is merit-based	100
% of students receiving paid internships	70
% of students receiving grants	17
Average award package	$6,000
Average grant	$1,750

ADMISSIONS

# of applications received	905
% applicants accepted	22
% acceptees attending	48
Average GMAT (range)	630 (580–660)
Minimum TOEFL	600
Average GPA (range)	3.12 (2.75–3.48)
Application fee (in/out-state)	$30/$30
Early decision program available	Yes
Early decision deadline	December 1, Jan 1
Early decision notification	January 15, Feb 15
Regular application deadline	February 1
Regular notification	4–6 weeks after receipt of application
Admission may be deferred?	Yes
Maximum length of deferment	1 year
Transfer students accepted?	No
Non-fall admission available?	Yes
Admissions process need-blind?	Yes

APPLICANTS ALSO LOOK AT

University of North Carolina at Chapel Hill, Emory University, University of Texas at Austin, Georgia Institute of Technology, Vanderbilt University, University of Virginia, Duke University, University of Tennessee at Knoxville

EMPLOYMENT PROFILE

Placement rate (%)	96
# of companies recruiting on-campus	55
% grads employed immediately	81
% grads employed within six months	97
Average starting salary	$55,601

Grads employed by field (avg. salary):

Accounting	3% ($40,000)
Consulting	17% ($57,846)
Finance	25% ($59,023)
General Management	12% ($60,760)
Marketing	27% ($52,055)
MIS	6% ($58,750)
Operations	4% ($54,575)
Other	6% ($59,300)

GEORGIA INSTITUTE OF TECHNOLOGY
DuPree School of Management

ACADEMICS

Georgia Tech's DuPree College of Management seeks to distinguish itself from the pack by emphasizing the technological aspects of business education. Even the degree it offers, a Master of Science in Management (MSM), sets the school apart from many other MBA programs (although the school brochure points out that "Georgia Tech's MSM is virtually identical to an MBA offered through a school of business administration"). Students tell us that DuPree's "emphasis on analytic skills and technology as a major driver of management techniques" persuaded them to choose the program. That and Tech's bargain-basement tuition, even for non-Georgians.

First-year students at DuPree must complete a full battery of foundation courses. A quarterly schedule that requires five courses guarantees that first-year is an extremely busy time for students. Students report favorably on the "range of topics covered by the core" and appreciate DuPree's commitment to small classes throughout the foundation sequence. One student notes approvingly that "many core courses consist of students with a background in the subject matter, which sets a fast pace for the rest of the class."

Second-year students give high grades to the finance, management, accounting, and operations departments ("the operations faculty," enthuses one student "is one of the school's great strengths"). They also appreciate the "flexibility" of second year, which stands in sharp contrast to the largely prescribed first-year program. Students give low marks to the marketing department, however. Professors are admired because "almost all do extensive work in their industries," yet remain "always available to students for support and advice." In assessing the administration, students concede to the often frustrating limitations state schools must navigate within, telling us that "the b-school is run well, given the restrictions placed on it," and acknowledging that the "administration has its hands tied by Tech bureaucracy." They are less understanding about such essential facilities as multimedia classrooms, computer labs, and the library, all of which "need a serious upgrade."

PLACEMENT AND RECRUITING

The Graduate Management Career Services (GMCS) office tells us that it "offers students a variety of services: a career seminar series, career planning and advising, mock interviews, and resume books. Additionally, alumni network contacts are available to students, as well as involvement in the New York and Atlanta consortiums. Recruiting companies making the most offers: Allied Signal, Citibank, Delta Airlines, Entergy Corporation, and Ernst and Young."

Students give Career Services merely average grades; detractors complain that the office "needs some help." Although our respondents feel that GMCS attracts high-quality recruiters, they also believe that more could be done to bring a greater quantity and diversity of recruiters to campus. Many students report that their experiences with mentors and alumni have been unhelpful.

Ann Johnston Scott, Director of the MSM Program
755 Ferst Drive, Atlanta, GA 30332
Admissions: 404-894-8713 • Fax: 404-894-4199
Email: msm@mgt.gatech.edu
Internet: mgt-sun1.iac.gatech.edu/dupree

Georgia Institute of Technology

STUDENT/CAMPUS LIFE

When 40 percent of a student body holds undergraduate degrees in engineering and computer science, it should come as no surprise that an unusually large proportion of these students have monster quantitative skills. Students report that their classmates buck the stereotype of the nerdy engineer, however, describing them as "surprisingly supportive and congenial, even though most of them are very competitive." One student expresses surprise that his classmates are "helpful, not as many Type A personalities as I expected. Very sharp!" The student body derives "from many different countries and backgrounds," although several students complain that there is "very little interaction between U.S. and international students." In general, "students hang out together during the day, play sports together, and socialize with each other at night."

Our respondents report heavy involvement in DuPree's many clubs, such as the Entrepreneur's Club, Honorary Accounting Organization, and Women in Business. All students are members of the Graduate Students in Management (GSM) organization, which arranges intramural sports, alumni events, and guest lecture series. The GSM also has input on curriculum changes, leading one student to write that there's "lots of student leadership" on campus. Students here also find time for community service. DuPree is conveniently located across the street from the university's Student Athletic Center, and reportedly its facilities are very good. Students also enjoy watching Tech's sixteen intercollegiate teams, especially its "great hockey team." Atlanta, ranked among the "top ten cities in the world for business" by Fortune magazine, is well loved by DuPree students. Writes one, "Atlanta and the surrounding area is a great place to live and provides numerous resources for current research and potential future employment." Other ambitious DuPree students cite the presence of Coca-Cola, CNN, and Bell South in the community as their reason for choosing Tech.

ADMISSIONS

If you're thinking of applying to GT straight out of college, reconsider. The vast majority of DuPree students have at least two years of work experience under their belts. Also of great concern to the admissions committee is your GMAT score: The average GMAT score of accepted applicants over the last four years is a smashing 632—way up in the 87th percentile. Also considered are undergraduate GPA, essays, and letters of recommendation.

FINANCIAL FACTS

Tuition (in/out-state)	$3,255/$11,040
Cost of books	$500
Room & Board (on/off-campus)	$10,200/$10,200
% of students receiving paid internships	95
% of students receiving grants	30

ADMISSIONS

# of applications received	500
% applicants accepted	45
% acceptees attending	39
Average GMAT (range)	632 (500–760)
Minimum TOEFL	600
Average GPA (range)	3.20 (2.10–3.90)
Application fee (in/out-state)	$50/$50
Early decision program available	No
Regular application deadline	May 15
Regular notification	Rolling
Admission may be deferred?	Yes
Maximum length of deferment	1 year
Transfer students accepted?	Yes
Non-fall admission available?	No
Admissions process need-blind?	Yes

APPLICANTS ALSO LOOK AT

Emory University, University of Georgia, University of Texas at Austin, Purdue University, Massachusetts Institute of Technology, Penn State University, Vanderbilt University, Carnegie Mellon University

EMPLOYMENT PROFILE

Placement rate (%)	93
# of companies recruiting on-campus	98
% grads employed immediately	93
% grads employed within six months	98
Average starting salary	$56,100

Grads employed by field (avg. salary):

Accounting	7% ($49,250)
Consulting	22% ($58,000)
Finance	18% ($55,000)
General Management	14% ($62,000)
Marketing	20% ($53,000)
MIS	17% ($58,300)
Operations	24% ($62,400)

HARVARD UNIVERSITY
Graduate School of Business Administration

ACADEMICS

Harvard Business School is indisputably the nation's most famous business school, and it is also one of the most selective. In 1994–95, a class of 900 students was admitted from among over 6,900 applicants. With these numbers and a worldwide reputation as the business school, HBS appears to be the envy of almost everybody in graduate business education. Unsurprisingly, the prevalent feeling here is summed up by one student's remarks: "If you're going to do an MBA, don't mess around. Come to the best b-school in the world." Those who are fortunate enough to be accepted usually do. More than 80 percent of last year's "admits" chose to enroll. Indeed, the school's "yield" (percentage of admitted candidates who choose to enroll) is the highest of any b-school in the United States.

How did Harvard come to occupy such an august position? First, as one of the oldest b-schools in the nation (founded in 1908), it got a head start on all the other programs. Second, as the biggest b-school—graduating roughly 800 MBAs per year—it's built a network of more than 60,000 alumni worldwide. And these are uncommonly loyal and generous alumni. Since 1980, the school's endowment has grown from $100 million to approximately $545 million in 1995. HBS also boasts more CEO alums than any other program, a nationally renowned faculty, and authorship of 90 percent of the case materials used worldwide.

HBS is known from coast to coast for its comprehensive coverage of the functional areas of business and how well it integrates them. General management is considered the cornerstone of the program, but all of the departments are strong. In recent years, however Harvard's programs have come under heavy criticism. The complaints: HBS has not been responsive to changes in the marketplace. Its rigid program has featured little of the international perspectives, teamwork, student consulting, or innovative learning experiences now characteristic of b-school education in the United States. Surprisingly, the venerable HBS has done what was considered unthinkable before and decided it's time for change. Recently, HBS has undertaken a stem-to-stern program overhaul called the Leadership Learning Initiative. It offers year-round classes (students can now enroll in September or January), sections of eighty instead of ninety, and greater emphasis on skill building and field-based learning delivered in a much more cross-functional context. The school also has been completely transformed by technology: relying heavily on the Internet and Harvard's own Intranet for everything from course materials to lecture examples.

PLACEMENT AND RECRUITING

HBS students get an average 3.8 job offers each—the most of any b-school. Ninety-nine percent have a job by graduation. On average, Harvard students earn some of the highest starting salaries. The big news: for the last few years, Harvard MBAs have been taking in six-figure-plus starting packages. That makes the tuition investment a little easier to handle now, doesn't it?

Jill Fadule, Director of Admissions
Soldiers Field Road, Boston, MA 02163
Admissions: 617-495-6127 • Fax: 617-495-0316
Email: admissions@hbs.edu
Internet: www.hbs.edu

Harvard University

STUDENT/CAMPUS LIFE

Harvard boasts one of the most beautiful, well-manicured campuses in the nation. It should. The school has plowed $200 million into its buildings and grounds over the last fifteen years. Over and over, students describe its "country club" ambiance and told us about groundskeepers obsessed with sod and shrubbery. "A plant died here last week," one student told us. "They replaced it within three days. And they use a snowblower to clear leaves." Students rave about the ever-popular Shad Hall, Harvard's gym, which is a veritable temple to sweat: "Shad is worth the tuition alone."

Harvard MBAs enjoy an active social life, although one notes, "There is no such thing as dating at HBS. Local undergrads aren't bad if you hide the fact that you go to Harvard." Fifty-six student clubs keep students fully engaged. Many of the clubs sponsor black-tie affairs such as the well-known Predator's Ball. A favorite spot for section gatherings is the Border Cafe. On warm days, students can be found hanging out on the sun-drenched patios of The Grille at Kresge, an on-campus eatery.

Harvard divides its 800 incoming students into sections of eighty; each section takes an entire year of courses together. Writes one MBA, "Section life is a great experience. You develop great camaraderie with classmates from diverse cultural and professional backgrounds." Most of the first-year social life revolves around the section, which schedule dozens of section events to ensure you get to know those eighty classmates well. The school highly recommends forming study groups. During orientation and the first week of class, students generally seek out classmates with whom to form a group. It's not uncommon for over-anxious types to begin doing this in the summer, to lock in someone smart.

Harvard's reputation for intensity and competitiveness is well earned. The first four months are the most difficult. As on student explains, "It ramps up quickly. Students who know zero about accounting and stats get left behind." The pressure to succeed is formidable.

ADMISSIONS

The admissions board at Harvard considers the following criteria (not ranked in order of importance): college GPA/transcripts, essays, letters of recommendation, and extracurricular activities. The essays are considered extremely important. Applicants are interviewed at Harvard's discretion only to further evaluate the student's candidacy. Applications are batched in rounds. A final note: after an eleven-year hiatus, Harvard has decided to add the GMAT as one more criterion in evaluating a candidate's admission to the school. This affects those applying for admission in September 1997 and beyond.

FINANCIAL FACTS

Tuition	$25,000
Fees	$2,540
Room & Board (on/off-campus)	$7,073/NR

ADMISSIONS

# of applications received	7,469
% applicants accepted	14
% acceptees attending	87
Average GPA	3.50
Application fee (in/out-state)	$160
Regular application deadline	March
Regular notification	Rolling
Admission may be deferred?	No
Transfer students accepted?	No
Non-fall admission available?	Yes
Admissions process need-blind?	Yes

APPLICANTS ALSO LOOK AT

Stanford University, Dartmouth College, University of Pennsylvania, Northwestern University, Massachusetts Institute of Technology, University of Chicago, University of California—Los Angeles, University of California—Berkeley

EMPLOYMENT PROFILE

Placement rate (%)	99
# of companies recruiting on-campus	330
% grads employed immediately	99
Average starting salary	$82,670

Grads employed by field (avg. salary):

Consulting	33% (NR)
Finance	33% (NR)
General Management	13% (NR)
Marketing	8% (NR)
MIS	4% (NR)
Strategic Planning	7% (NR)
Venture Capital	8% (NR)
Other	28% (NR)

HOFSTRA UNIVERSITY
Frank G. Zarb School of Business

ACADEMICS

One of the many strengths of Zarb is that it tailors its program to the individual needs of the student by taking into account prior education, graduate-degree objectives, and possible career goals. In addition, students can pursue the MBA full-time and complete degree requirements in only one calendar year by attending both summer sessions and the January session as well as fall and spring semesters.

The MBA program curriculum was recently completely revised to better reflect contemporary business management in a global environment. Included in the new curriculum are core competency courses, which must be completed by those students who have no previous business coursework but may be waived for those who have completed such courses prior to MBA enrollment. The core includes the common core of business subjects; a cluster of courses called "the contemporary business environment," which focus on ethics, the environment, and the global and diversity aspects of business; a final project, which may be completed either individually or as part of a team through case-oriented or consultancy-based projects, or using computer simulations as the main focus of learning.

One of the most noteworthy aspects of the Zarb School's MBA program is its use of the University's McGraw-Hill Technology Laboratory. MBA students use this software and database laboratory to support virtually every aspect of their studies. Zarb students also participate in consulting projects and engagements for companies ranging from small start-up shops to large, multinational firms.

The faculty for this "dynamic and intense" b-school, receive great reviews both for their brilliance and for their accessibility. Says one grad student, "The professors here are always willing to help, and their assistance has proven invaluable." On the downside, "too much stuff comes right out of the books, making class attendance, and therefore student interaction, merely optional." Students feel best prepared by their classes in marketing and finance, and assert that by "recruiting excellent students, both nationally and internationally, Hofstra creates an incredibly challenging environment."

PLACEMENT AND RECRUITING

The Career Development Office gives students assistance with resume preparation, interviewing skills, and job search strategies. Students may also place their resume in Hofstra's MBA resume book, which is distributed to Fortune 500 firms and small financial institutions in the New York City area.

In 1994, forty-five companies recruited on campus. Of all the students, 84 percent had a job within three months of graduation (four percent go on for additional education). The average starting salary for grads is $48,897. Forty-six percent of the class heads into finance, where the starting salary is higher than the average: $51,000. This is followed by marketing, with 15 percent of the class and salaries at the average mark. The big hires: KPMG Peat Marwick, Chase Manhattan, Citibank, and Andersen Consulting. Despite these stats, many students list career and internship placement as areas in which the school could use some improvement.

Susan McTiernan, Senior Assistant Dean
134 Hofstra University, Hempstead, NY 11550
Admissions: 516-463-5678•Fax: 516-463-5268
Email: humba@hofstra.edu
Internet: www.hofstra.edu

STUDENT/CAMPUS LIFE

Hofstra is located in Hempstead, New York, twenty-five miles from New York City. Situated right on the Hempstead Turnpike, the campus itself is lovely—tree-lined and dotted with sculpture. Less lovely is the parking situation, which students say can be next to impossible. This is a daily headache, since the school is dominated by Long Island commuters (a small number live on campus in the high-rise dorms, but more than one student begs for "a few on-campus bunga-lows where older students might feel more comfortable"). Classes are small, with an average of ten to twenty-five students in each. Hofstra MBAs bring diverse and interesting work perspectives to the classroom experience. Students call themselves competitive, but hardly the type to mow someone down. Instead, there is a sense of camaraderie, and students solve problems in a team environment. But, according to the survey, students don't necessarily intend to keep each other as long-terms buddies. Indeed, the social scene is subdued here, because students commute and aren't around on weekends. But at least one student notes a few on-campus activities: "There are many clubs for MBA students, such as the MBA club and the Consulting Group, and there are lots of Career Forums to attend. In addition, on Sundays we play sports like volleyball and basketball." For leaving it all behind, students organize tailgate parties before Hofstra football games, a spring picnic, and a graduate cruise around Manhattan. Overall, Hofstra MBAs are pleased with the administration: "The school makes a strong effort to meet each student's personal needs."

ADMISSIONS

According to the admissions office, the following are considered most important in your application: Leadership, communication skills, and levels of increasing professional responsibility. After that, in descending order of importance, are your college GPA, GMAT score, work experience, essay, letters of recommendation, and extracurricular activities. "Admission processes," writes the school, "tend to be very similar to the selective to highly selective schools in the United States. All [application] materials are evaluated carefully by a committee comprised of faculty and administrators. We offer perhaps one of the more timely application turnarounds among the group of selective schools; once an application is complete, we generally notify the applicant of a decision within four weeks. "Members of American minority groups, for example, African Americans, receive special consideration as do those students whose native language is not English."

Applicants may defer admission up to one year for medical reasons or to accrue additional work experience. There is an admission deferment program for college seniors.

FINANCIAL FACTS

Tuition	$16,000
Fees	$700
Cost of books	$1,500
Room & Board (on/off-campus)	$8,000/$7,500
% of students receiving aid	65
% first-year students receiving aid	60
% aid that is merit-based	65
% of students receiving loans	69
% of students receiving paid internships	25
% of students receiving grants	65
Average grant	$6,000

ADMISSIONS

# of applications received	696
% applicants accepted	57
% acceptees attending	34
Average GMAT (range)	570 (480–630)
Minimum TOEFL	600
Average GPA (range)	3.18 (2.80–3.40)
Application fee (in/out-state)	$40
Early decision program available	Yes
Early decision deadline	January
Early decision notification	January
Regular application deadline	June 1
Regular notification	Rolling
Admission may be deferred?	Yes
Maximum length of deferment	1 year
Transfer students accepted?	Yes
Non-fall admission available?	Yes
Admissions process need-blind?	Yes

APPLICANTS ALSO LOOK AT

New York University, Columbia University, CUNY Baruch College, Boston University, University of Connecticut, Babson College, University of Florida, Northeastern University

EMPLOYMENT PROFILE

# of companies recruiting on-campus	45
% grads employed immediately	91
% grads employed within six months	95
Average starting salary	$51,300

Grads employed by field (avg. salary):

Accounting	9% (NR)
Consulting	7% (NR)
Finance	46% (NR)
Human Resources	4% (NR)
Marketing	12% (NR)
MIS	7% (NR)
Operations	2% (NR)
Strategic Planning	5% (NR)

UNIVERSITY OF ILLINOIS AT URBANA-CHAMPAIGN
College of Commerce and Business Administration

OVERVIEW

Type of school	public
Affiliation	none
Environment	metropolis
Academic calendar	semester
Schedule	full-time only

STUDENTS

Enrollment of parent institution	36,000
Enrollment of business school	595
% male/female	69/31
% out-of-state	74
% minorities	14
% international (# countries represented)	47(39)
Average age at entry	27
Average years work experience at entry	4

ACADEMICS

Student/faculty ratio	47:1
% female faculty	13
% minority faculty	9
% part-time faculty	13
Hours of study per day	4.31

SPECIALTIES

Strengths in Accounting and Finance, Alliance with the College of Engineering and the National Center for Supercomputing Applications

JOINT DEGREES

MBA/MS Agriculture; MBA/MA Architecture; MBA/MS Computer Science; MBA/MS Electrical Engineering; MBA/MS Civil Engineering; MBA/MS General Engineering; MBA/MS Industrial Engineering; MBA/MS Mechanical Engineering; MBA/MS Journalism; MBA/M Education; MBA/JD; MBA/MD

SPECIAL PROGRAMS

Chief Financial Officer Lecture Series, Business Advisory Council, Executive in Residence Program, Internship, Development Program

STUDY ABROAD PROGRAMS

Mexico, France, Germany, Spain, Great Britain, Norway, Denmark, Canada, Netherlands, Brazil, Australia, Austria

SURVEY SAYS...

HITS
Off-campus housing
Gym
Library

MISSES
General management
Quantitative skills
MIS/operations

PROMINENT ALUMNI

Michael T. Tokarz, Partner, Kohlberg, Kravis, and Roberts; Wilma Smelcer, Vice President, Continental Bank

ACADEMICS

The University of Illinois at Urbana—Champaign recently retooled its MBA program, integrating the core curriculum and adding more options for "hands-on" learning. Students tell us that it is still "early in the reworking process of the Illinois MBA program. It will take a few years to work out the ticks," but they are pleased with the direction the school is pursuing. Of the integrated core, students tell us, "I like the integrated curriculum, which puts courses in order. During the first seven weeks, we study the foundation of business (strategic, marketing, decision-making). Then in the second seven weeks, we learn the managing process for internal organization (operations, organization, etc.)" The core includes two week-long seminars called Applying Business Perspectives (ABP). Students are "impressed with the ABPs. The student can apply material studies before [putting them] into a real business practice."

Some of the university's innovations take advantage of Urbana's prestigious engineering school. The Office for the Study of Business Issues (OSBI), for example, allows MBAs to work side by side with university engineers, computer researchers, and entrepeneures to evaluate the commercial potential of their innovations and to plan marketing strategies. Other innovations make an Illinois MBA more adaptable to the changing marketplace. Although students may enroll in traditional professional track majors focusing primarily on accounting, finance, marketing, and technology, the school also allows "tremendous flexibility in designing your own MBA if you only ask for it." Nearly one-quarter of the students here pursue joint degrees in such areas as education, computer engineering, law, medicine, and, even, Slavic languages.

Students give professors high marks, bragging, "The faculty are absolutely wonderful. Profs are always willing to help in and out of class. They make this program worthwhile." Finance and MIS are among students' favorite areas of study; accounting and marketing also earn high ratings among the b-schoolers. Students complain that the administration "needs to be more proactive in improving the program and show a genuine effort to help." They also warn that it can be difficult to get into popular courses. One student sums up the complaints, explaining, "although we are a small program we still deal with the bureaucracy of a big university."

PLACEMENT AND RECRUITING

Our survey shows continued improvement at Illinois' MBA Career Services Office (CSO). After years of very low levels of student satisfaction with the office, this year students give the office a "B-". The number and quality of companies recruiting on campus remains the students' chief bone of contention. Also, nearly a quarter of our respondents report that the alumni they contact are of "no help" in their search for jobs and internships.

The CSO publishes resume books for prospective employers and keeps students informed of "company presentations, workshops, interview schedules, deadlines, and important announcements," through a column in the bi-weekly student newsletter. The service also conducts mandatory career management classes for first-year students and voluntary forums for students to meet alumni and corporate reps. This fall, a new, comprehensive, web-based recruiting

Melanie Jarocki, Asst. Director of Admissions
410 David Kinley Hall, Champaign, IL 61820
Admissions: 217-244-8019 • Fax: 217-333-1156
Email: mba@uiuc.edu
Internet: www.mba.uiuc.edu

University of Illinois at Urbana-Champaign

system will streamline placement activities. Illinois participates in two major job fairs for international students. Companies that hire a great number of Illinois MBAs include AlliedSignal, Pillsbury, Hewlett-Packard, Procter & Gamble, Ford, GTE, Arthur Andersen, Andersen Consulting, Citibank, Dow Chemical, Eaton Corp., and Ernst & Young.

STUDENT/CAMPUS LIFE

Illinois boasts a "huge international population," resulting in a program that is "like studying abroad without going abroad. Very cool global business experience." However, as one African-American student notes, "we are culturally diverse, but not racially. Out of 286 first-years, only fourteen African-Americans." Students describe classmates as "friendly, outgoing, willing to work hard to improve the program for future students," but several told us that "many are young with little experience." As a result, there is a pervasive sense that the "top 25 percent are top-notch versus anybody. Bottom 25 percent are awful. Expected the class overall to be more competitive, disciplined, and professional."

Students give the school's hometown of Champaign mixed reviews. Proponents point out that it provides a "small town atmosphere good for studying" and is an "excellent, safe and quiet place to be with your family (I am married and have one child)." Detractors bemoan the fact that "Champaign is in the middle of nowhere" and that there is "not much entertainment near campus." One minority student came down hardest on Champaign, stating flat-out that "this city is horrible. There isn't much to do besides study and go to class. Socially numbing." Student opinion about campus life is more uniformly positive, owing to a "pretty campus" with "lots of restaurants, shops, and bars on campus." Sums up one student, "life here is great. Campus, intercollegiate sports, and the best libraries." The MBA program has "many clubs where we socialize and mix with classmates beyond the classroom." Our respondents recommend participation, explaining that "the workload here is tough, but it is worthwhile to get involved in MBA clubs and organizations. It will help you out in the long run."

ADMISSIONS

The admissions office considers your work experience to be most important; more than 85 percent of students have more than one year of significant work experience. After that, in descending order, they consider your GMAT scores, college GPA, essays, and letters of recommendation. Applicants are invited to present projects, portfolios, CDs, theses, and the like for review. Because of the quantitative components of the curriculum, applicants are advised to have completed a college-level calculus course. Writes the school, "The admissions program is client-oriented. An applicant can track his or her application through a 1-800-MBA-UIUC number."

Decisions are made on a rolling admissions basis. Applicants are notified of a decision two to three weeks from receipt of the completed application. Wait listed students are notified of a spot by June 15.

FINANCIAL FACTS

Tuition (in/out-state)	$8,546/$15,218
Fees (in-state/out-of-state)	$2,100/$2,100
Cost of books	$2,500
Room & Board (on/off-campus)	$6,000/$8,000
% of students receiving aid	66
% first-year students receiving aid	66
% aid that is merit-based	35
% of students receiving loans	61
% of students receiving paid internships	0
% of students receiving grants	35
Average award package	$24,000
Average grant	$6,000
Average graduation debt	$17,000

ADMISSIONS

# of applications received	1,322
% applicants accepted	53
% acceptees attending	41
Average GMAT (range)	600 (400–760)
Average GPA (range)	3.25 (2.20–4.00)
Application fee (in/out-state)	$40/$50
Early decision program available	Yes
Early decision deadline	January 1
Early decision notification	February 1
Regular application deadline	April 1
Regular notification	Rolling
Admission may be deferred?	Yes
Maximum length of deferment	1 year
Transfer students accepted?	No
Non-fall admission available?	No
Admissions process need-blind?	Yes

APPLICANTS ALSO LOOK AT

Indiana University, Northwestern University, University of Texas at Austin, University of Wisconsin—Madison, University of Michigan Business School, Ohio State University, New York University, Purdue University

EMPLOYMENT PROFILE

# of companies recruiting on-campus	110
% grads employed within six months	95
Average starting salary	$52,000

Grads employed by field (avg. salary):

Accounting	4% ($42,500)
Consulting	12% ($54,000)
Finance	30% ($53,250)
General Management	13% ($55,000)
Human Resources	7% ($49,000)
Marketing	14% ($47,000)
MIS	7% ($46,500)
Operations	7% ($53,500)
Other	6% ($61,320)

INDIANA UNIVERSITY
Kelly School of Business

OVERVIEW

Type of school	public
Affiliation	none
Environment	suburban
Academic calendar	semester
Schedule	full-time only

STUDENTS

Enrollment of parent institution	34,937
Enrollment of business school	543
% male/female	74/26
% out-of-state	87
% minorities	13
% international (# countries represented)	20(30)
Average age at entry	28
Average years work experience at entry	5

ACADEMICS

Student/faculty ratio	5:1
% female faculty	15
% minority faculty	11
Hours of study per day	5:17

SPECIALTIES

Finance and Marketing are most popular majors. Intergrated approach gives the curriculum an applied focus. Faculty emphasizes teamwork and skill development. Program taught by full-time experienced faculty.

JOINT DEGREES

MBA/JD, 4 years; MBA/MA in Area Studies, 3 years.

SPECIAL PROGRAMS

Team-based, integrative curriculum, opportunities to specialize in various majors or focus areas such as consulting. Company support and involvement in the programs is common with case competitions, simulations, and guest lectures.

STUDY ABROAD PROGRAMS

Spain, England, Norway, Australia, Mexico, Finland, France, Switzerland

SURVEY SAYS...

HITS
Alumni helpful in job search
Study groups
On-campus housing

MISSES
Safety
School clubs
Gym

PROMINENT ALUMNI

Harold Poling, former Chairperson and CEO, Ford Motor Company; James Lipate, CEO, Penzoil; Frank Popoff, CEO, Dow Chemical

ACADEMICS

Indiana University has enhanced its reputation as one of the best b-schools in the nation with a thorough overhaul of its curriculum. The new program incorporates modern-day themes such as a cross-functional curriculum, globalization, and team-building. In addition, it takes these themes one step ahead of the competition with a unique concept: "Academies" that prepare students for specific or unusual fields, such as consulting or sports and entertainment.

During the first semester of year one, there is a foundations core and a week-long industry analysis. During the second semester, there is a functional core and a global conference week. Compliments one student, "The cross-functional integration that IU pioneered has been tremendous in preparing me to analyze business issues from a broad perspective." During the second year, students focus on a specialization. We are especially impressed with Indiana's performance in teaching core courses. Remarks one student, "The core program is the reason I chose Indiana over Darden. Professors are really absorbed with teaching it." The most novel innovation at Indiana is that students receive only one grade in the first semester for the cores and one grade in the remaining core in the second semester. But students were fierce in their criticism of this grading system. Grouses one, "The 2-scored grading makes the exam periods competitive and uncertain. It can be hard to distinguish oneself academically due to the tight grading curve."

To enhance teamwork, the school year kicks off with a ten-day orientation, replete with team-building exercises and head-start classes in computers, accounting, and quantitative methods. The entering class is then divided into cohorts of sixty-five students each. Cohorts take first-semester courses together and are then reshuffled, giving the students the opportunity to meet as many classmates as possible. Five faculty members oversee each core, creating a personal learning environment. As one MBA put it: "Professors are intensely involved in a student's performance—all give out home phone numbers during the first class, and encourage us to use them!" Students unanimously praise professors for their fine teaching as well. Raves one, "The faculty are outstanding, instructors are willing to let the classroom have its own life." Overall, students reported they felt well prepared by their studies in accounting, marketing, and general management. Given the emphasis on collaborative learning, it's not surprising that students gave their teamwork skills near-perfect marks (among the highest in this book). Computer skills showed improvement this year: 80 percent of students now say they're good or better at computing. Students also reported excellent finance skills and told us, "IU has one of the best real estate programs in the country."

As for the administration, "they make every effort to ensure that the business school is run like a small business—and not a large bureaucracy." Prominent alumni who would agree: Harold Poling, former Chairperson and CEO, Ford Motor Company; James Lipate, CEO, Penzoil; Frank Popoff, CEO, Dow Chemical.

PLACEMENT AND RECRUITING

What do IU MBAs think of their placement office? It depends on whom you ask. While the majority say they're doing a good to great job, 23 percent would agree with this comment: "Placement Office is improving, but things could run more

James Holmen, Director of Admissions and Financial Aid
1309 East 10th Street, Room 254, Bloomington, IN 47405
Admissions: 812-855-8006 • Fax: 812-855-9039
Email: mbaoffice@indiana.edu
Internet: www.kelley.iu.edu/mba

smoothly." One MBA mentions, "The Placement office is very successful, but thinks it runs the school and likes to pat itself on the back." More constructive feedback came from this MBA who reports, "Most recruiters are for marketing. There is a shortage in investment banking and management consulting." But the numbers here are strong: 94 percent of grads had secured a position within three months of graduation. Most MBAs headed into marketing. The average starting salary for an Indiana alum is $65,000.

STUDENT/CAMPUS LIFE

Students still agree that IU's first-year piles on an "extremely demanding workload," requiring students to study/prepare an average of thirty-five to forty hours a week.The majority report it's important to do all or most assigned reading. Advises this MBA, "Time management is a key factor for success." Surprisingly, students are laid back and friendly; cutthroat central IU is not. In fact, says this student, "They are down-to-earth, unassuming, and very bright." In the complaint department, this student reports, "Not enough women—only 24 percent female population." However, that same student said women even out their representation by taking most of the leadership positions in clubs and activities.

On Thursday nights (there's no class on Friday) MBAs head to the designated bar of the week. Also popular are organized social events, such as picnics, barbecues, and the spring banquet. Many students become involved in the student-run career clubs, such as the Graduate Women of Business or the Finance Club. Students are psyched about all the career contacts they make through the Marketing Club, which features a "ROAD SHOW" that markets MBAs to targeted companies. Students are equally pumped about their "Brand-new gym facilities—amazing." In addition, this MBA reports, "Great support network for 'significant others'!" As for IU's hometown of Bloomington, prior survey respondents still describe it best: "like a mix of Ann Arbor, Berkeley, and Cambridge with a dash of Main Street, USA thrown in." Adds this current MBA, "Small town life is great!" Students report that on- and off-campus housing is cost-effective and attractive. The majority opt to live off-campus in Bloomington or surrounding neighborhoods. Public transportation is easily accessible. A car is helpful if you want to go exploring on the weekend, but students say parking is a nightmare. A final note: 30 percent of students are eligible for graduate assistantships (which subsidizes about 50 percent of tuition).

ADMISSIONS

Indiana looks for students whose academic background, work experience, leadership abilities, and comunication skills meet the demands of the program and promise a successful managerial career. The admissions committee takes a holistic look at each application as they consider the applicant's academic record, GMAT score, work experience, record of leadership, letters of recommendation, and essays. The committee searches for the strengths that balance any deficiency in each candidates's profile. Early application is encouraged, with three domesitc deadlines: December 1, January 15, and March 1. Interviews, though not required, are strongly encouraged.

FINANCIAL FACTS
Tuition (in/out-state)	$7,840/$15,686
Fees (in-state/out-of-state)	$543/$543
Cost of books	$4,342
Room & Board (on/off-campus)	$5,548/$5,548
% of students receiving aid	80
% first-year students receiving aid	86
% aid that is merit-based	100
% of students receiving loans	69
% of students receiving grants	19
Average award package	$18,449
Average grant	$5,455
Average graduation debt	$33,646

ADMISSIONS
# of applications received	1,790
% applicants accepted	37
% acceptees attending	39
Average GMAT (range)	630 (610–670)
Minimum TOEFL	580
Average GPA (range)	3.30 (3.03–3.40)
Application fee (in/out-state)	$50/$50
Early decision program available	Yes
Early decision deadline	December 1
Early decision notification	early February
Regular application deadline	March 1
Regular notification	April 1
Admission may be deferred?	Yes
Maximum length of deferment	1 year
Transfer students accepted?	No
Non-fall admission available?	No
Admissions process need-blind?	Yes

APPLICANTS ALSO LOOK AT
University of Michigan Business School, Northwestern University, University of North Carolina at Chapel Hill, University of Texas at Austin, University of Chicago, Duke University, University of Virginia, University of California—Berkeley

EMPLOYMENT PROFILE
Placement rate (%)	94
# of companies recruiting on-campus	230
% grads employed immediately	82
% grads employed within six months	94
Average starting salary	$65,000

Grads employed by field (avg. salary):
Accounting	($58,000)
Consulting	($75,000)
Finance	($65,000)
General Management	($65,000)
Human Resources	($58,000)
Marketing	($64,000)
MIS	($73,000)
Operations	($65,000)

UNIVERSITY OF IOWA
Iowa School of Management

OVERVIEW

Type of school	public
Affiliation	none
Environment	metropolis
Academic calendar	semester
Schedule	Full-time/part-time/evening

STUDENTS

Enrollment of parent institution	27,871
Enrollment of business school	657
% male/female	70/30
% out-of-state	14
% part-time	72
% minorities	2
% international (# countries represented)	10(19)
Average age at entry	27
Average years work experience at entry	3

ACADEMICS

Student/faculty ratio	6:1
% female faculty	18
% minority faculty	5
% part-time faculty	22
Hours of study per day	4.58

SPECIALTIES

Finance/Investments Marketing, Enterpreneurship and Management Information Systems. The curriculum effectively combines lecture, case analyses, and field projects.

JOINT DEGREES

Joint-degree MBA programs in Law, 4 years; Hospital and Health Administration, 3 years; Library Science, 3 years; Nursing, 3 years; MA in MIS 1.5 years

SPECIAL PROGRAMS

Summer internships with entrepreneurs

STUDY ABROAD PROGRAMS

France, Austria, United Kingdom, Germany

SURVEY SAYS...

HITS
Computer skills
Getting into courses a breeze
Quantitative skills

MISSES
Profs not great teachers
General management
School clubs

PROMINENT ALUMNI

Leonard A. Hadley, President and CEO, Maytag Corp.; John Pappajohn, President, Equity Dynamics, Inc.; Marvin A. Pomerantz, President and CEO, the Mid-America Group; Jerre Stead, Chairman and CEO, Ingram Micro; Kathleen A. Dore, President, Bravo/The Independent Film Channel/Much Music

ACADEMICS

The University of Iowa School of Management is "an MBA program on the rise." Spurred on by a new state-of-the-art facility ("incredibly advanced with the latest multimedia") and an administration that is "fantastic in working to provide a challenging and ever-improving atmosphere." Iowa continues its rise in national prominence as reported in previous editions of this book.

Many students are drawn to Iowa by the opportunity to diversify. "Most students seek dual concentrations," explains one student. Many others note the numerous dual degree offerings as their reason for choosing Iowa. Others come to study under "one of the brightest, most aggressive finance faculties in the nation." Finance remains Iowa's strongest discipline, benefiting from not only a strong faculty but also such innovative programs as "the Applied Securities Management program, which allows students to apply classroom ideas to manage real portfolios" and an online stock market game called the Iowa Electronic Market. Other highly rated departments include management, marketing, and management information systems. Among Iowa's other assets is the relatively small classes for a program of its size. Writes one student, "The dean and 90 percent of his staff knew my name in just six months. The class size here offers the opportunity to develop personal relationships with professors."

First year begins with Impact, a week-long Outward Bound-style orientation, "which fosters a climate of enthusiasm, cooperation, and camaraderie through various professional and recreational activities." Students then proceed to a comprehensive and demanding core that is reinforced at the end of the second year in the program's distinctive "capstone course." Students look favorably on the core, reporting that it builds teamwork skills and "creates good writers. Like it or not, you'll be an excellent report writer by the end of the program. There is a strong push to develop good written presentation skills." Second-year students must choose from among eight concentration areas.

Iowa professors receive high marks for accessibility but get mixed reviews for teaching ability. Although some write that the "faculty is on the cutting edge with their research and are able to express that in their lectures," others tell us that "some professors are excellent while others I question how they got to teach." Students are pleased that the "administration has made an outstanding effort to listen to students' concerns regarding teaching quality and to implement change."

PLACEMENT AND RECRUITING

Iowa's MBA Career Services Office (CSO) reports that its placement operation "has undergone dramatic changes in the recent past in response to requests and suggestions that its staff has solicited from employers, students, and alumni." To entice recruiters to the campus, the CSO has designed single-company "Showcase Days" that allow students to "learn firsthand what that company has to offer them." CSO supplements these efforts with an Internet job-listing service, an alumni network, videoconference interviews, and student efforts: "The student organizations plan multiple trips to disparate job markets to meet with top employers." In addition, "MBA Career Services has an Associate Director dedicated solely to internship placements and the School of Management's

Mary Spreen, Director of MBA Admissions
108 Pappajohn Business Administration Building, Iowa City, IA 52242-1000
Admissions: 319-335-1039 • Fax: 319-335-3604
Email: iowamba@uiowa.edu
Internet: www.biz.uiowa.edu/mba

University of Iowa

International Programs Office coordinates intern assignments for domestic students overseas and international students in the United States."

Student opinion of Iowa's CSO has improved since our last survey. Students are particularly satisfied with the number and quality of opportunities for off-campus projects and internships, and also report vast improvement in the quality of mentoring opportunities. The biggest complaint continues to be the school's difficulty in attracting recruiters from the coasts, particularly the East Coast.

STUDENT/CAMPUS LIFE

Iowa students think highly of their classmates, describing them as "immensely talented and cooperative. The students here have a balance that I have not encountered elsewhere. We are competitive, yet work well together in groups, teams, and organizations. There is a balance between coursework and organizational participation. The students here are very active in creating a better program." A "relaxed atmosphere here allows students to compete and learn from each other rather than just compete against each other." Students also "really enjoy the international perspective" added by the huge overseas segment, reporting that "Iowa's program fosters diversity. Recently a Chinese New Year celebration was held with a successful turnout." But, they add, the American students "mostly come from small cities, thereby limiting their perception of the world." Adds another, "there's only a small group of U.S. minorities, but I think it's typical of the Midwest."

Students report a heavy workload during the first-year, but note that "second-years have very light schedules, which leaves plenty of time for fun." For fun, they choose from among "a plethora of activities: academics, social, community service (both formal and informal)." The "very active" MBA Association organizes tailgate parties prior to sporting events, Spring Fling, faculty-student mixers, and lectures. It also manages the many popular student clubs, associations, and community service projects. On campus, the "unofficial hangout is the Dublin Underground" and one student cheerfully notes, "the large graduate population [at the university] means you are not stuck among a bunch of undergrads." Students have no qualms about leaving campus; Iowa City "is an excellent place to live while attending school. The town is beautiful, safe, and small yet can fill all the needs for those looking for big city conveniences." The town is also "very liberal and supports and embraces cultural diversity."

ADMISSIONS

According to the admissions office, the following components are all weighed equally: essays, college GPA, letters of recommendation, extracurriculars, work experience, and GMAT scores. The school advises, however, "Applicants are encouraged to pay particular attention to the essay component of the application process. In addition to considering quantitative factors such as GMAT scores and the undergraduate transcript, we look at prior work experience (responsibilities, not just titles), career focus and ambition, maturity, and individuality." The school recommends that applicants have some quantitative proficiency (i.e., calculus) before matriculating. Admissions decisions are made on a rolling basis until the final deadline. Students may defer admission for up to one year. Roughly one-third of all applicants are admitted.

FINANCIAL FACTS

Tuition (in/out-state)	$4,130/$11,246
Tuition per credit (in/out-state)	$230$230
Fees (in-state/out-of-state)	$202/$202
Cost of books	$1,362
Room & Board (on/off-campus)	$5,184/$5,184
% of students receiving aid	43
% first-year students receiving aid	45
% aid that is merit-based	60
% of students receiving paid internships	98
% of students receiving grants	37
Average award package	$6,671
Average grant	$2,127
Average graduation debt	$15,775

ADMISSIONS

# of applications received	762
% applicants accepted	34
% acceptees attending	30
Average GMAT (range)	610 (570–660)
Minimum TOEFL	600
Average GPA (range)	3.29 (2.93–3.58)
Application fee (in/out-state)	$20/$20
Early decision program available	No
Early decision deadline	April 15
Early decision notification	Rolling
Regular application deadline	July 15
Regular notification	Rolling
Admission may be deferred?	Yes
Maximum length of deferment	1 year
Transfer students accepted?	Yes
Non-fall admission available?	Yes
Admissions process need-blind?	Yes

APPLICANTS ALSO LOOK AT

University of Wisconsin—Madison, University of Texas at Austin, University of Michigan, University of Pennsylvania, UNC—Chapel Hill

EMPLOYMENT PROFILE

Placement rate (%)	100
# of companies recruiting on-campus	112
% grads employed immediately	75
% grads employed within six months	100
Average starting salary	$55,228

Grads employed by field (avg. salary):

Accounting	5% (NR)
Consulting	8% (NR)
Finance	40% ($64,563)
General Management	5% ($64,250)
Global Management	5% (44,000)
Human Resources	2% (NR)
Marketing	12% ($51,658)
MIS	10% ($41,500)
Operations	8% ($52,633)
Venture Capital	2% (NR)
Other	2% (NR)

UNIVERSITY OF KANSAS
School of Business

OVERVIEW

Type of school	public
Affiliation	none
Environment	suburban
Academic calendar	semester
Schedule	full-time/evening

STUDENTS

Enrollment of parent institution	27,639
Enrollment of business school	467
% male/female	68/32
% out-of-state	38
% part-time	66
% minorities	4
% international (# countries represented)	5(13)
Average age at entry	29
Average years work experience at entry	4

ACADEMICS

Student/faculty ratio	8:1
% female faculty	16
% minority faculty	12
% part-time faculty	3
Hours of study per day	4.35

SPECIALTIES

Strengths of faculty include strong research and consulting records and a genuine commitment to teaching.

JOINT DEGREES

JD/MBA, 4 years

STUDY ABROAD PROGRAMS

France, Italy, England, Japan, and Brazil

SURVEY SAYS...

HITS
Star faculty
On-campus housing
Small classes

MISSES
Social life
Quantitative skills
Presentation skills

PROMINENT ALUMNI

Jim Duff, President, U.S. Leasing International; Ed Kangas, National Managing Partner, Deloitte and Touche; Jeannine Strandjord, Vice President and controller, Sprint Corp.

ACADEMICS

Value and location are the reasons most MBAs give for choosing the University of Kansas School of Business. "The KU MBA program provides a great education for the money," sums up one student. Our survey shows that students are satisfied with the KU experience primarily because it will increase their earning power. Fewer say that the program lives up to their academic expectations, yet most report that they are happy to be earning their MBAs here, where costs are low and their prospects at graduation are high.

The KU MBA program begins with an orientation called "Challenge Week," during which students review basic computer and business research skills. Challenge Week also includes a business simulation contest and an outdoor Challenge Course, both of which are designed to foster "team-building" skills. The emphasis on teamwork carries over into the first-year curriculum, during which each student is assigned to a five-member team for all foundation core projects. Coursework is suspended twice during each of the first-year semesters for students to participate in "immersion weeks" in such subjects as Total Quality Management and Entrepreneurship. Students report that "the use of immersion weeks to present business ideas is creative. I think the weeks are excellent."

Second-year students choose from eight concentrations. They must also complete two required courses—one in business law and another in strategic management. All these requirements leave little time for electives, leading one student to write, "Overall I would say KU is conservative and wants us to stick to their laid out plan. However, there are some professors with maverick spirits that add a lot to our learning." Students give the highest marks to KUs management courses but complain that classes in marketing, accounting, information systems, and international business are weak.

KU professors receive mixed reviews. Although some students are "very pleased with the faculty's experience and talent," others complain that "some teachers think you should spend 80+ [hours] a week on school and assign an unreasonable amount of work." Several students write that they are frustrated by the "only moderate communication among administration, faculty, and students."

PLACEMENT AND RECRUITING

University of Kansas' Business Career Services Center, a placement center dedicated to both graduate and undergraduate business students, earns praise from Kansas MBAs. Writes one, "The Business Career Services Center is an excellent resource for students seeking professional employment. The quality, diversity, and number of hiring organizations is outstanding." Adds another happy customer, "The career services center has a very well-connected director and office staff. The past placement statistics are impressive and the possibilities ever-growing. If a company is not recruiting on campus, the center will put you in contact with someone in the home office."

The KU MBA program requires all students to fulfill a professional development requirement, usually by completing an internship or study abroad experience during the summer between their first and second years. The school has also recently created a new position—the career services coordinator—to

David O. Collins, Associate Director of Masters Programs
206 Summerfield Hall, Lawrence, KS 66045
Admissions: 785-864-4254 • Fax: 785-864-5328
Email: mba01@bschool.wpo.ukans.edu
Internet: www.bschool.ukans.edu/mba/mbalaw/info.htm

develop internship opportunities, provide career counseling and development activities, and market MBA students to recruiting organizations. According to the school, 200 national, regional, and local firms recruited on campus last year seeking undergraduate and/or MBA candidates. Top recruiters at KU include Sprint Corporation, Hallmark Cards, Arthur Andersen, Andersen Consulting, Deloitte & Touche, Ernst & Young, and Koch Industries.

STUDENT/CAMPUS LIFE

The majority of the Kansas student body is young. As one MBA explains, "students here are largely two to three years out of undergrad. They're a little naive." Others describe their classmates as "highly competitive," "ambitious and self-assured." Sums up one student, "There are a few students out for themselves. Overall, it's a good group of friendly, helpful colleagues. We see each other as teammates." According to our survey, KU MBAs perceive themselves as "a diverse group," but the numbers don't back this characterization up: international and minority populations are extremely low, and most students share a similar dearth of real-life work experience.

First-year students warn that "this program is time-consuming, and it is difficult to have an active personal life but that should be expected when entering an MBA program." When students' schedules open up during second year, most find that "student life is excellent. We have a great nightlife, excellent art productions, and a wide variety of activities to choose from." Agrees another, "Activities are varied. Sports events are good and fun. Cultural events are interesting. Louise's Downtown is popular for graduate students." Students enjoy Lawrence (pop. 70,000), which they describe as an "ideal college town," and also praise KU's "beautiful" campus. They warn, however, that housing can be a problem, both on- and off-campus. When small town life gets dull, students can head to "Kansas City, which is only thirty minutes away and has a lot to offer."

ADMISSIONS

According to the school, your college GPA, GMAT scores, letters of recommendation, and work experience are all weighted equally. Your extracurricular activities are also considered. Writes the admissions office, "There are no minimum scores for GPA/GMAT when considering candidates. The admissions board will also consider extra submissions, such as resumes and extra letters of recommendation." Decisions are made on a rolling admissions basis. Students are notified of a decision approximately three weeks after all application materials are received. Notes the school, "The application form, supplemental data form, and check for $50.00 must be received by the deadline. Other materials (GMAT, transcripts, letters of recommendation, TOEFL) can come in after the deadline, but a student will not be admitted without all. We have no auditing of classes for noncredit, no exceptions." Students may defer admission for up to one year with a written request.

FINANCIAL FACTS

Tuition (in/out-state)	$3,325/$10,926
Tuition per credit (in/out-state)	$98/$321
Fees (in-state/out-of-state)	$209/$209
Cost of books	$800
Room & Board (on/off-campus)	$3,736/$4,500
% aid that is merit-based	80
% of students receiving grants	10
Average grant	$1,200

ADMISSIONS

# of applications received	379
% applicants accepted	54
% acceptees attending	71
Average GMAT (range)	590 (550–640)
Minimum TOEFL	600
Average GPA (range)	3.22 (3.10–3.50)

Application fee (in/out-state)	$50/$50
Early decision program available	No
Regular application deadline	May 1
Regular notification	Rolling
Admission may be deferred?	Yes
Maximum length of deferment	1 year
Transfer students accepted?	Yes
Non-fall admission available?	Yes
Admissions process need-blind?	Yes

APPLICANTS ALSO LOOK AT

University of Texas at Austin, Arizona State University, University of Chicago, Indiana University, Harvard University, University of Wisconsin—Madison, University of Pennsylvania, Stanford University

EMPLOYMENT PROFILE

Placement rate (%)	85
# of companies recruiting on-campus	175
% grads employed immediately	85
Average starting salary	$44,518

Grads employed by field (avg. salary):

Consulting	37% ($47,133)
Entrepreneurship	2% (NR)
Finance	26% ($42,329)
General Management	4% ($42,000)
Human Resources	2% ($40,000)
Marketing	4% ($45,000)
Other	10% ($44,500)

UNIVERSITY OF KENTUCKY
Carol Martin Gatton College of Business and Economics

OVERVIEW

Type of school	public
Affiliation	none
Environment	metropolis
Academic calendar	semester
Schedule	full-time/part-time/evening

STUDENTS

Enrollment of parent institution	24,171
Enrollment of business school	254
% male/female	60/40
% out-of-state	41
% part-time	44
% minorities	8
% international (# countries represented)	16(10)
Average age at entry	27
Average years work experience at entry	3

ACADEMICS

Student/faculty ratio	5:1
% female faculty	14
% minority faculty	1
Hours of study per day	3.28

SPECIALTIES

School of Management (DSIS, Finance, Management/Organizational Behavior, Marketing) School of Accountancy, Department of Economics, Concentrations in International Business, Management Information Systems, Marketing Distribution, Finance, Real Estate and Banking, Accounting, Corporate Finance

JOINT DEGREES

MBA/JD, 4 years; BS Engineering/MBA, 5 years

SPECIAL PROGRAMS

Internships

STUDY ABROAD PROGRAMS

Austria, England, France, Germany, Australia, Wu-Wien, Heidelburg, ESC—Grenoble, RMIT Melbourne, Lancaster University, ISEP Schools worldwide. (200 through study abroad office)

SURVEY SAYS...

HITS
Star faculty
Small classes
Lexington

MISSES
Library
Finance
Presentation skills

PROMINENT ALUMNI

Edward T. Breathitt, Governor of Kentucky; Mr. Carol Martin Gatton, Donor to College of Business and Economics; James E. Rogers, Chairman, President, and CEO, PSI Holdings, Inc.

ACADEMICS

Across the board, students feel positive about their b-school experience at the University of Kentucky. Over and over, they enthused about the school's "excellent buy" in education. Indeed, relative to other schools in this book, UK features one of the lowest tuitions.

In terms of academics, UK's MBA program introduced three courses addressing contemporary issues in Global Business Management, Leadership in the Contemporary Business Environment, and Information Systems to replace older core courses. According to the school, the MBA program is considered two-track: "One track, the business track, is designed for business undergrads and emphasizes the development of a concentration in one of several areas: Finance, Real Estate and Banking, Marketing and Distribution, MIS, International Business, Accounting/Corporate Finance, and Production and Manufacturing." The other track is for those with non-business undergrad degrees who already have a concentration such as Engineering. Electives may also be taken in other university departments. Students feel the three-semester program does a good job of incorporating current events into the curriculum. We received several comments wishing for more rigor in the academic program. Ratings in several academic subjects fell last year. Although the marks students gave themselves for their academic preparedness were above average in all the major disciplines, the highest were in accounting, quantitative methods, teamwork skills, and general management. Still, students should do just fine when they take the b-school's required four-hour comprehensive exam in their final semester. No one has ever failed it.

The faculty received mixed reviews. One impressed student wrote, "Very tough, teachers are demanding and do not allow slackers." But others had less complimentary comments. "The professors are often difficult to understand, have overwhelming pride, or are just shoddy," wrote one student. Another griped that "the professors recognized in their field are not good teachers." Another student told us that "not one of my professors has been a female, or a minority." The administration got some high marks; one student claimed, "The MBA coordinator is the school's greatest strength. Marilyn Underwood is concerned that students get into classes and do well in the program." But a dissenter told us "The dean is a slacker." MBAs appreciate the school's up-to-date class facilities. Said one, "Every classroom has been networked with a state-of-the-art computing system." We heard a few complaints about the student body. One student said, "They're not as interested as I'd hoped." Another panned his classmates, saying that they're "too self-centered," and there was a general feeling that there is a lack of diverse professional experiences among classmates. One student noted, "Students with substantial business experience attend part-time, which makes it difficult to network." But all in all, the majority of students say taking time off to get a UK MBA is well worth it.

PLACEMENT AND RECRUITING

According to the school's placement office, Kentucky students follow a standard job placement procedure. The school reports: "The job search [process] starts in the first semester, when new students establish email addresses and prepare resumes for submission to the placement director. The placement director notifies all MBA students by email of full- or part-time job opportunities that arise

Dr. Michael G. Tearney, Associate Dean
237 Carol Martin Gatton College of Business and Economics, Lexington, KY 40506
Admissions: 606-257-3592 • Fax: 606-257-3293
Email: drball0l@pop.uky.edu
Internet: gatton.gws.uky.edu

University of Kentucky

and subsequently submits a file of resumes to recruiters for each advertised position. The placement director also gives aggressive supervision in a program that provides new students with internship opportunities." The school participates in the SEMBA consortium, which holds an annual job fair held in Atlanta. UK also encourages students to seek opportunities abroad through its student exchange program with "top-ranked business schools in England, France, and Austria." Many Kentucky students, it should be noted, are already employed before they come to school, and are seeking an MBA primarily to improve their prospects and rank with their current employers.

STUDENT/CAMPUS LIFE

At UK the workload is moderate, the pressure light. "It's not cutthroat, thank God," wrote one student, "I'll save that for work." The majority of students report that they hit the books an average of fifteen to twenty-five hours a week. The overwhelming majority of students use the collective expertise of their peers by working in study groups. As for those previously overstuffed classes, the administration has reduced class size dramatically, a critical improvement.

UK works hard to admit students from a variety of foreign countries, including the newly independent states of the former Soviet Union and from eastern Europe. Approximately 25 percent of the 100 students admitted each fall are international students. Yet one MBA griped, "Too many students don't have enough work experience to make valuable contributions." As for the social scene, the majority say it's lacking. There's only one student club, the MBA Association, which sponsors activities like student orientation, an MBA newsletter, a Thursday night supper club, and a few intramural sports. Students say the gym is pretty good and the "business lab and new classrooms are excellent." Other school attributes: A newly constructed Electronic Business and Economics Information Center, excellent computing facilities, an expansive library, and a summer-abroad program in Vienna, Austria, and Lancaster, England. There is also a semester-abroad exchange opportunity with ESC Grenoble and the Economics University in Vienna.

Students say one of the main advantages of UK is its location in a region of strong economic growth. Lexington is well-liked, and Louisville is only a short trip away. "Spring and fall meets at the world-renowned racetrack Keeneland are great!" raves one student. "Basketball is a huge part of the culture," said another MBA. The majority of students opt for off-campus living in the town of Lexington. But parking is a nightmare; students joke that after studying, looking for parking is their most time-consuming activity. Most students drop their cars at the football stadium and shuttlebus in.

ADMISSIONS

According to the admissions office, your GMAT score, college GPA/transcript, and the university you attended are considered most important. After that, in descending order, are your letters of recommendation, work experience, essays, and extracurricular activities. Notes the office of admissions: "Undergraduate degrees in engineering or science are considered a plus. The 100 best applications are accepted every year." Deferred admission is now possible.

FINANCIAL FACTS

Tuition (in/out-state)	$2,640/$7,920
Tuition per credit (in/out-state)	$147/$440
Fees (in-state/out-of-state)	$336/$336
Cost of books	$600
Room & Board (on/off-campus)	$5,834/$6,234
% of students receiving aid	46
% first-year students receiving aid	69
% aid that is merit-based	70
% of students receiving paid internships	50
% of students receiving grants	43
Average award package	$5,500
Average grant	$2,916

ADMISSIONS

# of applications received	341
% applicants accepted	46
% acceptees attending	64
Average GMAT (range)	590 (480–670)
Minimum TOEFL	550
Average GPA (range)	3.20 (2.60–3.90)
Application fee (in/out-state)	$30/$35
Regular application deadline	July 15
Regular notification	Rolling
Admission may be deferred?	Yes
Maximum length of deferment	3 years
Transfer students accepted?	Yes
Non-fall admission available?	No
Admissions process need-blind?	Yes

APPLICANTS ALSO LOOK AT

University of Tennessee at Knoxville, University of Georgia, Vanderbilt University, Indiana University, University of Alabama, Ohio State University, University of Texas at Austin, Arizona State University

EMPLOYMENT PROFILE

Placement rate (%)	67
# of companies recruiting on-campus	128
% grads employed immediately	67
% grads employed within six months	100
Average starting salary	$44,769

Grads employed by field (avg. salary):

Accounting	18% ($32,300)
Consulting	11% (NR)
Finance	22% ($32,125)
General Management	15% ($46,000)
Marketing	4% (NR)
MIS	33% ($51,000)
Operations	11% (NR)
Other	12% ($39,900)

LOYOLA UNIVERSITY
Chicago Graduate School of Business

ACADEMICS

Loyola University—Chicago offers an MBA program well-suited to the needs of working Chicagoans. The vast majority of Loyola MBAs are part-timers, who are drawn to the school by the availability of evening classes and a quarterly academic schedule that "allows you to complete the program faster." Students report that "Loyola accommodates the part-time student very well with extended office hours, career fairs in the evenings, evening and weekend classes, email announcements, etc."

Loyola is a Jesuit school, and according to the school "is strongly influenced by the Jesuit tradition, which stresses excellence in teaching and research . . . and the role of ethics in business decision making." Students report that Loyola meets these goals, giving professors good grades both for teaching ability and accessibility. Writes one student, "I have found very good teachers, especially in finance . . . they are accessible outside class, too." Adds another, "Professors are very knowledgeable and helpful, and the environment is very good." Ethical perspectives are interwoven in all course material; in addition, all students must complete one course dedicated entirely to ethical issues in business.

To serve the needs of its part-time student body, Loyola allows students a lot of leeway in creating their course schedules. Students are even given options in selecting their core courses, including the option of placing out if they can demonstrate proficiency. One student appreciates the "flexibility of the MBA program, permitting you to make your own schedule and thus concentrate in what you are really interested in." Second-year students may concentrate in a "field of specialization" but need not do so, if they choose instead to pursue a general curriculum. Students speak highly of Loyola's finance, health care administration, and information systems departments. Notes one student, "I chose Loyola because it offers technical MIS classes (e.g. C++). Most other schools do not." Loyola students also praise the school's "great facilities, especially the library and computer labs."

Loyola has recently changed its curriculum in an effort to place greater emphasis on international business studies, adding a required course in international business. The school also encourages students to take advantage of a two-week intensive summer course at its Rome campus, an option students describe as worthwhile. Opportunities to study in Bangkok and Greece are also available.

PLACEMENT AND RECRUITING

Loyola's MBA Career Services office coordinates workshops, job boards, an employer database, internships, and job fairs for its MBAs. In addition, students within six months of graduation can register with Career Services for inclusion in the Loyola resume books, resume referral program, on-campus interviews, and the Midwest MBA Consortium. Furthermore, the office conducts videotaped mock interview sessions twice a year and maintains an alumni database, accessible to students nearing graduation.

Paul Davidovitch, Director
820 North Michigan Avenue, Chicago, IL 60611
Admissions: 312-915-6120 • Fax: 312-915-7207
Email: mba-loyola@luc.edu
Internet: www.luc.edu/depts/mba

Loyola University

Students give the service average grades, telling us that "We need to expand career placement. They do a great job, but they could get more employers to recruit on campus." Students also complain that the "fellowship/assistantship program could use a more formal, organized structure." The burden on the service is lessened somewhat by the fact that some Loyola students pursue their MBAs to improve their stature at their current place of employment rather than to find new employers.

STUDENT/CAMPUS LIFE

Loyola's student body is "mainly [made up of] part-time students with a significant amount of work experience." They are a diverse group of people who "differ greatly in age, work experience, and cultural backgrounds," and include "many international students," which means "a lot of students from Thai Loyola University." Writes one student, "In my last four classes—all with group projects—we've had groups with students from the United States, Canada, Thailand, Korea, Ecuador, Venezuela, Colombia, and Brazil . . . we learn a lot." Students describe their classmates as "down-to-earth, intelligent, [and] motivated." African-American students warn, however, that their ranks are small; much of the minority population here is made up of Asian-Americans.

With so many students attending part-time—often while holding down full-time jobs—it is understandable that campus life at Loyola is subdued. Students report that the "GBA (Graduate Business Association) provides tons of social and professional events, for example a job fair, Cubs games, and wine-tasting." The Distinguished Speaker Series brings national leaders to campus to discuss current events and issues; recent topics have included business ethics, world trade agreements, banking reform, and the future of the American economy. Beyond campus, of course, is Chicago, one of the world's most active financial trading centers. Chicago is also one of the great American cities, offering a cornucopia of culture, entertainment, dining, and nightlife. One student explains, "This school is in the hub of the Chicagoland area and offers many opportunities to relax from the pressures of school." Adds another, "Social life is great. There's plenty to do in Chicago outside school, time permitting."

ADMISSIONS

Despite its generous 46 percent acceptance rate, Loyola places some exacting demands on its applicants. Academic strength, GMAT scores, work experience, recommendations, quality of undergraduate institution and difficulty of major, and extracurricular activities are considered, in that order. These fairly ordinary criteria become somewhat more daunting when you consider that the average Loyola MBA candidate has four years of work experience before enrollment—twice that of most other schools' applicants.

FINANCIAL FACTS

Tuition	$16,542
Tuition per credit	$613
Fees	$117
Cost of books	$900
Room & Board (on/off-campus)	$6,600/NR
% of students receiving loans	94
Average grant	$17,000

ADMISSIONS

# of applications received	646
% applicants accepted	46
% acceptees attending	72
Average GMAT (range)	530 (400–780)
Average GPA (range)	3.10 (2.50–4.00)
Application fee (in/out-state)	$20
Early decision program available	No
Early decision deadline	May 1
Regular application deadline	July 31
Regular notification	Rolling
Admission may be deferred?	Yes
Maximum length of deferment	1 year
Transfer students accepted?	Yes
Non-fall admission available?	Yes
Admissions process need-blind?	Yes

APPLICANTS ALSO LOOK AT

Northwestern University, University of Chicago, University of Illinois at Urbana-Champaign, University of Notre Dame, Georgetown University, University of Michigan Business School, University of California—Los Angeles, New York University

EMPLOYMENT PROFILE

Placement rate (%)	92
% grads employed immediately	84
% grads employed within six months	80
Average starting salary	$51,578

Grads employed by field (avg. salary):

Accounting	5% (NR)
Consulting	13% (NR)
Finance	42% ($46,543)
General Management	15% ($45,938)
Human Resources	8% (NR)
Marketing	22% ($41,042)
MIS	7% ($55,500)
Operations	9% ($58,800)
Strategic Planning	2% (NR)
Other	5% ($54,333)

UNIVERSITY OF MARYLAND
Robert H. Smith School of Business

OVERVIEW
Type of school	public
Affiliation	none
Environment	metropolis
Academic calendar	semester
Schedule	part-time/full-time

STUDENTS
Enrollment of parent institution	32,711
Enrollment of business school	927
% male/female	64/36
% part-time	46
% minorities	13
% international (# countries represented)	23(25)
Average age at entry	27
Average years work experience at entry	4

ACADEMICS
% part-time faculty	15
Hours of study per day	4.18

SPECIALTIES
Entrepreneurship, Transportation and Logistics, International Business, Management Science. Information Systems Statistics, Marketing , Finance, Accounting , Management Consulting, Organizational Change, Human Resources, Cross-functional Concentration: Financial engineering, Electronic Commerce, Logistics and Supply Chain Management, and Business Telecommunications

JOINT DEGREES
MBA/JD, MBA/Masters of Public Management, MBA/Master of Social Work, MBA/Master of Science

SPECIAL PROGRAMS
The Terrapin Fund is a year-long, seminar for 2nd years about: Portfolio Management Theory and Practice; Security Screening and Selection; Economic and Industry Analysis; Corporate Qualitative and Financial Analysis; Valuation Analysis; and Trading Strategies

STUDY ABROAD PROGRAMS
Norway; Belgium; France; Venezuela; England; Australia

SURVEY SAYS...
HITS
Diversity of work experience
Ethnic and racial diversity
Can't wait to network

MISSES
Safety
On-campus housing
MIS/operations

PROMINENT ALUMNI
Leo Van Munching, Jr., President of Van Munching and Co., Inc.; Robert H. Smith, Co-Chief Executive Officer and Co-chairman of the Board of Charles E. Smith Residential Realty Inc.

ACADEMICS

On a campus known to undergraduates as "Party Park," Maryland MBAs seem to be having a party of a very different kind. Cloistered in the southwest quadrant of this huge campus, the Maryland Business School inspires some extremely enthusiastic student responses. And the party is about to get better: a recent $15 million gift from Robert H. Smith, developer of Virginia's mammoth high-rise residential complex, Crystal City, is earmarked for upgrades in faculty, financial assistance to students, and the Graduate Career Management Center. The school was recently renamed in Smith's honor.

Add to this the business school's new, state-of-the-art facility and the full automation of cumbersome administrative tasks, and you can understand why students here are so cheerful. "The school runs like butter since the technology upgrade took effect," writes one student. "Registration, billing, everything is online." No wonder students here view the administration more charitably than do students at other state-run schools. "The school administration," writes one, "is responsive to student demands. If you have a point to make, you'll be heard." Another understanding student adds that the "administration seems understaffed, but they work hard."

Maryland stresses experiential learning, primarily through a series of required courses called, unsurprisingly, Experiential Learning Modules (ELM). Explains one student, "Every term we have two weeks of workshops in different topics (job search, teamwork and diversity, Washington experience). I find these ELMs to be outstanding." Second year requires fewer ELMs, but includes a Group Field Project, in which students are required to "balance theory with practical application." One student explains the difference between the two years this way: "First year carries a heavy workload, numerous team-building activities. Second year entails more career-focused activities, as well as excellent social and academic opportunities." Second-year students also have many more elective options than do first-years, who must complete the core curriculum.

Among the school's departments, students most often praise marketing, finance, and "the best entrepreneurship program locally available." Students also appreciate Maryland's focus on technology, telling us that "one of the reasons I chose MBS was its strong technology emphasis. As an engineer, I feel it's very important to stay current. At MBS, you can." Professors "are good at integrating theory and practice" but "should take a more active role in monitoring GAs/TAs and getting them involved with study groups." Some also complain that "visiting profs and adjunct staff leave a lot to be desired."

PLACEMENT AND RECRUITING

Maryland's Graduate Career Management Center (GCMC) earns high marks from students for its personal service and its ability to attract high-quality recruiters to campus. In addition to their approval of the GCMC's current services, students also note that the "placement office is undergoing substantial improvements."

The GCMC organizes workshops and "networking receptions" for first-year students, assists in the search for summer internships, and runs the Career Management ELM at the beginning of the second year. This program is designed to

Sabrina White, Director of MBA/MS Admission
MBA Office, College Park, MD 20742
Admissions: 301-405-2279 • Internet: www.mbs.umd.edu

University of Maryland

hone students' interviewing and communications skills by providing "hands-on instruction in everything from business etiquette to salary-offer negotiation." More than one hundred companies recruit on campus during a typical year at College Park. The school also participates in the MBA Career Forum in Chicago.

STUDENT/CAMPUS LIFE

As they are about all other aspects of their program, Maryland students are enthusiastic about their classmates. One student sums up the attitude: "The greatest thing about this school has to be the students. My classmates are of exceptional character. They are intelligent, fun, and personable. They bring a wide variety of experiences to the classroom, enriching my educational experience. They are also willing to help their classmates succeed. It is a great environment in which to go to school." Diversity comes in the form of "many foreign students and students from all over the U.S. A very good mix of people and experiences." A substantial portion of the "very competitive but friendly" student body "commute from long distances," and "a large portion are married/engaged." Some students warn that there is a "big rift between the part-time and full-time students."

Because so many students commute to College Park, relatively small portions of Maryland MBAs are active in extracurricular activities. Those who do participate report that there is an "abundance of clubs, social, and career activities." Another student confirms that "campus life offers me lots of options to enjoy my time outside of class. Gym facilities, the Marie Theater, dining halls, etc." Although College Park is a giant campus, students note that "the business school is like a campus in itself: tight-knit, easy to get to know others" and so boasts many of the assets of a smaller school. Once off-campus, students find that the "area near College Park sucks. You have to travel about a half-hour to go places that are fun and safe." Nearby Washington, DC, however, "the Mecca for high tech" as well as government, "provides plenty of cultural, political, and nightlife activities." Commuters are "pleased with the school's attention to commuter needs" but agree that "parking is a major hassle."

ADMISSIONS

According to the admissions office, your GMAT score, college GPA, and work experience are considered "very important." Your essays, interview, letters of recommendation, and extracurricular activities are considered "important."

Decisions are made on a rolling admissions basis. Typically applicants are notified of a decision eight weeks after the completed application has been received. Accepted applicants may defer admission for up to one year.

FINANCIAL FACTS

Tuition (in/out-state)	$8,730/$12,960
Fees (in-state/out-of-state)	$1,150/$1,150
Cost of books	$2,000
Room & Board (on/off-campus)	$2,899/NR
% of students receiving aid	175
% first-year students receiving aid	75
% aid that is merit-based	35
% of students receiving paid internships	95
Average award package	$14,000
Average grant	$5,000

ADMISSIONS

# of applications received	1,553
% applicants accepted	26
% acceptees attending	52
Average GMAT (range)	646 (600–680)
Minimum TOEFL	600
Average GPA (range)	3.34 (3.10–3.70)

Application fee (in/out-state)	$40
Early decision program available	Yes
Early decision deadline	February 1
Regular notification	Rolling
Admission may be deferred?	Yes
Maximum length of deferment	1 year
Transfer students accepted?	Yes
Non-fall admission available?	Yes
Admissions process need-blind?	Yes

APPLICANTS ALSO LOOK AT

Georgetown University, University of North Carolina at Chapel Hill, University of Virginia, University of Pennsylvania, Duke University, University of Texas at Austin, Wake Forest University, Indiana University

EMPLOYMENT PROFILE

Average starting salary	NR

Grads employed by field (avg. salary):

Consulting	NR ($58,703)
Finance	NR ($67,750)
Marketing	NR ($62,100)
MIS	NR ($60,758)
Operations	NR ($53,333)
Other	NR ($57,000)

UNIVERSITY OF MASSACHUSETTS AT AMHERST
Isenberg School of Management

OVERVIEW

Type of school	public
Affiliation	none
Environment	suburban
Academic calendar	semester

STUDENTS

Enrollment of parent institution	23,932
Enrollment of business school	66
% male/female	64/36
% out-of-state	14
% part-time	78
% minorities	8
% international (# countries represented)	33(11)
Average age at entry	28
Average years work experience at entry	4

ACADEMICS

Student/faculty ratio	35:1
% female faculty	18
% minority faculty	7
Hours of study per day	4.24

SPECIALTIES
Research orientation of the faculty, the small, intimate nature of the program; the quality of educational material; presentation of a very committed faculty.

JOINT DEGREES
none

STUDY ABROAD PROGRAMS
France — Roven; Sweden — Lund

SURVEY SAYS...
HITS
Getting into courses a breeze
Small classes
Marketing

MISSES
Finance
Presentation skills
Computer skills

PROMINENT ALUMNI
Roger Johnson, Administrator, General Service Administration; Peter Mawn, Senior Vice President, Fidelity Mgmt Trust Co.; Michael Philipp, Global Head of Sales; Deutsche Morgan Brenfell, London

ACADEMICS

The University of Massachusetts School of Management has only forty students in this year's class. You can know everyone's name in a day. SOM used to enroll ninety students a year, but downsized the enrollment so the administration could perform a review of the program. There's no word yet on when they'll re-inflate to their previous size.

The SOM trains its students to be general managers. During the first-year, students take eight required courses in the functional areas of business and have one elective. During the second year, students have up to four electives to specialize in fields such as accounting, finance, marketing, human resources management, and management information systems. Because courses emphasize quantitative methods, all students are expected to be proficient in math and to have previously taken a statistics and microeconomics course. In a unique program twist, students can supplement classwork with research and public service. Students report that their academic experience is "very sound." They feel well prepared in marketing, quantitative methods, accounting, and general management. Perhaps because teamwork is emphasized, or because the whole school is no bigger than an extended study group, students also said they possess strong teamwork skills. The small class size gives students a lot of interaction with the faculty. Several students cited the accounting faculty as particularly strong. Overall, teachers received mixed reviews. "Professors care about what they are teaching and that students are learning the material," said one MBA. "I strongly believe some of my professors could teach in any school in this country," wrote another supporter. But a critic noted "about half the professors are excellent, but I can't say anything good about the other half." The administration received mixed reviews as well. One student told us they had "a terrific dean," but another complained "the administration appears to be more committed to the professional MBA program (the night school) than the full-time, day MBA program." Students would like a larger selection of electives (including more MIS offerings), a bigger computer lab, and a little more work experience in their peers. But students are more than satisfied. "I look forward to going to class," wrote one. And the value can't be beat; it's almost free. As one MBA noted, "Ninety-nine percent of full-time students are fully funded. Tuition is waived, and we receive a modest stipend. Where else can you get a graduate degree for that price—plus access to all the other graduate programs across the campus?"

PLACEMENT AND RECRUITING

The placement office at U Mass has recently undergone some major changes in response to student dissatisfaction with the service. The school reports that the new office "provides individual career coaching, resume and cover letter workshops, corporate mock interview sessions, a career seminar at orientation, [and] recruitment and job postings. A strong relationship with other U Mass Amherst career centers allows for additional recruitment opportunities. A central component of the Career Management Office is the establishment of a new MBA Alumni Career Network. The response from alums has been impressive.

Heather Miller, Admissions Director
209 School of Management, Amherst, MA 01003
Admissions: 413-545-5608 • Fax: 413-545-3858
Email: gradprog@som.umass.edu
Internet: www.som.umass.edu

Additionally, a clear benefit of the small size of the MBA program is the exceptional career networking opportunities that exist with faculty, deans, and fellow students." The changes occurred too recently for our survey to gauge student reaction.

STUDENT/CAMPUS LIFE

The size of the UMass academic community is what makes it special. Many cite the sense of community as what they like best about the program. "It's not cutthroat at all," wrote one MBA. "The atmosphere is friendly, and learning is the common goal." "There's a good team spirit within the classes," concurred another student. "The class size reduces competition among peers because all students know each other on a personal level." Unusually for a b-school, the students report that the first and second year students are quite close. What this school lacks in size, it makes up for in academic rigor. A demanding and challenging curriculum keeps most students buried in their books an average of twenty to thirty hours a week. Although the majority of students say it's important to do all or most of the reading, some report they regularly skim assignments. But students are certainly up to the workload; their peers consider them "extremely intelligent," "professionally diverse," and, best of all, "down to earth."

Amherst is a quintessential college town in suburban Massachusetts. Students report that both on- and off-campus housing is more than adequate and affordable. They also say there's "plenty of opportunity to socialize outside of class," including "art and musical events, bar hopping, and intramural sports." Though SOM is small, the surrounding academic community is immense. "There's something for everyone here," agreed students, and most say they're "very happy."

ADMISSIONS

The admissions office considers your work experience most important. After that, in descending order, are your GMAT score, letters of recommendation, college GPA, and essays. Extracurricular activities and interviews are not considered. It is recommended that applicants complete courses in microeconomics and statistics before applying. Writes the school, "We are willing to make a number of academically 'high-risk' admissions decisions if we feel an individual has the potential to make a significant contribution to the business community. The strength of our program lies in its small size. Each student receives a great deal of individual attention from faculty and administrators."

FINANCIAL FACTS

Tuition (in/out-state)	$2,084/$6,637
Fees (in-state/out-of-state)	$2,773/$2,807
Cost of books	$1,900
Room & Board (on/off-campus)	$4,230/$6,500
% of students receiving aid	95
% first-year students receiving aid	95
% aid that is merit-based	85
% of students receiving loans	40
% of students receiving grants	5
Average award package	$15,000
Average grant	$11,870

ADMISSIONS

# of applications received	307
% applicants accepted	21
% acceptees attending	54
Average GMAT (range)	593 (520–720)
Minimum TOEFL	600
Average GPA (range)	3.30 (2.50–3.80)

Application fee (in/out-state)	$25/$40
Early decision program available	No
Regular application deadline	March 1
Regular notification	April 15
Admission may be deferred?	Yes
Maximum length of deferment	1 year
Transfer students accepted?	No
Non-fall admission available?	No
Admissions process need-blind?	Yes

APPLICANTS ALSO LOOK AT

University of Maryland, Boston University, Dartmouth College, University of California—Los Angeles, University of Connecticut, University of Michigan Business School, University of Texas at Austin, University of Virginia

MASSACHUSETTS INSTITUTE OF TECHNOLOGY
Sloan School of Management

OVERVIEW

Type of school	private
Affiliation	none
Environment	metropolis
Academic calendar	semester
Schedule	full-time only

STUDENTS

Enrollment of parent institution	9,947
Enrollment of business school	711
% male/female	73/27
% out-of-state	81
% minorities	18
% international (# countries represented)	38(61)
Average age at entry	28
Average years work experience at entry	5

ACADEMICS

Student/faculty ratio	10:1
% female faculty	12
% minority faculty	7
Hours of study per day	5.24

SPECIALTIES

Strengths of faculty and curriculum in Financial Engineering, Financial Management, Strategic Management/Consulting, Product and Venture Development, Strategic Information Technology, Operations Management/Manufacturing.

JOINT DEGREES

SM in Management/SM in Engineering (one of six departments), 2 years

SPECIAL PROGRAMS

The MIT-Japan Program in Science, Technology, and Management

STUDY ABROAD PROGRAMS

London Business School and I.E.S.E.

SURVEY SAYS...

HITS
Quantitative skills
Ethnic and racial diversity
Classmates are smart

MISSES
Gym
Campus is ugly
School clubs

PROMINENT ALUMNI

Richard Ayers, Chairman and CEO, Stanley Works; Judy Lewent, CFO, Merck and Co.; John Reed, Chairman, Citicorp; Mitchell Kapor, Founder, Lotus Development Co.; William Ford, Chairman, Ford Motor Co.; Benjamin Netanyahu, Prime Minister, Israel; Kofi Annan, General Secretary, United Nations.

ACADEMICS

The Sloan School of Management is not just the "top school for high-tech business," as would be expected of a school run under the auspices of MIT. Sloan is also a top performer in finance, management, manufacturing operations, international business, entrepreneurship, and economics (brags one student, "Our economics department has to be the best in the world!"). In fact, students give Sloan top grades in all academic disciplines here except marketing.

Technology, of course, is the bread and butter of parent institution MIT, and students on Sloan's information technology track benefit from the cutting-edge research being done within the university walls. So, too, do finance students, who have access to a $3.5 million trading floor that is virtually identical to the ones in the world's financial capitals. The trading floor not only allows students to gain practical trading experience, but also provides the data for MIT's pioneering research in financial engineering, a new field dedicated primarily to developing the tools with which to analyze the increasingly complex world markets. In manufacturing, the Leaders for Manufacturing program partners the b-school, the school of engineering, and thirteen corporations in a cooperative endeavor to develop new methods of manufacturing and manufacturing education.

Sloan's core requirements take up only a single semester's work, a system that yields mixed results. While students are pleased to get requirements out of the way quickly, they also suggest that the school "make the core courses wider, that is, make it a full year of required courses, not just one semester. The core currently does not require finance theory or marketing, but it should." Furthermore, under the current system "first semester is like boot camp at the Air Force Academy." Students note that the workload lightens appreciably after core courses are completed. They also have the opportunity to choose from more than 100 courses offered each semester.

In all areas at Sloan, "Teamwork is paramount, and group and academic projects reflect this philosophy." Students recognize that they are privileged to study with a "first-rate faculty, second to none." Writes one student, "We have classes with Nobel Prize winners and even get together with them at their places for a beer." They also report that "Administration and professors listen to student comments and complaints, and work to improve courses and overall course load. Professors will make changes mid-semester!"

PLACEMENT AND RECRUITING

Students at Sloan approve of the job done by the school's Career Development Office (CDO), with more than 70 percent expressing a high level of satisfaction with the range and diversity of companies recruiting on campus. Top recruiters here include Hewlett-Packard, McKinsey, A.T. Kearney, Booz-Allen & Hamilton, Motorola, Citibank, Merrill Lynch, and Lehman Brothers. Manufacturers, hi-tech, and bio-tech firms are also well represented among those hiring Sloan graduates.

Rod Garcia, Admissions Director
E52-126, Cambridge, MA 02139
Admissions: 617-253-3730 • Fax: 617-253-6405
Email: mbaadmissions@sloan.mit.edu
Internet: web.mit.edu/sloan/www

Massachusetts Institute of Technology

Sloan's CDO works hard to stay at the top of the heap, engaging in extensive market development work that has resulted in many new on-campus recruiting companies and an increase in job postings. Marketing is no doubt made easier by Sloan's extremely impressive list of alums, which includes: Judy Lewent, CFO, Merck; John Reed, Chair, Citicorp; Richard Avers, Chair and CEO, Stanley Works; Mitch Kapor, Founder, Lotus Development Group; and Kofi Annan, Secretary-General, United Nations.

STUDENT/CAMPUS LIFE

It should come as little surprise that most Sloan students find their classmates an impressive bunch: "Sloan's student body makes the school. People here are motivated, interested in a wide variety of subjects, and very willing to help their fellow students. They are collegial both in and out of class." Many describe fellow students as "incredibly intelligent." The student body at this "racially and ethnically diverse," "very international school" is made up of "one-half engineers, one-half from every walk of life." Most students "keep a good balance between private life and school," "working hard but in a friendly team environment. We make time to relax and have fun!"

Students at Sloan describe an active extracurricular scene. "Life at Sloan is a whirlwind of speakers, activities, lectures, and coursework." Another student adds, "You can get involved in as much as you want at Sloan, and can have an impact on the school and community. The variety of activities (speeches, workshops, parties, etc.) offered adds to the quality of life." A "great social life, with mixers and happy hours at least twice a week" is highlighted by Consumption Functions, known as "C-Functions" among students and faculty. "There is a strong sense of community at Sloan. Every Thursday we have a C-Function where almost the entire student community gets together. Most C-Functions have a theme (e.g., Latin America C-Function). Most are sponsored by companies." Students describe the campus as "fairly safe," but complain that "on-campus housing is poor," the "physical plant needs help," and "parking is a big problem." MIT is located in Cambridge, near Harvard and just across the Charles River from downtown Boston. Public transportation makes travel around the student-friendly city easy even for those without cars.

ADMISSIONS

Incoming students are expected to have completed calculus and economic theory before matriculating. If you wind up taking these courses at MIT, as one student put it, expect "math hell!" Gaining admission to MIT is no walk in the park. From an applicant pool of more than 3,400, Sloan fills a class with just over 350 strong. The admissions committee considers GMAT score, undergraduate GPA, quality of undergraduate school and coursework, recommendations, and essays.

FINANCIAL FACTS

Tuition	$25,800
Room & Board (on/off-campus)	$16,000/NR
% of students receiving loans	40
% of students receiving paid internships	50
% of students receiving grants	4

ADMISSIONS

# of applications received	3,394
% applicants accepted	14
% acceptees attending	75
Average GMAT (range)	663 (610–740)
Minimum TOEFL	600
Average GPA (range)	3.50 (3.20–3.90)

Application fee (in/out-state)	$125/$150
Early decision program available	No
Regular application deadline	January 31
Regular notification	March 30
Admission may be deferred?	Yes
Transfer students accepted?	No
Non-fall admission available?	No
Admissions process need-blind?	Yes

APPLICANTS ALSO LOOK AT

Harvard University, Stanford University, University of Pennsylvania, University of Chicago, Columbia University, Northwestern University, Dartmouth College, University of California—Berkeley

EMPLOYMENT PROFILE

Placement rate (%)	100
# of companies recruiting on-campus	214
% grads employed immediately	96
% grads employed within six months	98
Average starting salary	$78,200

Grads employed by field (avg. salary):

Communications	3% ($76,200)
Consulting	46% ($84,700)
Finance	26% ($74,100)
Marketing	6% ($74,700)
Operations	17% ($74,900)
Strategic Planning	3% ($84,700)
Other	

UNIVERSITY OF MICHIGAN
University of Michigan Business School

OVERVIEW

Type of school	public
Affiliation	none
Environment	metropolis
Academic calendar	semester
Schedule	full-time only

STUDENTS

Enrollment of parent institution	21,971
Enrollment of business school	862
% male/female	74/26
% out-of-state	90
% minorities	25
% international (# countries represented)	28(40)
Average age at entry	27
Average years work experience at entry	5

ACADEMICS

Student/faculty ratio	17:1
% female faculty	23
% minority faculty	20
% part-time faculty	40
Hours of study per day	4.66

SPECIALTIES

General Management, Finance, Marketing, Accounting. Curriculum allows student specialization or general management focus and combines academic excellence with in-depth professional development.

JOINT DEGREES

Manufacturing; Environmental Management

SPECIAL PROGRAMS

Executive Skills Seminars; Leadership Development Program; International in-company learning (Europe, Asia, Africa, S. America); required in-company; international network of corporate partnerships

STUDY ABROAD PROGRAMS

Australia, Austria, Costa Rica, Denmark, Finland, France, Germany, Italy, The Netherlands, Singapore, Spain, Sweden, Switzerland, United Kingdom

SURVEY SAYS...

HITS
Alumni helpful in job search
Study groups
Library

MISSES
Campus is ugly
Safety
School clubs

PROMINENT ALUMNI

Steve Sanger, Chairman and CEO, General Mills; Robert Shaye, Chairman and CEO, New Line Cinema; George Farr, Vice Chairman, American Express

ACADEMICS

Michigan has a well-deserved reputation as one of the best b-schools in the nation, boasting strong academic programs across the board and a general management focus. But Michigan has decided to go one step further and teach students what they'll need to know in the coming decades. The result is a progressive curriculum that incorporates interdisciplinary approaches, team-teaching, action-based learning, and 1990's themes like global business and citizenship. A cornerstone of the program is the Multidisciplinary Action Project (MAP), a seven-week business apprenticeship that puts first-year students to work for real-life companies doing a multidisciplinary exercise in process analysis. The MAP exercise often ends with a presentation to the CEO and other top executives. Students love the exercise for its hands-on training. They're also wild about their dean, whom students credit with the trail-blazing direction of the school. Students brag about Dean White's strong vision. White has introduced the Michigan MBA program to intensive professional and leadership development that maximizes graduates' effectiveness plus gives them extensive experiential learning opportunities outside of the United States.

Students told us Michigan had prepared them well in subjects across the board. General management and teamwork skills were rated highest. Almost 70 percent of the students say that the program taught teamwork skills "very well." Fifty-six percent say Michigan taught them excellent general management skills; the sizable remainder describe them as "very good." Only 8 percent say their training in this area was "okay" or "less than okay." Marketing and Finance received high scores as well. Operations lagged, still it showed improvement from how it fared in our last survey. Here's the actual operations breakdown: 20 percent of students thought they developed "excellent" operations skills, 36 percent describe them as "very good," while 25 percent say they were just "okay." Quantitative skills, on the other hand, not only showed an improvement, but seemed to be over the top, with 82 percent of students describing them as "very good" or "better." MBAs are unanimous, however, in their overall opinion of this program: This is an outstanding program that is more than meeting their academic needs.

PLACEMENT AND RECRUITING

Students saw an improvement in the Placement Office this year, with 71 percent ranking the office good or excellent, up from 64 percent last year. Forty-seven percent of students say the quality of campus recruiting is excellent. Brand management gets highest marks for representation; investment banking, the lowest. In 1995, 360 companies recruited on-campus for permanent positions. Ninety-five percent of graduating MBAs reported accepting a position by July.

STUDENT/CAMPUS LIFE

The Michigan b-school boasts a sleek, modern, multi-building structure and amazing facilities. To foster strong academic and social relationships, Michigan sections the entering class of 400 into a more manageable size of six groups of roughly seventy students each. Reveals one MBA, "At first I was reluctant to come here because the school is relatively large, and I thought I wouldn't receive personal attention. My fears were completely unfounded as things here are very

Jeanne Wilt, Director of Admissions
701 Tappan Street, Ann Arbor, MI 48109
Admissions: 734-763-5796 • Fax: 313-763-7804
Email: umbusmba@umich.edu
Internet: www.bus.umich.edu

personal." Students take all their first-year classes with their section mates, and travel in packs from classroom to classroom. Popular classes are reportedly easy to get into. Students endure a heavy workload and spend an average of thirty to forty hours a week studying. Says one student, "I am constantly challenged to develop my skills, yet the atmosphere here is not overly competitive (except during interview time)." Says another on constant pressure to do the job search, "The emphasis at the school on the whole job search process is totally nauseating." Agrees another, "From the first day, the school starts working as an employment agency." Students say their classmates are competitive, extremely smart, very friendly, and genuinely interested in helping each other. Indeed, about the only time this place gets competitive, students say, is during "interview time."

As for Michigan's home town of Ann Arbor, commonly referred to as A2, students were very enthusiastic: "It's small enough to be easy to deal with while offering a rich array of cultural events." Obviously, the winters are brutal. To get through the winters, you'd better like football and basketball: "It's the only top 10 MBA program with a top 10 basketball and football team." Always popular are the pre-game tailgate parties. In addition, an active student body gets involved in intramural sports such as football, racquetball, and soccer. Two favorite events are the b-school Faculty Auction and the Spring Swing formal. Michigan offers more than twenty-two student clubs that focus on practical business issues. Whether it's arranging a panel discussion with Apple Computer founder Steven Jobs or organizing a fundraiser for developing countries, students learn as much outside of the classroom as they do in it. One MBA says, "The honor code is impressive. The students value it and act accordingly in the classroom." They also say they appreciate and benefit from Michigan's diversity. If you're looking to broaden your experiences and go to school with a diverse and happily integrated student body, this is the place. This school attracts more minorities than any other b-school profiled in this book.

ADMISSIONS

According to the admissions office, the following criteria are considered: essays, college GPA, letters of recommendation, extracurricular activities, work experience, interview, and GMAT score. A college-level calculus course must be completed before enrollment. Applicants are strongly encouraged to interview. The school asks applicants to note alumni ties in their applications, but does not reserve places in the class for those related to alumni. The school notes, "We do not use any 'formulas' or numerical cutoffs in admitting students." Michigan uses a batch admissions system with three deadlines: December 1, January 15, and March 1. There is an advantage to applicants who apply well before the March 1 deadline. Applications past the deadline are considered on a space-available basis. There is not a fixed allocation of space for in-state and out-of-state students.

FINANCIAL FACTS

Tuition (in/out-state)	$18,400/$24,000
Cost of books	$1,000
Room & Board (on/off-campus)	$7,800/$7,800
% of students receiving aid	65
% first-year students receiving aid	60
% of students receiving loans	60
Average award package	$22,000
Average grant	$13,700
Average graduation debt	$22,000

ADMISSIONS

# of applications received	4,145
% applicants accepted	22
% acceptees attending	46
Average GMAT (range)	662 (600–720)
Minimum TOEFL	600
Average GPA (range)	3.32 (2.90–3.80)
Application fee (in/out-state)	$100/$100
Early decision program available	No
Early decision notification	December 1
Regular application deadline	Dec 1; Jan 15; Mar 1
Regular notification	Feb 1; Mar 15; May 1
Admission may be deferred?	No
Transfer students accepted?	No
Non-fall admission available?	No
Admissions process need-blind?	Yes

APPLICANTS ALSO LOOK AT
Northwestern University, University of Chicago, Harvard University, University of Virginia, Stanford University, University of Pennsylvania

EMPLOYMENT PROFILE

Placement rate (%)	100
# of companies recruiting on-campus	308
% grads employed immediately	94
% grads employed within six months	100
Average starting salary	NR

Grads employed by field (avg. salary):

Consulting	28% ($109,000)
Finance	31% ($84,000)
General Management	11% ($82,000)
Human Resources	2% ($69,000)
Marketing	19% ($78,000)
MIS	2% ($85,000)
Operations	2% ($95,000)
Strategic Planning	2% ($86,000)
Venture Capital	2% ($75,000)

MICHIGAN STATE UNIVERSITY
Eli Broad Graduate School of Management

ACADEMICS

A strong national reputation, low tuition, and "a program that involves all the important concepts to be an efficient manager" attract applicants from all over the world to the Eli Broad Graduate School of Management at Michigan State University. Broad MBAs report a high degree of satisfaction with their program, telling us that "diversity and the team concept are the greatest strengths of this school. They are ably supported by a very responsive faculty and staff."

The Broad MBA program is a program in transition. It has recently improved many of its facilities, adding high-tech classrooms with a computer interface and power source at every desk, computer labs, and a brand new business library with three times the capacity of its predecessor. Even more importantly, the Broad School has revamped its curriculum to more fully integrate core courses and to increase in-class opportunities for team study and problem solving. The new curriculum notably includes the Leadership Alliance Program: a learning opportunity in which first-year students work with an experienced upper-level executive "from a leading-edge organization" in order to "bring the real-world business environment into the classroom and to demonstrate how academic concepts and theories are implemented in progressive organizations." Of these changes, students tell us, "Coordination of the new curriculum needs work, but there has been considerable improvement already. While there have been problems, the changes have also been very rewarding." Helping to iron out the kinks is an administration that "is extremely receptive to student feedback. The school is very committed to the MBA program."

First-year at Broad begins with two weeks of quantitative review (required of students with poor quant backgrounds and for fast-track students, voluntary for all others) followed by a required orientation, during which students are divided into cohort study teams. The core curriculum is organized by concept, with students focusing on the role of the firm during first semester, and on the value chain during second semester. Second-year students are encouraged to develop dual concentrations. Among Broad's eight areas of concentration, general management, manufacturing, and supply-chain management earn students' highest praises. Broad MBAs give their professors high marks for teaching ability and accessibility, adding that, "teachers are good at directing us to alternative information sources." Writes one student, "Professors really care. Most are approachable. They have the relevant experience." Overall, Broad students appreciate the fact that their school works to foster a "friendly environment. Faculty, staff, and students work together to make this a better program."

PLACEMENT AND RECRUITING

The Broad School's Placement and Career Center (PCC) offers MBAs an assortment of counseling and recruitment services, including seminars and personal consultations covering resume building, interviewing and networking skills, and salary negotiation. The PCC maintains a resume database, which recruiters can access through the school's website. Students and graduates can tap into BroadNet, an exclusive internet site that lists on-campus interview dates, job postings, and alumni contacts. Students may also use the university-wide Career Services and Placement (CS&P) office. The Broad School claims to be

Brenda Hernandez, Assistant Director
215 Eppley Center, East Lansing, MI 48824-1221
Admissions: 517-355-7604 • Fax: 517-353-1649
Internet: www.bus.msu.edu

"one of the very few top thirty MBA programs to have a career advisor focus on international students."

Students give the PCC average marks, touting "a solid alumni base around the world" but complain that "more national companies" are needed for on-campus recruitment. According to the school, this year "more than sixty nationally and internationally known firms will recruit MBA students [on-campus] for full time positions."

STUDENT/CAMPUS LIFE

Broad MBAs describe their student body as diverse, citing a population of foreign nationals that constitutes more than one-third of the student body. Others point out, however, that student demographics break down to "a big portion of people from Michigan, a big portion of Asians, then smaller portions of the rest." Among the international students is a large contingent of Korean managers, studying at MSU through a program run in conjunction with Korea's Kyung Hee University. One Asian MBA notes that students here are "very understanding of different cultures," while an American student described his classmates as "generally friendly, although there are some whiners who very much enjoy complaining." Many students arrive at the Broad School with considerable work experience, leading one to report that "because of their experience, they really add to the learning in our program. And, they're a lot of fun to hang out with."

Students describe academics at the Broad School as rigorous, and as a result "life at school is challenging and fun. The constant learning maintains the challenging atmosphere and the camaraderie of the students, staff, and faculty provide the fun." Students are "very involved in activities, especially in community service and making changes and improvements to the program." Student clubs are less popular but are readily available, and those who take advantage of them report that "they are good to be involved with." East Lansing receives high marks from Broad MBAs, who tell us, "There are more things to do in this town than time to do them. The East Lansing area is a great place to live." Included among social activities is "lots of drinking by students," as "bars abound in this very social atmosphere." For those seeking a more urban environment, Detroit is 90 minutes away by car. Students tell us that the campus is very safe, adding that the 5,000-acre campus is "shockingly beautiful." One of the few quality-of-life complaints concerned parking facilities. Gripes one student, "Parking space is the biggest problem here. Something has to be done urgently."

ADMISSIONS

The Broad MBA Program considers applicants on the basis of their academic record, GMAT scores, work experience, personal accomplishments, essays, and interviews. full-time students need not demonstrate extensive prior business experience either in the workplace or in academia, but must "appear well-suited for management careers based upon academic ability, maturity, motivation, leadership, and communication skills..." Applicants for the Fast-Track MBA Program, however, must have at least two years of 'quality' work experience. International applicants must score a minimum of 600 on the TOEFL and a minimum of 24 on the verbal section of the GMAT.

FINANCIAL FACTS

Tuition (in/out-state)	$8,128/$11,800
Cost of books	$1,362
Room & Board (on/off-campus)	$3,856/$5,085
% aid that is merit-based	50
% of students receiving paid internships	85
Average grant	$7,700
Average graduation debt	$62,303

ADMISSIONS

# of applications received	655
% applicants accepted	43
% acceptees attending	50
Average GMAT (range)	614 (480–750)
Minimum TOEFL	600
Average GPA (range)	3.30 (2.20–4.00)
Application fee (in/out-state)	$30/$30
Early decision program available	No
Regular application deadline	June 15
Regular notification	NR
Admission may be deferred?	Yes
Maximum length of deferment	1 year
Transfer students accepted?	No
Non-fall admission available?	Yes
Admissions process need-blind?	NR

APPLICANTS ALSO LOOK AT

University of Michigan, The Ohio State University, Cornell University, Indiana University, University of Texas—Austin, Thunderbird, Notre Dame, University of Illinois

EMPLOYMENT PROFILE

Placement rate (%)	95
# of companies recruiting on-campus	85
% grads employed immediately	95
% grads employed within six months	98
Average starting salary	NR

Grads employed by field (avg. salary):

Consulting	14% ($77,286)
Finance	25% ($52,250)
Human Resources	8% ($53,500)
Marketing	17% ($52,000)
Operations	19% ($62,150)
Strategic Planning	14% ($60,500)

UNIVERSITY OF MINNESOTA
Curtis L. Carlson School of Management

OVERVIEW

Type of school	public
Affiliation	none
Environment	metropolis
Academic calendar	quarter

STUDENTS

Enrollment of parent institution	18,487
Enrollment of business school	1,158
% male/female	68/32
% out-of-state	41
% minorities	11
% international (# countries represented)	17(NR)
Average age at entry	28
Average years work experience at entry	5

ACADEMICS

Student/faculty ratio	53:1
% female faculty	11
Hours of study per day	4.34

SPECIALTIES

General Management, Information Systems, Marketing

SPECIAL PROGRAMS

International Study in France, Germany, Sweden, Japan, Italy, Spain, Australia, Austria; International Management Exchange

STUDY ABROAD PROGRAMS

Australia, Japan, Austria, Belgium, England, France, Italy, Spain, Sweden, Switzerland, Brazil

SURVEY SAYS...

HITS
Gym
Minneapolis
Small classes

MISSES
Profs not great teachers
Quantitative skills
Campus is ugly

PROMINENT ALUMNI

Duane L. Burnham, Chairman and CEO, Abbott Laboratories; James Campbell, Chairman and Executive Vice President, Commercial Banking Services and Specialized Lending, Northwest Bank Minnesota, N.A.; David Hubers, President and CEO, American Express Financial Advisors; Robert Jaedicke, PhD, Retired Dean, Stanford University Graduate School of Business

ACADEMICS

MBAs tend to view a business school's competition for a higher national ranking in terms of a horse race. Applying that metaphor here, one would have to say that the Carlson School of Management is "making its move." Efforts to seriously upgrade the program's national stature are manifest in its new home, a "state-of-the-art building with great facilities (computers, food, study rooms dedicated to groups)." Students agree that the "new building is fantastic. It should really help to develop a sense of community now that the school facilities are very good." Moreover, students "appreciate the administration's efforts to bring this school into the top twenty. Investments in faculty, technology, new buildings, and attracting top students all have played a significant role."

At its heart, Carlson remains the school that first earned national attention as a "small program with accessible professors and helpful students that makes for very cooperative learning environment." First-year students enjoy the program's integrated core, although several warn, "the quarter system is extremely fast-paced. Winter Quarter is hell but the best learning experience around. More Harvard Business School case analysis than you can shake a stick at. Be sure to learn how to 'power nap.'" Second-year students must complete a fourteen-week field project and a lab in Managerial Communications but are otherwise free to pursue coursework in their fields of concentration and electives.

Students report favorably on the "excellent technology and strategy programs" and give management courses high marks as well. They give their professors mixed grades, although their rating of professors has improved since our last survey. Explains one student, "all the recently hired professors are 'A++'—as the old guard retires, the teaching gets better and better." Others are even more enthusiastic, asserting that "Professors are excellent! Very responsive—I've gotten answers to email questions after midnight! Exceeded my expectations!" Still, students also complain that the "faculty must improve its 'bench.' The 'starters' are the best round, but beyond that the profs should spend more time teaching than publishing."

PLACEMENT AND RECRUITING

According to the students we surveyed, Minnesota's Career Services Center (CSC) is doing an adequate job. On the up side, the CSC maintains a "strong relationship with an extensive network of corporations in the Twin Cities area." Students report that "the Mentor Program w/local CEOs is fantastic." On the down side, students complain that too few out-of-state companies make recruiting trips to their campus. The school reports that "approximately 150 companies come to campus to interview graduating students. Fall and winter interviewing is fairly heavy while spring interviewing is very light."

Carlson offers a standard array of career services: one-on-one counseling, Internet job databases, career nights, and assistance in contacting alumni. Companies hiring Carlson MBAs include Kimberly Clark, Andersen Consulting, Deloitte & Touche, Northwest Airlines, and Pillsbury.

Sandra Kalzenberg, Associate Director of MBA Programs
271 19th Avenue South, Minneapolis, MN 55455
Admissions: 612-625-5555 • Fax: 612-626-7785
Email: mbaoffice@csom.umn.edu
Internet: www.csom.umn.edu

University of Minnesota

STUDENT/CAMPUS LIFE

Carlson students are "mature, helpful, friendly, and have diverse experiences. They're typical Midwesterners." Although "about one-third of the students are international or minority students," a considerable number of students believe that ethnic and racial minorities are underrepresented. "Even with all the attention given to diversity, the student body is not very diverse ethnically," reports one typical student. Many respondents note a wide disparity between the best and worst students in the program, complaining that "we need stronger students to round out the lower half of the class."

Student life at Carlson is "active! Most students are involved in a broad variety of activities (both school and non-school related)." Studies demand "a rigorous schedule," writes one student. "I'm usually on campus at least twelve hours a day, between classes, group work, study, and work in organizations. Fun days though!" Students agree that "life at school is very community-oriented. Classmates enjoy being in activities with each other outside of class." Those activities include "regular happy hours on Thursday, Friday, or both" and "many clubs and organizations." One such organization is the student government, which works effectively with an "accommodating administration" to improve this program: "Students have driven ninety percent of the changes that will be attributable to this school's success." Although "U of M is a huge campus," students don't mind because "the Carlson School is small and comfortable." Students also appreciated the availability of "inexpensive housing." Their chief complaint: "The winter here is too long and too cold. Except for this, it is a nice place."

ADMISSIONS

The admissions office considers your GMAT score, work experience, and college GPA most important. Then, in descending order, they consider your letters of recommendation, essays, and extracurricular activities. Applications are processed in semibatches. According to the school, "Applications are reviewed when they become complete. Those not offered admission at the time at which they are received are reviewed again within six weeks of the April 1st deadline." Students may defer admission for one year.

FINANCIAL FACTS

Tuition (in/out-state)	$9,775/$14,525
Fees (in-state/out-of-state)	$800/$800
Cost of books	$1,300
Room & Board (on/off-campus)	$4,600/NR
Average grant	$5,300

ADMISSIONS

# of applications received	718
% applicants accepted	37
% acceptees attending	39
Average GMAT (range)	600 (420–750)
Minimum TOEFL	580
Average GPA (range)	3.20 (2.39–4.00)

Application fee (in/out-state)	$60/$90
Early decision program available	Yes
Early decision deadline	January 1
Early decision notification	February 15
Regular application deadline	April 1
Regular notification	May 15
Admission may be deferred?	Yes
Maximum length of deferment	1 year
Transfer students accepted?	No
Non-fall admission available?	No
Admissions process need-blind?	Yes

APPLICANTS ALSO LOOK AT

Northwestern University, University of Wisconsin—Madison, University of Michigan Business School, University of Chicago, New York University, University of North Carolina at Chapel Hill, University of Texas at Austin, Georgetown University

EMPLOYMENT PROFILE

# of companies recruiting on-campus	94
% grads employed immediately	98
% grads employed within six months	100
Average starting salary	$61,499

Grads employed by field (avg. salary):

Consulting	19% ($64,414)
Finance	36% ($59,070)
General Management	6% ($69,613)
Marketing	23% ($59,932)
MIS	13% ($62,071)
Operations	3% ($60,125)

New York University

Leonard N. Stern School of Business

OVERVIEW

Type of school	private
Affiliation	none
Environment	metropolis
Academic calendar	semester
Schedule	full-time/part-time/evening

STUDENTS

Enrollment of parent institution	15,871
Enrollment of business school	3,030
% male/female	67/33
% out-of-state	44
% part-time	73
% minorities	15
% international (# countries represented)	33(49)
Average age at entry	27
Average years work experience at entry	4

ACADEMICS

Student/faculty ratio	10:1
% female faculty	16
% minority faculty	11
Hours of study per day	4.35

SPECIALTIES

Finance, Information Systems, Marketing, International Business

JOINT DEGREES

JD/MBA, 4 years.; MBA/MA French Studies, 2.5 years; MBA/MA Journalism, 2.5 years; MBA/MA Politics, 2.5 years

SPECIAL PROGRAMS

Major tracks in Enterpreneurial Studies, Management Consulting, Financial Engineering, Entertainment, Media and Telecommunications

STUDY ABROAD PROGRAMS

Australia, Austria, Belgium, Brazil, Chile, China, Costa Rica, Denmark, England, France, Germany, Hong Kong, Israel, Italy, Japan, Korea, Mexico, Netherlands, Norway, Singapore, South Africa, Spain, Sweden, and Switzerland.

SURVEY SAYS...

HITS

Finance
Ethnic and racial diversity
Alumni helpful in job search

MISSES

Campus is ugly
Library
Safety

PROMINENT ALUMNI

Alan Greenspan, Chairman, Federal Reserve; Harvey Golub, Chairman, American Express; Richard Kogan, Chairman, Schering Plough

ACADEMICS

New York University's international management and finance departments are widely regarded as among the best in the country and give NYU a national profile. With twenty-nine foreign exchange programs and international research centers of worldwide renown in its arsenal, the international business area is especially strong. Stern is truly global: more than 30 percent of the full-time student body is foreign. The first-year consists of a prescribed program of eleven core courses, all with a global angle, plus two electives. A year-end capstone course, in the form of a team project, pulls together learning from all the core courses. The second year is more flexible—only two required courses that emphasize business strategy and management communication. Students take eight electives and declare a major, a double major, or even a co-major. For would-be entrepreneurs, there are appealing courses from the Center for Entrepreneurial Studies. Particularly noteworthy is the consulting specialization and the Management Consulting Program, in which corporations such as Reebok, Campbell Soup, and IBM hire teams of students to do consulting work. Other Stern perks include study tours of Europe, Africa, Asia, and Latin America, and a Chief Executive speaker series.

Not surprisingly, students rate each other's acumen in the school's power subjects—finance and quantitative analysis—as exceptional. But Stern MBAs aren't digitheads; they rate their classmates' teamwork skills equally high. As for the remaining areas—marketing, accounting, general management, and computers—students rate themselves strong but not stellar. The marketing department and operations lag behind other disciplines. As for the faculty, which includes one Nobel Laureate and members of the National Academy of Science, one MBA claimed, "Teachers are committed to seeing us master the material; they care that we really learn." Half of the students surveyed say professors are "good," but a third rate them "outstanding!" Eighty-five percent say teachers are accessible. All this leads students to describe Stern as, "On its way to becoming a top-ten school." They feel the school is underrated but many agreed that "there is a strong desire in the dean's office to improve Stern's competitive standing among business schools."

PLACEMENT AND RECRUITING

Stern's Office of Career Development (OCD) receives a natural boost from the school's location in "the heart of New York City's bustling financial, consumer-products, and media industries." More than 200 corporations make the trip to the Stern campus (many are only a short taxicab ride away). Stern's location likewise facilitates alumni networking, since many graduates remain in the city. The school takes advantage of its access to alumni through its Career Advisory Program, which makes more than 1,500 Stern graduates available to students for "informational interviews."

Stern was a pioneer in publishing student resumes on the Internet, and it administers a state-of-the-art database of available positions and internships. The school reports that, through its efforts, students have online access to more than 2,500 job postings each year. OCD also maintains a video conferencing center so students can interview with prospective employers anywhere in the world. OCD delivers a Career Management Series, which is designed to provide MBA students with the tools necessary to conduct a successful job search: personal skills and values assessment, resume writing, interview training, and networking are just a few examples.

Mary Miller, Admissions
Management Education Center, 44 West 4th Street, New York, NY 10012
Admissions: 212-998-0600 • Fax: 212-995-4231
Email: stenmba@stern.nyu.edu
Internet: www.stern.nyu.edu/External.html

STUDENT/CAMPUS LIFE

"You name it, we've got it," say students about the diversity of people and activities at Stern. "It's easy to find a niche for yourself." "NYU is New York City," remarked one student. "People either love or hate New York—with very few people in between." And, in truth, the climate at Stern seems to represent the best and worst of the Big Apple itself: Diverse, intense, international, and glittering with opportunity. Students describe their classmates as "street-smart, focused, and self-centered," and often complain of overcrowding and isolation.

To foster academic and social bonds between students, NYU divides the entering class into "blocks" of about sixty students who spend the first-year together. By the second year, students take just one class per semester with their "block." Students describe a heavy workload and spend an average of twenty to forty hours a week studying. To get newcomers up and running, the "Stern Pre-Term" provides students a skills-building session before school begins.

On the downside, students complained that the school needs to "maintain a better balance between full-time and part-time student life." Observed one MBA, "There is a lack of participation in team-building and school spirit activities with the part-time students, which leads to a generally lackluster sense of community." full-time students gripe that "too many classes are given at night to accommodate the schedules of part-timers." Though one MBA noted that "the administration has worked hard to change the schools image as a commuter school," others observed that "after class people disperse into the vast city of New York." More and more students, however, are living on campus, as housing prices skyrocket and NYU accomodates graduate students with better housing—they are building a new graduate dorm on 14th Street on the site of the old Palladium. One student remarked, "The new Management Education Center building has enhanced the school greatly. It has state-of-the-art presentation equipment, comfortable lecture halls, and small meeting rooms. The new uptown location creates a much friendlier and collegiate atmosphere."

The campus social scene centers on student-run clubs such as the Asian Business Society, Entrepreneurs' Exchange, Emerging Markets Association, and Stern Women in Business, which organize conferences, parties, and outings. Student government plays a big part in student life and how the program is run. In New York, there are millions of things to do outside of club life, such as hanging out in Washington Square Park and frequenting the many cafes and musical venues in Greenwich Village. Warns one MBA, "New York City is a very expensive place to go to school." Fortunately Stern students do have the opportunity to do a lot of activities right on campus. The Cole Sports Center features an outdoor track, basketball courts, and an Olympic-size swimming pool: A virtual oasis in this city of concrete and steel. Stern MBAs don't do a lot of in-class dating.

ADMISSIONS

According to the admissions office, the following criteria are considered (in order of importance): GPA and GMAT scores, work experience, letters of recommendation, essays, and extracurricular activities. Applicants whose native language is not English are required to submit TOEFL scores. Interviews are conducted by invitation.

FINANCIAL FACTS

Tuition	$26,250
Fees	$1,030
Cost of books	$3,153
Room & Board (on/off-campus)	$10,700/NR
% of students receiving aid	85
% first-year students receiving aid	70
% aid that is merit-based	100
% of students receiving loans	70
% of students receiving paid internships	95
% of students receiving grants	53
Average award package	$41,133
Average graduation debt	$35,000

ADMISSIONS

# of applications received	4,244
% applicants accepted	20
% acceptees attending	49
Average GMAT	657
Minimum TOEFL	600
Average GPA (range)	3.30
Application fee (in/out-state)	$75/$75
Early decision program available	Yes
Early decision deadline	January 15
Early decision notification	March 15
Regular application deadline	March 15
Regular notification	Rolling
Admission may be deferred?	No
Transfer students accepted?	No
Non-fall admission available?	No
Admissions process need-blind?	Yes

APPLICANTS ALSO LOOK AT

Columbia University, University of Pennsylvania, Northwestern University, University of Chicago, Harvard University, University of California—Los Angeles, University of Michigan Business School, Stanford University

EMPLOYMENT PROFILE

Placement rate (%)	97
# of companies recruiting on-campus	250
% grads employed immediately	95
% grads employed within six months	97
Average starting salary	$92,503

Grads employed by field (avg. salary):

Accounting	2% ($86,117)
Consulting	18% ($97,511)
Finance	51% ($91,981)
Marketing	17% ($75,182)
MIS	1% ($83,000)
Operations	1% ($77,500)
Strategic Planning	6% ($91,229)
Other	4% ($85,848)

UNIVERSITY OF NORTH CAROLINA AT CHAPEL HILL

Kenan-Flagler Business School   JD# 42926

ACADEMICS

Kenan-Flagler is one of the nation's most highly regarded state b-schools. KFBS's innovative curriculum focuses on business issues and problems, not functional areas. The curriculum is designed around seven-week modules ("mods"), four per year. This approach allows KFBS to offer a variety of topics—such as consulting and environmental issues—not possible under a semester system. Because the multi-function courses cram so much learning into one program, students told us KFBS is not for lightweights. Wrote one, "The workload is heavy, but, as they say, 'What doesn't kill you makes you stronger'!"

Students raved about the variety of learning opportunities. Wrote one, "UNC has great business contact with the state and general business community. There are excellent opportunities to get in 'real' work situations—practicums, case development, consulting." Teamwork is the motto at UNC. Students are pre-assigned mandatory study groups organized around members' experience and backgrounds. Ninety-eight percent of the class also participates in the optional MBA Adventure, an Outward Bound-style exercise designed to enhance the team approach to problem solving. But, according to one MBA, "Sometimes you don't get enough of a chance to develop individual skills."

Students couldn't say enough good things about the faculty, which they rated "exceptional." "Professors at KFBS are attuned to student needs and create synergies between core classes," said one student. "The teaching caliber of the faculty has far exceeded all expectations," gushed another. "All of the professors have consulting gigs outside of school, which enriches the classroom experience." A few mentioned they would like "more rigorous cold-calling in class" and "more emphasis on international issues and perspectives." They'd like to improve the bidding system, too. "Good classes need to be offered more often," remarked one MBA. But reportedly, "students are very involved" in shaping the program, and feel their comments are well received by the administration. UNC-Chapel Hill—as of October 1997—boasts a brand new, $44 million business school building. Students feel this facility makes Kenan-Flagler an indisputable top choice for prospective MBAs.

PLACEMENT AND RECRUITING

Students at Kenan-Flagler report that the Office of Career Services (OCS) has "improved vastly" in recent years. OCS adds that its 106:1 ratio of students to counselors is "one of the strongest across top business schools" nationwide. Counselors set goals here, striving "for an average of at least three [job offers] per student" so that graduates will have several jobs to choose from. They also encourage first-year students to seek internships abroad: more than 15 percent take this advice.

OCS supplements on-campus interviewing with a resume book, Internet job postings, and a video-conferencing facility. The school also sponsors a unique 'Student Ambassador' program, in which "a group of second-year students [visit] key corporations to share their experiences at Kenan-Flagler. We have found that our students are our best salespeople, and their work increases our exposure with corporations."

Anne-Marie Summers, Chairperson, MBA Admissions C[...]
CB #3490, McCoil Building, Chapel Hill, NC 27599
Admissions: 919-962-3236 • Fax: 919-962-0898
Email: lynn_loomis@unc.edu
Internet: www.bschool.unc.edu

STUDENT/CAMPUS LIFE

"The quality of life at Carolina is unmatched," brag[...] students seem to agree. They report working hard, es[...] say the academic pressure is mild. Grading is based [...] papers, class participation, and project-based work.

Cooperation is the rule, not the exception. As one stude[...] work with your team can affect your grades." But stud[...] get along. "The students here are not just a bunch of rich [...] "they're real people." "Most of my classmates are wel[...] who do not view an MBA as an identifier of who they are, [...] Married students report being happy at UNC and feel th[...] spected." They report that the spouse support group is [...] describe their classmates as "mature" and "highly intellig[...] information quickly, so that we can use our time to get ou[...] mountain bike," said one student.

UNC-Chapel Hill boasts a stately, tree-lined campus and bu[...] the National Historic Register. Because Chapel Hill is a uni[...] with extensive apartment developments, it's a renter's market. Public bus lines make off-campus living especially convenient. For a little adventure you can take a short road trip to the coastal beaches to the east, or the Appalachian mountains to the north and west.

On campus, sports, particularly the Tarheels basketball team, are popular. "With tailgate parties, basketball games in the Dean Dome, and the Franklin Street social scene, student life doesn't get much better than Chapel Hill," wrote one student. Students describe an active student community. There's a variety of student clubs, and a strong tradition of social service. The annual mini-biathlon sponsored by the MBA Student Association raises thousands of dollars for charities, as does a Habitat for Humanity student golf tournament. In summary one MBA said, "Carolina is a slice of heaven. The surroundings are beautiful, the people are friendly, and everyone is willing to help everyone."

ADMISSIONS

According to the admissions department, "work experience" is considered most important. After that, the following criteria are weighed equally: essays, college GPA, GMAT scores, letters of recommendation, interview (which is required), extracurricular activities, and leadership capabilities. The admissions office notes that, "because of our large applicant pool, applicants are encouraged to apply as early as possible." Only 18 percent of those who apply are accepted, establishing KFSB as one of the five most selective schools profiled in this book. Applicants are strongly encouraged to schedule an on-campus interview, sit in on classes, and meet with current MBA students.

NORTHEASTERN UNIVERSITY
Graduate School of Business

OVERVIEW

Type of school	private
Affiliation	none
Environment	metro
Academic calendar	
Schedule	full-time/par[...]

STUDENT[...]

Enrollment of parent instit[...]	
Enrollment of business [...]	
% male/female	
% part-time	
% min[...]	
	600
Average GPA (range)	3.20 (2.80–3.40)

Application fee (in/out-state)	$60/$60
Early decision program available	No
Regular application deadline	March 1
Regular notification	May 1
Admission may be deferred?	Yes
Maximum length of deferment	1 year
Transfer students accepted?	No
Non-fall admission available?	No
Admissions process need-blind?	Yes

APPLICANTS ALSO LOOK AT

Duke University, University of Virginia, Northwestern University, University of Michigan Business School, University of Pennsylvania, Dartmouth College, Wharton (Pennsylvania), Stanford University

EMPLOYMENT PROFILE

Placement rate (%)	97
# of companies recruiting on-campus	142
% grads employed immediately	91
% grads employed within six months	97
Average starting salary	$70,568

Grads employed by field (avg. salary):

Consulting	28% ($81,975)
Finance	35% ($64,300)
General Management	5% ($62,571)
Human Resources	2% ($67,333)
Marketing	22% ($65,130)
Operations	5% ($67,714)
Strategic Planning	3% ($66,900)

	polis
	quarter
	time/evening
tion	24,325
s school	1,138
	55/45
	72
rities	6
nternational (# countries represented)	8(26)
Average age at entry	26
Average years work experience at entry	3

ACADEMICS

Student/faculty ratio	12:1
% part-time faculty	25
Hours of study per day	4.28

SPECIALTIES

Finance, Accounting, Marketing, Logistical and Transportation Management, Information Resources Management, International Business, Enterpreneurship

JOINT DEGREES

JD/MBA; MS/MBA Nursing Administration; MD/MBA; MS/MBA Accounting

SPECIAL PROGRAMS

Executive MBA Program, Cooperative MBA Program, MS in Finance, High Technology MBA

STUDY ABROAD PROGRAMS

France, Eastern Europe, Southeast Asia

SURVEY SAYS...

HITS
Star faculty
Alumni helpful in job search
Study groups

MISSES
School clubs
Unfriendly students
Profs not great teachers

PROMINENT ALUMNI

Dennis J. Picard, Chairman and CEO, Raytheon Co; J. Philip Johnson, President and CEO, CARE; Richard Egan, Chairman of the Board, EMC Corporation.

ACADEMICS

A hallmark of Northeastern's business program is that it provides opportunities to combine paid professional work with study. There are five different MBA programs: a part-time program, an Executive MBA, the two-year full-time MBA, the Cooperative Education MBA, and the High Technology MBA. The High Tech MBA is the first of its kind in the nation. In this program, technical professionals take classes one night a week and on alternate Saturdays, and focus on management in the high-tech industry. Observes one student, "High-tech attracts high-caliber, excellent students." Perhaps the most popular and unique of the five programs is the Cooperative Education MBA, which begins in January and June. One MBA's comments typified the feeling among fans: "The Co-op program is excellent! The pace is fast, challenging, and rewarding." This may be because it offers students paid, MBA-level employment for six months during twenty-one months of accelerated study. Raves this happy MBA, "The main reason I chose this business school is because of the Co-op program, which allowed me to gain invaluable work experience while attending school." Especially noteworthy at Northeastern is the MS-MBA in accounting, which enjoys corporate support from major accounting firms. Indeed, it boasts a 100 percent placement rate for its most recent classes. Another academic strength: "The Finance department is strong!"

Northeastern's MBA programs offer generalist perspectives and contain a core of the basic business subjects. Electives are used to broaden or deepen the course of study. Prior to class, a week-long orientation jump-starts the programs with a team-building exercise and a foray into case study. Among the extras: an executive mentoring program that allows students to form personal relationships with CEOs and the like. Also, there are "great options for studying abroad."

The overwhelming majority of MBAs say this program is worth the investment of time and money, with 73 percent saying it's more than meeting their academic expectations. As one student put it: "The MBA program is excellent and very practical—coursework involves lots of 'real life' examples and cases." By all accounts, this allows students to feel proficient in a number of areas. For example, 80 percent of NU MBAs feel well prepared by their studies in finance, accounting, and general management—the school's dominion. Students award themselves even higher marks for their teamwork abilities. There is improvement from last year in students' marketing and computer acumen—52 percent say they're good or better in these subjects. One repeater weak spot is the efficiency of the school. Unhappily, things have gotten worse. Gripes one MBA, "Unfortunately, the administration has not taken any efforts to ensure quality control." On the upside, 70 percent rated the faculty good or better teachers. Most MBAs agree: "The quality of instruction here is as good as it is at other Boston schools." Reports another, "NU's faculty favor class participation, debates, and adopts a very practical methodology. This is very rewarding." Students gave professors particularly high marks for their after-class availability. But one MBA sounds off: "Some professors use the classroom as a bully pulpit for conservative...views." Nineteen percent gave the school average or worse marks for its equitable treatment of minorities. Foreign students are quite happy: "Being a French student at NU, I really appreciate interacting in class with this ethnically diverse student body." Adds another, "Great program for international students."

Daniel A. Gilbert, Manager, Full-Time MBA Programs
360 Huntington Avenue, Boston, MA 02115
Admissions: 617-373-2714 • Fax: 617-373-8564
Email: gsbac@cba.neu.edu
Internet: w.cba.neu.edu/gsba

Northeastern University

PLACEMENT AND RECRUITING

This go 'round, our survey shows that more students feel the MBA Career Center has improved. Thirty-seven percent of NU students say the range of companies recruiting on campus is now good to excellent. For some extra help, the remainder might suggest you head over to the university's main career office in Stearn's Hall. The majority of students go into finance and consulting. The average starting salary is $54,457. The major recruiters: State Street Bank, Texas Instruments, Lucent Technologies, M&M Mars, Digital, and Staples.

STUDENT/CAMPUS LIFE

Northeastern relies on the case-study method, which tends to produce late-night, intensive study sessions. Students here study an average of twenty-five to thirty-five hours a week. The vast majority report there are few corners to cut; it's important to do all or most of the assigned reading. Depending on the program you're in, the pressure ranges from manageable to formidable. Fortunately, study groups play an integral part in case preparation. Class participation counts for 20 to 40 percent of the grade. Classes are generally kept to twenty-five to fifty students. Students here are fairly competitive, in fact, 73 percent say very competitive, but this does not necessarily translate into one-upmanship. Cooperation and teamwork are the accepted mode of behavior. Northeastern MBAs say the student body is both professionally and racially diverse, a claim that most b-schools can't make. Seventy-seven percent also say fellow students are very bright. However, 27 percent report that classmates aren't the type of people they like to hang with a whole lot. In all likelihood, this has to do with the influx of part- and semi-full-time attendees who tend to be focused on their own thing. Still, the majority report an active social life. Observes this student, "The campus is exciting, and it's easy to make friends." B-school classes are held in Dodge Hall, a recently unveiled, gleaming new facility, which features state-of-the-art classrooms, high-tech computer facilities, a student lounge, case rooms, and a modern Career Center office. As for Boston, everyone loves this preppy East Coast city, which one student describes as an "intellectually exciting place to be." (But finding affordable housing is difficult, and almost no one lives on campus.) For extracurriculars, the MBA Association sponsors corporate speaker events, as well as barbecues. Students advise: "Participation is important."

ADMISSIONS

The admissions office considers the following criteria (in no particular order): essays, college GPA, letters of recommendation, work experience, and GMAT scores. The office of admissions notes, "Decisions are made by small committees after an application has been read by at least three professionals who independently assess several factors: academic preparation (GMAT scores and transcripts), maturity, motivation, and direction (essays, recommendations, and work experience). These factors are considered equally important."

FINANCIAL FACTS

Tuition	$21,000
Tuition per credit	$500
Fees	$250
Cost of books	$850
Room & Board (on/off-campus)	$10,380/$10,380
% aid that is merit-based	1
% of students receiving loans	19
% of students receiving paid internships	16
Average award package	$18,500

ADMISSIONS

# of applications received	NR
% applicants accepted	60
% acceptees attending	NR
Average GMAT	550
Minimum TOEFL	600
Average GPA	3.22

Application fee (in/out-state)	$50/$50
Early decision program available	Yes
Early decision deadline	February 15
Early decision notification	March 1
Regular application deadline	Rolling
Regular notification	Rolling
Admission may be deferred?	Yes
Maximum length of deferment	1 year
Transfer students accepted?	Yes
Non-fall admission available?	Yes
Admissions process need-blind?	Yes

APPLICANTS ALSO LOOK AT

Boston University, Babson College, Harvard University, New York University, University of Connecticut, Loyola University, University of Massachusetts, Northwestern University

EMPLOYMENT PROFILE

# of companies recruiting on-campus	117
% grads employed immediately	86
% grads employed within six months	95
Average starting salary	$54,457

Grads employed by field (avg. salary):

Consulting	25% (NR)
Finance	37% (NR)
General Management	2% (NR)
Marketing	16% (NR)
MIS	12% (NR)
Operations	4% (NR)
Strategic Planning	2% (NR)
Other	2% (NR)

NORTHWESTERN UNIVERSITY
J. L. Kellogg Graduate School of Management

OVERVIEW

Type of school	private
Affiliation	none
Environment	metropolis
Academic calendar	quarter
Schedule	full-time only

STUDENTS

Enrollment of parent institution	7,570
Enrollment of business school	2,900
% male/female	71/29
% part-time	48
% minorities	15
% international (# countries represented)	25 (45)
Average age at entry	27
Average years work experience at entry	5

ACADEMICS

Student/faculty ratio	9:1
Hours of study per day	4.16

SPECIALTIES

All areas of business and entrepreneurship. Special strengths—General Management, Finance, and Marketing.

JOINT DEGREES

MM/RN (nursing school, 4 years); MM/MD (medical school, 4 years); MM/JD (law school, 4 years); and MM/M (engineering school, 4 years)

SPECIAL PROGRAMS

Pre-enrollment math "Prep"; Foreign study in nine countries

SURVEY SAYS...

HITS
Marketing
Quality of recruiting
Administration

MISSES
Quantitative skills
Computer skills
School clubs

ACADEMICS

Kellogg, an extremely popular and top-ranked b-school in the last five years, offers the Master of Management (MM) degree. Students pursue a general management curriculum and "specialize in one or more of the professional fields: general business, public and nonprofit, health services, transportation, and real estate management." First-years take nine required courses and three electives. Happily, students who have completed prior study in a core course may apply for a waiver. Students with enough prior coursework may even complete their MMs in one year. Group work dominates everything at Kellogg—studying, classwork, even social life—which cements Kellogg's preeminent reputation for developing first-rate teamwork skills in its MMs. In fact, 78 percent of students rate their teamwork skills as superior, dominating other schools in this category.

Kellogg has a seemingly unshakable reputation as a marketing school, although more students enroll for classes in finance (another power subject) than in any other department. But the program has many other strong suits, notably: transportation management, real estate management, public and nonprofit management, and manufacturing. Tons of international business courses, a global focus in the core, and nine foreign study programs in Europe and Thailand make the study of international business a priority. An equally exciting area of study at Kellogg is entrepreneurship. Budding entrepreneurs may now "major" in the subject as well as join the hugely popular Entrepreneurship and New Venture Club. Students are still wild about the Master in Manufacturing Program (MMM), designed primarily for engineers who are in manufacturing/operations: "The MMM program is a hidden jewel." Exclaimed another, "The MMM program is positioning itself as a leading national operations/manufacturing program and is recognized among leading companies as a feeder to management training programs. Professors teaching the core courses are excellent."

Kellogg suffers from the reputation of being an easy school. However, one student suggests doing a reality check: "Kellogg is more hard work and more competitive than I assumed it was before my arrival here." The academic year at Kellogg is divided into three quarters. Most classes are kept somewhere in the range of twenty-five to fifty students. The first-year kicks off with Conceptual Issues in Management (CIM), a week-long orientation organized by returning second-years; CIM features get-to-know-you teamwork exercises but, thankfully, no high-anxiety ropes courses. Faculty and administration come out to press flesh and greet new students. Married students are treated to several married-only events.

How well is Kellogg preparing its students? Here's the report card: 37 percent of Kellogg MBAs rate their quantitative skills "good." But a third say their number-crunching skills are average or worse, not what you'd expect to find at a top-ranked program. Lack of confidence in this area may be driven by the school's emphasis on areas such as marketing and teamwork. Indeed, more than 80 percent of students say their marketing acumen is sharp enough to launch any product to success. Students also rate their accounting, general management, and finance skills as strong. Another positive: "Students get tremendous flexibility in structuring their first-year courses." Enthuses one MBA, "Kellogg really offers a program 'a la carte.' This, combined with the availability of the faculty allows the

Michele Rogers, Assistant Dean and Director of Admissions
2001 Sheridan Road, 2nd Floor, Evanston, IL 60208
Admissions: 847-491-3308 • Fax: 847-491-4960
Email: kellogg-admissions@nwe.edu
Internet: www.kellogg.nwu.edu

school to meet all kinds of expectations." As for how well the faculty teaches, almost 50 percent of students rate them outstanding, and the balance say they're good. A final point about Kellogg you can't miss: this school is predominantly student-run and driven. Over and over, MMs told us, "What makes Kellogg unique is that each student has the power to initiate change from Day 1." Sums up this student, "I love the people here. I love this school. I love my life here. Period."

PLACEMENT AND RECRUITING

More than 300 companies recruit on-campus. As for placement rates, in 1996 more than 90 percent of the graduates had reported placement three months after graduation. Students are happy with the quality and number of companies recruiting on-campus and satisfied with the Office of Career Development itself.

STUDENT/CAMPUS LIFE

The 440 entering students are divided into eight sections, creating a "homeroom" of about fifty-five students each. This lasts for the fall quarter only. After that, disbanded sectionmates keep in touch via numerous planned events. Much of the social scene revolves around activities successfully sponsored by the Graduate Management Association (GMA). These range from the academic (they compile quarterly teacher-course evaluations) to the social (weekly Friday afternoon beer bashes and parties, like the Halloween Bash). The GMA also coordinates Kellogg's two largest social events: the Charity Ball in February and the Black Tie Spring Fling. The Northwestern campus itself is beautiful, located along a half-mile stretch of Lake Michigan, twelve miles from downtown Chicago in the suburb of Evanston. On-campus housing is fair, with space available to 250 single students and fifty apartments for the wedded.

One MM says, "This is a school for people who like people. Back-stabbing is not tolerated. Kellogg develops leaders who have the simultaneous ability of being team members." Perhaps, but the biggest surprise, according to our survey, is that one-third of students say the competition is rigorous, contrasting sharply with the school's all-for-one, one-for-all image. Also surprising, almost 50 percent describe average or lackluster social lives, though the majority say classmates are the type of people with whom they like to network. In the plus column, a main selling point of this school is "student diversity (especially in terms of the numbers of international students)." Ninety-three percent of Kellogg students also say their peers have highly diverse professional backgrounds. Several students praise Kellogg for its admissions policy of interviewing everyone, which produces a school full of "high-caliber students."

ADMISSIONS

According to the Kellogg admissions office, your GPA, GMAT score, essays, work experience, extracurricular activities, recommendations, and interviews (which are required) are all "equally important." GMAT scores of applicants are typically high, undergrad grades are strong, and applicants have several years of impressive work experience. Applications are reviewed in rounds. As for when to apply, applicants are advised, "The earlier the better." Admission deferrals are considered on a case-by-case basis, but professional circumstances may be considered.

FINANCIAL FACTS

Tuition	$23,025
Cost of books	$1,200
Room & Board (on/off-campus)	$9,630/$9,630
% of students receiving aid	60
% first-year students receiving aid	60
% of students receiving loans	60
% of students receiving grants	40
Average award package	$25,000
Average grant	$4,500

ADMISSIONS

# of applications received	6,180
% applicants accepted	16
% acceptees attending	61
Average GMAT (range)	660 (490–790)
Average GPA (range)	3.40 (2.50–4.00)
Application fee (in/out-state)	$125/$125
Early decision program available	No
Early decision deadline	December 1
Regular application deadline	January 15
Regular notification	Rolling
Admission may be deferred?	Yes
Transfer students accepted?	No
Non-fall admission available?	No
Admissions process need-blind?	Yes

APPLICANTS ALSO LOOK AT

Harvard University, Stanford University, University of Pennsylvania, University of Chicago, University of Michigan Business School, Duke University, Dartmouth College, University of California—Los Angeles

EMPLOYMENT PROFILE

# of companies recruiting on-campus	291
% grads employed immediately	91
% grads employed within six months	93
Average starting salary	$58,000

Grads employed by field (avg. salary):

Accounting	1% (NR)
Communications	3% ($70,000)
Consulting	37% ($85,000)
Entrepreneurship	1% (NR)
Finance	25% ($65,000)
General Management	8% ($70,000)
Marketing	21% ($64,000)
MIS	1% (NR)
Operations	2% ($73,200)
Strategic Planning	3% ($68,000)
Venture Capital	1% ($80,000)
Other	

UNIVERSITY OF NOTRE DAME
College of Business Administration

OVERVIEW

Type of school	private
Affiliation	Catholic
Environment	metropolis
Academic calendar	semester

STUDENTS

Enrollment of parent institution	10,281
Enrollment of business school	254
% male/female	80/20
% minorities	6
% international (# countries represented)	30(19)
Average age at entry	26
Average years work experience at entry	3

ACADEMICS

Student/faculty ratio	3:1
% female faculty	6
% minority faculty	4
Hours of study per day	4.63

SPECIALTIES

General Management has long been the strength of Notre Dame's MBA program. Many MBA students go on to careers in Finance & Marketing with much success.

JOINT DEGREES

JD/MBA, 5 years; Engineering/MBA, 5 years, (Notre Dame undergrads only); Science/MBA, 5 years, (Notre Dame undergrads only).

SPECIAL PROGRAMS

The London and Santiago Program: Notre Dame has its own campus and faculty in the heart of each city.

STUDY ABROAD PROGRAMS

England, Chile, Mexico

SURVEY SAYS...

HITS
On-campus housing
Social life
Library

MISSES
Quantitative skills
School clubs
Computer skills

ACADEMICS

Notre Dame takes a traditional approach to the MBA. The first-year of its two-year program is crammed with intensive review courses in management, operations, and quantitative skills. Notre Dame then allows students a great deal of freedom in their second year, requiring study in two disciplines (ethics and international business) and a course in corporate strategy, but otherwise giving students free rein of the course catalogue. Even though the program doesn't include some of the bells and whistles that other schools add so they stand out in the MBA crowd, that doesn't seem to bother students here, most of whom prefer conservative, traditional approaches. Says one student, "The school itself has a lot of history and lore. The tradition inspires you to contribute and do well."

One unique feature of the Notre Dame MBA is the optional three-semester program, which is available only to students with an undergraduate degree in business. It takes one full year to complete the three-semester program. Participants cover the material taught in the traditional first-year MBA curriculum during an intensive nine-week summer semester, then join the second-year students in the fall. According to one student in the program, "three-semester students are extremely motivated, friendly, fun, and helpful. Traditional MBA students are nice, too, but I wouldn't trade my three-semester friends for the world."

Among the academic departments, finance gets the highest marks. Typical among our respondents is the one who writes "In finance and investment, I believe that our faculty is second to none." Management also scores high, while entrepreneurship is given low grades, although one student notes that "while the entrepreneurship program is very weak, it's expected to improve with the new dean." Students describe the administration as "extremely approachable. If you need any problem addressed, there is someone available to listen and help." Professors and facilities also get the students' thumbs up. About the only complaint students register is that the program "could use more and better course selection. [The] school's small size prohibits some electives that would have been nice."

PLACEMENT AND RECRUITING

Notre Dame students are satisfied with their prospects upon graduation; this is due more to "one of the strongest alumni networks in the world" and "name recognition" than to the Career Development Office (CDO), to which students give an average grade. Alumni return to campus to participate in career panels, serve as mock interviewers, volunteer as mentors, provide career advice, and support the recruitment of Notre Dame MBAs.

The CDO manages popular off-campus projects and internships, which the majority of our respondents find both plentiful and useful. Students wishing to use the services of the CDO must attend career management seminars, essentially making these seminars mandatory.

Notre Dame participates in several MBA recruiting consortia, including two aimed specifically at placement in the international market. Among the

Brian T. Lohr, Assistant Director of Admissions
College of Business Administration Complex, Suite 276, Notre Dame, IN 46556
Admissions: 219-631-8488 • Fax: 219-631-8800
Email: lohr.1@nd.edu
Internet: www.nd.edu:80/~mbawww

University of Notre Dame

companies that have recently recruited on campus are: Andersen Consulting, Citibank NA, Fidelity Investments, GE, Kimberly-Clark, Nissan Motor Company, Price Waterhouse, and Whirlpool.

STUDENT/CAMPUS LIFE

Notre Dame students report a high degree of satisfaction with their classmates and social lives. "The people are, without question, the greatest strength of this school," writes a typical student, adding, "this place is a community. People care about each other and all learning takes place in that context. The community has heart, spirit, and soul. We emphasize a well-rounded, balanced life." The "vast majority" has "excellent professional credentials, which provides for very challenging class and teamwork discussions." Students are friendly ("spontaneous review sessions form in the team rooms before exams, and you can drop in on any group and be welcome"). One student describes her peers thusly: "Blue-collar type people. They have all worked very hard to achieve their successes. They are the most personable people I've met." A detractor complains that "there is zero diversity in this program. My classmates are the poster children for the Young Republicans."

MBAs form a "very close-knit group" at Notre Dame: "Students work hard during the week and stick together over the weekend." Our survey confirms one student's opinion that "the workload is challenging yet not overwhelming. There is a good balance between academics and quality of life." Athletic events figure prominently into students' spare time, in the form of intramurals ("Everyone is really athletic. The athletic facilities are awesome, and the intramural leagues are really competitive, but you should know that we consistently beat the law school in intramurals") and intercollegiate sports ("Football season is killer at Notre Dame."). The campus even has its own golf course. The school and student organizations maintain a full-slate of "outstanding on-campus social activities including a talent show, holiday dance, weekly TGIT (Thank Goodness it's Thursday!), and spring formal." Students also praise the "weekly happy hour with profs." All these events help mitigate the fact that the closest town, South Bend, is "boring" and "not very attractive."

ADMISSIONS

The admissions committee considers the following criteria (not necessarily in order of importance): work experience, GMAT scores, college GPA, extracurricular activities, letters of recommendation, and the required essays. According to the admissions office, "We require a minimum of two years of work experience, but prefer three or more, particularly for our three-semester program. An undergraduate business degree is required for our three-semester program. There are no specific curricular requirements for our two-year MBA, although the school does advise applicants to have academic preparation in statistics. We highly recommend interviewing; we conduct off-campus interviews with MBA alumni as well as schedule on-campus interviews. Applicants should have a demonstrated history of leadership through professional or community activities. Students are advised to apply as early as possible, especially if requesting fellowship consideration.

FINANCIAL FACTS

Tuition	$21,500
Fees	$250
Cost of books	$925
Room & Board (on/off-campus)	$4,800/$4,800
% of students receiving aid	73
% first-year students receiving aid	63
% aid that is merit-based	100
% of students receiving loans	50
% of students receiving paid internships	85
Average graduation debt	$36,500

ADMISSIONS

# of applications received	512
% applicants accepted	42
% acceptees attending	42
Average GMAT (range)	615 (520–720)
Minimum TOEFL	600
Average GPA (range)	3.10 (2.40–3.80)

Application fee (in/out-state)	$75/$75
Regular application deadline	May 10
Regular notification	May 23
Admission may be deferred?	Yes
Maximum length of deferment	1 year
Transfer students accepted?	No
Non-fall admission available?	Yes
Admissions process need-blind?	Yes

APPLICANTS ALSO LOOK AT

Northwestern University, Georgetown University, Michigan State University, Duke University, Vanderbilt University, Indiana University, University of Texas at Austin, University of Michigan Business School

EMPLOYMENT PROFILE

Placement rate (%)	93
# of companies recruiting on-campus	92
Average starting salary	$57,052

Grads employed by field (avg. salary):

Accounting	7% ($47,071)
Consulting	25% ($65,887)
Finance	37% ($54,185)
General Management	6% ($67,134)
Human Resources	2% ($37,000)
Marketing	14% ($57,413)
MIS	1% ($52,860)
Operations	5% ($53,432)
Other	3% ($54,800)

OHIO STATE UNIVERSITY
Fisher College of Business

OVERVIEW

Type of school	public
Affiliation	none
Environment	metropolis
Academic calendar	quarter
Schedule	full-time/evening

STUDENTS

Enrollment of parent institution	55,787
Enrollment of business school	414
% male/female	74/26
% out-of-state	31
% part-time	38
% minorities	12
% international (# countries represented)	19(17)
Average age at entry	27
Average years work experience at entry	4

ACADEMICS

Student/faculty ratio	5:1
% female faculty	15
% minority faculty	16
Hours of study per day	4.09

SPECIALTIES

Academic Specialties are represented in our major & minor areas—Accounting, Finance, Consulting, Human Resources, International Business, Logistics, MIS, Marketing, Operations, & Real Estate

JOINT DEGREES

MBA/JD, 4 years; MBA/MHA, 3 years

SPECIAL PROGRAMS

Business Solution Team; Student Investment Management; Executive Luncheon Series

SURVEY SAYS...

HITS
Finance
Getting into courses a breeze
Accounting

MISSES
Library
Safety
Campus is ugly

PROMINENT ALUMNI

Jeff R. Rodak, Worldwide President and COO, Ingram Micro; John C. Easton, Chairman, Sensotec Inc.; John L. Giering, Senior Vice President and CFO, NCR Corp

ACADEMICS

Ohio State has rightly earned a reputation for the quantitative emphasis of its curriculum. In all areas, students at the Fisher College of Business "really develop a knack for quantifying criteria and evaluating situations and alternatives effectively." To ensure that entering students are prepared for this aspect of the program, Fisher requires a pre-enrollment review of accounting, economics, statistics, and computer literacy. It's a rigorous start to a program that remains extremely challenging throughout the first-year core curriculum; an exhaustive, tightly integrated overview of essential business skills and concepts. In the final quarter of their first-year, students must select a major in one of four areas or craft their own "interdisciplinary studies" major from among eleven areas of minor concentration. The latter option requires faculty approval.

Students give the highest marks to the finance department, describing its faculty as "top-notch." They also praise accounting, marketing, supply management, consulting, operations and logistics, and real estate studies. Professors are "very knowledgeable" and are "great in one-on-one interaction with students," but our respondents also warned that "teaching ability is very wide! Some are great, others are terrible." Explains one student, "professors are brilliant and accessible, yet a little too research-oriented." An administration that "is always helpful and supportive" and an awareness that the education they receive is "very cost-effective for such high quality" contribute to a high level of student satisfaction with the Fisher MBA program.

Fisher's physical plant gets mixed reviews. Students explain that "the computer labs are great; the classroom facilities are not" and also complain that "the library needs improvement." Hopes are up, however: "A state-of-the-art, new business complex is expected to be ready by June 1999, and then we will have the best of the best facilities in the world." Students would like to see OSU add programs in entrepreneurship and international business. Also on the student wish-list are smaller core classes and abandoning the frantic quarterly academic schedule.

PLACEMENT AND RECRUITING

Ohio State students give their Career Services office average grades, complaining that "The office is overworked and has trouble helping all students adequately. The school needs to devote more resources to this office." Another student offers a slightly more positive spin, noting that the "Career office seems confused and inactive, but opportunities are available in spite of them." That's probably because of "very strong corporate involvement. A lot of companies are coming to campus."

Almost 200 companies conduct on-campus interviews with OSU MBAs, according to Career Services statistics. Other employment opportunities are made available through the school's participation in the National MBA Consortium in Chicago, the International MBA Consortium Employment Conference, Ohio State Career Day, and the Ohio State Minority Job Fair.

Cindy Holodnak, Director
Hagerty Hall, 1775 College Road, Columbus, OH 43210
Admissions: 614-292-8511 • Fax: 614-292-1651
Email: cobgrd@cob.ohio-state.edu
Internet: www.cob.ohio-state.edu

Ohio State University

STUDENT/CAMPUS LIFE

Fisher MBAs describe their classmates as a "homogenous, Midwestern, married" group. Students enjoy the fact that their peers are friendly and not overly competitive, but some worry about an overall lack of work experience. "Many students don't really have 'real work' experience," laments one student. "Many are right out of four-year college, and they act like it." Another agrees, "The maturity level varies considerably. The people with no work experience, or out only a year or two, tend to be less mature."

OSU's quarterly academic schedule results in increased but manageable pressure. Students report that "this is a rigorous program, yet diligent work allows for a good balance between work and social affairs. You make time and integrate the two: study groups over dinner, for example." Adds another, "First-year has a heavy workload. Second year is less time consuming, allowing time for job search." Participation in student organizations and school activities is relatively low. Still, numerous clubs based on academic major, minority standing, and extracurricular interests are available for those who are interested. Campus life is "fun, especially during football season. Football, in fact, is the greatest unifying factor here. Also, the campus is beautiful during spring and summer." Another student is especially pleased to note that the "golf facilities are fantastic!" Unmarried students agree that "social life is good. MBAs often go out in packs of five to ten for fun activities." Hometown Columbus offers "all the luxuries of a metropolitan urban economic center with the feeling of a small town in the Midwest. Great place for families, education, and employment," although it's "a little depressing in the winter." Incoming students, be forewarned: the parking situation on campus is "horrifying."

ADMISSIONS

The admissions office at Ohio State considers your work experience most important. The school then considers, in descending order of importance, your GMAT scores, college GPA, work experience, letters of recommendation, essays, and extracurricular activities. Decisions are made in five blocks. The school adds, "Our self-completing application allows applicants to manage their files. Once they submit a completed application, an admission decision will be sent to them within four weeks. Early application completion and a campus visit are strongly recommended."

FINANCIAL FACTS

Tuition (in/out-state)	$5,683/$13,969
Fees (in-state/out-of-state)	$360/$360
Cost of books	$1,000
Room & Board (on/off-campus)	$4,332/$7,200
% of students receiving aid	56
% first-year students receiving aid	31
% aid that is merit-based	100
% of students receiving paid internships	90
% of students receiving grants	20
Average award package	$4,500

ADMISSIONS

# of applications received	1,326
% applicants accepted	25
% acceptees attending	40
Average GMAT (range)	621 (570–690)
Minimum TOEFL	600
Average GPA (range)	3.20 (2.60–3.80)
Application fee (in/out-state)	$30/$40
Early decision program available	Yes
Early decision deadline	January 15
Early decision notification	February 28
Regular application deadline	April 30
Regular notification	May 30
Admission may be deferred?	Yes
Maximum length of deferment	1 year
Transfer students accepted?	No
Non-fall admission available?	No
Admissions process need-blind?	Yes

APPLICANTS ALSO LOOK AT

University of Texas at Austin, University of Michigan Business School, Case Western Reserve, Penn State University, Indiana University, Northwestern University, Purdue University, University of Illinois

EMPLOYMENT PROFILE

Placement rate (%)	98
# of companies recruiting on-campus	198
% grads employed immediately	90
% grads employed within six months	98
Average starting salary	$63,656

Grads employed by field (avg. salary):

Accounting	3% ($63,000)
Consulting	17% ($63,040)
Finance	30% ($72,594)
General Management	1% ($65,000)
Human Resources	4% ($40,000)
Marketing	17% ($68,160)
MIS	10% ($54,670)
Operations	15% ($57,375)
Strategic Planning	1% ($67,000)
Other	

PENN STATE UNIVERSITY
Mary Jean and Frank P. Smeal College of Business Administration

OVERVIEW

Type of school	public
Affiliation	none
Environment	suburban
Academic calendar	semester
Schedule	full-time only

STUDENTS

Enrollment of parent institution	40,471
Enrollment of business school	257
% male/female	74/26
% out-of-state	60
% minorities	20
% international (# countries represented)	23(24)
Average age at entry	27
Average years work experience at entry	4

ACADEMICS

Student/faculty ratio	40:1
% female faculty	17
% minority faculty	17
% part-time faculty	3
Hours of study per day	4.84

SPECIALTIES

Financial Services, Manufacturing, Supply Chain Management, and Entrepreneurship and Innovation

JOINT DEGREES

Science BS/MBA, Quality and Manufacturing Management; MHA/MBA; MBA with manufacturing option; JD/MBA

SPECIAL PROGRAMS

Global Business, Logistics Research, Management of Technological and Organizational Change, Research in Conflict and Negotiation, Study of Business and Public Issues, Real Estate Studies, Study of Business Markets, Study of Organizational Effectiveness, and Risk Management

STUDY ABROAD PROGRAMS

Australia, Austria, Belgium, Denmark, England, Finland, France, Germany, Mexico, New Zealand, Norway, Singapore, and Spain

SURVEY SAYS...

HITS
Presentation skills
Interpersonal skills prep
Marketing

MISSES
School clubs
General management
Gym

PROMINENT ALUMNI

Brain E. Falch, President and Chief Executive Officer, H.J. Heinz Company of Canada, Ltd.; Alexander Goldberg, President of Ford Motor Land Services Corporation

ACADEMICS

Great value could be the mantra of all Smeal MBAs, whose high level of satisfaction with their program stems from the combined effects of low tuition and a small but effective program. The tiny student body guarantees that students can't fall through the cracks, while state support keeps tuition low, especially for Pennsylvania State residents.

Team teaching and the substitution of seven-week course "blocks" for traditional semesters keeps things fast-paced and dynamic. Smeal loads the first-year of its MBA program with thirteen core courses in quantitative analysis, accounting, management, finance, and communications, and then opens up the second year to a surprisingly wide choice of electives and concentrations. Students give the highest grades to "the communications department. The three components —speech, visual, and writing—get you ready for just about anything that could happen to you in your job." They are also pleased with the marketing, logistics, and finance departments. One student writes, "One of the best kept secrets is our finance department. We have a strong Wall Street alumni network. If you are interested in investment banking but don't want to pay $35,000 a year to get there, then Penn State is the place to go." Students give their lowest marks to the accounting department, although somewhat contradictorily they report that they believe themselves "very well prepared" in quantitative skills. Regardless of the department, students here feel that "the practical nature of the majority of classes is a strength . . . the professors use practical and useful course materials." Professors, according to almost everyone, are "great," providing "one-on-one interaction when needed. Very accessible and willing to offer help." The administration is similarly "nice, helpful, and friendly." The school's multimedia classrooms and facilities are universally considered "excellent."

Smeal offers a number of options to particularly ambitious students. Because Penn State offers study in practically every academic discipline under the sun, Smeal can provide many opportunities for dual degrees. Most popular among these is a combined MBA/MHA (Masters in Health Administration), offered in conjunction with the College of Health and Human Development. Students are also encouraged to study abroad during the fall semester of their second year; Smeal currently sponsors study in Australia, Europe, and East Asia.

PLACEMENT AND RECRUITING

Smeal students report that "Student/alumni relations are one of Penn State's strengths. There is a strong sense of pride in PSU. Everyone helps each other so that we all succeed together." It should come as no surprise, then, that alumni contacts are a primary resource for Penn State MBAs as they enter the job market. The network is huge: as the school often boasts, "one in every 700 Americans holds a Penn State degree."

Companies that regularly hire Smeal graduates include AMP, Andersen Consulting, AT&T, Citibank/Citicorp, Ford Motor Company, Hewlett-Packard, IBM, Intel, and Pfizer. The MBA Professional Development staff emphasize intensive, personal attention and work closely with alumni, faculty, and corporate partners to mentor students. Students participate in MBA consortia and job fairs

Roger Dagen, Marketing, Recruitment & Admissions Director
801 Business Administration Building, University Park, PA 16802
Admissions: 814-863-0474 • Fax: 814-863-8072
Email: jhh2@psu.edu
Internet: www.smeal.psu.edu/mba

Penn State University

to supplement the active on-campus recruiting. Smeal students often find job opportunities most plentiful in the automotive, consulting, electronics and computer technology, and pharmaceutical and health care industries.

STUDENT/CAMPUS LIFE

The tiny student body at Smeal means that "everybody knows everybody well. Profs know every student by first name. Being in a small program helps us all." One student reports, "There is a concerted attempt to include spouses and significant others in activities," which not only helps married students adjust to graduate life but also helps to flesh out the crowds a little. Students describe each other as "conservative" and "down-to-earth." Most agree that the student body represents an "excellent mix of various countries, ages, [and] races."

Although Smeal is a small program, the university system it occupies is anything but. Penn State is enormous; as one student explains, "The small college has the personal benefits of a small cutting-edge program with the resources of one of the largest universities in the nation." Adds another, "The large campus, which is one of the most beautiful in the country, allows each student to pursue hobbies and interests in numerous ways. Large events, such as school-sponsored tailgates, add to an enjoyable experience outside the classroom." Social life "is very available in this college town . . . the problem is finding time for it" since "academics is the primary focus of most students and it needs to be. Plan on working." When it's time to blow off steam, students can find plenty going on. "Sports teams and concerts provide entertainment . . . the restaurant and bar scene is great, and cheap!" Penn State's perennially successful football team "adds an esprit de corps like I have never felt before. That enthusiasm gets carried over into our academic and social lives." Many students report participation in sports as their primary diversion. On the downside, off-campus housing "is too expensive" and parking "is a major problem throughout Penn State. Oh, and the weather can be rough, too." Students also warn that University Park is "inconvenient to major cities and airports."

ADMISSIONS

According to the admissions office, your GMAT score, work experience, and college GPA are considered most important, and then, in descending order, your interview, essays, and letters of recommendation. They note, "Interviews are strongly encouraged and considered on a par with work experience." Applications are handled on a rolling admissions basis. It generally takes two to six weeks "depending on the backlog" for a student to be notified of a decision after receiving the completed application. Students may defer admissions for up to one year for personal reasons.

FINANCIAL FACTS

Tuition (in/out-state)	$6,636/$13,314
Fees (in-state/out-of-state)	$450/$450
Cost of books	$1,200
Room & Board (on/off-campus)	$4,500/$5,000
% of students receiving aid	35
% first-year students receiving aid	25
% aid that is merit-based	100
% of students receiving grants	7
Average award package	$10,000
Average grant	$10,000

ADMISSIONS

# of applications received	1,376
% applicants accepted	25
% acceptees attending	38
Average GMAT (range)	601 (570–630)
Minimum TOEFL	585
Average GPA (range)	3.15 (3.94–3.41)
Application fee (in/out-state)	$40/$40
Early decision program available	Yes
Early decision deadline	February 1
Early decision notification	March 1
Regular application deadline	April 1
Regular notification	June 1
Admission may be deferred?	Yes
Maximum length of deferment	1 year
Transfer students accepted?	No
Non-fall admission available?	No
Admissions process need-blind?	Yes

APPLICANTS ALSO LOOK AT

University of Virginia, University of Maryland, University of Pittsburgh, University of North Carolina at Chapel Hill, New York University, University of Texas at Austin, Duke University, University of Pennsylvania

EMPLOYMENT PROFILE

Placement rate (%)	96
# of companies recruiting on-campus	138
% grads employed immediately	88
% grads employed within six months	98
Average starting salary	$62,200

Grads employed by field (avg. salary):
Consulting	15% ($64,000)
Finance	42% ($62,800)
General Management	4% ($52,300)
Marketing	20% ($61,300)
Operations	7% ($58,500)
Other	12% ($61,700)

UNIVERSITY OF PENNSYLVANIA
The Wharton School Graduate Division

OVERVIEW

Type of school	private
Affiliation	none
Environment	metropolis
Academic calendar	semester

STUDENTS

Enrollment of parent institution	9,493
Enrollment of business school	1,539
% male/female	73/27
% minorities	17
% international (# countries represented)	31(48)
Average age at entry	27
Average years work experience at entry	6

ACADEMICS

Student/faculty ratio	8:1
% female faculty	15
Hours of study per day	4.55

JOINT DEGREES

MBA/JD; MBA/MD; MBA/DMD-Dental; MBA/MSE Engineering; MBA/MA Communication; MBA/MA, MBA/MA; MBA/MSW; MBA/PhD; MBA/Animal Health Economics Training Program

SPECIAL PROGRAMS

Wharton's Sol C. Snider Entrepreneurial Center; the Lauder Institute's Program in International Studies: paid consulting available; summer pre-enrollment "pre-term," foreign study

STUDY ABROAD PROGRAMS

10 countries

SURVEY SAYS...

HITS
Wide range of recruiters
Quality of recruiting
Finance

MISSES
Safety
On-campus housing
Gym

PROMINENT ALUMNI

Lewis E. Platt, Chairman, President & CEO, Hewlett-Packard; Peter Lynch, Vice Chairman, Fidelity Management & Research Co.; Yotaro Kabayashi, Chairman & CEO, Fuji Xerox Ltd.

ACADEMICS

Long considered a bastion of finance, Wharton now boasts first-rate academics in general management, marketing, accounting, real estate, entrepreneurship, nonprofit, business management, insurance/risk management, and business law. Equally important is the emphasis on global study. This is supported by an international student body, international courses, two international joint-degree programs, and a global immersion program in China, the ASEAN countries, and Latin America. Courses at Wharton have a quantitative orientation and require well-developed math skills. Advises one student, "It helps if you were quantitative before coming to this program."

Wharton's MBA program provides a "curriculum for the twenty-first century." Instead of the traditional two-term academic structure, the first-year consists of four intensive six-week modules. Single-discipline instruction has been replaced by "team-taught courses and integrative case study projects that draw together cross-functional insights." Reports one student, "Wharton is working very hard to change, incorporating leadership, teamwork, and increasing teaching quality through constant feedback." Entering first-years start off with a four-week preterm in August. Students are "prepped" in courses such as economics and statistics so that all first-years begin on an equal footing. Thus far students report a heavier workload and more papers and exams, due to the more compact schedule of modules. They also told us the that the non-disclosure grading policy has mellowed the competitive atmosphere.

First-years take nine core courses and must complete a Management Communications course and demonstrate proficiency in LOTUS and basic math before progressing to the second year. The second year offers students a choice of of twenty-eight majors in eleven departments. A dizzying collection of 200 electives offers opportunities for specialization or eclectic sampling. Here are some favorites: Innovation and Entrepreneurship, Geopolitics, Risk and Crisis Management, and Environment of the Firm. Students praised the ethics offerings and the guest speakers program. The current facilities appear to be cramping their style, however, and there was a cry for "additional computer resources!" The school tells us that they plan to alleviate such concerns with a new building tentatively slated for completion in 2002. Another hot topic: Teaching quality, which has reportedly been subpar in the last few years. Apparently, superstars and duds walk the same hallways. Wrote one student, "The best researchers don't mean the best teachers."

PLACEMENT AND RECRUITING

Students are quite happy with the quality, range, and number of companies recruiting on campus. Students also gave high marks to the career placement center itself, and rated the alumni network as vital and helpful. In 1997, a total of 630 firms, representing over fifty industries, made offers to Wharton graduates and summer interns. Wharton has upped its placement rate in recent years to an acceptable 90 percent.

The leading recruiters in 1997 in descending order were McKinsey, Goldman Sachs, Bain & Co., and Morgan Stanley. Average starting salaries were sky-high, putting UPenn in the top five b-schools profiled in this book.

Robert Alig, Director of Admissions and Financial Aid
102 Vance Hall, 3733 Spruce Street, Philadelphia, PA 19104-6361
Admissions: 215-898-6183 • Fax: 215-898-0120
Email: mba.admissions@wharton.upenn.edu
Internet: www.wharton.upenn.edu/mba

University of Pennsylvania

STUDENT/CAMPUS LIFE

Each fall, 750 students enter Wharton, making it the second-largest MBA program in the nation. To create a more intimate environment, the entering class is now divided into lettered "cohorts," each made up of sixty students who remain together through the core courses. Classes are held in amphitheater-style rooms where students are identified by their name plates. An average class numbers forty to fifty. Students are competitive. However, given the school's emphasis on group work, competitive students are at a disadvantage: Shark-like behavior is frowned upon, and pegs someone as undesirable for group projects. "The best part of Wharton is the student body," goes a typical student comment. "They're very diverse, from professional athletes and singers to I-bankers. Much more helpful than I thought they would be." Others disagree: "There is a highly visible minority that fulfills all the negative stereotypes—vain, self-centered, selfish—that give the rest of us a bad name."

Part of the University of Pennsylvania's 260-acre campus, Wharton is bordered by historic buildings and spacious lawns. The official Wharton building is Vance Hall, an outdated four-story structure. (Stay tuned—Vance should receive a facelift in the near future.) The new Steinberg-Deitrich Hall is shared with (and really home to) Wharton undergrads. It's hard to characterize a Wharton type. Traditionally, the school has been described as a feeder to the financial community but, in recent years, students have been as likely to go into management consulting or marketing as investment banking. Despite the diverse student body, Wharton has an East Coast, Ivy League feel. But that doesn't mean students don't know how to go crazy. There is a huge social scene here (more geared to groups than to dates, we were told). Examples: The Walnut Walk (in which students don boxer shorts and bar-hop down Philly's Walnut Street), cohort theme parties, weekly all-you-can-eat pizza nights at the pub, the Holiday Ball and Spring Ball, and "ding" night at Cavanaugh's, where an employment rejection letter gets you free beer. In between are the Wharton Follies, intramural sports, the activities of over 100 student clubs, and several volunteer events such as Christmas in April and Wharton into the Streets. As for housing, married or single students can live in the Graduate Towers, in which twelve floors have been set aside for MBA students. Many students opt to live off-campus in Center City or West Philly, where apartments are plentiful and reasonably priced.

ADMISSIONS

The admissions office considers the following criteria (in no particular order): essays, GMAT score, undergraduate or graduate transcripts, letters of recommendation, extracurricular activities, and work experience. The interview is optional. Writes the school, "The admissions committee evaluates applicants individually. Selection of students is not driven by categories or quotas. Applicants should represent themselves as they truly are versus what they may feel Wharton wants to hear. Applicants should also help the committee fully understand any unusual or nontraditional aspects of their candidacy." It is advisable to apply early in the rolling admissions cycle.

FINANCIAL FACTS

Tuition	$26,290
Cost of books	$1,641
Room & Board (on/off-campus)	$9,070/NR
% of students receiving aid	70
% aid that is merit-based	1
% of students receiving loans	60
% of students receiving grants	40
Average grant	$3,500
Average graduation debt	$40,000

ADMISSIONS

# of applications received	7,461
% applicants accepted	15
% acceptees attending	73
Average GMAT (range)	674 (580–750)
Average GPA	3.40
Application fee (in/out-state)	$125/$125
Early decision program available	No
Regular application deadline	April 10
Regular notification	Rolling
Admission may be deferred?	Yes
Transfer students accepted?	No
Non-fall admission available?	No
Admissions process need-blind?	Yes

APPLICANTS ALSO LOOK AT

Stanford University, Harvard University, University of Chicago, Columbia University, Northwestern University, University of California—Los Angeles, University of Michigan Business School, New York University

EMPLOYMENT PROFILE

Placement rate (%)	97
# of companies recruiting on-campus	317
% grads employed immediately	98
% grads employed within six months	98
Average starting salary	$95,000

Grads employed by field (avg. salary):

Accounting	3% ($77,500)
Communications	2% ($72,000)
Consulting	35% ($85,000)
Entrepreneurship	2% (NR)
Finance	43% ($65,000)
General Management	6% ($75,000)
Human Resources	1% (NR)
Marketing	8% ($65,000)
MIS	0% (NR)
Operations	1% (NR)
Strategic Planning	32% ($75,000)
Venture Capital	2% ($72,500)
Other	4% (NR)

PEPPERDINE UNIVERSITY
The George L. Graziadio School of Business and Management

OVERVIEW

Type of school	private
Affiliation	Church of Christ
Environment	suburban
Academic calendar	trimester

STUDENTS

Enrollment of parent institution	7802
Enrollment of business school	982
% male/female	NR
% full-time	17
% part-time	83
% minorities	NR
% international (# countries represented)	NR(28)
Average age at entry	26
Averge years work experience at entry	3

ACADEMICS

student/faculty ratio	6:1
Hours of study per day	4.05

SPECIALTIES

Marketing & Finance, Organizational Development, Global/International Business, Practical Application, Real-world business experience

JOINT DEGREE

JD/MBA—4 yrs., MBA/Master of Public Policy—3 yrs.

SPECIAL PROGRAMS

Mentorship, executive internship, nonprofit civic leadership, buisness foreign language, communication workshop

STUDY ABROAD

Belgium, France, Germany, Italy, Spain, Netherlands, Mexico, Philippines, Thailand, Hong Kong, China, England.

SURVEY SAYS...

HITS
Placement
Campus is attractive
On-campus housing

MISSES
Profs not great teachers
General management
Quantitative skills

PROMINENT ALUMNI

Christos Cotsakos, President and CEO, E-Trade Group, Inc.; Donald Skinner, President and CEO, Eltron International, Inc.; David A. Mount, Chairman and CEO, Warner Electric Atlanta, Inc.

ACADEMICS

Pepperdine's Graziadio School of Management and Business provides "practical approaches to the business world" alongside an emphasis on the "rapidly expanding global marketplace." According to students we surveyed, these attributes combine with a powerful job networking system—both local and abroad—to make Pepperdine an appealing choice for business students.

Students appreciate the fact that in both its traditional MBA program and its Masters in International Business (MIB) program, Pepperdine integrates international issues into the curriculum. Students in both programs are encouraged to pursue summer internships abroad. MIB students, who complete their second-year studies overseas, describe the "intensive language program" here as "very effective," preparing them well to spend their second year at schools in France, Germany, or Mexico. One MIB tells us, "One great strength is the quality of schools with which Pepperdine is affiliated abroad. They're the best schools in Europe and Mexico." The second year of the MIB track culminates in a four-month internship in the European Union, Switzerland, or Mexico.

Students also praise Pepperdine's "conservative curriculum" that "prioritizes practical knowledge ahead of theory." (Pepperdine's conservatism should come as no surprise, given its affiliation with the Churches of Christ and the fact that the university once offered Whitewater special prosecutor Kenneth Starr the deanship of its law school.) Explains one student approvingly, "My professors are able to apply real-life situations to most of my assignments and readings." Teachers are "very knowledgeable and always accessible through home phone or email." However, students give professors merely average grades for teaching ability. In fact, their assessment of academics here are generally lukewarm, with most departments earning only middling marks. Students are much more enthusiastic about Pepperdine's ability to place them in the job market (see Placement and Recruiting below), with many citing this knack for placement as their main reason for choosing the school. They also appreciate the school's personal touch, noting that "the faculty and staff are extremely supportive to all students. Almost all staff members know your name, and they are always ready and willing to help." Among the complaints most frequently voiced: "We need a new building with a library." Pepperdine offers a one-year MBA program to students with undergraduate business experience. Respondents in the program describe it as "very fast-paced. It has involved a lot of hard work." Pepperdine also offers a joint JD/MBA.

PLACEMENT AND RECRUITING

Students at Pepperdine are pleased with the school's "excellent career development program." In fact, a considerable number of survey respondents list the school's placement services among their top reasons for choosing Pepperdine. They are particularly happy with the quality and selection of opportunities for off-campus projects and internships, both in the L.A. area and abroad. Furthermore, they tout a "wonderful alumni network" and applaud the fact that "the school has strong relationships with businesses in the L.A. area." These factors mitigate students' relative dissatisfaction with the number of companies that recruit on-campus.

Darrel Eriksen, Director of Admissions
400 Corporate Pointe, Culver City, CA 90230
Admissions: (310) 568-5525 • Fax: (310) 568-5779
Email: gsbm@pepperdine.edu
Internet: bschool.pepperdine.edu

Pepperdine University

Pepperdine's Career Development Center (CDC) offers the standard assortment of career counseling services, including skills development seminars and an extensive resource library. The CDC hosts numerous industry forums and "career exploration events" throughout the year and also coordinates Pepperdine's participation in the West Coast MBA Consortium. The school's automated resume service matches incoming job offers with student resumes, which students may update via the Internet.

STUDENT/CAMPUS LIFE

Pepperdine's student body consists of two groups: students in the MBA program, and a smaller contingent pursuing the MIB. Minority and international enrollment is greater among MBAs, of whom Asian students constitute the greatest part of the minority population. Nearly half the MBA students are foreign nationals; in contrast, only 13 percent of MIB students arrive from overseas. Hispanic students make up the largest minority among Pepperdine MIBs. Students in both programs "come from all different backgrounds ranging from accounting and finance to hospital employees." One student describes his classmates as "the most eclectic group of people I've ever been surrounded by. Brilliant people, eccentric, successful, children of interesting parents and others contribute to the mix." Pepperdine's emphasis on team learning results in a student body that is "very collaborative, taking a team approach to problem solving." Notes one student, "Our entering class was small. The communications workshop united us very quickly. As classes began, we were very comfortable with each other." Students also happily report that their classmates are "leaders, entrepreneurs, people with excellent international connections and excellent local networking connections."

Pepperdine's Malibu paradise offers a pleasant mix of quiet surroundings and beautiful weather complemented by its proximity to Los Angeles. Although a few (insane?) students complain that Malibu is "boring and a far distance from any real nightlife activities," the majority love the town. Writes one student, "Life in Malibu is like a dream for an East Coaster like myself. Sun, ocean, campus—I'm very happy here." A Michigan native praises the "outstanding opportunities for me to be exposed to many new experiences, such as surfing," others point out that because L.A. is only about 30 miles from campus, it's an easy drive and "there is so much to do in the L.A. area." "Most students live in the Valley and commute to Malibu. The cost of living is cheaper in the Valley." On campus, students tell us about "copious amounts of social activities," community service opportunities, and student organizations. They describe the 830-acre campus as "one of the most beautiful settings in the world."

ADMISSIONS

The admissions office at Pepperdine considers an applicant's GMAT scores, completed application including three personal essays, transcripts, letters of recommendation, and current resume. A personal interview, although not required, is recommended. In addition, international students must score a minimum of 550 on the TOEFL and submit an Evidence of Financial Support Form. MIB applicants are strongly encouraged to enter with intermediate level proficiency in a foreign language. Applicants to the one-year MBA program must demonstrate at least two years of professional work experience and hold a business-related undergraduate degree.

FINANCIAL FACTS

Tuition (in/out):	$22,050/$22,050
Tuition (per credit):	$705/$705
Fees:	NR
Cost of books	$1500
Room & Board (on/off)	$7450
% receiving aid	50%
% first-year receiving aid	50%
Average award package	$18,500
Average loans	$18,500

ADMISSIONS

# of applications received	409
% applicants accepted	60%
% acceptees attending	39%
Minimum TOEFL	550
Average GPA	3.1
Average GMAT	580
Application fee (in/out)	$45/$45
Early decision	Yes
Early decision deadline	December 15
Early decision notification	January 31
Regular app. deadline	February 15
Regular notification	Rolling
Admission may be deferred?	Yes
Maximum length of deferment	1 year
Transfers accepted?	Yes
Non-fall admission?	Yes
Admissions need-blind?	NR

APPLICANTS ALSO LOOK AT

Indiana University, University of Michigan Business School, University of Texas at Austin, Cornell University, Ohio State University, Penn State University, Case Western Reserve, University of Notre Dame

EMPLOYMENT PROFILE

Placement rate (%)	84
# companies recruiting on-campus	NR
% of graduates employed immedietly	NR
% employed within six months	100
Average starting salary	$46,500

Grads employed by field (avg. salary):

Consulting	5.4% ($58,000)
Entrepreneurship	19% (NR)
Finance	19% ($41,000)
General Management	16% ($47,000)
Marketing	NR ($44,500)
MIS	NR ($55,000)
Quantitative	2.7% (47,000)
Strategic Planning	2.7% ($40,000)

UNIVERSITY OF PITTSBURGH
Katz Graduate School of Business

OVERVIEW

Type of school	public
Affiliation	none
Environment	metropolis
Academic calendar	modules

STUDENTS

Enrollment of parent institution	12,901
Enrollment of business school	1,127
% male/female	32/68
% out-of-state	70
% part-time	68
% minorities	12
% international (# countries represented)	41(21)
Average age at entry	27
Average years work experience at entry	5

ACADEMICS

Student/faculty ratio	4:1
% female faculty	16
% minority faculty	2
% part-time faculty	31
Hours of study per day	4.57

SPECIALTIES
Finance, Marketing, Information Systems, Strategy

JOINT DEGREES
MBA/MA in areas of specialization such as East Asia, Latin America, and Eastern Europe; MBA/Masters International Business; MBA/MS Information Systems; Master of Health Administration; joint degree in Business and Law

SPECIAL PROGRAMS
Foreign study in Prague and Budapest; intensive foreign language instruction

SURVEY SAYS...
HITS
Pressure
Placement
Ethnic and racial diversity

MISSES
Presentation skills
General management
Gym

PROMINENT ALUMNI
Ray Smith, CEO, Bell Atlantic; John J. Shea, President and CEO, Speigel Inc.; Donald R. Beall, Chairman and CEO, Rockwell International; Thomas E. Frank, President and CEO, Hickory Farms.

ACADEMICS

Katz "offers an MBA program that is unique, enabling you to earn your MBA in eleven months, over three terms of study rather than in the two years usually required elsewhere." This is made possible by the program's pace, breadth of study, and integrated curriculum, the last of which prevents duplication of course material. The obvious advantages of an eleven-month program are, as one student put it, "low opportunity cost and half the tuition!" The disadvantages are that you miss out on a summer internship and have little time to digest what you've learned. (Many students enroll in a dual degree program, however, and spend two years at UPitt in the end anyway; those students have a required intership as part of their studies.) To prepare for the July through June sprint, students can take optional pre-program workshops to improve their skills in areas in which they are weak. Still another highlight of the program is the Project Course, in which students solve actual corporate problems and see their solutions implemented. The student-run management learning organizations complete an internship-like assignment where they consult on a real world project, combining skills they learn in economics and strategic performance classes. All students take a "strategy envelope" of three courses: Competing in a Global Environment, Organizational Transformation, and Managing Strategic Performance. Summed up this happy MBA, "Katz is continually trying to improve, which is excellent."

Students say the faculty are extremely accessible, but the teaching quality got mixed reviews. "The majority of faculty are excellent—they use real world situations to apply theories," one MBA told us, "but a few are really bad. "The tenured profs are behind the times," said another. The administration didn't score well either. "The dual degree program administration needs better continuity," advised one student. But the biggest complaint was the antiquated registration process: "This school is ranked as a top ten techno-MBA, but the registration system is manual, not computerized!" exclaimed a student. MBAs petitioned for a facility upgrade, including increased library resources—and won. The school recently improved library resources by establishing separate facilities for undergrads, improved library database equipment, and upgraded computer facilities. The program is clearly working better for some than others. "It's an eleven-month program, but they try to run it like a two-year program, which is ineffective—there's too much emphasis on homework and not enough on teaching business," wrote one student. But another said, "It's a real MBA in half the time. It's great." All students agreed the program is "rigorous" and "not for people who want a two-year vacation from work."

PLACEMENT AND RECRUITING

Katz's Career Services Center (CSC) describes itself as "one of the most ambitious MBA placement offices in the nation," an assessment with which most students concur. The CSC "goes the extra mile," reported one satisfied student. Because a Katz MBA is completed in a brief eleven months, the CSC hits the ground running, meeting with all students during the first week of classes. "It's important that our students get up to speed quickly," says Joan Craig, director of the Career Services Center. "We put a premium on getting to know every student who wants to compete in the job market, and helping them to develop an effective job search strategy."

Kathleen Rickle Valentine, Director of Admissions
276 Mervis Hall, Roberto Clemente Drive, Pittsburgh, PA 15260
Admissions: 412-648-1700 • Fax: 412-648-1659
Email: mba-admissions@katz.business.pitt.edu
Internet: www.pitt.edu/~business

University of Pittsburgh

The CSC program includes abundant one-on-one counseling, mandatory interview workshops, an on-campus career fair featuring the school's top twenty-five recruiters, and national MBA consortia. More than 100 companies recruit on campus. Placements are strongest in the region immediately surrounding Pittsburgh, but the CSC reports that the number of placements in the Southwest and on the West Coast is increasing.

STUDENT/CAMPUS LIFE

Life at Katz is lived at a breakneck pace. One tired MBA complained, "The seven-week courses are tough." Said another, "It is very hectic. Trying to balance class work with interviewing schedules and social activities is extremely difficult." A value-added program for students is the Executive Briefings series, hour-long presentations held several times a month at which chief executives from major corporations come to Katz to speak on career and industry issues. Afterward, a handful of students join the exec and the dean for lunch. Equally exciting is the American Assembly Dialogue, which brings business leaders to campus to discuss major economic and social issues of the day. Katz is the only school in the nation to hold this event. Past participants include Ivan W. Gorr, chairman of Cooper Tire and Rubber Co.; Ted Turner of Turner Broadcasting System; and Robert Maloney, chairman, Diebold, Inc.

Despite the workload, many students told us "I love life at Katz!" The atmosphere is reportedly cooperative. "My fellow students are willing to help each other and still maintain a sense of competition," wrote one MBA. The students report their classmates are diverse, and there is a large number of international students. One MBA criticized his classmates as "heavily quantitative . . . not problem solvers." But an enthusiast told us, "There is a big sense of 'family' at Katz," Married people reported being happy at here, too.

Students described the Katz facilities as "very modern and technologically advanced," though there was more than one pitch for "healthier food!" The campus itself is located in Oakland, a small, college-town part of Pittsburgh. Students say it's "very livable—a clean, safe, comfortable city with good cultural events—plays, Steelers, festivals, etc." MBAs seem to have a good time out of the classroom. "It isn't unusual to find thirty to fifty of us at a bar on the weekend blowing off a little steam," wrote one student. Choice on-campus activities include intramural sports, and going to watch the Pitt's nationally rated football and basketball teams. Community service ranks high on the scorecard of favorite extracurriculars. A large number of students are involved in ABBEY (Going ABove and BEYond).

ADMISSIONS

Katz first considers your work experience and then, in descending order, GMAT score (TOEFL for international students), college GPA, essays, interview, letters of recommendation, and extracurricular activities. According to the school, "Quantitative information is important, but a student's work background and experiences through their college years can be as important as actual performance numbers on the GMAT or academic record." Minorities, international, and handicapped students are given special consideration. Each application is individually considered, then evaluated in groups of 100 or more.

FINANCIAL FACTS

Tuition (in/out-state)	$15,375/$26,190
Tuition per credit (in/out-state)	$446/$834
Fees (in-state/out-of-state)	$2,164/$2,164
Cost of books	$1,000
Room & Board (on/off-campus)	NR/$14,000
% of students receiving aid	28
% first–year students receiving aid	27
% aid that is merit-based	80
% of students receiving loans	40
% of students receiving paid internships	8
% of students receiving grants	58

ADMISSIONS

# of applications received	800
% applicants accepted	63
% acceptees attending	48
Minimum TOEFL	600
Average GPA (range)	3.36
Application fee (in/out-state)	$50/$50
Early decision program available	Yes
Early decision deadline	January 15
Early decision notification	March 1
Regular application deadline	March 15
Regular notification	Rolling
Admission may be deferred?	Yes
Maximum length of deferment	1 year
Transfer students accepted?	Yes
Admissions process need-blind?	Yes

APPLICANTS ALSO LOOK AT

Penn State University, New York University, University of Pennsylvania, University of Maryland, University of North Carolina at Chapel Hill, University of Chicago, Ohio State University, University of Texas at Austin

EMPLOYMENT PROFILE

Placement rate (%)	98
# of companies recruiting on-campus	100
% grads employed immediately	94
% grads employed within six months	95
Average starting salary	$58,000

Grads employed by field (avg. salary):

Accounting	12% ($56,322)
Consulting	($54,220)
Finance	40% ($58,800)
General Management	3% ($61,000)
Human Resources	1% ($52,500)
Marketing	19% ($50,457)
MIS	24% ($56,400)
Operations	7% ($58,300)
Strategic Planning	2% ($50,000)
Other	8% ($69,150)

PURDUE UNIVERSITY
Krannert Graduate School of Management

OVERVIEW
Type of school	public
Affiliation	none
Environment	suburban
Academic calendar	moduled
Schedule	full-time only

STUDENTS
Enrollment of parent institution	33,033
Enrollment of business school	262
% male/female	74/26
% minorities	14
% international (# countries represented)	27 (27)
Average age at entry	27
Average years work experience at entry	4

ACADEMICS
Student/faculty ratio	5:1
% female faculty	10
% minority faculty	18
Hours of study per day	5.02

SPECIALTIES
Business–to–Business Marketing, Organizational Behavior & Human Resource Mgmt., Strategic Mgmt., Manufacturing Mgmt., Corporate Finance, Info. Tech.; All major functional areas represented. In addition, programs in Entrepreneurship, International Management and Manufacturing Management are available. Especially strong in Operations Management, Corporate Finance, and Applications of Information Technology.

JOINT DEGREES
Agribusiness MBA (in approval process now)

SPECIAL PROGRAMS
Washington Campus Program, Externship Program, Big Ten MBA Job Fair, MS in Human Resources Mgmt; Plus Leadership Program, Management Volunteer Program, Business Opportunity Program

STUDY ABROAD PROGRAMS
None yet

SURVEY SAYS...
HITS
Computer skills
Placement
Pressure

MISSES
Profs not great teachers
School clubs
MIS/operations

PROMINENT ALUMNI
Karl Krapek, President, United Technologies Pratt & Whitney Division; Thomas Page, Chairman of the Board, Enova Corporation and San Diego G&E; James Perrella; Chairman, Preisdent and CEO, Ingersoll-Rand Company

ACADEMICS

Krannert offers a degree in Management (MSM) that emphasizes an analytical approach with a heavy focus on information technology. Purdue also offers a degree in Industrial Administration (MSIA), which is completed in eleven months, including a summer session. Students in both programs share the same core course requirements. However, MSIAs take four electives. MSMs take up to eight, and have the opportunity to declare an "options area."

Students at Krannert gave the administration good marks. Wrote one, "The school now considers students' concerns and problems. Decision makers are accessible and they're genuinely concerned." This sense of satisfaction apparently has much to do with the recently restructured curriculum, which now features two eight-week modules instead of the traditional sixteen-week semester. The shorter modules lighten up the core requirement load, provide students greater exposure to a variety of courses, and permit them to take more electives during the first-year.

One of the assets that draws students to Krannert is a national reputation in operations management. "We are the strongest in the country when it comes to using computers for quantitative analysis," asserted one student. But students also gave top scores to their general management skills. Another MBA remarked, "The finance department is very underrated." High marks went to the administration for their efforts to involve students in shaping Krannert. "The program is making a concerted effort to improve its quality and publicity." The teaching at Krannert got unfavorable reviews, however. One student told us the instruction was "nothing to write home about," and another called it "a weak spot." Students seem satisfied with their overall experience, however. Many agreed with the classmate who said: "Krannert is a top-twenty school for the money. I'd choose it again."

PLACEMENT AND RECRUITING

Students are satisfied with the Krannert Management Placement Office (MPO), and no wonder. In past years it has ranked among the ten most effective in placing students, according to our survey. Small class size works to students' advantage here, resulting in a great deal of personal attention from career counselors.

Like many other placement offices, MPO has developed an Internet-based approach to marketing its graduates, posting student resumes, and submitting them electronically to any (and all) of the 1600 companies in its database that students choose. Top recruiters at Krannert in 1998 included Air Products, Andersen Consulting, Booz-Allen, Deloitte & Touche, Ernst & Young, Ford, General Motors, Hewlett-Packard, Hines Interests, IBM, Ingersoll-Rand, Intel, Price Waterhouse, Procter & Gamble, SAP, Tektronix, and United Technologies.

STUDENT/CAMPUS LIFE

The Krannert School is small, which fosters a cooperative team atmosphere. First-years take core courses together. "I know everyone in my class," wrote one MBA, "We're like a family." People are competitive, but "there are no cut-throat-sell-your-mother-for-a-buck-types," according to one student.

Dr. Ward D. Snearly, Associate Director Prof. Master's Programs
1310 Krannert Building, West Lafayette, IN 47907
Admissions: 765-494-4365 • Fax: 765-494-9841
Email: krannert_ms@mgmt.purdue.edu
Internet: www.mgmt.purdue.edu

MBAs report they have "met friends for life" at Krannert. Students do have criticisms for their fellow classmates, however. The primary one is lack of work experience. Diversity is not a strength of the student body either. Said one student, "my classmates are all white, male, engineers from the Midwest. There is no diversity of thought." Another MBA told us he was "disappointed with the overall low caliber of students and their complete ignorance of anything that's not operations oriented, that is, politics, news, grammar, etc."

The b-school computers and classrooms at Krannert are state of the art. Unfortunately, the course load can be a grind. "We work like dogs," reported one MBA. But another disagreed: "It's certainly manageable if you have a little discipline and the ability to manage time." Nonetheless, students agree, "Krannert is not a country club b-school." Perhaps that's why recruiters attribute a Midwest work ethic to Krannert grads: newly minted MBAs don't expect to start at the top, they expect to work hard to get where they want to go.

The good news: a social life can be found at Krannert. As one student put it: "A school full of engineers does not create 'Animal House,' but evenings are fun." Another agreed, "Social life is what you make of it. There are plenty of activities football—tailgates, movies with student discounts, parties. You can always find a group of friends at Harry's (the campus bar)." Students work out at the "Co-Rec," an impressive gym featuring amusement-park-like facilities—from bowling to golf courses to archery. Planned events include school picnics in the fall, the annual alumni/student banquet, tailgate parties, a talent show, and a charity ball. If all else fails, big city delights can be found in Indianapolis and Chicago, a one-hour and two-hour drive, respectively.

ADMISSIONS

The admissions office reports, "Although applicants come from diverse backgrounds in terms of education, experience, and cultures, they tend to have in common a strong analytical and problem-solving background." Krannert first considers an applicant's GPA, then in descending order of importance: GMAT scores, work experience, interview, letters of recommendation, essays, and extracurriculars. Applications are handled on a rolling admissions basis; students are notified of a decision three to six weeks after their file is completed. Students can defer admission up to two years, and 10 percent of applicants are accepted with no work experience. Krannert uses a self-managed application (you accumulate documents and submit them all together), so applicants know the application is complete at the time of submission.

FINANCIAL FACTS

Tuition (in/out-state)	$6,825/$14,708
Cost of books	$800
Room & Board (on/off-campus)	$5,005/$4,500
% of students receiving aid	50
% first-year students receiving aid	20
% aid that is merit-based	50
% of students receiving loans	38
% of students receiving paid internships	99
% of students receiving grants	21
Average award package	$10,000
Average grant	$6,000

ADMISSIONS

# of applications received	1,304
% applicants accepted	25
% acceptees attending	39
Average GMAT (range)	615 (590–650)
Minimum TOEFL	575
Average GPA (range)	3.11 (2.80–3.40)

Application fee (in/out-state)	$30/$30
Early decision program available	Yes
Early decision deadline	November 1 then rolling
Early decision notification	December 15 then rolling
Regular application deadline	April 15
Regular notification	April 15
Admission may be deferred?	Yes
Maximum length of deferment	2 years
Transfer students accepted?	No
Non-fall admission available?	No
Admissions process need-blind?	Yes

APPLICANTS ALSO LOOK AT

University of Texas at Austin, University of Michigan Business School, Duke University, University of Illinois at Urbana-Champaign, Northwestern University, Indiana University, Penn State University, University of North Carolina at Chapel Hill

EMPLOYMENT PROFILE

Placement rate (%)	94
# of companies recruiting on-campus	95
% grads employed immediately	94
% grads employed within six months	100
Average starting salary	$62,134

Grads employed by field (avg. salary):

Accounting	0% (NR)
Consulting	14% ($68,500)
Finance	32% ($62,205)
General Management	12% ($59,230)
Human Resources	0% (NR)
Marketing	15% ($59,636)
MIS	5% ($67,400)
Operations	22% ($59,982)
Strategic Planning	0% (NR)
Other	0% (NR)

RENSSELAER POLYTECHNIC INSTITUTE
Lally School of Management and Technology

OVERVIEW

Type of school	private
Affiliation	none
Environment	suburban
Academic calendar	semester
Schedule	full-time/part-time/evening

STUDENTS

Enrollment of parent institution	1,929
Enrollment of business school	328
% male/female	77/23
% out-of-state	75
% part-time	46
% minorities	11
% international (# countries represented)	28(30)
Average age at entry	28
Average years work experience at entry	4

ACADEMICS

Student/faculty ratio	12:1
% female faculty	12
% minority faculty	3
% part-time faculty	9
Hours of study per day	4.52

SPECIALTIES

Management and Technology, with particular emphasis on Entrpreneurship, Management Information Systems, Value Creation, and Financial Technology.

JOINT DEGREES

BS/MBA, 5 years; MBA/MS, 2.5–3 years; MBA/Masters in Engineering, 2.5–3; MBA/JD, 3–4 years

SPECIAL PROGRAMS

International Exchange in seven countries, Sino-U.S. MBA, Executive MBA

STUDY ABROAD PROGRAMS

Denmark, Finland, Hong Kong, Australia, France, Italy

SURVEY SAYS...

HITS
On-campus housing
MIS/operations
Computer skills

MISSES
Social life
Profs not great teachers
Gym

PROMINENT ALUMNI

Sal Alfiero, CEO, Mark IV Industries; Robert Bozzone, Vice Chairman of the Board, Allegheny Ludlum Corp.; John Broadbent, Vice President-Finance, Treasurer, and director, Arrow International Corp.; Warren Bruggerman, former vice president, General Electric Company; William C.W. Mow, chairman and CEO, Bugle Boy Industries; Paul Servino, founder and Former Chairman, Bay Networks

ACADEMICS

Rensselaer Polytechnic Institute Lally School of Management and Technology offers only a Management & Technology (M&T) MBA. The M&T program, which has attracted a good deal of attention, emphasizes the integration of the traditional business areas with each other and with technology. As one might expect, the program features a heavy technical/quantitative slant and attracts engineering types with strong math and computer backgrounds.

The single most exciting aspect about the program is that "it involves lots of student consulting in technological areas" according to one MBA, and is a "hot-bed for new ventures." Enthused one student, "The strongest contribution to my education has been the yearlong, team-based, product development program." Another MBA praised the entrepreneurial activities of the Incubator Project and Technology Park which "provide students real-life experience in working with start-up, high-tech companies."

To bolster "softer" skills, RPI has designed a program that relies heavily on group work, and requires its techie types to take a leadership seminar. Thus the focus on technology remains a strength, while not dominating the curriculum. Though RPI MBAs rate their quantitative, operations, and computer skills very strong, they rate their general management and presentation skills equally strong, and their teamwork skills the strongest of all. According to one M&T MBA "not having a technical background has not hindered my status in the program." The professors at Rensselaer receive strong ratings. "The good ones are truly top-notch," wrote one student, "although there are a few duds." More impressive, given the dedication to cutting-edge research, is that the "faculty is very accessible and assist students outside of class." All in all, students agreed, "RPI's new M&T program is one of the most innovative programs around."

PLACEMENT AND RECRUITING

RPI MBAs are satisfied with the job offers they receive at graduation. This is due in part to the high demand for M&T graduates, who make a great fit for growing technological companies. The Career Resources Office (CRO) can take credit for student satisfaction as well because it takes advantage of the small size of the student body by making sure students are given personal attention. The CRO reports that they "seek out" those students who don't visit the office, especially as graduation approaches. This practice is barely imaginable at larger schools. The placement office works as hard on summer internships, participating in the Kauffman Summer Intern Program, which places ten students with start-up companies. According to the CRO, the program provides "a real entrepreneurial summer experience, followed by a fall term independent study when students write a business plan for the company." The CRO works cooperatively with RPI's larger Career Center, creating opportunities for M&T students to seek employment with businesses that might not originally have thought to hire an MBA.

David J. Bohan, Director of Management and Technology Masters Program
Troy, NY 12180
Admissions: 518-276-4800 • Fax: 518-276-8661
Email: management@rpi.edu
Internet: www.lallyschool.rpi.edu

Rensselaer Polytechnic Institute

STUDENT/CAMPUS LIFE

A small school, RPI boasts small classes, great computing facilities, and a lot of student/faculty interaction. The workload, however, is a killer. The vast majority of students study outside of class a whopping thirty to forty hours a week. Study groups provide an opportunity for commiseration and collaboration. Though RPI students rate each other as intensely competitive, the emphasis on teamwork lightens up the industrious mentality of the driven types. Students appreciate a helping hand from their peers and frequently reciprocate. More than one MBA, however, pleaded for "more tutoring sessions!" The second-years workload is lighter, but they're kept busy with a practicum in a local industry, which usually entails fifteen to twenty-five hours a week of work. At least it's not homework.

Rensselaer's program is very group-oriented, and students agree their classmates are both professionally and ethnically diverse. Over 40 percent of students hail from overseas, and minorities comprise nearly 12 percent of the school. While the majority of MBAs report they enjoy each other's company, they told us the social scene is hindered by the number of academic activities in and out of the classroom. Most events are scheduled through the MBA Association and include happy hours, barbecues, golf events, and guest speaker series. About 30 percent of the students live on campus in graduate housing, which is considered extremely attractive and safe. The majority of students, though, live off-campus in Troy. Though no one reported a great love for the town, they said the public transportation was pretty good.

ADMISSIONS

The admissions office considers candidates with strong technical, quantitative, leadership, and teamwork skills. All components of the application–college GPA, GMAT score, work experience, extracurricular activities, interview, letters of recommendation, and essays–are equally weighed. A TOEFL of 570 or greater is required of those who speak English as a second language. The school favors applicants with a technically oriented undergraduate background: "Our focus is the intersection of management and technology. Everything we do begins with the conviction that for all firms in all future markets, sustainable competitive advantage is built upon a technological foundation."

FINANCIAL FACTS

Tuition	$18,900
Tuition per credit	$630
Fees	$1,045
Cost of books	$1,605
Room & Board (on/off-campus)	$7,125/$7,125
% of students receiving aid	70
% first-year students receiving aid	50
% aid that is merit-based	100
% of students receiving loans	75
% of students receiving paid internships	25
% of students receiving grants	35
Average grant	$15,120

ADMISSIONS

# of applications received	244
% applicants accepted	65
% acceptees attending	48
Average GMAT	593
Minimum TOEFL	570
Average GPA	3.20
Application fee (in/out-state)	$35
Early decision program available	Yes
Early decision deadline	February 1
Early decision notification	March 1
Regular application deadline	April 1
Regular notification	Rolling
Admission may be deferred?	Yes
Maximum length of deferment	1 year
Transfer students accepted?	Yes
Non-fall admission available?	Yes
Admissions process need-blind?	Yes

APPLICANTS ALSO LOOK AT

Cornell University, Massachusetts Institute of Technology, Carnegie Mellon University, Columbia, University of Maryland, New York University, George Washington University, Purdue

EMPLOYMENT PROFILE

Placement rate (%)	98
# of companies recruiting on-campus	115
% grads employed immediately	76
% grads employed within six months	100
Average starting salary	$55,934

Grads employed by field (avg. salary):

Consulting	22% ($45,100)
Finance	20% ($56,055)
General Management	4% ($42,500)
Marketing	10% ($49,125)
MIS	20% ($50,967)
Operations	8% ($55,433)
Other	16% ($43,500)

RICE UNIVERSITY
Jesse H. Jones Graduate School of Management

ACADEMICS

Rice University's Jones School of Administration may be on the threshold of some major changes. In March of 1997 a blue-ribbon steering committee of senior business executives and prominent academicians published its suggestions for the school's future. Among those recommendations: increase the size of the student body and faculty, establish an Executive MBA program, pursue more joint ventures with area hospitals, businesses, and other departments at Rice, and secure national accreditation from the American Assembly of Collegiate Schools of Business. The following July, the school appointed Gilbert Whitaker Jr. as dean of the program. Whitaker, a Rice graduate, previously piloted the University of Michigan School of Business's rise to national prominence.

All of these changes are intended to address the only perceived shortcoming in this highly regarded program, namely that its size and lack of American Assembly of Collegiate Schools of Business accreditation (all top–fifty ranked schools have this accreditation) have prevented the Jones School from entering the top echelon of national MBA programs. Even so, the Jones School currently enjoys a well-deserved reputation as an excellent program, albeit one that draws students primarily from its immediate region. Students attribute the school's standing to an "excellent faculty, challenging curriculum, and beneficial utilization of the case-study method." Students here also benefit from the fact that "the new dean and administration are very focused on student concerns and improving the program" and a "very low student-faculty ratio," where "students and professors spend time outside of class discussing business and topical matters. There are many opportunities to be involved." Students give professors high marks for teaching ability as well as accessibility.

Jones MBAs praise the school's finance department and entrepreneurship program. They also approve of the marketing and accounting departments. In all departments, students report that professors rely heavily on quantitative analysis and the case method. Writes one, "Almost all classes use the case method. Classes that use it most extensively—marketing and economics—are more difficult, but immensely more rewarding. It is hard work but it pays off." The result is a "major work load with many group projects," especially during the first-year core curriculum.

Several features distinguish the Jones program. Among them are required courses in entrepreneurship and global strategy/operations. Another is its unusual focus on legal, ethical, and governmental issues in business administration. Rice offers a joint MBA/Masters in Engineering through the Jones School and the George R. Brown School of Engineering. Rice's location in Houston, national headquarters of the energy industry, greatly enhances the value of this degree.

PLACEMENT AND RECRUITING

Students at Rice University give their Career Planning Center above average marks, although a sizable minority feels that the service needs substantial improvement. In the plus column are Rice's "great connection to oil and gas industry, as well as to [the] Houston business community" and a "strong alumni network." In the debit column, students complain that the school does not do

Jill L. Deutser, Director of Admissions and Marketing
6100 Main Street, Houston, TX 77005-1892
Admissions: 713-527-4918 • Fax: 713-285-5251
Email: enterjgs@rice.edu
Internet: www.ruf.rice.edu/~jgs

Rice University

enough to attract on-campus recruiters from outside the Texas region. Writes one typical respondent, "There is a need for more national recognition and an increase in the number of companies recruiting at Rice University."

In addition to on-campus recruiting, Rice creates recruitment opportunities through participation in the Atlanta MBA Consortium and the Foreign National MBA Career Forums in Miami and Orlando.

STUDENT/CAMPUS LIFE

As would be expected at so highly regarded an academic institution, students at Rice are "highly intelligent." Many are "competitive in nature, sometimes overly concerned with grades, but mostly very friendly, sociable, and fun." The student demographic is "very mixed-all ages, all backgrounds" with "lots of married students." Furthermore, "Rice has a great mix of quantitative students (former engineers) and qualitative students that makes for great class discussions." The minority population, however, is small. Although "extremely hardworking, Rice students are also "involved in non-school activities."

A large married contingent and a demanding academic schedule result in low participation levels in school activities and clubs, although those with the available time note that the Rice community provides "a lot of clubs and organizations. A real sense of community among students, faculty, and staff." Although a few students complain that they "have no life other than school," most agree that "life at Rice is good. Plenty of learning, lots of networking, tons of opportunity, and an active social scene." During a typical week, "Monday to Wednesday is serious and then the weekend kicks off Thursday afternoon with a party on the back patio [called a partio]- fun!" Furthermore, "social activities happen often and in big groups. It is very common for a group of twenty plus students to meet for drinks on Friday night." Located in a residential section of Houston, Rice offers a surprisingly tranquil and beautiful 300-acre campus encircled by a tree-lined jogging path.

ADMISSIONS

The Jones admissions department considers the following criteria most important: essays, college GPA, letters of recommendation, and work experience. Extracurricular activities and leadership skills are also considered. An interview is strongly encouraged; the school plans to make interviews mandatory for all applicants and schedule them in conjunction with weekly information sessions. According to the school, "Each applicant receives a comprehensive evaluation due to the composition of our admissions committee, which includes two graduating MBA students, a recent alumnus or alumna, a tenured faculty member, and the admissions directors. We do not select or reject an applicant based solely on his or her academic record or GMAT score; instead we evaluate each applicant in the context of the entire application." Decisions are made on a rolling basis with four major deadlines: December 1, January 15, March 1, and April 15.

FINANCIAL FACTS

Tuition	$15,750
Tuition per credit	$795
Fees	$420
Cost of books	$1,200
Room & Board (on/off-campus)	$7,200/$9,000
% of students receiving aid	70
% first-year students receiving aid	70
% aid that is merit-based	50
% of students receiving loans	70
% of students receiving paid internships	100
% of students receiving grants	40
Average grant	$5,100

ADMISSIONS

# of applications received	571
% applicants accepted	45
% acceptees attending	56
Average GMAT (range)	632 (550–770)
Minimum TOEFL	600
Average GPA (range)	3.17 (2.70–4.00)
Application fee (in/out-state)	$25/$25
Early decision program available	No
Regular application deadline	March 1
Regular notification	April 30
Admission may be deferred?	Yes
Maximum length of deferment	1 year
Transfer students accepted?	No
Non-fall admission available?	No
Admissions process need-blind?	Yes

APPLICANTS ALSO LOOK AT

University of Texas at Austin, University of Pennsylvania, University of Virginia, Harvard University, Northwestern University, University of North Carolina at Chapel Hill, Stanford University, University of California—Los Angeles

EMPLOYMENT PROFILE

Placement rate (%)	100
# of companies recruiting on-campus	71
% grads employed immediately	85
% grads employed within six months	100
Average starting salary	$61,000

Grads employed by field (avg. salary):

Accounting	7% ($41,333)
Consulting	8% ($70,714)
Finance	43% ($61,541)
Marketing	13% ($55,000)
MIS	7% ($56,333)
Operations	7% ($64,021)
Strategic Planning	5% ($63,000)
Other	

UNIVERSITY OF ROCHESTER
William E. Simon Graduate School of Business Administration

OVERVIEW

Type of school	private
Affiliation	none
Environment	metropolis
Academic calendar	quarter
Schedule	full-time/part-time/evening

STUDENTS

Enrollment of parent institution	7,832
Enrollment of business school	814
% male/female	73/27
% out-of-state	30
% part-time	30
% minorities	12
% international (# countries represented)	32(48)
Average age at entry	27
Average years work experience at entry	5

ACADEMICS

Student/faculty ratio	15:1
% female faculty	15
% minority faculty	0
% part-time faculty	11
Hours of study per day	4.80

SPECIALTIES
The Simon School offers 13 concentrations, ranging from the more broad-based, i.e. finance, to the more specialized, i.e. health care mgmt. The hallmarks of a Simon School ed. are its integration around economic principles & its long-term applicability.

JOINT DEGREES
MBA/MS in Microbiology and Immunology, 2 years; MBA/MS in Nursing, 2.5 years; MBA/Master of Public Health, 3 years, MD/MBA, 5 years

SPECIAL PROGRAMS
VISION, Broaden Your Horizons Intercultural Seminar Series, the Executive Seminar Series, International Exchange Programs, Coach-Mentor Program

STUDY ABROAD PROGRAMS
8 foreign exchange programs available

SURVEY SAYS...
HITS
Finance
Ethnic and racial diversity
Quantitative skills

MISSES
Social life
Gym
General management

PROMINENT ALUMNI
Paul A. Brands, CEO, American Mgmt Systems; Charles R Hughes, CEO and President, Land Rover North America; Charles A. Dowd '69, President, MASCO Corporation

ACADEMICS

"Finance" is the magic word at the Simon School of Graduate Business Administration, where a staggering eighty-two percent of all students give the finance department our highest rating. The department is the most-often cited reason students give for choosing the Rochester MBA program. Explains one student, "The finance teachers are great and present current research that can be used in real-world situations." Another articulates the belief commonly held here, that "in finance and data analysis we are unequaled, with the possible exception of Chicago."

The Simon School's strength lies in its world-class, research-oriented faculty who, unlike many researchers, also happen to be excellent teachers. At Simon, "the big name professors actually teach, and they do it well." One student noted that these "world-famous professors devote incredible energy to teaching, and you can walk into their offices and have a chat any time!" The vaunted finance faculty features Gregg A. Jarrell, one-time chief economist of the U.S. Securities and Exchange Commission, and Clifford W. Smith Jr., author of numerous books and winner of even more teaching awards. Accounting is the other standout department here. Students also give good marks to courses in management and operations.

School brochures boast "the most integrated MBA curriculum" of all business schools, and students apparently agree. Explains one, "The other day I was reading a case for econometrics. One of the case questions was from my finance professor who thought it would be interesting for us to explore a couple of finance issues. That's integration! The profs are always on top of who's doing what in each class." First-year studies emphasize teamwork through five-member cohorts and student management teams. Students remain in their assigned cohort throughout the three-quarter long core sequence and collectively tackle numerous case studies and group projects. Our respondents appreciated the "strong grounding in economic theory" they received through the core but warn that the sequence is "very quantitative-challenging, especially for non-quant folks." Students agree that "the experience is worth it!" Second-year students choose from among thirteen areas of concentration, and many pursue a double concentration. Grade-conscious students, beware. "The Simon School's relative grading system (curve) is very competitive," complains a student.

PLACEMENT AND RECRUITING

Simon's Career Services Office (CSO) writes that the program's small size allows it to offer "uniquely personal and individualized assistance to all Simon students during the recruiting and placement process." Among the "full range of services" offered are individual counseling, mock interviews, career workshops, resume books, and alumni programs. In addition to scheduling on-campus recruiting, the CSO organizes the New York Recruiting Program, "which gives students an opportunity to interview in Manhattan with New York City-area firms," and participation in MBA consortia and international student recruiting events.

Pamela Black-Colton, Assistant Dean for Admissions and Administration
Schlegel Hall, Rochester, NY 14627
Admissions: 716-275-3533 • Fax: 716-271-3907
Email: mbaadm@mail.ssb.rochester.edu
Internet: www.ssb.rochester.edu

Our survey revealed dissatisfaction with the CSO, "especially for non-finance students." Students complain that the school needs to "bring more recruiters on campus. We don't advertise our product—the student—enough. We need to show corporations that the trip to Rochester is worthwhile, because we are!" Other students agree that "the school is making an effort to improve its placement office," and "its reputation...it is paying off–literally."

STUDENT/CAMPUS LIFE

The student body at the Simon School is "a true embodiment of positive diversity. They draw from almost all countries, all educational and professional backgrounds." The nearly fifty percent from overseas meet with the approval of all the students, who feel that "the diversity of the student body really prepares us to work in global environments." Students are "surprisingly helpful despite the relative grading system." The first-year emphasis on teamwork helps, fashioning a group that is "very teamwork oriented, and willing to learn about the cultural backgrounds of all students." According to one student, another reason that "students are generally helpful" is the "sense that the school is underrated, and by helping each other we will have greater collective success that will eventually reflect on the school." Finally, students grow close during this program because "it's a small group; we all know each other."

Students write that "it is a challenge to find a balance between school, social, sports" because "the workload can be intense." This is especially true during the first-year, when "you practically live with your study team." A second-year student reflects, "social life is a sore subject the first year. The second-year students seem to have a lot more fun because the workload eases up dramatically." In their spare time, students become "highly involved in a diverse range of academic/club activities. Simon has everything big schools offer in a small package with top facilities." The "administration and student government have worked to improve social life by arranging school-funded ski trips, sporting events, parties." Snowy during winter, but located in a beautiful part of upstate New York, the weather does not hurt an active social life. One student commented,"There is always something going on in Rochester to take a break from the challenging and rewarding Simon Program."

ADMISSIONS

Three-fourths of the full-time graduating class start in September; the remaining one-fourth start in January and complete the program in an accelerated eighteen-month schedule.

The admissions committee considers the following criteria (not listed in order of importance): Quality of undergraduate school; academic accomplishments and ability; essays, college GPA, letters of recommendation, and GMAT. Interviews are suggested for all students. Decisions are made on a rolling admissions basis. Applicants are notified of a decision within three weeks of applying.

Accepted students may defer admission for up to one year.

FINANCIAL FACTS

Tuition	$22,620
Tuition per credit	$754
Fees	$530
Cost of books	$1,200
Room & Board (on/off-campus)	$7,160/$7,160
% aid that is merit-based	100
% of students receiving paid internships	99
% of students receiving grants	69
Average grant	$9,952

ADMISSIONS

# of applications received	1,419
% applicants accepted	32
% acceptees attending	37
Average GMAT (range)	631 (560–670)
Minimum TOEFL	600
Average GPA (range)	3.22 (2.90–3.60)
Application fee (in/out-state)	$75/$75
Early decision program available	No
Regular application deadline	June 1
Regular notification	Rolling
Admission may be deferred?	Yes
Maximum length of deferment	1 year
Transfer students accepted?	Yes
Non-fall admission available?	Yes
Admissions process need-blind?	Yes

APPLICANTS ALSO LOOK AT

New York University, Cornell University, Columbia University, University of Pennsylvania, University of Chicago, University of Michigan—Ann Arbor, Dartmouth College, Duke University

EMPLOYMENT PROFILE

Placement rate (%)	87
# of companies recruiting on-campus	99
% grads employed immediately	87
% grads employed within six months	99
Average starting salary	$69,513

Grads employed by field (avg. salary):

Accounting	6% ($60,000)
Consulting	17% ($78,731)
Finance	43% ($74,310)
General Management	3% ($64,500)
Marketing	16% ($64,081)
MIS	6% ($62,358)
Operations	6% ($60,708)
Strategic Planning	3% ($53,236)
Other	

UNIVERSITY OF SOUTHERN CALIFORNIA
Marshall School of Business

OVERVIEW

Type of school	private
Affiliation	none
Environment	metropolis
Academic calendar	semester
Schedule	full-time/part-time/evening

STUDENTS

Enrollment of parent institution	27,000
Enrollment of business school	1,360
% male/female	
% part-time	62
% minorities	
% international (# countries represented)	(21)
Average age at entry	27
Average years work experience at entry	5

ACADEMICS

Student/faculty ratio	6:1
Hours of study per day	4.68

SPECIALTIES

International business in all of its aspects, including coursework in Accounting, Finance, Marketing, Management, and Information Systems/Operations Management, Global Business

JOINT DEGREES

JD/MBA; JD/Master of Business Taxation; Doctor of Pharmacy/MBA; MBA/Doctor of Dental Surgery; MBA/Master of Planning; MBA/Master of Real Estate Development; MBA/Master of Science in Industrial and Systems Engineering; MBA/Master of Science in Nursing, Gerontology, or East Asian Area Studies

SPECIAL PROGRAMS

International Exchange, MBA Enterprise Corps, Entrepreneurship Program, Program in Real Estate; All first-year MBA students in the full time program travel abroad for 1 week to China, Japan, Mexico or Indonesia

STUDY ABROAD PROGRAMS

Argentina, Australia, Austria, Brazil, Chile, China, Costa Rica, Denmark, France, Germany, Hong Kong, Indonesia, Japan, Korea, Mexico, Phillipines, Singapore, Spain, Switzerland, Taiwan, Thailand, UK

SURVEY SAYS...

HITS
Marketing
Teamwork skills
Interpersonal skills prep

MISSES
Safety
On-campus housing
School clubs

PROMINENT ALUMNI

Gordon Marshall, Chairman, Marshall Industries

ACADEMICS

The Marshall School of Business boasts strength in an impressive array of areas for a program of its size. Students praise the "strong academic programs in finance, accounting, and marketing," an "excellent information systems program," and the school's entrepreneurship program, which is consistently among the top-ranked in the nation. In addition, Marshall's Los Angeles location is a huge boon for those seeking opportunity in the entertainment business.

Many students tell us that they chose USC primarily because of its Pacific Rim Education (PRIME) program, a recent addition to the Marshall curriculum. PRIME consists of a four-week course covering business practices and management styles on the Pacific Rim. Team-taught by Marshall professors and faculty from "Pacific Rim partner institutions," PRIME exemplifies Marshall's emphasis on a "global perspective" in business. PRIME concludes with a trip to China, Japan, or Mexico, where students visit and study overseas businesses and financial institutions.

First-year courses at Marshall are organized sequentially so that concepts and skills build on each other. Courses are staggered to maximize the integration of the curriculum and may begin or end in the middle of a semester. Marshall's core curriculum emphasizes case studies, student presentations, and team projects, while trying to minimize the amount of class time spent in conventional lectures. Students are assigned to six-member teams during the orientation "team-building retreat" and remain with their team throughout first-year, completing core assignments and studying together. The result is a close-knit and happy student body.

Marshall professors earn high marks from their students, who tell us that their professors are "clearly experts, yet extremely approachable and personable." The prominence of the faculty has other benefits as well. As one student puts it, "I love talking about my professors' research while in my job interviews." Students caution that "professors expect you to work very hard, and they reward for hard work." According to our survey, students are also happy with their administration. "The administration is very responsive to student input and is working very hard to attract more recruiters and better-qualified students," writes one. Another explains, "When I applied, I inquired about a joint MBA/MA in Asian Studies. In response, the school created the dual degree. This is an example of how responsive they are!" No wonder students tell us "the program is student service-oriented, with lots of personal attention."

PLACEMENT AND RECRUITING

Our previous surveys indicated increased student satisfaction with Marshall's Career Resource Center, a trend that continues this year. Student opinion of on-campus recruiting, internship opportunities, and mentoring opportunities all reached new peaks this year. Our respondents save their highest praise for the "tremendous" alumni network "that is active and eager to help students."

Keith Vaughn, Director of MBA Admissions
BRI 100, Los Angeles, CA 90089
Admissions: 213-740-7846 • Fax: 213-749-8520
Email: uscmba@bus.usc.edu
Internet: www.marshall.usc.edu

The top full-time employers of recent graduates include Ernst & Young, Deloitte & Touche, AlliedSignal, Price Waterhouse, Intel, Hunt-Wesson, Arthur Andersen, Bank of America, Hewlett-Packard, HPM-Stadco, and IBM. Top employers of recent summer interns included Avery Dennison, Walt Disney Co., Wells Fargo Bank, and Intel.

STUDENT/CAMPUS LIFE

Marshall students think highly of their classmates, whom they describe as "intelligent, congenial, and teamwork oriented." Students come from a variety of business backgrounds. As a result, "everyone brings something different to the table, which is essential because so much of the work is team-based." Students of Asian descent make up a large portion of the student body: nearly one-quarter are Asian-American, and a substantial portion of the international contingent arrives from the Far East. Our respondents agree that "international students add significantly to the quality of education," reinforcing the feeling that the "students are one of the great strengths of the school." Although the workload here is heavy, students "seem to be able to balance their academic and social lives very well."

USC began construction on Popovich Hall, a new facility to house the MBA program, in the fall of 1997. Students believe that the facility, when completed, will remedy current concerns about classroom space and access to computer labs (which MBAs currently share with undergraduates). Campus life at USC is active, with students reporting strong participation in school activities and organizations such as the Graduate Marketing Association and the Graduate Latin Business Leaders. MBA candidates enjoy "great mixers every week, sponsored by companies that provide excellent opportunities for networking with potential employers and second years. The same applies to the scheduled 'brown bag' lunches every week." Sums up one student, "There are more resources available to me than I could possibly take advantage of. Life at school is all about time management." USC's park-like 150-acre campus is another of the program's many assets. Beyond the classroom, students agree that "social life is excellent," abetted by easy access to all that Los Angeles has to offer. Students give on-campus housing low marks, and most students here live off-campus in the beach communities of Manhattan, Hermosa, and Redondo Beach.

ADMISSIONS

According to the school, USC considers essays, college GPA, letters of recommendation, extracurricular activities, work experience, GMAT scores, leadership, and interviews. USC recommends that applicants be proficient in mathematics through calculus. Students are notified of a decision approximately three weeks after receipt of the completed application, including test scores. The final deadline for applicants is April 15. Students who are placed on a waitlist decision are notified of a post by June 30. On a case-by-case basis, students may defer admission for one year. According to the school, "We are a member of the Consortium for Graduate Study in Management, offering fellowships for talented minorities."

Room & bo...	
% of students receiving ...	
% first-year students receiving aid	
% aid that is merit-based	
% of students receiving loans	95
% of students receiving grants	30
Average award package	$39,000
Average grant	$19,000

ADMISSIONS

# of applications received	1,835
% applicants accepted	35
% acceptees attending	45
Average GMAT (range)	640 (580–700)
Minimum TOEFL	600
Average GPA (range)	3.20 (2.70–3.60)
Application fee (in/out-state)	$90/$90
Early decision program available	Yes
Early decision deadline	December
Early decision notification	December
Regular application deadline	April 1
Regular notification	April 15
Admission may be deferred?	Yes
Maximum length of deferment	1 year
Transfer students accepted?	No
Non-fall admission available?	Yes
Admissions process need-blind?	Yes

APPLICANTS ALSO LOOK AT
University of California—Los Angeles, University of California—Berkeley, Stanford University, Northwestern University, University of Texas at Austin, Georgetown University, New York University, University of Michigan Business School

EMPLOYMENT PROFILE

Placement rate (%)	96
# of companies recruiting on-campus	153
% grads employed immediately	87
% grads employed within six months	98
Average starting salary	$70,000

Grads employed by field (avg. salary):
Consulting	33% ($75,000)
Finance	29% ($66,000)
General Management	10% ($65,000)
Marketing	19% ($60,000)
MIS	1% ($63,000)
Operations	4% ($65,000)
Other	4% ($63,000)

METHODIST UNIVERSITY
Cox School of Business

ACADEMICS

The Edwin L. Cox School of Business at Southern Methodist University (SMU) sports "outstanding ties to the Dallas business community" and a progressive curriculum. In 1992 the school transitioned from a one-year to a traditional two-year program, and students report that they like belonging to "an up-and-coming organization." The program is comprised of demanding and qualitatively rigorous courses that provide students with a broad graduate management education with opportunities to concentrate in specific areas. Classes are taught in both lecture and case-study style. Cox encourages its MBAs to interact with the business community through formal interaction and by other informal networking opportunites with high-level business executives. The formal curriculum includes: the Business Leadership Center (BLC) and the Executive Mentor Program. The BLC was created to hone leadership and team skills. BLC workshops and seminars build strategic, interpersonal, communication, team-building, and leadership skills—the very skills that are prized in organizations but overlooked in many MBA programs. Courses are organized by outside consultants from some of today's most progressive corporations. Over and over, students praised this "innovative soft-skill curriculum." The Mentor program matches MBA students with a professional mentor from the Dallas business community. The mentor-student relationship begins from the very start of the MBA program. Students appreciate this structured networking program and say, "It's of incredible personal and professional value."

Students at SMU told us the "administrative staff is top-notch." "This place runs like a well-oiled machine," wrote one student. "The administration is very responsive and student-oriented," observed another, "They are willing to restructure at all levels based on student request." A smoothly run school no doubt contributes to the popularity of the MA/MBA—an option several students cited as their reason for coming here. The professors got high marks too, particularly in accounting and economics. However, one student remarked, "the teaching quality seems to be bipolar: Some professors are outstanding, others mediocre." MBAs appreciated professors' outside consulting experience, but one suggested that "professors should use computers more." Students also praised the integration of the curriculum. More than one agreed with the classmate who wrote "I feel truly challenged." Though students would like "more study rooms!" and a little more diversity and work experience in their ranks, they are more than satisfied with their experience at SMU. "Life at the Cox school is great" summed up a happy MBA.

PLACEMENT AND RECRUITING

Initiated in 1997, the MBA Career Management Office at Cox offers the Careeer Management Training Program, a series of required and optional workshops to equip students with job search skills. Students report that the alumni network is great, although limited geographically. Wrote one, "Few graduates move throughout the country and thus SMU's reputation is very localized." Last year more than 130 corporations recruited on campus. Cox also participates in the MBA Consortium, which organizes annual national interviewing events in New York and Atlanta. SMU grads most frequently move on to work at Ernst & Young, American Airlines, SABRE Goup, and Chase Bank of Texas.

Monica Powell, Director of MBA Programs
P.O. Box 750333, Dallas, TX 75275
Admissions: 214-768-2630 • Fax: 214-768-3956
Email: mbainfo@mail.cox.smu.edu
Internet: www.cox.smu.edu

STUDENT/CAMPUS LIFE

The small size of Cox's MBA program promotes an intimate learning environment. "At a school of this size, you really get to meet everyone," remarked one MBA. "I learn as much from the other students as I do from my classes." MBAs give themselves high grades for teamwork: "If someone has a superb study sheet they have made, they'll share it with others," claims one student. "There is a strong sense of cooperation at our school balanced by a fierce competitiveness . . . an interesting dichotomy," noted another. Although students say it's critical to do all the assigned reading, the workload is manageable, the pressure moderate. Students say their classmates are "smart and confident in their ability to succeed." MBAs say the student body is internationally diverse, which provides "an interesting mix of cultures," though a few wish there were "more women!" "I couldn't ask for better classmates!" enthused a happy student.

The Cox school is housed in a three-building complex. Reported a student, "The classroom facilities are first rate, though the damn air conditioning is too cold!" The electronic resources of the Business Information Center are considered outstanding. "A bigger snack bar would be nice," mused one MBA, "but I think the many benefits of being a Cox student outweigh having to go next door for lunch." Both off-campus and on-campus housing is reportedly attractive and readily available.

Students at Cox spend their time outside of class playing intramural tennis and volleyball. A favorite event is the spring golf tournament. Every Thursday night is drink-and-be-happy hour. On weekends, groups of students venture off-campus to enjoy the city delights of Dallas. According to students, "there are lots of places in Dallas to blow off steam," and most consider it a "nice city."

ADMISSIONS

The SMU admissions office told us, "We look for students who will take advantage of the variety of professional growth opportunities offered by the school for it is these inidividuals who can most clearly contribue to and benefit from our MBA Program." They enroll such students by searching out individuals who are well rounded, have clearly demonstrated academic achievement, and have a commitment and a capacity for leadership in business. Cox school admissions committee also emphasizes a strong GPA and GMAT score and prior work experience as important factors in their decision.

FINANCIAL FACTS

Tuition	$19,350
Tuition per credit	$677
Fees	$2,194
Cost of books	$1,200
Room & Board (on/off-campus)	$7,040/$12,000
% of students receiving aid	75
% first-year students receiving aid	75
% of students receiving loans	56
% of students receiving grants	54
Average award package	$13,500
Average grant	$19,306

ADMISSIONS

# of applications received	491
% applicants accepted	58
% acceptees attending	49
Average GMAT (range)	611 (570–650)
Minimum TOEFL	600
Average GPA (range)	3.10 (2.77–3.34)
Application fee (in/out-state)	$50/$50
Early decision program available	Yes
Early decision deadline	December 1
Early decision notification	January 31
Regular application deadline	Rolling
Regular notification	Rolling
Admission may be deferred?	No
Transfer students accepted?	No
Non-fall admission available?	No
Admissions process need-blind?	Yes

APPLICANTS ALSO LOOK AT

University of Texas at Austin, Vanderbilt University, Rice University, Duke University, Texas Christian University, University of California—Los Angeles, Northwestern University, University of Pennsylvania

EMPLOYMENT PROFILE

Placement rate (%)	91
# of companies recruiting on-campus	142
% grads employed immediately	78
% grads employed within six months	96
Average starting salary	$57,170

Grads employed by field (avg. salary):
Consulting	29% ($63,272)
Finance	38% ($59,993)
General Management	9% ($56,880)
Marketing	18% ($53,553)
Operations	5% ($49,800)
Other	

STANFORD UNIVERSITY
Stanford Graduate School of Business

OVERVIEW

Type of school	private
Affiliation	none
Environment	suburban
Academic calendar	quarter
Schedule	full-time only

STUDENTS

Enrollment of parent institution	6,561
Enrollment of business school	745
% male/female	71/29
% minorities	25
% international (# countries represented)	29(31)
Average age at entry	26
Average years work experience at entry	4

ACADEMICS

Student/faculty ratio	8:1
% female faculty	17
% part-time faculty	14
Hours of study per day	4.09

SPECIALTIES

General Management—includes all majors disciplines. Finance, Economics, Strategic Management, Marketing, Accounting, Human Resources/Organizational Behavior, Operations, Information & Technology, Political Science, and Entrepreneurship.

JOINT DEGREES

It is possible to earn dual degrees with many other departments. Most common areas are JD/MBA, 3 years and MSE/MBA.

SPECIAL PROGRAMS

Health Services Management option, the Speakers Platform, Global Management Program, Public Management Program

SURVEY SAYS...

HITS
Classmates are smart
Social life
Placement

MISSES
Gym
Safety
Profs not great teachers

PROMINENT ALUMNI

Scott McNealy, Chairman & CEO, Sun Microsystems; Charles Schwab, CEO & Chairman, Charles Schwab Inc.; Robert M. Bass, President, Keystone, Inc.; John Morgridge, Chairman, CISCO Systems.

ACADEMICS

The Stanford Graduate School of Business is indisputably one of America's great b-schools. If you study here, you will study among the nation's best and brightest, learn from Nobel Prize-winning faculty, and gain access to power employers. The first-year curriculum features a quantitative orientation and is extremely demanding. It's common for first-years to experience panic attacks about whether they'll make it or not. Despite their fears, almost no one flunks out. An extensive first-year mentoring and support system eases the way.

Stanford breaks its year into three quarters: fall, winter, and spring. The core curriculm has been designed to develop understanding and competence in four broad areas: internal environment of the organization (organizational behavior and human resource management); external environment (economics, political economy); functional areas (accounting, finance, marketing, production); and quantitative techniques (computer methods, decision analysis, statistics). The first-year core includes fourteen classes covering these topics. Students can take exemption exams to place out of cores. During the second year, students may choose from more than 100 electives. Favorites are: Strategic Management in the Nonprofit Environment, Personal Creativity in Business, Strategy and Action in the Information Processing Industry, and Power and Politics in Organizations. The interest in nonprofit topics is related to the popularity of the school's Public Management Program (PMP), which students describe as excellent. PMP is a certificate that is earned by taking three public management electives in addition to their required courses. Stanford also offers a Global Management Program within the MBA.

One of the hottest courses of study at Stanford is entrepreneurship. In fact, MBAs who take Entrepreneurship: Formation of New Ventures, have been known to come out with original and successful start-ups. Unique to Stanford is a de-emphasis on grades: Notes this MBA: "No-disclosure grading allows you to focus on what's most important/interesting to you." As for the faculty, while our prior survey revealed that students found less-than-exciting teaching in the core, much has been done to remedy this. A significant majority now rate professors good or better teachers. Some of the best learning experiences are found in the visiting speakers program, which features a greater number of speakers than most schools have in faculty. In a span of just nine days, Stanford was host to the following celebrities of the cyberworld: Apple Founder Steve Jobs, Jim Barksdale of Netscape, Ed McCracken, CEO of Silicon Graphics, Michael Nevens, leader of Mckinsey's worldwide electronics practice, and Andrew Grove, CEO of Intel. If that's not enough, in a creative pairing of expertise, Stanford Professor Robert A. Burgelman and Andrew Grove, CEO of Intel, team-teach Strategy and Action in the Information Processing Industry.

PLACEMENT AND RECRUITING

In 1997, more than 270 companies interviewed on-campus. A large number of graduates go to work for smaller, high-growth ventures and computer businesses in both Silicon Valley and elsewhere. Ninety-nine percent of the class had a job within three months of graduation. Average starting salaries were among the three highest of schools profiled in this book—$80,000 (which does not include lucrative sign-on bonuses)—a solid return on one's investment.

Marie Mookini, Director of Admissions
518 Memorial Way, Stanford, CA 94305-5015
Admissions: 650-723-2146 • Fax: 650-725-7831
Email: mbainquiries@gsb.stanford.edu
Internet: gsb-www.stanford.edu

STUDENT/CAMPUS LIFE

As one former student put it, several factors make Stanford stand out: "The absolute irrelevance of grades, the entrepreneurial spirit of the class, the supportive and comfortable atmosphere, the emphasis on social life, and the access to Silicon Valley." Much of student life revolves around the student clubs, of which there are over 100, including one for spouses and partners, The High Tech Club, and the I Have a Dream Program, unique to the Stanford Business School. Indeed, there is "A lot of emphasis on social and community responsibility." To judge by the responses to our survey, students are "the crown jewel of this program." Compliments this MBA: "The people are what makes the place. Friendly, happy, intelligent, fun classmates." Raves another, "The most impressive group of people I've ever been with!" But they eye Harvard warily for which school deserves to be King of the Hill. According to these students, Stanford has a certain edge on Harvard: "All the benefits of Harvard (i.e., great jobs) but nicer people, and almost no academic pressure." Indeed, what students find at Stanford is an informal, noncompetitive, intimate type of environment. All that, and a world class education. Located in suburban Palo Alto, Stanford MBAs are treated to an amazing atmosphere: sunny days, breathtaking views, hot tubs, year-round swimming in the school's outdoor pool, and, just a few hours' drive away, skiing in Lake Tahoe. A sprawling golf course on campus makes golf clubs de rigueur. Friday afternoons are reserved for Liquidity Preference Functions (LPF). Tuesday nights it's the "Friends of Arjay Miller," a.k.a. FOAM (which includes everyone). As for the campus, it's beautiful. The Spanish-style, red-tiled roofs are "a Stanford trademark." Facilities—including the research center and the library—are considered top-notch. On-campus housing for MBAs is available in a new facility, which opened in the summer of 1997. Most second-year students opt to rent shared houses in the hilly communities nearby. Many of these belong on the cover of Architectural Digest and verge on expensive (a four bedroom runs $1,800–$2,400 per month). However, all this atmosphere doesn't go to Stanford MBA's heads: according to our survey, students spend twenty to thirty hours per week studying. There is a major emphasis on teamwork and group projects. Students say classmates are ethnically and socially diverse. Recent classes boasted two Jesuit priests, an Olympic Medalist from New Zealand, a stand-up comic, a Washington lobbyist, and a shrimp farmer from Ecuador. All in all, students are in agreement with this very happy classmate: "I wouldn't want to be anywhere else!"

ADMISSIONS

Notes the admissions office, "We do not interview individual applicants. We ask that you treat your essay as an interview on paper. We have tried to design our essays to elicit the same type of information that you would share in a face-to-face meeting. Focus on the essays. We want to get to know you, so don't simply reiterate information we find elsewhere in your application. We use the nation's most selective admissions process to admit students who represent a broad range of professional and personal achievement." Affirmative action is considered for Native Americans, Mexican-Americans, African-Americans, and Puerto Ricans. Applications are batched in one of three rounds. According to the school, "The earlier you apply, the better." College seniors are admitted with a mandatory two-year deferral.

FINANCIAL FACTS

Tuition	$24,000
Cost of books	$2,290
Room & Board (on/off-campus)	$9,225/$11,409
% of students receiving aid	70
Average graduation debt	$46,416

ADMISSIONS

# of applications received	6,559
% applicants accepted	NR
% acceptees attending	NR
Average GMAT	711
Average GPA	3.60
Application fee (in/out-state)	$140/$140
Early decision program available	No
Regular application deadline	Nov 5, Jan 7, Mar 18
Regular notification	Jan 14, Mar 25, May 27
Admission may be deferred?	Yes
Transfer students accepted?	No
Non-fall admission available?	No
Admissions process need-blind?	Yes

APPLICANTS ALSO LOOK AT

Harvard University, Northwestern University, University of Pennsylvania, University of California–Los Angeles, University of Chicago, University of California–Berkeley, Massachusetts Institute of Technology, University of Michigan Business School

EMPLOYMENT PROFILE

Placement rate (%)	99
# of companies recruiting on-campus	392
% grads employed immediately	99
% grads employed within six months	99
Average starting salary	$113,250

Grads employed by field (avg. salary):

Communications	4% (NR)
Consulting	22% (NR)
Entrepreneurship	6% (NR)
Finance	19% (NR)
General Management	4% (NR)
Marketing	13% ($125,000)
Operations	4% ($140,000)
Strategic Planning	7% ($137,500)
Venture Capital	6% ($229,000)
Other	15% (NR)

SYRACUSE UNIVERSITY
School of Management

ACADEMICS

Like many b-schools, Syracuse has retooled its program to reflect the times. The updated curriculum addresses topics such as globalization, social responsibility, ethics, technology, diversity, and managing total quality. Distinct to Syracuse is the "management and the natural environment" theme, which focuses on the responsibilities of business in environmental issues. Also new and exciting: the Entrepreneurship and Emerging Enterprises Center, and a distinguished lecture series. A lot of credit goes to Syracuse's new dean, who spearheaded much of the change and a focus on curriculum quality. Said one satisfied MBA, "Syracuse has been working hard to improve the MBA experience."

Another added, "The new program is very innovative." The first-year curriculum is extremely regimented. This consists of the unifying theme courses, personal skills development courses such as "teamwork and groups" and "computer proficiency," and professional core courses. During the second year, students choose seven elective courses from a possible fifty and complete their remaining core courses. Students can also pursue interdisciplinary studies—from law to engineering and computer science, a bonus for MBAs who want to broaden their marketability by studying at Syracuse's top-rated Newhouse Graduate School of Public Communications or Maxwell School of Citizenship and Public Affairs.

Students are pleased with the program overall. They cited a strong finance department and guest speakers program as sources of satisfaction. "I'm thrilled to have the opportunity to better myself and my earning potential in this setting," gushed one MBA. "Opportunities for consulting projects for local businesses abound," reported another happy MBA. An unusual feature of Syracuse is that a large portion of the student body is in the Army. "ACP students are a valuable presence," asserted one MBA. "They offer discipline and a diversity of experiences which improve the program as a whole." A few students had complaints about each other's "lack of work experience" and "shoddy work ethics."

The students also had reservations about the quality of instruction. "Too many foreign teachers," complained one MBA. "It creates language barriers." Another student remarked "The professors are overly academic. They lack real-life experiences—they teach strictly from the text." A few respondents mentioned problems with "unprofessional" behavior in the faculty, such as petty infighting, which dragged down the quality of their experience.

PLACEMENT AND RECRUITING

The Syracuse Career Center points out that its strength is in the numbers: that is, the low ratio of students to staffers, which allows the school to "focus on the needs and skills of each of our students." On-campus recruiting is supplemented by two off-campus events, an MBA consortium in Washington, DC, and a recruitment meeting held in New York City exclusively for Syracuse students. The school also maintains offices in Shanghai, South Africa, Hong Kong, London, and Singapore, through which it provides students with opportunities for internships abroad. According to Career Center reports, the average starting salary of Syracuse graduates (see sidebar) is especially impressive because "a number of our graduates prefer to work with regional or entrepreneurial companies where the starting salaries are generally lower on a gross basis than those obtained in the larger metropolitan areas or with larger firms."

Paula Charland, Assistant Dean, Master's Enrollment
100 School of Management, Syracuse, NY 13244
Admissions: 315-443-9214 • Fax: 315-443-9517
Email: mbainfo@som.syr.edu
Internet: sominfo.syr.edu

Syracuse University

STUDENT/CAMPUS LIFE

The Syracuse campus is beautiful—a 200-acre spread of grassy lawns and historical, landmark buildings. The town of Syracuse has a secluded, rural feel that's conducive to hitting the books. And hit the books they do. Students report they are burdened with a heavy workload. The pace and breadth of the new curriculum keeps them studying an average of twenty-five to thirty hours a week. Papers and class participation are the preferred instruments of the grading system. MBAs report a moderate level of pressure and competition. Students report they find the pressure "stimulating" and they feel their classmates are interested in helping each other. "Syracuse is very teamwork oriented," agreed most MBAs. Over and over, students raved about how this school "has made major strides over the last two years—it's an up-and-comer!"

A decent, though not robust, social scene exists here. Students partake of the "Friday Shared Experience," where recent speakers include: Alan Greenspan, Jack Kemp, and Carmen Poicy (San Francisco 49'ers), and network through informal gatherings. Also garnering star reviews: Orange Consulting Group, a student-run organization that arranges for MBAs to consult with area corporations. Students are paid for their consulting work, but altruism is taught early here; monies go to a scholarship fund for other students. For the second-year MBAs, Fridays are held open for job fairs, reviews of exam topics with profs, or just catching up on some downtime. Overall, students' quality of life ratings zipped up from last year's survey. They report being happier, more involved with school clubs and activities, more impressed with their fellow students, and more warmly received by school alumni.

ADMISSIONS

The admissions office considers (not listed in order of importance) your essays, college GPA, letters of recommendation, extracurricular activities, work experience, and GMAT score. An interview is encouraged. Writes the school, "Each candidate is evaluated individually. Acceptance is based on the ability to excel in the classroom and eventually the career in business. We evaluate intellectual compatibility and academic potential through an in-depth review of the applicant's educational record, references, and performance on the GMAT exam. Program selection, major, and undergraduate institution are also considered. full-time work experience is highly recommended. Evidence of leadership potential, perseverance, and teamwork ability is also a plus." Decisions are made on a rolling admissions basis. Candidates may defer admission for up to one year.

FINANCIAL FACTS

Tuition	$16,650
Fees	NR
Cost of Books	$969
Room & Board (on/off-campus)	NR/$8,956
% aid that is merit-based	100
% of students receiving loans	30
% of students receiving grants	27
Average award package	$15,000
Average grant	$8,000
Average graduation debt	$9,633

ADMISSIONS

# of applications received	659
% applicants accepted	36
% acceptees attending	58
Average GMAT (range)	551 (470–670)
Minimum TOEFL	580
Average GPA (range)	3.10 (2.50–3.70)

Application fee (in/out-state)	$40/$40
Early decision program available	No
Regular application deadline	May 1
Regular notification	Rolling
Admission may be deferred?	Yes
Maximum length of deferment	1 year
Transfer students accepted?	No
Non-fall admission available?	Yes
Admissions process need-blind?	Yes

APPLICANTS ALSO LOOK AT

Boston University, New York University, University of Texas at Austin, George Washington University, University of Buffalo/SUNY, University of Rochester, Cornell University, Duke University

EMPLOYMENT PROFILE

Placement rate (%)	97
# of companies recruiting on-campus	130
% grads employed immediately	75
% grads employed within six months	99
Average starting salary	$57,000

Grads employed by field (avg. salary):

Accounting	8% ($57,000)
Communications	4% (NR)
Consulting	21% ($51,000)
Finance	15% ($57,000)
General Management	5% ($49,000)
Human Resources	12% ($47,000)
Marketing	17% ($61,000)
MIS	13% ($54,000)
Operations	5% ($55,000)
Strategic Planning	1% (NR)

UNIVERSITY OF TENNESSEE AT KNOXVILLE
College of Business Administration

OVERVIEW

Type of school	public
Affiliation	none
Environment	metropolis
Academic calendar	semester
Schedule	full-time only

STUDENTS

Enrollment of parent institution	26,000
Enrollment of business school	181
% male/female	70/30
% out-of-state	70
% minorities	10
% international (# countries represented)	11(7)
Average age at entry	26
Average years work experience at entry	4.5

ACADEMICS

Student/faculty ratio	15:1
% female faculty	10
% minority faculty	5
Hours of study per day	5.38

SPECIALTIES

Technology, Entrepreneurship, Logistics/Transportation

JOINT DEGREES

JD/MBA, 4—4.4years; BA/MBA, 5 years; MBA/Masters in Industrial Engineering, 2 years and 1/2 summer session.

SPECIAL PROGRAMS

The MBA Symposia, TOMBA, The Oak Ridge National Library, Summer Internships, Corporate Connections, Community Connections

SURVEY SAYS...

HITS
Presentation skills
Interpersonal skills prep
Marketing

MISSES
Quantitative skills
On-campus housing
Gym

ACADEMICS

The University of Tennessee at Knoxville b-school has overhauled its program to introduce a new paradigm for learning: Cross-functional courses, team-teaching, team-building, global study, and experiential exercises. This roll-up-your-shirtsleeves, activity-based program offers students more real-world experience than they could hope to find at most other b-schools. Distinct to UTK is the Oak Ridge National Laboratory (ORNL), which offers students access to pioneering technology. According to the school, "Students develop marketing strategies for commercializing technologies developed by ORNL. Selected students from any concentration may serve as consultants and market analysts who work with scientists from ORNL to identify, research and, when possible, market technologies with commercial potential."

UTK has the most innovative program in its regional area, and students rave about the academics. "Beyond expectations—the best learning experience I ever enjoyed," enthused one student. "Very strong academic program," advised another, "Its great value for the money." The core curriculum centers on a year-long case experience in which students run their own businesses. Working in teams, students make the management decisions necessary to keep the business in operation. At the end of the year they give presentations about their experience to companies who have faced similar problems. Students report that "taking a company from its birth through the entire business cycle" is one of their favorite aspects of the first-year experience.

The second year is less structured. Students take eight specialized electives to build an area of concentration. UTK MBAs give themselves strong ratings in marketing, management, finance, operations and teamwork skills. In fact, ratings went up from last year's survey in all academic areas, including professorial quality and accessibility. "Faculty is 100 percent behind student success," asserted one MBA. The only items on student wish lists were a stronger international business curriculum and better facilities. "The business building should either be renovated or demolished," wrote one student. Complaints in prior surveys focus on computer facilities, now that each MBA student is required to own a computer, there is little or no need to visit a computer lab and hang out with the undergrads. Overall, students are satisfied at UTK and want to get the word out about what a good time they're having.

PLACEMENT AND RECRUITING

The small number of Tennessee MBAs ensures that students receive plenty of individual attention from career counselors. The downside of a small program, of course, is that many companies pass it over during their recruitment drives, but the Career Services (CS) office claims to have countered this problem through its cooperative efforts with the campus-wide placement office (the university as a whole is huge) and 95 percent of 1998 MBAs were placed at graduation. CS also maintains a video-conferencing center to facilitate interviews with businesses that do not visit the campus, as well as a web-based resume book for employers to peruse. In 1998 the employers most aggressively recruiting UTK MBAs were Andersen Consulting, Coopers & Lybrand SysteCon, Cummins Engin, FedEx, Fleetguard, IBM, Lexmark International, and Lowe's.

Donna Potts, Director of Admissions, Graduate Business Programs
527 Stokely Management Center, Knoxville, TN 37996-0552
Admissions: 423-974-5033 • Fax: 423-974-3826
Email: gchampa1@utk.edu
Internet: mba.bus.utk.edu

University of Tennessee at Knoxville

STUDENT/CAMPUS LIFE

UTK sports a very small program. All entering students participate in the same yearlong first-year program. The small size promotes an "intimate" atmosphere and a cooperative learning environment. Remarked one student, "There is a strong all-for-one attitude here." A unique grading system also encourages cooperation in which "grading is based on team and individual performance and comprehensive written evaluations, NOT exams." Students have a heavy workload and hit the books an average of thirty to forty hours a week. This results in a fair amount of pressure, though not enough to cause a heart attack. To lighten the load, the majority of students work in study groups. MBAs agree that minorities are easily accepted, though they don't make up a high percentage of the student body.

Students report a high quality of life. This is due in part to the terrific social scene. "There's plenty to do here," wrote one MBA, "concerts, intramurals. Clubs and bars are also hot spots. We have a great time." The campus also boasts state-of-the-art facilities. TOMBA, the Tennessee Organization of MBAs, is the professional and social association for full- and part-time MBA students. The heart and soul of student life, TOMBA not only organizes the social events for students, but also organizes the network of UTK MBA alums, runs a professional speaker series, and orchestrates a major community service project. All MBA students are expected to join. As for Knoxville, one student wrote, "It's a great little city. Excellent restaurants—and the Smoky Mountains within one hour, a huge plus!" UT is known for its great basketball and football teams. One student told us, "Sports are huge. Football has a big impact on daily life."

ADMISSIONS

According to the admissions office, your work experience is considered to be the most important criteria for admission followed by GPA, GMAT score, interview, essays, extracurricular activities, and letters of recommendation come into play. "Since the UTK program is relatively small," writes the office of admissions, "we can give a good deal of individual attention to our applicants in order to determine whether ours is the right program for them and whether they are right for our program. As often as possible, we invite students to visit the campus, sit in on classes, and talk with current MBA students. In addition, we involve the faculty and administration in the admissions process."

FINANCIAL FACTS

Tuition (in/out-state)	$2,942/$7,382
Tuition per credit (in/out-state)	$150/$408
Fees (in-state/out-of-state)	$244/$244
Cost of books	$1,622
Room & Board (on/off-campus)	$3,000/$6,000
% of students receiving aid	50
% first-year students receiving aid	50
% aid that is merit-based	20
% of students receiving loans	80
% of students receiving paid internships	100
% of students receiving grants	10
Average grant	$4,000
Average graduation debt	$6,000

ADMISSIONS

# of applications received	565
% applicants accepted	27%
% acceptees attending	55%
Average GMAT (range)	610 (480–760)
Minimum TOEFL	550
Average GPA (range)	3.33 (2.60–4.00)
Application fee (in/out-state)	$35/$35
Early decision program available	No
Early decision deadline	Rolling
Early decision notification	Rolling
Regular application deadline	March 1
Regular notification	Rolling
Admission may be deferred?	No
Transfer students accepted?	No
Non-fall admission available?	No
Admissions process need-blind?	No

APPLICANTS ALSO LOOK AT

Vanderbilt University, University of Georgia, University of North Carolina at Chapel Hill, University of Virginia, Duke University, University of Alabama, University of Texas at Austin, Wake Forest University

EMPLOYMENT PROFILE

placement rate(%)	100
# of companies recruiting on-campus	NR
% grads employed immediately	87
% grads employed within six months	100
Average starting salary	$59,092

Grads employed by field (avg. salary):

Consulting	37% ($63,394)
Finance	11% ($38,560)
Human Resources	2% ($43,000)
Marketing	19% ($49,125)
MIS	2% ($62,000)
Operations	2% ($69,700)
Strategic Planning	NR ($85,000)
Other	32% ($56,500)

TEXAS A & M UNIVERSITY
Lowry Mays College Graduate School of Business

OVERVIEW

Type of school	public
Affiliation	none
Environment	suburban
Academic calendar	semester
Schedule	full-time only

STUDENTS

Enrollment of parent institution	41,892
Enrollment of business school	224
% male/female	75/25
% out-of-state	17
% minorities	11
% international (# countries represented)	33(19)
Average age at entry	25
Average years work experience at entry	2

ACADEMICS

Student/faculty ratio	10:1
% female faculty	20
% minority faculty	10
Hours of study per day	3.93

SPECIALTIES

Strengths of faculty and curriculum in Accounting, Taxation, Finance, Marketing, Management, Information Hystems, Human Resources Management, Real Estate, Organizational Behavior, Business/Public Policy, International Business, Management Science.

JOINT DEGREES

MBA/MA in International Management with Johannes Kepler University; MBA with Ecole Superieur de Commerce; MS in five business fields

SPECIAL PROGRAMS

Study Abroad in seven countries

STUDY ABROAD PROGRAMS

Austria, France, Germany, Mexico, Southeast Asia, England, Netherlands

SURVEY SAYS...

HITS
Gym
Off-campus housing
Presentation skills

MISSES
Quantitative skills
On-campus housing
Computer skills

ACADEMICS

Plenty of Lowry Mays College Graduate School of Business b-school students agreed with the Aggie (as they like to call themselves) who wrote, "A bargain!" Even for out-of-state residents, this school offers one of the lowest tuition rates in the country.

But Texas A&M has more than price going for it. It also boasts a national reputation and, according to students, "a great location" in the heart of the oil, gas, and power industries. The school's new updated curriculum starts off with "Challenge Week," an Outward Bound-style orientation. Students also take a two-semester leadership and development program, which focuses on ethics, cultural diversity, and leadership. A Cross Discipline Project (the CDP) gets students working on real-world problems and solutions. MBA teams study an existing company and then do an analysis on each of its functional areas. Elective hours can be earned through internships or study abroad. Everything here features a global slant. The latest addition to the program is "Aggies on Wall Street." Students get to travel to the Big Apple, glad-hand industry leaders, and tour the major exchanges and commercial banks.

Students praised the schools "top-of-the-line amenities" and gave themselves above average marks for academic preparedness in all the major disciplines. High scores were in the areas of accounting, general management, and teamwork. Students thought there should be stricter admissions requirements to select "brighter students." The Mays MBA program does now require students to have prior work experience before they can enroll in the program, which should improve the quality of matriculates. The faculty received decent marks for being "concerned with student success and well-being." The student loan office was described as "horrible" but generally the administration is well-regarded. Said one student; "There is a very strong commitment on the part of the administration to improving the school and its image." Overall, Aggies say this school is "taking major strides in the right direction," and providing students with a career-enhancing boost.

PLACEMENT AND RECRUITING

In response to prior complaints, Mays MBA now boasts a placement office dedicated solely to the needs of only MBA students. The small class size allows placement officers to get to know students personally. The aggressive approach the school takes in securing relationships with corporations results in high placement for grads, as does services such as resume books, recruiting events, and job search seminars. Indeed connections help, too. Students compliment the "Aggie network" and say alumni are responsive. Top employers include Exxon, Andersen Consulting, Koch Industries, and Houston Industries.

Wendy Boggs, Academic Advisor
212 Wehner Building, College Station, TX 77843-4117
Admissions: 409-845-4714 • Fax: 409-862-2393
Email: mba-office@cgsb.tamu.edu
Internet: mba-grad.tamu.edu

Texas A & M University

STUDENT/CAMPUS LIFE

Students at Texas A&M describe each other as "all around good old boys and girls" who relish "tradition." Students report that the atmosphere is competitive, but assert that "no sharks" swim in their ranks. By all accounts, the workload is heavy, but it's not overwhelming. The majority of students study an average of twenty to twenty-five hours a week. The MBA facilities are state of the art, though students wish there were a separate business library because "the bookstore is a rip-off." The new recreation center features an Olympic-size pool, a weight and fitness room, an aerobics room, an indoor track, and, for those with no fear of heights, an indoor climbing wall a first among b-school athletic centers.

College Station is described as a "small town" where there is "nothing to do but study and drink beer." The majority of students live off-campus in housing that is affordable, though not especially beautiful. Parking is reportedly "atrocious." Extracurriculars are sponsored by the MBA Association, which holds a case competition, executive lecture series, and recruiter/faculty/student golf tournament. Of course, sports are big—football, basketball, and baseball. An alumni mentor program quickly gets Mays MBA students hooked into the famed "Aggie alumni network," providing them a competitive advantage in the job search. Overall, students wish their ranks were more diverse and their digs cosmopolitan. But they report that the campus is friendly and safe, and the locale has great weather. One MBA challenged, "Let's see Harvard beat 70 degrees in January."

ADMISSIONS

While Texas A&M has no cut-and-dried formula for selecting MBA applicants, they do hold them to fairly rigorous standards. Above all, your GPA and GMAT score ought to be well above average. Beyond those, your work experience (they like to see a resume and require two years' post-baccalaureate work), personal essay, recommendations, and the quality and rigor of your undergraduate program are all taken into consideration. Leadership in any pursuit makes a good impression. There are no set math requirements, but A&M appreciates a strong quantitative background in its applicants. The Mays MBA program requires all candidates under consideration for admission to interview. Decisions are made on a rolling admissions basis.

FINANCIAL FACTS

Tuition (in/out-state)	$2,984/$8,552
Tuition per credit (in/out-state)	$68/$282
Fees (in-state/out-of-state)	$1,663/$1,663
Cost of books	$1,000
Room & Board (on/off-campus)	NR/$7,000
% of students receiving aid	50
% first-year students receiving aid	50
% aid that is merit-based	100
% of students receiving paid internships	40
% of students receiving grants	50
Average grant	$2,000
Average graduation debt	$2,000

ADMISSIONS

# of applications received	528
% applicants accepted	46
% acceptees attending	50
Average GMAT	608
Minimum TOEFL	600
Average GPA	3.27
Application fee (in/out-state)	$35/$35
Early decision program available	No
Regular application deadline	May 1
Regular notification	Rolling
Admission may be deferred?	Yes
Maximum length of deferment	1 year
Transfer students accepted?	No
Non-fall admission available?	No
Admissions process need-blind?	Yes

APPLICANTS ALSO LOOK AT

University of Texas at Austin, Rice University, Southern Methodist University, Arizona State University, Texas Christian University, Duke University, University of North Carolina at Chapel Hill, Purdue University

EMPLOYMENT PROFILE

Placement rate (%)	92
# of companies recruiting on-campus	110
% grads employed immediately	78
% grads employed within six months	92
Average starting salary	$50,500

Grads employed by field (avg. salary):

Accounting	5% ($42,500)
Consulting	27% ($49,800)
Finance	28% ($51,900)
General Management	14% ($52,625)
Human Resources	4% ($52,700)
Marketing	18% ($52,100)
MIS	2% ($41,500)

THE UNIVERSITY OF TEXAS AT ARLINGTON
College of Business Administration

OVERVIEW

Type of school	public
Affiliation	none
Environment	metropolis
Academic calendar	semester
Schedule	full-time/part-time/evening

STUDENTS

Enrollment of parent institution	19,286
Enrollment of business school	491
% male/female	65/35
% part-time	61
% minorities	10
% international (# countries represented)	23(41)
Average age at entry	30
Average years work experience at entry	2

ACADEMICS

Student/faculty ratio	7:1
% female faculty	11
% minority faculty	15
% part-time faculty	2
Hours of study per day	3.02

SPECIALTIES
Finance, Accounting, Information Systems, International Business

JOINT DEGREES
Accounting, Eonomics,Information Systems, Marketing Research, Personnel and Human Resource Management, Real Estate, and Taxation. Other graduate degrees including Engineering, Architecture, Science, etc.

SPECIAL PROGRAMS
Careers Program that includes comprehensive assessment, industry analysis, career exploration and interviews, managing in a diverse environment, career-focused academic advising, and internships.

STUDY ABROAD PROGRAMS
Norway, England, France, Australia, Mexico, Germany, and Korea.

SURVEY SAYS...

HITS
Star faculty
Small classes
Ethnic and racial diversity

MISSES
Unfriendly students
Social life
General management

ACADEMICS

The University of Texas Arlington (UTA) has tailored its MBA program to create a "good fit" for a particular niche of prospective business grads. Chief among UTA's assets is its location in the Metroplex region, which along with Houston is the center of the active, high-stakes Texas business world. This location allows UTA not only to feed area businesses but also to draw students from them, and accordingly the school has created a program that suits the needs of both full and part-timers well. Writes one student, "I like how UTA offers flexibility to MBA students, with most classes held in the evening." UTA is also extremely accessible to students with limited business experience, although the school prefers applicants with prior work experience. Finally, UTA provides all this without a heavy price tag, allowing graduates, unlike many MBAs, to enter the business world unencumbered by debt.

For incoming students with little or no academic business background, UTA provides "deficiency courses" in mathematics, computer information systems, and statistics. More experienced students may begin with "core" courses in accounting, finance, marketing, management, and computers and information systems. Students who have completed courses similar to the foundation courses may place out of them and proceed directly to advanced study, which includes several required courses, concentration in one academic field, and a number of electives that must be spread across several academic disciplines. Students report that, within these parameters, UTA is quite flexible. Writes one student, "The administration has supported me through numerous curriculum changes that have enabled me to enhance my market value."

The UTA faculty consists of "a good mix of 'academic' professors and part-time instructors with 'real-world' experience." Our survey shows a widespread perception that "Some professors are very good, others are awful. Lots of variation in quality." At one end of the spectrum are those who are "excellent and seem very concerned about the students;" at the other are professors who "don't really care if students learn. They're just interested in putting out the information." Students are most complimentary of the marketing and accounting departments. They also approve of UTA's "excellent resources: library, health facilities, student center, etc.," and report happily that "UTA is upgrading b-school facilities, computer labs, and adding a much-needed, MBA-only placement center."

PLACEMENT AND RECRUITING

UTA tells us, "The Dallas/Fort Worth Metroplex, with more than 115,000 businesses, provides a fertile lab for the exploration and pursuit of hundreds of career alternatives. The University annually hosts one of the largest 'career day events' in Texas and also serves as a co-sponsor of the Metroplex Area Consortium of Career Centers' (MAC3) semi-annual career day programs that attract top employers throughout the region. These events help maintain one of the nations largest student employment services, which offers daily 8,000–10,000 part-time jobs, co-ops, and internships. These opportunities are available year-round to students. A core of career professionals participate in a comprehensive MBA careers program and present an array of seminars designed to enhance the student's mobility skills and improve their circle of opportunities. Traditional

Alisa Johnson, Assistant Director of Graduate Business Programs
Box 19376, Arlington, TX 76019
Admissions: 817-272-3005 • Fax: 817-794-5799
Email: question@utarlg.uta.edu
Internet: www.uta.edu/gradbiz/gradweb.htm

University of Texas at Arlington

on-campus interviews are complemented by cooperative career fairs, extended electronic job listings, and an interactive resume data bank."

Our survey reveals that UTA students are only mildly satisfied with the school's placement office, approving of internship opportunities but expressing disappointment with on-campus recruiting. One student complains about the "lack of business jobs [listed at the career center]. Most of the job postings I saw were for engineers or were computer-related." Students also remark that UTA alumni are rarely helpful when contacted for assistance with job searches.

STUDENT/CAMPUS LIFE

While half of the classroom consists of full-time students, many of UTA's MBAs are part time and "commuter students. Most work; some have families. The part-time students bring a wide range of experiences to the classroom." These "hard-working, hard-earning, future-focused professionals" include a large international contingent that is "open and receptive." The result of this combination is that students receive "a lot of exposure to international perspectives and [input] from professionals [who are] working and taking courses at the same time." Because many students come to campus only to attend class and study, students find "very little opportunity to get to know each other." Notes one student, "I was not expecting such a commuter school. Also, I just graduated with my BA from Texas. I was not expecting to be the only one in my early twenties in most of my classes." Those who make the effort, however, do make contacts among the student body: "The best aspect of this program is the networking relationship I have formed with my classmates."

Typically, UTA students feel that "due to doing the MBA part time, overall life is a bit stressed. It would be better doing this full time." Part-time students warn that " because the MBA program runs in the evenings and Saturdays, campus life is nonexistent," although full-time students tell us, "There are lots of activities going on on-campus. One usually gets involved in extra-curricular activities." For those who have the time to appreciate it, UTA's "lovely campus" is also an asset. Students can access a wide range of extracurricular options in the Metroplex area. Arlington is a city of nearly 300,000, and is home to the American League's Texas Rangers as well as two huge amusement parks, numerous theaters, and several museums and art galleries. Fifteen miles to the east is Dallas, one of the cultural and retail centers of Texas. Forth Worth, twenty minutes to the west by car, boasts a world-renowned art museum as well as many historical remnants of the region's pioneering and cattle-herding heritage.

ADMISSIONS

While it accepts more applicants than it rejects, Arlington does expect its entering class to have a great deal of work experience to draw from. GMAT scores followed by undergraduate GPA and letters of recommendation rank highest in admissions importance.

FINANCIAL FACTS

Tuition (in/out-state)	$3,691/$10,411
Tuition per credit (in/out-state)	$98/$322
Cost of books	$800
Room & Board (on/off-campus)	$9,000/$9,000

ADMISSIONS

# of applications received	486
% applicants accepted	49
% acceptees attending	51
Average GMAT (range)	552 (490–610)
Minimum TOEFL	550
Average GPA (range)	3.13 (2.80–3.60)

Application fee (in/out-state)	$25
Early decision program available	No
Regular notification	Rolling
Admission may be deferred?	Yes
Maximum length of deferment	1 year
Transfer students accepted?	Yes
Non-fall admission available?	Yes
Admissions process need-blind?	Yes

APPLICANTS ALSO LOOK AT

University of Texas at Austin, Texas Christian University, Southern Methodist University, Texas A & M University, Arizona State University, Rice University, Ohio State University, Columbia University

EMPLOYMENT PROFILE

# of companies recruiting on-campus	851
% grads employed within six months	84
Average starting salary	$40,000

UNIVERSITY OF TEXAS AT AUSTIN
Graduate School of Business

OVERVIEW

Type of school	public
Affiliation	none
Environment	metropolis
Academic calendar	semester
Schedule	full-time only

STUDENTS

Enrollment of parent institution	50,000
Enrollment of business school	837
% male/female	75/25
% out-of-state	63
% minorities	11
% international (# countries represented)	15(40)
Average age at entry	28
Average years work experience at entry	5

ACADEMICS

Student/faculty ratio	10:1
% female faculty	20
% minority faculty	6
% part-time faculty	18
Hours of study per day	4.39

SPECIALTIES

Accounting, Finance, Information Systems, Marketing, Human Resources, Entrepreneurship

JOINT DEGREES

MBA/Master of Public Accounting; MBA/MA Asian Studies; MBA/MA Latin American Studies; MBA/MA Middle Eastern Studies; MBA/MA Public Affairs; MBA/MA Post-Soviet Studies; MBA/MA Communications; MBA/MS Manufacturing Systems Engineering; MBA/MS Nursing; MBA/JD, most are 72–75 credit hours, JD/MBA is 134 credit hours.

SPECIAL PROGRAMS

Spanish Language Track, Foreign Study, Masters in Professional Accounting Program, Investment Fund, Energy Finance, Quality Management Consortium, MOOT Corp.

STUDY ABROAD PROGRAMS

Germany, France, Mexico, Brazil, Chile

SURVEY SAYS...

HITS
Austin
School clubs
Accounting

MISSES
On-campus housing
Quantitative skills
Computer skills

PROMINENT ALUMNI

Kenneth M. Jastrow II, CFO, Temple-Inland; William R. Johnson, President and CEO, HJ Heinz; and James J. Mulva, President, Phillips Petroleum Co.

ACADEMICS

Over the past several years, the University of Texas at Austin (UT) MBA program has made a major commitment to upgrading its information resources, an effort appreciated by students. Writes one, "UT is dedicated to continuous improvement and it shows. You can't beat the bang for the buck you get at UT." Among these improvements is the EDS Financial Trading and Technology Center, a state-of-the-art research facility that, according to UT, uses technology tht is "more advanced than what you would find in the leading investment houses." UT Austin is also home to the IC2 (Innovation, Creativity, Capital) Institute, a "virtual organization" that links research institutes to businesses in an effort to develop and test modern business practices. IC2 includes the "Austin Technology Incubator," which assists start-up technology entrepreneurs and in so doing provides more than 150 students with hands-on entrepreneurial experience.

UT Austin boasts a number of other notable features. Students manage the TEXASMBA Investment Fund, which has managed more than $3 million in investments (the fund brought in an annualized return of 21 percent during its first two years of operation). Other students serve as paid consultants to area businesses through the Quality Management Consortia (also student-managed). A unique feature of QMC is that its internships run for an entire year, rather than three months (as is typical of many internship programs). The extended period allows interns to "accumulate in-depth, practical experience," according to the university.

UT Austin places its first-year students in cohorts of sixty students, who as a group complete the year-long core curriculum. Students approve, noting that "the cohort system fosters cooperation and networking and sharing of knowledge" and that "professors in the core are very good: great lecturers and terrific preparers." Second-year students may pursue any of a number of traditional majors and fields of concentration, or they may design their own courses of study. Students praise UT's "practical approach to business" in the marketing, entrepreneurship, finance, and IT programs, also asserting that UT is a "strong quantitative school." Professors, who earn very good marks from our respondents, are described as "excellent, experienced, and accessible," and "very supportive . . . They motivate you to investigate, analyze, and to carry through your own ideas and projects." Although "there are a few lemons [on the faculty], there are a lot more stars." Students warn that "the administration is somewhat bureaucratic, but it still gets the job done"

PLACEMENT AND RECRUITING

Students give the UT Austin Business Career Services office better-than-average grades, noting that the office does a good job of organizing "lots of recruiting receptions, career panels, and career workshops." According to the school, "The Career Services Office at UT Austin begins working with students before they enroll on resume and job search issues to help them get a jump start on the internship search."

UT Austin also reports that in recent years as many as 575 companies conducted on-campus interviews for MBAs at UT Austin. Past top recruiters have

Dr. Carl H. Harris, Director of Admissions, MBA Programs
CBA 2.316, Austin, TX 78712
Admissions: 512-471-7612 • Fax: 512-471-4243
Email: texasmba@bus.utexas.edu
Internet: texasinfo.bus.utexas.edu

University of Texas at Austin

included: Ernst & Young Consulting, Intel, Procter & Gamble, Deloitte & Touche Consulting, Exxon, Ford, IBM Consulting, AT Kearney, Citibank, NationsBank, SAP America, and Morgan Stanley. Students expressed great satisfaction with both the quantity and quality of companies performing on-campus searches. Our survey results indicate that UT Austin alumni were very helpful to those MBAs who contacted them for help in their job searches.

STUDENT/CAMPUS LIFE

Austin MBAs describe a friendly atmosphere: "People are genuinely helpful. We have great networking opportunities, and we foster a cooperative, not competitive, spirit." Incoming students appreciate a "great support system set up by second-years for first-years," and African-American students report that "African Americans form a great support network" for each other. An entrepreneurial spirit pervades the student body; as one student explains, "While the big dream at Wharton may be to make millions working for a prestigious firm, the big dream at UT is to make millions working for yourself." More than three-fifths of the students arrive with four or more years of work experience under their belts, bringing with them "diverse backgrounds that contribute to excellent classroom discussions."

The student-friendly town of Austin contributes heavily to the high level of overall happiness reported by the respondents in our survey; the majority of students rate the town "excellent." "The city of Austin has a wonderful culture of live music and arts in a beautiful setting," explains one student. Others comment on the city's vibrant bar scene, and others still praise a climate that "allows us to participate in outdoor sports all year." On campus, there's "tons going on," because "there are so many interesting courses to take, companies to do projects with, clubs to join, [and] activities to do, that you have to learn to set priorities and optimize your use of time." Many students meet every Thursday at an event called "Think and Drink," and clubs and organizations are "always organizing a get-together ranging from UT athletics events to a charitable fund raiser." Students also appreciate the "newly renovated campus recreation facilities," including an excellent gym "right across the street from the school." Although "everyone here is very focused . . . and puts school/job search first," they're also "always up for a good time."

ADMISSIONS

The admissions office uses the following criteria to evaluate applicants (not listed in order of importance): GMAT scores, essays, academic record and college GPA, work experience, and letters of recommendation. Interviews are not required, but a visit to the campus is encouraged if at all possible. Writes the school: "Although grades and GMAT scores are important, other areas receive substantial consideration. Personal and professional goals, achievements, extracurriculars, community involvement, and evidence of leadership and management abilities are considered in the admissions decision." The school places a high priority on increasing the representation of qualified women and minorities in the program. Decisions are made on a rolling admissions basis. Advises the school, "Apply as early as possible." After their files have been referred to the admissions committee, applicants are notified of the decision within six to eight weeks. On a case-by-case basis, admission may be deferred for one year.

FINANCIAL FACTS
Tuition (in/out-state)	$3,240/$12,450
Tuition per credit (in/out-state)	$108/$415
Fees (in-state/out-of-state)	$1,527/$1,527
Cost of books	$850
Room & Board (on/off-campus)	$5,372/$6,414
% of students receiving aid	82
% first-year students receiving aid	82
% aid that is merit-based	10
% of students receiving loans	72
% of students receiving paid internships	85
% of students receiving grants	10
Average award package	$16,000
Average grant	$1,000
Average graduation debt	$22,191

ADMISSIONS
# of applications received	2,552
% applicants accepted	32
% acceptees attending	49
Average GMAT (range)	645 (500–780)
Minimum TOEFL	550
Average GPA (range)	3.30 (2.00–4.00)
Application fee (in/out-state)	$80/$100
Early decision program available	No
Regular application deadline	April 15
Regular notification	May 1
Admission may be deferred?	Yes
Maximum length of deferment	1 year
Transfer students accepted?	No
Non-fall admission available?	No
Admissions process need-blind?	Yes

APPLICANTS ALSO LOOK AT
University of North Carolina at Chapel Hill, University of Michigan Business School, University of California—Los Angeles, University of California—Berkeley, Stanford University, Texas A&M, Northwestern University, University of Pennsylvania

EMPLOYMENT PROFILE
Placement rate (%)	95
# of companies recruiting on-campus	575
% grads employed immediately	90
% grads employed within six months	98
Average starting salary	$65,637

Grads employed by field (avg. salary):
Accounting	1% ($55,333)
Communications	2% ($70,200)
Consulting	25% ($74,381)
Entrepreneurship	2% ($63,350)
Finance	35% ($66,251)
General Management	13% ($69,841)
Human Resources	2% ($49,350)
Marketing	28% ($63,190)
MIS	18% ($67,025)
Operations	3% ($68,634)

TEXAS CHRISTIAN UNIVERSITY
M. J. Neeley School of Business

OVERVIEW

Type of school	private
Affiliation	independent
Environment	metropolis
Academic calendar	semester
Schedule	full-time/part-time/evening

STUDENTS

Enrollment of parent institution	7,273
Enrollment of business school	298
% male/female	70/30
% out-of-state	30
% part-time	40
% minorities	7
% international (# countries represented)	22(26)
Average age at entry	28
Average years work experience at entry	5

ACADEMICS

Student/faculty ratio	12:1
% female faculty	16
% minority faculty	3
Hours of study per day	3.86

SPECIALTIES

Applied learning opportunities and an emphasis on effective communication skills.

JOINT DEGREES

3/2 Program for TCU undergraduates

SPECIAL PROGRAMS

Educational Investment Fund, Student Enterprise Program, Semester Study Abroad Programs.

STUDY ABROAD PROGRAMS

Germany, France, Hungary, Mexico

SURVEY SAYS...

HITS
Presentation skills
Interpersonal skills prep
Getting into courses a breeze

MISSES
MIS/operations
On-campus housing
Quantitative skills

PROMINENT ALUMNI

John Roach, CEO, Tandy Corp; Roger King, Executive Vice President for Human Resources, Frito-Lay; Webb Joiner, CEO, Bell Helicopter-Textron, Inc.

ACADEMICS

As one student put it, Texas Christian University is "under recognized. It has been improving its standards and courses over the past few years." TCU offers students a two-year generalist MBA. During the second year of the program, students can concentrate their studies in one of five areas: decision sciences, finance, management, management information systems, or marketing. Across the board, students report they feel well-prepared by their training in areas such as finance, accounting, general management, and teamwork and communication skills. Students consider the Center for Productive Communication one of the great assets of TCU. Raved one MBA, "The Center is a wonderful facility and is very receptive to assisting students with their team projects and presentations." Another major asset, literally, is the Educational Investment Fund, with cash and securities totaling $1.3 million—one of the largest student-run portfolios in the nation. Here, students are offered incomparable hands-on experience in investment management. For more hands-on experience, students can participate in the Student Enterprise Program, wherein teams of students act as paid consultants to various for-profit and not-for-profit organizations.

More than half of the students surveyed rated their teachers as "good," and one-quarter said they were "outstanding!" One student wrote, "Faculty are ALWAYS available for discussion outside of class," though a few others lobbed accusations of favoritism. Students appreciate the opportunity to "get practical experience" and think the location in the Dallas/Fort Worth metroplex gives the school strong corporate ties and provides good opportunities to network. "Business leaders from the area speak to us regularly," said one MBA. TCU students were not without their complaints, however. Several MBAs thought the physical resources of the school could be improved. "We need better classroom facilities," said one. Agreed another, "Computer labs need updating." The school administration draws major criticism from the students. "Conflicts between department chairs, the dean, and Admissions are common," wrote one MBA, "there's a lot of beaurocracy." In response to student concerns, the dean has organized scheduled forums with students. Overall, students wished the school would do more to promote itself, since "it has a lot to offer."

PLACEMENT AND RECRUITING

The Career Services office at Neeley provides all the standard services to students, such as career counseling, mock interviews, and a video-conferencing center. It also features some unique programs, such as Student Enterprises, in which students "compete for 'real' consulting projects for 'real' corporate clients." The Career Services office points out that students manage the school's $1.5 million Educational Investment Fund, through which they can establish contacts among Fund alumni and investment professionals.

According to students, TCU is the best school to go to for "GREAT connections to businesses in the Dallas/Fort Worth area." (It should be noted, however, that students at SMU feel the same about their school.) In 1997 the biggest employers of Neeley grads were GTE, Harris Methodist Health Systems, American Airlines, the SABRE Group, Andersen Consulting, Burlington Northern-Santa Fe, Frito-Lay, EDS, and Sprinx Health Systems.

Peggy Conway, Director of MBA Admissions
P.O. Box 298540, Fort Worth, TX 76129
Admissions: 817-257-7531 • Fax: 817-921-7227
Email: mbainfo@tcu.edu
Internet: www.neeley.tcu.edu

Texas Christian University

STUDENT/CAMPUS LIFE

TCU is a small school. Total enrollment is kept to 300 students—half the size of the national average. The workload can be substantial. One student complained, "Emphasis is on the quantity of the work instead of its quality." But a classmate countered, "The pressure is light by b-school standards." Indeed, the majority of students study only fifteen to twenty-five hours a week.

The social scene is handled by the MBA Association, which organizes parties and a designated eatery or bar of the week for Thursday night get-togethers. Reported one student, "There's plenty to do and most students take time out from their work to socialize." Students were favorably disposed to TCU's hometown of Fort Worth. Only one apartment complex is within walking distance of school, though. Most MBAs live off campus in apartment complexes in the Hulen area of Fort Worth, a ten-minute commute by car from campus. The average for living expenses is $8,500 per year.

The students report the atmosphere at TCU is competitive, but not cutthroat. Enthused one MBA, "The community is friendly and accessible. It's easy to meet people." The school's emphasis on teamwork creates a supportive and friendly atmosphere. TCU students said classmates are smart and professionally diverse, but, unfortunately, not racially diverse. Also, several MBAs commented that the student body seems unseasoned and "the school is more geared toward people with little or no work experience."

ADMISSIONS

According to the school, no single criterion is most important. The admissions committee considers the composite application of each student. Prerequisites include: quantitative proficiency and a foundation in macroeconomics and microeconomics. Writes the school, "Consistent with TCU's emphasis on the individual, our admissions staff looks closely at the specific merits of each application. No single admissions formula is used. Our goal is to select applicants from a variety of backgrounds who possess a balanced set of credentials: strong academic aptitude, demonstrated leadership skills, and meaningful work and lifetime experiences."

FINANCIAL FACTS

Tuition	$8,040
Tuition per credit	$335
Fees	$1,190
Cost of books	$750
Room & Board (on/off-campus)	NR/$8,500
% of students receiving aid	76
% first-year students receiving aid	70
% aid that is merit-based	24
% of students receiving loans	46
% of students receiving paid internships	95
% of students receiving grants	48
Average award package	$10,426
Average grant	$6,200

ADMISSIONS

# of applications received	314
% applicants accepted	73
% acceptees attending	54
Average GMAT (range)	560 (510–600)
Minimum TOEFL	550
Average GPA (range)	3.10 (2.80–3.50)
Application fee (in/out-state)	$50/$50
Early decision program available	Yes
Early decision notification	rolling
Regular application deadline	April 30
Regular notification	rolling
Admission may be deferred?	Yes
Maximum length of deferment	1 year
Transfer students accepted?	Yes
Non-fall admission available?	No
Admissions process need-blind?	Yes

APPLICANTS ALSO LOOK AT

University of Texas at Austin, Southern Methodist University, Texas A & M University, University of Texas at Arlington, Rice University, Vanderbilt University, Wake Forest University, University of Colorado at Boulder

EMPLOYMENT PROFILE

Placement rate (%)	100
# of companies recruiting on-campus	80
% grads employed immediately	31
% grads employed within six months	90
Average starting salary	$44,000

Grads employed by field (avg. salary):

Accounting	3% ($57,000)
Consulting	5% ($53,500)
Finance	29% ($51,000)
General Management	3% ($47,300)
Human Resources	8% ($36,100)
Marketing	39% ($44,500)
MIS	5% ($37,500)
Operations	2% (NR)
Other	8% (NR)

THUNDERBIRD
The American Graduate School of International Management

OVERVIEW

Type of school	private
Affiliation	none
Environment	metropolis
Academic calendar	semesters

STUDENTS

Enrollment of parent institution	1,508
Enrollment of business school	1,508
% male/female	65/35
% out-of-state	88
% minorities	12
% international (# countries represented)	44(79)
Average age at entry	28
Average years work experience at entry	4

ACADEMICS

Student/faculty ratio	14:1
% female faculty	33
% minority faculty	27
% part-time faculty	13
Hours of study per day	4.75

SPECIALTIES

All aspects of International Management: Cross-Cultural Communication, Global Strategy, Emerging Market, and Regional Market Development. Corporate Marketing and Finance.

JOINT DEGREES

MIM/MBA, AZ State University, AZ State University West, University of AZ, Case Western Reserve University, University of Colorado at Denver, Drury College, University of Florida, University of Houston, and The University of Texas at Arlington.

STUDY ABROAD PROGRAMS

Japan, France/Geneva, Mexico, Republic of China, Czech Republic, and Russia

SURVEY SAYS...

HITS
Ethnic and racial diversity
Social life
Diversity of work experience

MISSES
Gym
Safety
General management

PROMINENT ALUMNI

W.L. Lyons Brown Jr., Fincastle; George Fugelseng, CEO, North America Dresdner, Bank AG

ACADEMICS

Like a great steak house that serves only one dish but does so exceedingly well, Thunderbird—officially, Thunderbird, The American Graduate School of International Management—focuses on doing one thing right: international business. Students at Thunderbird can study all the traditional b-school disciplines of management, finance, marketing, consulting, and information systems, but they do so in the context of the international market. Students who choose Thunderbird know what they're coming for. Writes one, "It is exactly the type of curriculum I was looking for, and you can finish the program in one year!"

One year at Thunderbird is the exception rather than the norm, since the program requires forty-two course hours. However, students qualified to place out of some foundation courses can finish their MIMs (Masters in International Management; Thunderbird does not offer a traditional MBA) in twelve months by attending the summer session. The Thunderbird curriculum consists of three components: international studies, which is actually a series of foundation courses covering the international economy and the characteristics of regional markets overseas; modern languages, which requires proficiency in a foreign language; and world business, which makes up the bulk of MIM's coursework at Thunderbird and covers a wide range of business studies. Students write that the curriculum's "strength lies in tailored classes on global business, recommended by the Board of Trustees and the Thunderbird Global Council—real-world execs with Fortune 500 companies." Among the few complaints about the curriculum is that it "should put greater emphasis on quantitative skills."

Thunderbird offers students many opportunities for study overseas, with centers in Tokyo and Geneva. The school also sponsors summer programs in Mexico, the People's Republic of China, the Czech Republic, and Russia. Cooperative education programs take Thunderbird students to b-schools on four continents.

Students tell us, "Some teachers here are outstanding, truly leaders in their fields, and some aren't. If you get into the best teachers' classes, you're going to learn a lot." Another student notes that "profs' doors are always open." The administration, "like many, is bureaucratic. Some organizational skills are lacking." On the positive side, "the administration is constantly changing the curriculum to remain competitive."

PLACEMENT AND RECRUITING

Thunderbird's Career Services Center (CSC) faces a singular challenge in that "everyone [in the program] wants to work internationally." The explosive growth of nearby Phoenix, now the nation's 6th largest city–has provided new opportunities, and Thunderbirds are increasingly finding positions in Arizona at major firms such as Motorola, Intel, Amex, and Hneywell. Somehow, though, Thunderbird attracts nearly 300 companies to recruit on campus. The school uses extensive video-teleconferencing, telephone, email, and an Internet-based resume book to market its students to more than 400 off-campus recruiters. The school also boasts an alumni list of more than 30,000; students in our survey who contacted alums for help in their job search found them to be helpful.

Judy Johnson, Associate Vice President
15249 North 59th Avenue, Glendale, AZ 85306
Admissions: 602-978-7210 • Fax: 602-439-5432
Email: tbird@t-bird.edu
Internet: www.t-bird.edu

Students give the CSC average grades, even though they are highly satisfied with the quality and quantity of recruiters and with their opportunities for off-campus projects and internships. Furthermore, the perception on campus is that the CSC has gotten better in recent years. Writes one student, "Thunderbird has improved dramatically in internship and job placement, but they could still probably do better."

STUDENT/CAMPUS LIFE

Thunderbird students, who refer to themselves as T-Birds, are a "very diverse group . . . we come from all walks of life and experiences." Notes one student, "Ethnic diversity is our strength. Half the students here are foreign nationals." According to another T-Bird, students here are "very teamwork-oriented. We're all in this together! They are very talented and intelligent, and they're willing to share knowledge." Adds still another, "Overall, people are very interesting here—not your usual 'serious accountant' type of MBA."

Thunderbird students participate in more than sixty campus clubs and organizations, a number of which serve students of common national or ethnic origin. International theme events are common, and students report that there are "so many activities on campus, you're always missing one to attend another." Students also lead active social lives, which "take place primarily in clubs. We also have a pub that many T-birds find themselves at on Thursdays." Many of respondents mention the on-campus pub, noting with approval that it serves an unusually wide variety of imported beers. Students agree that there are "more than enough choices of what to do on any given night between Thursday and Sunday," but also tell us that "Some people work. Some people work and play. Some people play. You do with it what you want. But if you come to work, it will definitely pay off." Students are less pleased with Glendale, which they describe as "a little behind the times," and "in need of a charm transfusion." When they leave campus, T-Birds head for nearby Phoenix or take "bonding trips to California and Vegas."

ADMISSIONS

Thunderbird considers GMAT scores, TOEFL test scores for non-native English speakers, undergrad and graduate education, a personal essay, and references in evaluating a prospective students candidacy. The minimum TOEFL score for consideration is 550.

FINANCIAL FACTS

Tuition	$9,970
Fees	$200
Cost of books	$600
Room & Board (on/off-campus)	$5,380/$6,000
% of students receiving aid	70
% first-year students receiving aid	65
% aid that is merit-based	20
% of students receiving loans	68
% of students receiving paid internships	32
Average award package	$20,000
Average grant	$5,400
Average graduation debt	$35,000

ADMISSIONS

# of applications received	1,333
% applicants accepted	56
% acceptees attending	62
Average GMAT (range)	590 (490–750)
Minimum TOEFL	550
Average GPA (range)	3.44 (2.60–4.00)
Application fee (in/out-state)	$50/$50
Early decision program available	No
Regular application deadline	January 31
Regular notification	January 31
Admission may be deferred?	Yes
Maximum length of deferment	1 year
Transfer students accepted?	Yes
Non-fall admission available?	Yes
Admissions process need-blind?	Yes

APPLICANTS ALSO LOOK AT

Columbia University, Harvard University, University of Texas at Austin, Georgetown University, University of California—Berkeley, Stanford University, University of California—Los Angeles, New York University

EMPLOYMENT PROFILE

Placement rate (%)	92
# of companies recruiting on-campus	269
% grads employed immediately	85
% grads employed within six months	95
Average starting salary	$59,123

Grads employed by field (avg. salary):

Accounting	1% (NR)
Communications	1% (NR)
Finance	25% ($62,440)
General Management	1% (NR)
Marketing	41% ($57,383)
MIS	3% (NR)
Operations	3% (NR)
Other	22% ($58,691)

TULANE UNIVERSITY
A. B. Freeman School of Business

OVERVIEW

Type of school	private
Affiliation	none
Environment	metropolis
Academic calendar	semester
Schedule	full-time/part-time/evening

STUDENTS

Enrollment of parent institution	11,424
Enrollment of business school	374
% male/female	67/33
% part-time	49
% minorities	16
% international (# countries represented)	19(21)
Average age at entry	26
Average years work experience at entry	4

ACADEMICS

Student/faculty ratio	20:1
% female faculty	14
% minority faculty	15
% part-time faculty	42
Hours of study per day	4.37

SPECIALTIES
International business and finance and Latin American studies.

JOINT DEGREES
MBA/JD, 4 years; MBA/Master of Arts in Latin American Studies, 2.5 years; MBA/Master of Public Health, 3 years

SPECIAL PROGRAMS
Study Abroad, International Internships

STUDY ABROAD PROGRAMS
Argentina, Austria, Brazil, Chile, Colombia, Czech Republic, Ecuador, England, France, Germany, Hong Kong, Hungary, Mexico, Spain, Taiwan, and Venezuela.

SURVEY SAYS...
HITS
Gym
Ethnic and racial diversity
Presentation skills

MISSES
MIS/operations
On-campus housing
Computer skills

PROMINENT ALUMNI
Lawrence A. Gordon, President, Lawrence Gordon Entertainment, motion picture industry; Frank B. Stewart, Jr., Chairman, Stewart Enterprises, nation's 3rd-largest deathcare corp; Francis Fraenkel, President, Delta Capital Corp.; Shannon Burchett, President, Ameren Energy.

ACADEMICS

Touted as an "up-and-comer," Tulane has retooled its curriculum to focus more on global business, the managerial role, and the social and political environment in business. The result is a unique course of study. First-years now take three "focus modules," which encourage collegial bonding among students. The first module is called the Job of the Executive and is delivered during the first two weeks of school. Students learn why they need to study all the disciplines and how that multifunctional knowledge is used in the workplace. Computer Skills, Team Leadership, and Business Perspectives comprise the subsequent modules. First-years also take the more traditional core courses and participate in a career development series. Popular b-school electives include Cases in Finance, Negotiations, International Business, and Strategic Marketing, which features a business simulation game. For some real-life experience, students can participate in the production of The Burkenroad Reports. MBAs analyze publicly traded Louisiana companies for the reports which are then circulated through the financial community. Students say this exercise also provides great opportunities for networking.

Students deem professors "astute" and "approachable." One student wrote, "The faculty here is interested in students learning skills as opposed to raking us over the coals of a grade curve distribution." Overall, MBAs agree that their academic experience is "blissfully challenging." But there were a few weak spots: Entrepreneurial studies and marketing could use improvement, and students wanted more offerings in the MIS area and more female faculty. On the plus side, they gave themselves high marks for their proficiency in general management, finance, accounting, and quantitative skills. Most agree: "Tulane students can compete against any MBAs."

Tulane creates a strong international environment with coursework and foreign study, but also with the very makeup of its student body. A huge percentage of the student population hails from overseas. Students rave about the real-life perspective this provides their international curriculum. To assist international students in their transition to American studies, the school offers a special International Student Orientation Program.

PLACEMENT AND RECRUITING

When it comes to placement, Tulane students benefit from their school's location: what recruiter, after all, is going to pass up a visit to New Orleans? The Career Development Center (CDC) exploits this advantage by holding a "Mardi Gras Job Fair." The CDC adds that "in addition to inviting companies to visit us with our active on-campus recruiting program and the popular Mardi Gras Job Fair, we bring our students directly to them, as well. Events such as the New York MBA Internship Consortium, the Atlanta MBA Consortium, Freeman Days in New York, and the International Job Fairs in Miami and Orlando showcase our students...." Freeman MBAs also have the advantage of the school's "superior experiential learning opportunities," such as the hands-on research they conduct to produce reports on select publicly traded companies in the area. In addition to consulting for local businesses, networking with alumni is "a major resource" for Freeman grads.

John C. Silbernagel, Assistant Dean for Admissions and Financial Aid
7 McAlister Drive, Suite 400, New Orleans, LA 70118
Admissions: 504-865-5410 • Fax: 504-865-6770
Email: admissions@freeman.tulane.edu
Internet: freeman.tulane.edu

Tulane University

STUDENT/CAMPUS LIFE

According to the school, Tulane's location in New Orleans plays a critical role in the success of the program. Students strongly agree. Wrote one, "Hanging out on Bourbon Street is a great break from the rigors of Tulane." Ready yourself for a diet of crawfish, po' boys, and a nightlife that applicants regularly travel thousands of miles to partake in.

Tulane is housed in a spectacular building. Goldring/Woldenberg Hall is a seven-story complex featuring an auditorium, group-study rooms, classrooms, and a three-story atrium. "Hang time" is enhanced by a second-floor outdoor patio that surrounds the entire building. The building also houses a state-of-the-art technology/computer center, a library, an audio-visual studio complete with television studio and editing and viewing room, a computer classroom with forty-four networked laptops, and a computer-integrated manufacturing laboratory used for simulating manufacturing processes. Wrote one student, "The physical facilities—building, classrooms, services—are superb." Students say the administration and faculty are personable and "most of them know you by name." And that's not all. One grateful MBA told us that when the Director of Admissions spotted him looking for an apartment on foot, the administrator insisted on driving him around the area for two hours. Now that's a responsive administration!

The majority of students work in study groups, and the student body seems tight-knit. "I feel like our class is a club," remarked one MBA. Another offered "It's a small community where everyone has a specific skill or talent that benefits the entire program." Students' impressions of their classmates' competitiveness ranged from "competitive only with themselves" to "grade hungry CUTTHROATS!" Most students feel the atmosphere is competitive, but manageable. One wrote, "Fellow students inspire me to a healthy pressure to excel." As for the workload, students report, "The first-year was very time-consuming, but we all helped each other over the rough spots." Students rated each other smart and highly diverse, and most importantly, "damn goodlookin'!" Overall, the MBAs surveyed agree with the classmate who said, "I would do it all over again and choose Freeman!"

ADMISSIONS

The admissions committee considers work experience, GMAT scores, and college GPA most important, and then, in descending order of importance, the interview (required for all domestic applicants), letters of recommendation, essays, and extracurricular activities. Quantitative coursework is highly recommended, but not mandatory. Tulane uses a rolling admissions process. All applicants are automatically considered for merit-based fellowships at the time of admission. College seniors who are admitted may defer for up to two years. Tulane features a combined five-year baccalaureate/MBA program. Wrote one student, "The five-year program is excellent and extremely competitive. Students in this program were among Tulane's best undergraduates."

FINANCIAL FACTS

Tuition	$21,719
Tuition per credit	$724
Fees	$1,576
Cost of books	$800
Room & Board (on/off-campus)	$6,920/$6,920
% first-year students receiving aid	58
% of students receiving loans	43
% of students receiving paid internships	34
% of students receiving grants	40
Average grant	$15,000

ADMISSIONS

# of applications received	778
% applicants accepted	34
% acceptees attending	36
Average GMAT (range)	637 (550–660)
Average GPA (range)	3.40 (3.04–3.60)
Application fee (in/out-state)	$40/$40
Early decision program available	No
Regular application deadline	May 1
Regular notification	Rolling
Admission may be deferred?	Yes
Maximum length of deferment	2 years
Transfer students accepted?	No
Non-fall admission available?	Yes
Admissions process need-blind?	Yes

APPLICANTS ALSO LOOK AT

University of Texas at Austin, Vanderbilt University, Duke University, University of North Carolina at Chapel Hill, New York University, Georgetown University, Emory University, University of Virginia

EMPLOYMENT PROFILE

Placement rate (%)	89
# of companies recruiting on-campus	282
% grads employed immediately	89
% grads employed within six months	98
Average starting salary	$60,625

Grads employed by field (avg. salary):

Accounting	8% ($46,800)
Consulting	11% ($53,000)
Finance	43% ($63,500)
General Management	11% ($73,178)
Human Resources	3% ($51,500)
Marketing	15% ($57,528)
MIS	2% ($73,500)
Operations	4% ($53,000)
Other	3% ($64,500)

VANDERBILT UNIVERSITY
Owen Graduate School of Management

ACADEMICS

The Owen Graduate School of Management has recently burst onto the national b-school scene. And indeed, Owen delivers a solid education. Professors teach the major disciplines from a cross-functional point of view. Managerial Problem Solving and Communication, serves up the kind of fare that allows managers to translate ideas into actionable programs. Students can opt to add an "international emphasis" by taking three international electives. One of the international electives, International Management and Seminars, features a visit to a foreign country with the dean and several faculty members. Each year students in this course decide where they want to go, and whom they want to meet with. Owen MBAs may also earn degree credit for advanced language study. Much praise was also heaped on the school's human resources management program, which students say is "tops."

Overall, Owen MBAs are happy with their academic experience. "Owen has succeeded at providing top-notch students, professors, and surroundings while avoiding the 'cutthroat' traits of other top programs," writes one student. MBAs are pleased with the accessibility of the faculty and the physical and financial resources of the school. Students feel very well prepared by their studies in marketing, finance, human resources, quantitative methods, computers, and presentation skills. One student wrote, "As a finance major, I'm convinced my training is superior to that at almost all other schools." Several students mentioned that the "new module system still needs to get the kinks from the semester system knocked out." But, the administration was deemed "responsive," and, overall, students say this program exceeds their expectations.

PLACEMENT AND RECRUITING

The placement office at Vanderbilt was cited as a strength in our student surveys. "They pay close, individual attention to students," wrote one MBA. In 1997, 232 companies interviewed Owen students. Ninety percent of the class had a permanent job offer within three months of graduation. The major recruiters were: AT&T, American Airlines, Andersen Consulting, MCI, GE, PepsiCo, Northern Telecom, Deloitte & Touche LLP, Eli Lilly, Taco Bell, Federal Express, Sara Lee, and Procter & Gamble. Students believe that placement will only improve as Owen's reputation goes national because Nashville is, after all "an out-of-the-way place for many big companies." This too, should provide more West Coast contacts.

STUDENT/CAMPUS LIFE

Like many small schools, Owen provides its students with an intimate learning environment. "Students are extremely collegial here," wrote one student, "lots of smiling faces, and you can't walk two inches without people engaging you in conversation. If you're a gunner or a jerk don't come here!" Another offered, "The one aspect of Owen that has greatly exceeded all expectations is the quality of the friendships I've made." Over and over in our surveys, students made references to "the family thing," "community," and told us they "do everything together." A few thought the atmosphere bordered on cliquey. We heard from minorities and gays, however, that the administration was supportive and that they had experienced "no problems."

Hayden Estrada, Director of Admissions and marketing
401 21st Avenue South, Nashville, TN 37203
Admissions: 615-322-2534 • Fax: 615-343-7110
Email: motzsm@ctrvax.vanderbilt.edu
Internet: mba.vanderbilt.edu

Vanderbilt University

Students describe their classmates as "supportive and hard working." "They 'set the bar' high, which adds to the desire to produce excellent work." The workload, while not up-all-night impossible, can be tough. Students hit the books roughly thirty hours a week. The overwhelming majority use study groups to get the benefit of many heads applied to a single problem. As hard as they study, Owen students strike a balance between work and play. "There is time to work out, socialize, and enjoy Nashville—a great city," writes one MBA. On-campus, the student-run clubs sponsor many activities: a lecture series, community service, student-consulting projects, baseball games, a golf tournament, and the Fall Ball. The school is housed in one building, which students describe as "outstanding." Equally awesome is the recreation center, which, in addition to every piece of exercise equipment you can imagine, also features an indoor climbing wall. Many Vanderbilt MBAs agree with the classmate who wrote, "I couldn't have picked a better place."

ADMISSIONS

The admissions office considers your work experience most important, then, in descending order, your college GPA, interview, GMAT scores, essays, letters of recommendation, and extracurricular activities. The school adds, however, this order "differs according to the background of each candidate."

The interview is an "integral part of the admissions process," according to the school. "It allows a candidate to present key aspects of her background, character, and aspirations that are not easily conveyed in writing. The primary objectives in the interview are to assess career goals and explore motivation and clarity of purpose." Students must take a calculus course to demonstrate strong quantitative skills. The school goes by rolling admissions. The final deadline is March 15.

Applicants with two or more years' work experience who get their applications in by the first Friday in December will have a decision by the end of January. Applicants who would benefit from additional work experience may defer admission for up to two years.

FINANCIAL FACTS

Tuition	$22,900
Room & Board (on/off-campus)	$8,200/NR
% of students receiving aid	60
% first-year students receiving aid	66
% aid that is merit-based	100
% of students receiving loans	50
% of students receiving grants	30
Average award package	$33,000

ADMISSIONS

# of applications received	1,313
% applicants accepted	38
% acceptees attending	40
Average GMAT (range)	625 (550–700)
Average GPA (range)	3.10 (2.53–3.55)
Application fee (in/out-state)	$50
Early decision program available	No
Regular application deadline	March 15
Regular notification	Rolling
Admission may be deferred?	Yes
Transfer students accepted?	Yes
Non-fall admission available?	No
Admissions process need-blind?	Yes

APPLICANTS ALSO LOOK AT

Duke University, University of Virginia, Northwestern University, University of Texas at Austin, University of North Carolina at Chapel Hill, University of Chicago

EMPLOYMENT PROFILE

Placement rate (%)	95
# of companies recruiting on-campus	108
% grads employed immediately	85
% grads employed within six months	95
Average starting salary	$65,043

Grads employed by field (avg. salary):

Accounting	3% ($71,667)
Consulting	25% ($70,840)
Finance	9% ($58,613)
Human Resources	4% ($61,500)
Marketing	21% ($61,379)
MIS	2% ($52,000)
Operations	8% ($66,389)
Venture Capital	18% ($66,398)
Other	12% ($59,200)

UNIVERSITY OF VIRGINIA
Deadline 11/2/98 + decision 12/15
12/1

Darden Graduate School of Business Administration

ETS cat = 5820   http://www2.darden.edu/admissions

OVERVIEW

Type of school	public
Affiliation	none
Environment	suburban
Academic calendar	semester
Schedule	full-time only

STUDENTS

Enrollment of parent institution	18,000
Enrollment of business school	487
% male/female	70/30
% out-of-state	57
% minorities	26
% international (# countries represented)	16(37)
Average age at entry	28
Average years work experience at entry	5

ACADEMICS

Student/faculty ratio	8:1
% female faculty	26
% minority faculty	2
% part-time faculty	39
Hours of study per day	5.86

SPECIALTIES

Excellent teachers; most have business experience; more than half have taught overseas; 14% international. Curriculum strengths: general mgmt.; case method; integrated, holistic curriculum; required ethic course; teamwork; student centered learning.

JOINT DEGREES

MBA/JD, 4 years; MBA/MA in Asian Studies 3 years; MBA/MA in Government, Foreign Affairs, or Public Administration, 3 years; MBA/ME, 3 years; MBA/MSN, 3 years; MBA/Ph.D., 4 years

STUDY ABROAD PROGRAMS

Hong Kong U. of Science and Technology; Salvary Business School; Universite Libre de Bruxelles; Internationa U. of Japan; Sweden, Finland, Mexico, Australia, Canada.

SURVEY SAYS...

HITS
Profs are great teachers
General management
Pressure

MISSES
Social life
Computer skills
On-campus housing

PROMINENT ALUMNI

George David, President, CEO, and COO, United Technologies; Steven S. Reinemund, President and CEO, Frito-Lay; Henri A.M. Termeer, President, and CEO, and Chairman, Genzyme Corporation.

ACADEMICS

Darden is part of a state-affiliated university and has a well-deserved reputation as one of the best b-schools in the nation. The program offers a strong general management education, although the student body has many budding entrepreneurs. "More than 40 percent of Darden grads start or buy their own businesses," said one student. The foundation for this is the case-study method. Notes the school, "In analyzing each case, students learn how to define important issues, when and how to apply analytical techniques, and how to make decisions after evaluating alternatives."

First-year MBAs take ten required courses, but this feels more like one nine-month multifunctional course. Alas, no electives allowed. Second-years take two required courses and can choose from among eighty electives. A major component of the second year is the Business Project, which involves working with a faculty member on a managerial issue involving field research, teamwork, and consulting. Students tell us, "Darden ranks top in the nation for academic excellence, and it deserves this reputation. The cases are tough, but interesting and manageable." The curriculum features a strong emphasis on quantitative applications and is known for its intense schedule: "The workload is heavy and diverse, requiring the development of varied skills." But one student griped, "There is too much focus on doing and not enough on learning. A little more down time might lead to better student performance." Another agreed, "Darden is a bootcamp. It's a great education, but the process is painful."

Darden MBAs raved about their profs, who they described as "dynamic." "The teaching quality is outstanding!" exclaimed one student. "Professors know all of their students by name, have an open-door policy, and often email or call students at home to offer congratulations for a job well done in class!" "Their energy is a great motivator," agreed another. The administration received their share of kudos too. MBAs told us that "the administration makes a great effort to promote a 'Darden community' with events from morning coffee to awards presentations." Despite all these perks, the cost of tuition is still relatively low. What's more, a new state-of-the-art building now shelters this academic powerhouse. All these ingredients add up to "an experience beyond my expectations," in the words of one student, and "a once in a lifetime chance" to "learn a lot and meet brilliant people." All in all students feel "there is an unusually strong loyalty to Darden and a view that 'this is the best place for me to earn an MBA'."

PLACEMENT AND RECRUITING

One hundred and eighty-nine companies recruited on-campus in 1998. The major recruiters: McKinsey, Microsoft, Merrill Lynch, Procter & Gamble, and Lucent Technologies. One student wrote, "We should have more medium-sized and small companies available on-campus or through correspondence opportunities." "We need more high-tech companies," added a second. "Also, more West Coast recruiters." Another MBA recommended "more mandatory interview-prep sessions." Though the alumni network is not as large as it is at other top-tier schools, students agree that "the alumni loyalty is overwhelming."

A. John Megibow, Director of Public Relations
P.O. Box 6550, Charlottesville, VA 22906
Admissions: 804-924-3220 • Fax: 804-924-4859
Email: darden@virginia.edu
Internet: www.darden.virginia.edu

University of Virginia

STUDENT/CAMPUS LIFE

Located in the college town of Charlottesville, the UVA campus is beautiful, and the b-school recently moved into a new, state-of-the-art facility, designed by Robert A. M. Stern. "The new building is amazing—it makes a huge difference!" enthused one student. "If you're going to work your ass off, it may as well be in a great setting," concluded another. Almost half of the first-year class lives in a nearby apartment complex, christened Darden Gardens. Several other apartment complexes are within "spitting distance," which alleviates some of Darden's parking problems. Many students rent shared farmhouses near the Blue Ridge Mountains, only a ten-minute commute.

Despite this idyllic setting, student life is quite challenging. Students spend many hours studying every week. Though some thrive on the challenge, others feel that a lack of "time to reflect or review," hampers their academic experience. "You are always, always, always on the go," writes one student. "It's a non-stop barrage of work and commitments that empties you out physically, mentally, and emotionally." Still, another reported, "Darden is not as difficult as people say. You have to be disciplined and keep up with the work so as not to be killed by cold calls. Second year is a lot less stressful." Students are preassigned to study groups intentionally structured to create a mix of skills and expertise, as well as offer support. Darden's small size fosters a close-knit, homey atmosphere. Wrote one MBA, "Classmates are bright and supportive. They're not out to get each other." Though not racially diverse, the students like each other: "People here are friendly, and genuinely down-to-earth. The Southern atmosphere softens the destructive forms of competition that appear at some grad schools." There's an intense social scene, though. "We work hard, but we know when to blow it off," says one student. "We party every weekend," agreed another, "though there's little or no activity weekday nights." "You're within striking distance of DC, yet outdoor activities are plentiful," say Dardenites. "You can mountain bike, hike, rock climb, or camp."

ADMISSIONS

Each of the following components count for roughly one-third in the admissions decision: Academics (GPA, GMAT); work/professional experience; personal attributes (essays, interview, extracurriculars). The interview is strongly encouraged but not required. The committee explains, "We look for evidence of competitive academic performance, intellectual ability, significant work and life experiences, as well as other qualities of character that cannot be quantitatively measured. Factors such as breadth of perspective, international exposure, and diversity are also taken into consideration." Applications are processed in one of three rounds. Students are rarely granted a deferral; possible reasons for one are military obligation or visa restrictions.

FINANCIAL FACTS

Tuition (in/out-state)	$16,060/$21,480
Room & Board (on/off-campus)	NR/NR
% of students receiving aid	65
% aid that is merit-based	10
% of students receiving loans	70
% of students receiving grants	50
Average grant	$2,000

ADMISSIONS

# of applications received	3,111
% applicants accepted	15
% acceptees attending	50
Average GMAT	660
Average GPA	3.30
Application fee (in/out-state)	$100/$100
Early decision program available	No
Regular application deadline	April 1
Regular notification	Rolling
Admission may be deferred?	No
Transfer students accepted?	No
Non-fall admission available?	No
Admissions process need-blind?	Yes

APPLICANTS ALSO LOOK AT

Northwestern University, Duke University, Stanford University, Harvard University, Dartmouth College, University of Pennsylvania, University of North Carolina at Chapel Hill, University of Michigan Business School

EMPLOYMENT PROFILE

Placement rate (%)	100
# of companies recruiting on-campus	191
% grads employed immediately	94
% grads employed within six months	100
Average starting salary	$74,000

Grads employed by field (avg. salary):

Consulting	28% (NR)
Finance	33% (NR)
General Management	13% (NR)
Marketing	12% (NR)
Operations	5% (NR)
Strategic Planning	5% (NR)
Other	4% (NR)

WAKE FOREST UNIVERSITY
Babcock Graduate School of Management

OVERVIEW

Type of school	private
Affiliation	none
Environment	metropolis
Academic calendar	semester
Schedule	full-time/part-time/evening

STUDENTS

Enrollment of parent institution	6,015
Enrollment of business school	672
% male/female	76/24
% out-of-state	16
% part-time	64
% minorities	9
% international (# countries represented)	7(15)
Average age at entry	26
Average years work experience at entry	3

ACADEMICS

Student/faculty ratio	7:1
% female faculty	15
% minority faculty	10
% part-time faculty	10
Hours of study per day	5.41

SPECIALTIES
Operations, Finance, Marketing, Management Consulting, Entrepreneurship, and Family Business.

JOINT DEGREES
JD/MBA Law and Business, 4 years; MD/MBA Medicine and Business, 5 years

SPECIAL PROGRAMS
Babcock Leadership Series; Mentor Program; Field Study Program

STUDY ABROAD PROGRAMS
England, Latin America, Japan, China, Continental Europe

SURVEY SAYS...

HITS
Administration
Computer skills
Teamwork skills

MISSES
On-campus housing
Gym
School clubs

PROMINENT ALUMNI
Ann Morrison, Author "Breaking the Glass Ceiling"; Charles Ergen, founder & CEO, Echo Start Communication; Peter Daks, President, GTE Florida; Steve Lineberger, President, Sara Lee Casualwear

ACADEMICS

Babcock students agree that of their program's many assets, the greatest is "its size. It is small enough to have good relationships with the professors. The team-oriented environment encourages students to help one another." It is an asset that just got even better: in 1998, the school introduced its "3/38 Plan," which divides incoming students into three sections of thirty-eight. The goal is to create "the smallest section sizes of any major MBA program" in the country.

The first-year at Babcock entails a mandatory integrated core curriculum with courses that are frequently team-taught and require student teams to complete assignments collectively. Students speak approvingly of the core, reporting that "the combination of lecture and case analysis is ideal, and contributions from the students add great value to the classroom experience." The core includes two courses in international business and another in 'Law and Ethics,' perhaps explaining why one student describes Babcock as "a business school with ethics."

Second-year students must complete two required courses: one in management control and yet another in international business. Those with fewer than three years of relevant work experience must also complete a field study project in which student teams undertake a consulting project with a local or national company. Otherwise, however, second-year students are free to focus on their concentration of choice. Students speak highly of the Finance, Management Consulting, and Operations departments. They also rave about the program's international focus.

Most students like the faculty, whom they describe as "real people—not at all bookish. They are brilliant in the classroom but fun to go to lunch with, too." Adds another: "Professors are very willing to help and will put all else aside for students. They truly take an interest in each individual." Students are particularly impressed with how accessible professors—many of whom remain active in the business world—make themselves to students. Says one: "Professors do not post office hours because they are available all the time and are willing to talk about subjects ranging from classes to careers to personal issues." Academic facilities here are top-notch, and students appreciate the fact that the school "provides laptops for everybody. Tech system is first rate."

PLACEMENT AND RECRUITING

The Babcock Career Services Office (CSO) provides a combination of personal counseling and computer support to students searching for internships and post-graduate employment. Counselors use workshops, mock interviews, and one-on-one meetings to prepare students for their job search. They also maintain an Internet site of student resumes and an intranet system, accessible to Babcock students only, to post potential career opportunities. CSO staff meet with more than 350 companies a year in their efforts to market the Babcock program.

Our survey shows a high level of student satisfaction with the CSO. Says one student, "Career services didn't hand me my job. But, they did give me the tools I needed to land a great job. They taught me how to network, interview, follow up, and negotiate compensation. Outstanding preparation!" More than sixty

Mary Goss, Assistant Dean
P.O. Box 7659, Winston-Salem, NC 27109
Admissions: 336-758-5422 • Fax: 910-758-5830
Email: edwina_groves@mail.mba.wfu.edu
Internet: www.mba.wfu.edu

companies visited the campus to interview prospective Babcock graduates last year. However, the survey also reveals a vocal minority who feel strongly that Babcock must attract more recruiters from beyond the immediate region. Wake Forest helps conduct MBA Consortia in Atlanta and New York and participates in several smaller international consortia held by private vendors. Companies hiring Babcock grads last year included KPMG Peat Marwick, Pepsico Foods, Bear Sterns, Merck, and NationsBank.

STUDENT/CAMPUS LIFE

Because of the size of the program, Babcock students form a tight-knit group. Writes one, "Due to our small class size, students get to know each other pretty well. This creates an environment of free interaction where we can learn from other students' backgrounds and experiences." The intimacy of the program means that students also get a close-up look at each others' flaws, leading one to describe classmates as "young, yuppie, financially stable, not the most aggressive." Several respondents mentioned the relative inexperience of Babcock MBAs, noting that they "wish they had a few more years of experience. Sometimes the youth of the class shows in classroom discussion." The student who writes this is quick to add, however, this his classmates are "overall a great group of supportive, intelligent people." Many students note that they "really enjoy" the "large number of international students. There is much to gain from other cultures."

MBAs here spend a lot of time together outside the classroom. Clubs and student government-run activities are very popular, and students here frequently socialize with each other off campus. Basketball games are particularly popular, since Wake Forest competes in one of the most talent-rich conferences in the country. Married students happily find that their spouses are invited to "become active in all school functions. It has been the best two years of our lives!" All this explains why students say, "there is a genuine sense of community here that extends to faculty, staff, students, and their families, and even their pets! Everyone helps each other however they can. We really like each other here!" Because there is only limited on-campus housing available to graduate students, most MBAs live off campus, where housing is reportedly comfortable and affordable. The campus itself ranks among the safest and prettiest in the country. Of their adopted hometown, Babcock students write that "there is not much nightlife in Winston-Salem, but we make the best of it with road trips to Greensboro and Charlotte."

ADMISSIONS

GMAT scores tops the list of admissions criteria at Babcock, followed by work experience, undergrad GPA, interview, recommendations, and leadership abilities. Writes the school, "The admissions committee evaluates the applicant's scholastic ability for graduate study, character qualities, motivation, and managerial potential. Interviews are strongly recommended and required for applicants who lack full-time work experience. Applicants who schedule interviews are matched with a student host who takes them to class, gives them a tour of the facility, and takes them to lunch."

FINANCIAL FACTS

Tuition	$20,400
Tuition per credit	$666
Fees	$100
Cost of books	$1,500
Room & Board (on/off-campus)	NR/$5,600
% of students receiving aid	71
% first-year students receiving aid	82
% aid that is merit-based	100
% of students receiving loans	55
% of students receiving paid internships	98
% of students receiving grants	51
Average award package	$23,366
Average grant	$7,924
Average graduation debt	$37,785

ADMISSIONS

# of applications received	610
% applicants accepted	44
% acceptees attending	45
Average GMAT (range)	615 (580–650)
Minimum TOEFL	600
Average GPA (range)	3.20 (2.90–3.60)
Application fee (in/out-state)	$50/$50
Early decision program available	Yes
Early decision deadline	December 1
Early decision notification	December 25
Regular application deadline	April 1
Regular notification	Rolling
Admission may be deferred?	Yes
Maximum length of deferment	1 year
Transfer students accepted?	No
Non-fall admission available?	No
Admissions process need-blind?	Yes

APPLICANTS ALSO LOOK AT
University of North Carolina at Chapel Hill, Duke University, Vanderbilt University, Emory University, University of Virginia, College of William and Mary, Georgetown University, University of Maryland

EMPLOYMENT PROFILE

Placement rate (%)	89
# of companies recruiting on-campus	85
% grads employed immediately	89
% grads employed within six months	99
Average starting salary	$59,000

Grads employed by field (avg. salary):

Consulting	21% ($55,858)
Entrepreneurship	2% (NR)
Finance	29% ($53,125)
Marketing	26% ($51,200)
Operations	10% ($50,587)
Other	14% ($42,900)

UNIVERSITY OF WASHINGTON
Graduate School of Business Administration

OVERVIEW

Type of school	public
Affiliation	none
Environment	metropolis
Academic calendar	quarter

STUDENTS

Enrollment of parent institution	32,198
Enrollment of business school	387
% male/female	66/34
% out-of-state	42
% part-time	24
% minorities	13
% international (# countries represented)	18(20)
Average age at entry	29
Average years work experience at entry	5

ACADEMICS

Student/faculty ratio	35:1
% female faculty	13
% minority faculty	9
Hours of study per day	4.68

SPECIALTIES

Marketing, Finance, Entrepreneurship, International Business.

JOINT DEGREES

MP Accounting; JD/MBA; MBA/MAIS; MBA/MHA Health Administration; MBA/MS Engineering; Program in Engineering and Manufacturing Management

SPECIAL PROGRAMS

Overseas Study, International Management Certificate Program

STUDY ABROAD PROGRAMS

Chile, Mexico, China, Denmark, England, Finland, France, Germany, India, Japan, Spain, Switzerland

SURVEY SAYS...

HITS
Seattle
Campus is attractive
Star faculty

MISSES
Finance
General management
MIS/operations

ACADEMICS

There is little mystery to the popularity of the University of Washington's MBA Program. As one student succinctly puts it, "It has a great reputation, and the tuition is cheap." UW adds a third asset to the mix: "proximity to a high-tech and rapidly growing economy" in a fun, growing city. The substantial Japanese presence in the Seattle business community means greater "ties to Asian markets" for this MBA program and outstanding opportunities for students interested in international business studies.

UW MBAs praise the "coordinated first-year-core curriculum," described in the catalogue as a "year-long sequence of three courses taught by an interdisciplinary team of professors." Students describe the "excellent, rounded first core year with all of the best instructors" as "academically challenging but still friendly" and particularly like the "emphasis on group work." One student writes, "the work is intense and challenging, and the amount we're learning is amazing. Even so, the pressure is manageable because everyone's so motivated. The administration is full of great, innovative ideas."

Second-year students have numerous choices. They may take electives in any of the program's eleven disciplines, or they may pursue the more structured "special-study options," which award certificates in International Management; Management of Technology; Environmental Management; Global Trade, Transportation, and Logistics Studies; and Entrepreneurship and Innovation. Furthermore, students also have the option of pursuing concurrent degrees in Law; International Studies; Engineering; and Public Health and Community Medicine. Students praise professors in all departments for their teaching ability and accessibility, although some warn that students "need to do some selective hunting for second-year profs."

About the only consistent bone of contention at UW are the facilities. The new Seafirst Executive Center is "great, but some of the classrooms could be improved," as could computer labs. One student complains, "Although rooms are equipped with multimedia resources, they are often not functioning, and most people are not capable of using them because the system is convoluted." The School of Business is currently undergoing renovations—it already has "a great new library, remodeled lounge, and a new restaurant"—that may remedy this situation. Among those who complain, many concede that the "University is well on its way" toward necessary improvements.

PLACEMENT AND RECRUITING

The University of Washington Business Career Center writes, "University of Washington students gravitate toward high-tech companies and get experience in the industry through internships. In return, high-tech companies seek out students interested and experienced in the field. The Business Career Center staff works closely with students to help them assess and identify their interests. The program staff also organizes a number of networking events geared to put students in touch with hard-to-locate constituencies such as entrepreneurs." Among those events is on-campus recruiting visits from sixty-one companies and MBA consortia in Chicago; Irvine, CA; and Michigan. Top employers include Andersen Consulting, ATL Ultrasound, Deloitte & Touche, Ernst &

David Williams, Acting Director of MBA Program
110 Mackenzie Hall, Box 353200, Seattle, WA 98195
Admissions: 206-543-4661 • Fax: 206-616-7351
Email: mba@u.washington.edu
Internet: www.weber.u.washington.edu/~bschool/mba

University of Washington

Young, Fluke Corporation, Hewlett-Packard Company, Intel Corporation, and Price Waterhouse.

Washington students give their career center average grades, telling us that the school does a good job of attracting high-quality area companies, but that it "needs to diversify recruiting beyond the Pacific Northwest." Students also give low marks to the school's mentoring system.

STUDENT/CAMPUS LIFE

University of Washington draws heavily from the Pacific Rim, a situation agreeable to students from both sides of the Pacific. One American student notes that "international students add a much needed layer of depth and insight to our education." A Japanese student observes that "many students are open to foreign students. They call us to their parties often. In group academic projects, basically they are helpful." Regardless of their national origin, students praise their classmates as "smart," "friendly," and "awesome! Bright, energetic, hardworking, diverse in interests and backgrounds." One MBA with an unusual facility for class demographics writes, "I like the fact that there are 'older' people (average age: 29) with work experience (average 5.5 years)." Not surprisingly for a predominantly West Coast group, UW students are both "high-tech oriented" and "outdoorsy, more environmentally concerned than motivated by money."

Life on the UW campus is "very busy. Too much to do, too little time to enjoy the experience." The amount of time students devote to study here is above the national average, especially during the first-year, which is "stressful but with a congenial atmosphere and many group projects." Adds one student, "You feel the camaraderie the moment you arrive. My class is a tight group—you know they care about your academic and professional success." Our survey shows that "most students socialize and work together in clubs and other activities," of which there are "lots." They love their beautiful 700-acre campus and they also love Seattle, which they describe as "safe," "fun-filled," and "growing economically." They especially love their proximity to "hundreds of little software firms in the area, including mother Microsoft." On the downside, campus housing "needs improvement" and off-campus housing is "very expensive."

ADMISSIONS

The admissions office considers the following criteria (in no particular order): essays, college GPA, extracurricular activities, work experience, the interview, GMAT scores, and letters of recommendation. Notes the school, "We look closely at GPA and GMAT scores, but high quantitative measures do not ensure admissions—strong work experience or extensive extracurricular or community activities can significantly improve an applicant's chances of admission." The admissions office has implemented a round-based admission cycle, with an early deadline of December 1, and early notification by January 15. Decisions are made on a rolling basis. Notes the office, "We strongly encourage early application." The final deadline is March 15, but students are encouraged to apply by the January 8 or February 1 dates. Notification is generally received in six to eight weeks. Students must complete a college-level calculus course before enrollment.

FINANCIAL FACTS

Tuition (in/out-state)	$5,424/$13,470
Cost of books	$2,000
Room & Board (on/off-campus)	$7,458/NR
% of students receiving aid	80
% first-year students receiving aid	63
% aid that is merit-based	5
% of students receiving grants	15
Average grant	$3,568

ADMISSIONS

# of applications received	1,106
% applicants accepted	33
% acceptees attending	39
Average GMAT (range)	630 (520–770)
Minimum TOEFL	600
Average GPA (range)	3.28 (2.20–4.00)
Application fee (in/out-state)	$45/$45
Early decision program available	Yes
Early decision deadline	December 1
Early decision notification	January 15
Regular application deadline	Rolling
Regular notification	Rolling
Admission may be deferred?	No
Transfer students accepted?	No
Non-fall admission available?	No
Admissions process need-blind?	Yes

APPLICANTS ALSO LOOK AT

University of California—Berkeley, University of California—Davis, University of California—Los Angeles, University of California—Santa Barbara, Brigham Young University, University of Michigan Business School, Dartmouth College, Duke University

EMPLOYMENT PROFILE

Placement rate (%)	84
# of companies recruiting on-campus	61
% grads employed immediately	84
Average starting salary	$53,556

Grads employed by field (avg. salary):

Accounting	10% (NR)
Consulting	17% ($56,240)
Finance	22% ($56,030)
General Management	14% ($43,240)
Marketing	27% ($55,960)
MIS	4% ($43,500)
Operations	3% (NR)
Other	2% (NR)

WASHINGTON UNIVERSITY
John M. Olin School of Business

ACADEMICS

Students in our survey were very satisfied with their academic experience at Washington University. The program that everyone talks about is Olin's Management Center. Here companies pay for teams of MBAs to come on-site and consult on matters ranging from marketing to strategy. At the conclusion of this practicum, students make a formal presentation to the client company. Thus far, fifty-seven organizations, including Enterprise Rent-A-Car, Ford Motor Company, Price Waterhouse, Ralston Purina, Apple Computer, and Monsanto, have asked Olin students to advise them on select issues. Social responsibility is also promoted—student teams perform pro-bono consulting to organizations in the nonprofit sector. Almost twenty-five percent of Olin MBA students returned from winter break a week early last term and partnered with Ernst & Young consultants on these projects. The Management Center also runs The Hatchery, a program in which budding entrepreneurs work with fledgling companies to draw up business plans to present to potential investors. Prospective traders can participate in Investment Praxis, a semester-long program where students act as portfolio managers for a portion of the school's reserve fund. A program called Total Quality Schools allows MBAs to consult to local public schools for credit. Another experiential learning program that has received a lot of press is SuperTYCOON, a one-week simulated management program taught in conjunction with a strategy course. The dual-degree MBA/MA in East Asian studies, in which students study Japanese or Mandarin Chinese and complete a semester or internship in their target country (China, Taiwan, or Japan) is another successful program. Finally, a "close encounter" series brings small groups of students face to face with top executives such as John Pepper, President of Procter & Gamble.

The administration earned very high marks this year. Students agree "The school is extremely responsive to student input" and has a "high 'student-service' attitude." A wheelchair user confirmed this, writing "the school has been very proactive about being accessible." "We are able to make an impact on policies and programs" reported a happy MBA. Another stated simply "Dean Stuart Greenbaum—he's the man." Professors got decent grades for their teaching and were praised for their accessibility. The majority of Olin MBAs said this program meets their academic expectations. One student noted that "the large international constituency makes the learning experience more interesting." A satisfied student summed up his experience at Olin by saying, "This MBA program is the smartest investment I've ever made."

PLACEMENT AND RECRUITING

Olin's approach to career placement is "touchy-feely" as compared to the hard-nosed approach of many of the top b-schools. This school takes steps to ensure that their MBAs realize their interests and values and in turn place them-often through nontraditional means-in a job that will "make [their dreams] come true." Olin offers some unique career placement services, including a mandatory half-credit course in Professional Development Planning during students' first weeks and a later non-credit Career Management Series. The main goal of such services is to focus on students on an individual basis to teach them how to market themselves according to their strengths and goals.

Deborah Booker, Director of MBA Admissions
Campus Box 1133, One Brookings Drive, St. Louis, MO 63130
Admissions: 314-935-7301 • Fax: 314-935-6309
Email: mba@wuolin.wustl.edu
Internet: www.olin.wustl.edu

Washington University

In 1997 major recruiters at Olin were Ernst & Young, Price Waterhouse, Monsanto, Emerson Electric, Procter & Gamble, Deloitte & Touche, Bank of Nova Scotia, A.G. Edwards & Sons, Hallmark, and Stifel Nicolaus; by August 1997, 89 percent of that year's graduating class was employed.

STUDENT/CAMPUS LIFE

Olin MBAs report a high quality of life. "Olin is a comfortable place," wrote one student, "not at all pretentious." The campus is amazingly beautiful. The academic facilities are also well-appointed, though several students reported they were already outgrowing the space, particularly the computer lab. Students report that housing is plentiful and attractive. Most live off-campus in nearby apartments. The heavy social scene at WU ranges from weekly Friday afternoon keg parties to student fund-raisers. This year an "Olin Walk for Charity" raised money for Paraquad and Canine Companions. Other major clubs are: Entrepreneurs Club, Business Minority Council, International Business Council, Operations and Manufacturing Club, Voluntary Action Committee, and Women in Management.

The associate dean at Olin is a woman, one of the few in that position in the nation. Most agree there could be more racial and geographic diversity in the student body, but overall the students seems to like each other. "Best experience I've ever had," writes one, "I've met lifetime friends." Olin MBAs describe their classmates as "high-quality." Roughly one-third of the students are foreign. "I was surprised how much the international population influences this environment," remarked another MBA. Still another recommended admitting "fewer students with one to two years of work experience."

Olin MBAs report a steady, heavy dose of work, especially during the first-year. Students prepare for class roughly twenty-five hours a week and describe the academic pressure as intense, forcing the efficient use of study groups, which are considered integral to student life. The small size of the school (approximately 150 students in each full-time class) offers many advantages: small classes, personal attention, and a supportive environment. Students say this school is competitive but, not surprisingly, teamwork is the overriding theme here. Confirmed one MBA, "There's a strong family-like atmosphere here."

ADMISSIONS

According to the admissions office, a candidate's setting and achieving challenging goals in all aspects of their lives is the most important criterion. After that, the school considers, in descending order, your college GPA, GMAT scores, interview, letters of recommendation, and essay. Writes the school, "The interview is not required, but strongly recommended, and can be a determining factor." The school also requires students to submit a very detailed work history. Olin's Consortium for Graduate Study in Management is dedicated to funding fellowships for talented minorities. Admissions are handled on a rolling basis; students are notified of a decision three to five weeks after their applications are received.

FINANCIAL FACTS

Tuition	$23,800
Tuition per credit	$670
Cost of books	$2,500
Room & Board (on/off-campus)	NR/$11,000
% of students receiving aid	63
% first-year students receiving aid	62
% aid that is merit-based	47
% of students receiving loans	49
% of students receiving grants	72
Average award package	$26,869
Average grant	$7,000
Average graduation debt	$38,880

ADMISSIONS

# of applications received	1,165
% applicants accepted	39
% acceptees attending	50
Average GMAT (range)	606 (570–690)
Minimum TOEFL	570
Average GPA (range)	3.20 (2.80–3.60)
Application fee (in/out-state)	$80/$80
Early decision program available	No
Regular application deadline	March 30
Regular notification	Rolling
Admission may be deferred?	No
Transfer students accepted?	No
Non-fall admission available?	No
Admissions process need-blind?	Yes

APPLICANTS ALSO LOOK AT

Northwestern University, University of Michigan Business School, University of Chicago, Duke University, New York University, Vanderbilt University, Indiana University, University of Virginia

EMPLOYMENT PROFILE

Placement rate (%)	89
# of companies recruiting on-campus	124
% grads employed immediately	83
Average starting salary	$59,200

Grads employed by field (avg. salary):
Accounting	5% ($50,000)
Consulting	30% ($62,000)
Finance	36% ($61,290)
Marketing	11% ($59,500)
Operations	5% ($60,750)
Strategic Planning	7% ($56,900)
Other	6% ($45,700)

UNIVERSITY OF WESTERN ONTARIO
Ivey Business School

OVERVIEW

Type of school	public
Affiliation	none
Environment	NR
Academic calendar	semester

STUDENTS

Enrollment of parent institution	25,000
Enrollment of business school	200
% male/female	75/25
% out-of- state	42
% minorities	NR
% international (# countries represented)	20(100)
Average age at entry	29
Average years work experience at entry	5

ACADEMICS

Student/faculty ratio	2:1
% female faculty	18
Hours of study per day	5.71

SPECIALTIES
Global orientation, General Management, Extensive Exchange Program, Intergrated Program

JOINT DEGREES
MBA/ LLB — 4 years

SPECIAL PROGRAMS
Enterprenuership, Consulting Streams

STUDY ABROAD PROGRAMS
Australia, Austria, Brazil, Denmark, France, Germany, Hong Kong, Japan, Mexico, The Netherlands, Philippines, Singapore, Spain, Sweden, South Korea, Switzerland

ACADEMICS*

The Richard C. Ivey School of Business at the University of Western Ontario distinguishes itself with a generalist approach to management issues, taught through an unusually heavy reliance on case studies. In fact, the school boasts that Ivey is one of the largest producers of case studies in the world. Notes the school's promotional material: "Over the duration of the Western MBA Program, [students] tackle more than 600 real-world business cases."

Entering MBAs are divided into sections of from sixty to seventy students and then into smaller learning teams, within which students tackle many of the program's case studies. Ivey's "highly integrated core" incorporates international and local business issues as well as aspects of the many fields of business study: marketing, operations, communications, finance, information technology, statistics, and accounting. In addition, "From the very start of the program students work with executives and managers from a major corporation in addressing one or more current issues facing that corporation." Learning teams and case studies not only teach students how to solve business problems but also how to foster teamwork skills.

Second-year students are given wide berth to design their own programs. Elective choices include traditional, single-subject courses as well as many interdisciplinary courses. The school catalog notes, "Many of these electives have field-based projects associated with them, giving [students] the opportunity not only to get out into that real world but also to explore industries and companies in which [they] may be considering building [their] careers." Students focusing on international business are encouraged to take language and cultural studies courses outside the MBA program to supplement their education. Exchange programs are available with schools in Asia, Latin America, Scandinavia, Europe, and Australia. Other interesting international opportunities include the Leader Project and the China Project, which send fifty MBA candidates to Eastern Europe and China to teach basic management skills to "selected officials and entrepreneurs."

PLACEMENT AND RECRUITING

At the beginning of the fall semester, the Ivey School's Career Services Office (CSO) conducts a week-long seminar in job-search skills for incoming students. Skills covered include resume writing, planning job searches, and interviewing. The CSO compiles a resume book for second-year students, which it sends to "hundreds of employers." The Ivey School attracts more than 150 recruiting companies to its campus each year; visits occur year-round for full-time job offerings and in the spring for summer internships. Among the companies that have visited the Ivey campus in the past are Deloitte and Touche; Goldman Sachs; Morgan Stanley; Citibank; Bank of Montreal; Scotiabank; Procter and Gamble; Unilever; General Electric; Ford Motor Company; and Parke-Davis. In addition, the school hosts an autumn Job Fair—which attracted 30 companies in 1997—for all second-year students. The school claims more than 11,000 alumni in over 60 countries, creating a potentially strong job network for Ivey MBAs.

Larysa Gamula, Admissions Director
London, Ontario
Canada N6A 3K7
Admissions: 519-661-3212
Email: info@ivey.uwo.ca
Internet: www.ivey.uwo.ca

University of Western Ontario

STUDENT/CAMPUS LIFE

Two-thirds of Ivey MBAs are native to Canada; the rest are drawn from more than twenty countries, including the United States, Switzerland, Germany, France, Taiwan, Singapore, China, Hong Kong, Mexico, Colombia, Venezuela, Russia, Ukraine, United Kingdom, and Ireland. The average incoming student is twenty-nine and has five years of work experience. According to the school, "Many have substantial work experience outside North America. Many come from occupations totally unrelated to business, including the health professions, education, and government service. Some come from more traditional business backgrounds, having earned degrees in business, commerce, or economics, and then completed an entry-level position before deciding that now was the time to earn an M.B.A." Nearly one-quarter studied engineering as undergraduates.

The Ivey School is located in London, Ontario, a town with a population just over 300,000. London is a quaint, picturesque town with many parks and tree-lined streets, thus earning it the nickname "The Forest City." The university, construction, and light manufacturing drive the London economy; the city is host to manufacturing plants owned by GM, Serco, Siemens Automotive, and 3M, among others. London offers little in the way of big-city entertainment, but is large enough to support a pleasant variety of restaurants, bars, and night-clubs. The university is large (25,000 students) and accordingly provides many of the social opportunities available at big schools in the United States. MBAs constitute their own sub-population within the university, forming clubs that sponsor various professional and social events, as well as guest lectures and recruiting trips. Toronto and Detroit are within 130 miles of London; Great Lakes resorts are within an hour's drive.

ADMISSIONS

According to the program's promotional materials, Ivey's "admissions committee takes into account as many factors as possible. Considerable weight is placed on [applicants'] intellectual performance and potential, full-time work experience and accomplishments, leadership, and interpersonal skills." All applicants must take the GMAT; in addition, ESL applicants must score at least a 600 on the TOEFL. The Ivey School considers candidates on a rolling basis. Admissions officers begin evaluating applications in November; applications are usually processed within eight weeks of receipt. The deadline for applications from outside Canada is April 1, and applicants are encouraged to submit well before this deadline. The Ivey school occasionally admits students lacking an undergraduate degree; such students, however, "must have a minimum of seven years of challenging full-time work experience, some university courses with a very solid academic standing and other strong management qualities."

FINANCIAL FACTS

Tuition (in/out-state)	$12,000/NR
Cost of books	$2,000
Room & Board (on/off-campus)	$6,000/$6,000
% aid that is merit-based	100

ADMISSIONS

# of applications received	926
% applicants accepted	46
% acceptees attending	50
Average GMAT (range)	632 (560–730)
Minimum TOEFL	600
Average GPA (range)	3.30 (2.70–3.90)
Application fee (in/out-state)	$100/$100
Early decision deadline	Rolling Admission
Regular application deadline	May 15
Regular notification	NR
Admission may be deferred?	Yes
Maximum length of deferment	1 year
Transfer students accepted?	No
Non-fall admission available?	No
Admissions process need-blind?	Yes

EMPLOYMENT PROFILE

Placement rate (%)	91
# of companies recruiting on-campus	485
Average starting salary	$88,736

Grads employed by field (avg. salary):

Accounting	NR ($61,462)
Consulting	NR ($77,371)
Finance	NR ($82,600)
Global Management	NR ($60,000)
Marketing	NR ($70,000)
MIS	NR ($58,000)
Operations	NR ($40,000)
Other	NR ($66,000)

*NOTE: University of Western Ontario was chosen for inclusion in this book at too late a date for The Princeton Review to survey a representative sample of students. We feel that the program is too good to overlook; therefore, this profile is based on the school's promotional materials. We plan to survey students to include a more thorough profile in next year's edition of *The Best 75 Business Schools*.

COLLEGE OF WILLIAM AND MARY
Graduate School of Business

OVERVIEW

Type of school	public
Affiliation	none
Environment	town
Academic calendar	semester

STUDENTS

Enrollment of parent institution	5,326
Enrollment of business school	361
% male/female	65/35
% out-of-state	40
% part-time	40
% minorities	17
% international (# countries represented)	12(12)
Average age at entry	28
Average years work experience at entry	5

ACADEMICS

Student/faculty ratio	4:1
% female faculty	20
% minority faculty	5
Hours of study per day	5.48

SPECIALTIES

Special strengths in Finance, Operations Management and Information Technology; Marketing, Leadership.

JOINT DEGREES

MBA/JD, 4 years; MBA/MPP, 3 years

SPECIAL PROGRAMS

Field Studies

STUDY ABROAD PROGRAMS

Norway, Costa Rica

SURVEY SAYS...

HITS
Marketing
MIS/operations
Cozy student community

MISSES
Social life
School clubs
Computer skills

PROMINENT ALUMNI

William P. Fricks, Chairman, President and CEO, Newport News Shipbuilding; Daniel J. Ludman, Chairman and CEO, Moentor Investment Group; Robert J. Murphy, Senior Vice President, Hard News, ABC News

ACADEMICS

An intense, intimate program at state-school prices is what attracts MBAs to the College of William and Mary Graduate School of Business. A little more than 100 students are admitted each year, making this program ideal for those who want a "smaller program with personal attention and non-competitive attitude" at an "excellent value for in-state students."

William and Mary emphasizes building teamwork even before the first day of classes. Incoming students participate in an Outward Bound-style Orientation Week, during which they divide into teams of six and meet the challenges of a high ropes course, zip-line water crossing, and a raft-building competition. The six-member teams remain in place throughout first-year to serve as study groups; the college takes care to build teams of students whose diverse areas of expertise supplement each others'. First-year students must complete a twelve-course core, sequenced "to provide the greatest crossover benefits among courses and disciplines." Case studies, computer simulations, and lectures (by both faculty and visiting speakers) are integrated throughout the year. Writesone student, "the case/lecture method is very effective."

Second-year students may choose from a variety of electives in accounting, finance and economics, marketing, and operations and information technology. Respondents give these departments high grades across the board, citing a uniformly excellent faculty as the school's distinguishing trait. Professors "are very enthusiastic, very capable," and offer each student "a great deal of personal attention. Teachers are very responsive to performances of students." They're hardly pushovers, however; as one student explains, "The professors are great. They really want you to learn the material. They are very tough though, and they will push you very hard." Students hold the administration and staff in similarly high regard. Major complaints concern facilities—the library is considered "weak" and the computer labs "need more computers and more frequent upgrades"—and a grading system that "is too severe and puts us at a disadvantage with grads from other schools."

PLACEMENT AND RECRUITING

Students at William and Mary agree that the "placement office is the weak link here," although some feel that "perhaps as the stature of the school grows, the placement office will become more effective." Most common among student complaints is the feeling that "we need increased on-campus recruiting opportunities." Among the companies that visit Williamsburg are Andersen Consulting, Bristol-Myers Squibb, Champion, Delta Airlines, GE, Merrill Lynch, and Whirlpool.

The placement office tries to supplement on-campus recruiting through participation in MBA consortia in Atlanta and New York City. The Office of Career and Employer Development also manages two programs designed to interweave "real-life experience" into the MBA experience: the Mentor Program, "which enables students to form professional relationships with business leaders chosen from a nationwide list"; and the Internship Program, "which provides hands-on experience in the students' field of choice."

Susan Rivera, Director of MBA Admissions/Student Services
Blow Hall, Room 255, Williamsburg, VA 23187
Admissions: 757-221-2898 • Fax: 757-221-2958
Email: sgrive@dogwood.tyler.wm.edu
Internet: www.business.tyler.wm.edu

College of William and Mary

STUDENT/CAMPUS LIFE

The rigorous academics required for a William and Mary MBA demand that students be "bright," "very serious about their careers," and ready to "study, study, study." They're a driven group, but "not competitive to the point [that] they aren't friendly. Everyone here wants their fellow students to succeed." Students spend a lot of time working together in groups, so it's a good thing that they're "very team-oriented. For example, if information is received individually from a professor, students will email all relevant facts to classmates on a given assignment." Our survey shows their work experiences to be "very diverse, ranging from banking and consulting to the Peace Corps," but also shows little ethnic/racial diversity in the program. Although students are "sometimes pretty stressed out," they are generally "tremendously professional, helpful, and cooperative." Most would agree with the student who tells us that "my fellow students have become my extended family. They help me when I need it, I help them when they need it, and everyone is supportive of each other!"

The school is located in historic Williamsburg, a re-creation of a colonial town that is more tourist trap than thriving metropolis. "The town is a graveyard," is how one MBA bluntly puts it. Another warns that "nightlife is scarce." It should be noted, however, that at least one student thinks that "the historic setting is a big plus," and that others point out that the town is "very safe and friendly, if a little boring at times." For most, the school's setting is irrelevant, since "life is school. We work so much there is little time to spend doing other activities." In fact, the most frequent complaint about the program is that it is too time-consuming. "We need a better balance between academic work and social events," is typical of responses. "Only half of the phrase work hard, play hard applies to the W&M b-school environment." Students occasionally find time to participate in a "great intramural sports program that allows us to interact with students from other programs." They also take advantage of "tremendous opportunities for personal growth in the many clubs available on campus." Occasionally students slip out of Williamsburg. Their destinations? "Virginia Beach is only 45 minutes away. The Blue Ridge Mountains are only 1 + hours away. D.C. is not far."

ADMISSIONS

According to the admissions office, work experience is considered most important. Then the following in descending order: GMAT scores, required interview (phone interviews are arranged for those unable to travel to Williamsburg), letters of recommendation and essays, and college GPA. William and Mary features a rolling admissions process beginning early October and running through May 1. The school advises prospective students to submit applications prior to February 1.

FINANCIAL FACTS

Tuition (in/out-state)	$6,500/$16,200
Tuition per credit (in/out-state)	$200/$510
Fees (in-state/out-of-state)	$80/$80
Cost of books	$1,600
Room & Board (on/off-campus)	$7,500/$7,500
% of students receiving aid	90
% first-year students receiving aid	60
% aid that is merit-based	25
% of students receiving loans	90
% of students receiving paid internships	100
% of students receiving grants	85
Average award package	$30,000
Average grant	$5,000
Average graduation debt	$30,000

ADMISSIONS

# of applications received	450
% applicants accepted	33
% acceptees attending	70
Average GMAT (range)	620 (580–680)
Minimum TOEFL	600
Average GPA (range)	3.20 (2.70–3.80)
Application fee (in/out-state)	$50/$50
Early decision program available	Yes
Early decision deadline	December 1
Early decision notification	December 15
Regular application deadline	May 1
Regular notification	Rolling
Admission may be deferred?	Yes
Maximum length of deferment	1 year
Transfer students accepted?	No
Admissions process need-blind?	Yes

APPLICANTS ALSO LOOK AT

University of Virginia, Wake Forest University, Duke University, University of North Carolina at Chapel Hill, Georgetown University, University of Texas at Austin

EMPLOYMENT PROFILE

Placement rate (%)	90
# of companies recruiting on-campus	72
% grads employed immediately	90
% grads employed within six months	95
Average starting salary	$59,000

Grads employed by field (avg. salary):

Accounting	1% ($60,860)
Consulting	37% ($54,610)
Entrepreneurship	1% (NR)
Finance	39% ($60,860)
General Management	4% ($64,200)
Global Management	1% (NR)
Human Resources	($64,000)
Marketing	9% ($58,500)
MIS	2% ($56,600)
Operations	4% ($64,500)

UNIVERSITY OF WISCONSIN-MADISON
Business School

OVERVIEW

Type of school	public
Affiliation	none
Environment	metropolis
Academic calendar	semester

STUDENTS

Enrollment of parent institution	40,000
Enrollment of business school	457
% male/female	67/33
% out-of-state	55
% minorities	13
% international (# countries represented)	25(30)
Average age at entry	28
Average years work experience at entry	4

ACADEMICS

Student/faculty ratio	6:1
% female faculty	13
% minority faculty	3
Hours of study per day	4.35

SPECIALTIES

Faculty are strong in all areas of teaching and research. New MBA curriculum enables students to build on their strengths. Seven-week modules combined with semester courses allows for the best mix of core courses and electives. The shorter segments allow material to be more current and tailored to the individual needs. Schedule also allows greater opportunity for students to take electives in their majors, both inside and outside of the Business School.

JOINT DEGREES

JD/MBA (4 years)

SPECIAL PROGRAMS

Marketing Research, Arts Administration, Applied Security Analysis, Real Estate, Enterprise, Distribution Management, Manufacturing & Technology Management, and Agribusiness.

STUDY ABROAD PROGRAMS

Germany, France, Chile, Mexico, Denmark, Austria, Thailand, China, England

SURVEY SAYS...

HITS
Small classes
Campus is attractive
Madison

MISSES
MIS/operations
General management
On-campus housing

PROMINENT ALUMNI

John Morgridge, Chairman of the Board, Cisco Systems; Charles Robb, U.S. Senator from Virginia, Former Governor of VA.

ACADEMICS

University of Wisconsin MBA students consider their b-school top-tier: "We have great niche programs, such as the A.C. Nielsen Center for Marketing Research, which provide top-notch training," raved one student. "The Real Estate program is ranked #1!" cheered another. There are also top programs in Applied Securities Analysis and Distribution Management. "This program is very underrated," remarked one MBA. Students are equally fired up about the quality and productivity curriculum and the Joyce Erdman Center for Manufacturing and Technology.

Students expressed disappointment only about the core course program they're required to complete. Other than recent additions to the curriculum—including an infusion of hip courses on ethics, negotiation and bargaining, strategy and policy, and managing innovation and technology—students describe core courses as mediocre. Fortunately, there's a way out. Although first-years must complete a foundation core of nineteen credits, up to thirteen credits can be waived without replacements. Students who have completed relevant coursework may be passed into higher-level (and presumably more interesting) courses. Electives can be taken as early as the first-year. A huge emphasis is placed on international business, with many international course offerings, summer and semester abroad programs, yearly student/faculty trips to destinations like the Pacific Rim and Latin America, and foreign language classes in other UW departments to prep for it all.

For most MBAs, the first two semesters are spent fulfilling the core requirements. A warning to the mathematically challenged: The heavy quantitative focus sends many students running for help. (The school strongly advises students to bolster their number-crunching skills before applying.) Fortunately, students can brush up during the week-long math camp offered before orientation or take tutorial sessions at the Learning Center during the school year.

MBAs feel they have very good access to the faculty, but the quality of their teaching is inconsistent. Said one student, "There are some great profs, but a few bad apples, too." Several people griped about the focus at UWisconsin on undergrads. "I feel they shouldn't let honors undergrads take first-year MBA courses," said one respondent. But overall, students are more than satisfied. "I gave up a great job in sunny California to come to school in Wisconsin, and it's proving to be one of the best decisions I've ever made," attested one. Others agree: "Wisconsin is an up-and-coming program on the verge of becoming a top-ranked business school."

PLACEMENT AND RECRUITING

Students report that the Business Career Center (BCC) is among U Wisconsin's greatest assets. "The placement office bends over backwards for us," enthused one student. The BCC provides many of the services that are standard at the best b-schools: continual counseling, mock interviews, job fairs, MBA consortia, and video-conferencing all fit into the mix. Small classes and an effective BCC staff allow counselors to give students that extra bit of attention that almost always results in a high level of student satisfaction.

Lisa Urban, Director of Marketing and Recruiting
2266 Grainger Hall, 975 University Avenue, Madison, WI 53706
Admissions: 608-262-1555 • Fax: 608-265-4192
Email: uwmadmba@bus.wisc.edu
Internet: www.wisc.edu/bschool

More than 230 companies visited the Madison campus to recruit MBAs for full-time positions and internships during 1996–97. MBAs here place primarily in the Midwest: nearly forty percent stay in Wisconsin, while another 25 percent head for either Chicago or Minneapolis.

STUDENT/CAMPUS LIFE

According to students, Madison is practically a utopia. One student offered this glowing report: "Madison is a wonderful place to be a student. There is a plethora of restaurants, bars, and arts activities that can't be sampled in just two years." Another remarked, "The city is great for outdoor enthusiasts. There are bike paths, parks, and lakes for all kinds of activities." Indeed, everyone seems to agree that this a college town where the quality of living is high.

Wisconsin's students are pleased with their classmates and the laid-back atmosphere of the school. "The people here are down-to-earth and more cooperative than competitive." Students described each other as "very sociable" and "always willing to help each other out." Despite the number of international students, many feel the school could be more diverse, and recruit more minority students and faculty.

Social activities abound. During the long winters, parties proliferate, especially for the majority of students who live near campus. When it warms up, everyone hangs out at Memorial Union on "the Terrace" facing Lake Mendota. Thursday nights are accompanied by bands and beer. Intramural sports are popular: basketball, volleyball, and six-man football. Great golf is a priority-students get half off at the University Ridge Golf Course—one of the top courses in the state. But not everyone is a jock. Roughly forty student clubs offer ample opportunity for group involvement, such as Women in Business, Graduate Marketing Network, and Toastmasters.

Over and over, students raved about their "awesome new $45 million school building" which is specially equipped with multimedia applications in the classroom. Remarked one MBA, "Having all your classes in one building is a real bonus during a Wisconsin winter." Campus parking, however, was reported to be dreadful.

ADMISSIONS

UW considers a prospective student's work experience an important factor in the selection process. Wisconsin is also looking for students with strong GMAT scores, good grade point averages, good references, and a dynamite essay. Wisconsin admits by major, so essays should address the student's interest in a specific field of study. Interviews are not required, but a campus visit is encouraged. Students with exceptional academic qualifications should apply by January 1 to be considered for All-University Fellowships. Wisconsin is a founding member of the Consortium for Graduate Study in Mangement, which offers full-tuition scholarships for talented minority students.

FINANCIAL FACTS
Tuition (in/out-state)	$5,666/$15,380
Cost of books	$665
Room & Board (on/off-campus)	NR/$6,756
% of students receiving aid	33
% aid that is merit-based	100
% of students receiving paid internships	54
% of students receiving grants	34
Average grant	$5,438
Average graduation debt	$0

ADMISSIONS
# of applications received	854
% applicants accepted	39
% acceptees attending	56
Average GMAT (range)	596 (550–640)
Minimum TOEFL	600
Average GPA (range)	3.30 (3.10–3.55)
Application fee (in/out-state)	$45/$45
Early decision program available	Yes
Early decision deadline	Rolling
Regular application deadline	May 1
Regular notification	Rolling
Admission may be deferred?	No
Transfer students accepted?	Yes
Non-fall admission available?	Yes
Admissions process need-blind?	Yes

APPLICANTS ALSO LOOK AT
Northwestern University, University of Texas at Austin, University of Michigan Business School, Indiana University, University of Chicago, University of Minnesota, University of North Carolina at Chapel Hill, Ohio State University

EMPLOYMENT PROFILE
Placement rate (%)	98
# of companies recruiting on-campus	213
% grads employed immediately	93
% grads employed within six months	96
Average starting salary	$50,935

Grads employed by field (avg. salary):
Accounting	5% ($37,950)
Communications	0% (NR)
Consulting	16% ($55,152)
Entrepreneurship	2% ($61,285)
Finance	30% ($50,403)
General Management	8% ($46,001)
Global Management	0% (NR)
Human Resources	1% ($53,400)
Marketing	20% ($49,815)
MIS	4% ($51,366)
Operations	1% ($46,500)
Quantitative	2% ($52,025)
Strategic Planning	1% ($60,480)
Venture Capital	2% ($61,000)
Other	8% ($48,360)

UNIVERSITY OF WYOMING
College of Business

OVERVIEW

Type of school	public
Affiliation	none
Environment	suburban
Academic calendar	semester
Schedule	full-time/part-time/evening

STUDENTS

Enrollment of parent institution	10,774
Enrollment of business school	71
% male/female	46/54
% out-of-state	57
% part-time	62
% minorities	6
% international (# countries represented)	7 (NR)
Average age at entry	30

ACADEMICS

Student/faculty ratio	2:1
% female faculty	20
% minority faculty	2
Hours of study per day	3.79

SPECIALTIES

Strengths of faculty and curriculum in solving business problems, decision-making, interpersonal skills, balancing human and quantitative management tools.

STUDY ABROAD PROGRAMS

France- Ecole Superieure de Commerce Tours

SURVEY SAYS...

HITS
Small classes
Star faculty
On-campus housing

MISSES
School clubs
Profs not great teachers
Quantitative skills

ACADEMICS

Students looking for an intimate, low-pressure, and cost-effective MBA program would do well to consider the University of Wyoming's College of Business. With just a little more than seventy full-time students, Wyoming fosters camaraderie among classmates and between students and professors. "The most outstanding asset of this school is the student/teacher ratio. You really get to know your professors," explains one student. The workload at Wyoming is manageable, according to our respondents, while an "administration that works smoothly" and "professors who take an interest in the students, thanks to the small classes" help keep the school atmosphere friendly and relaxed. Wyoming is also a bargain-even for out-of-state students—with low tuition and costs offset by "generous assistantships."

Wyoming is also a good choice for students with extensive undergraduate business experience, as it is possible for students to place out of some or all of the first-year foundation courses. Foundation year covers the basics in accounting, finance, business law, operations, management, marketing, microeconomics, and business math. Students describe it as "a broad program, good for a person with a more focused background," although some complain that "[foundation] classes are geared too heavily towards the quantitative aspects of business. More qualitative courses should be available to balance the two." Wyoming calls its second year the "core year," which is highly structured like the first-year. Not surprisingly for a program this small, "electives are scarce," leaving some students to wish for more options. Second-year students are required to complete the Business Ventures Course, during which they form teams and plan a new Wyoming-based business. Some of these projects make it beyond the classroom and have flourished as operating enterprises. Other second-year requirements include the Strategy and Policy Course, in which students design mid-sized manufacturing businesses and then simulate their management. Finally, Wyoming students must write a traditional master's-style thesis at the conclusion of their second year.

Students give their professors average grades for teaching ability, praising them for "providing real-life examples to prepare us for the business world" and "one-on-one teaching," but also complain that "some just do not care about teaching." One critic goes further, deriding instructors as "biased, old-school professors with a 'good old boys' mindset." The highest marks go to instructors in general management, operations, and accounting. Wyoming students think less of their marketing, international business, and entrepreneurial studies instructors.

The University of Wyoming offers state residents the unusual opportunity of completing a part-time MBA off-campus. Through the use of compressed video and computer communication, students may earn a Laramie MBA at one of a dozen sites around the state, where they meet to attend 'virtual classes.'

Director of MBA Program
P.O. Box 3275, Laramie, WY 82071
Admissions: 307-766-2449
Email: mba@uwyo.edu
Internet: www.uwyo.edu/bu/mba/mba.htm

University of Wyoming

PLACEMENT AND RECRUITING

Wyoming students give their career placement office poor marks across the board, expressing particular disappointment with the number and quality of companies that make on-campus recruiting trips. They also complain about the alumni network, more than half of whom our respondents find to be "no help" in their employment searches. Students are somewhat more positive about the quality of opportunities for off-campus projects, internships, and mentoring.

Approximately seventy companies visit the Laramie campus to recruit Wyoming MBAs each year. The school also markets its graduates through a resume book, which it mails to more than two hundred companies, alumni, advisory board members, and university trustees.

STUDENT/CAMPUS LIFE

The small student body at Wyoming is made up of "mostly white, middle-class, traditional students." Students knock their classmates because they "lack work experience," but otherwise describe them as friendly, helpful, and intelligent.

Students describe life in Wyoming as "peaceful, safe, but dull." With "the entire program in one building, with the library and other services close by," students enjoy a "relaxed atmosphere" in which it is "easy to gain assistance and to work in groups." It's a good thing facilities are close together, since "it is very cold here." Laramie offers students a "nice small town life." Notes one student, "Due to the limited locations in town, the life after school is highly dependent on private meetings and activities." Such activities are frequent, leading one student to report that "life is good but very busy. There is just so much to do at school and outside of school." The region surrounding Laramie is conducive to most outdoor activities, and students enjoy hiking, climbing, and skiing.

ADMISSIONS

Wyoming accepts about 26 percent of its MBA applicants (about two-thirds of whom wind up enrolling) on the basis of GPA, GMAT score, personal interviews, work experience, quality of undergraduate curriculum, and essays. Approximately one-third are from Wyoming. Writes the school, "The others are from the U.S., China, and Europe."

FINANCIAL FACTS

Tuition (in/out-state)	$2,260/$6,994
Fees	$332
Cost of books	$300
Room & Board (on/off-campus)	NR/NR
% of students receiving aid	53
% first-year students receiving aid	85
% aid that is merit-based	43
% of students receiving loans	34
% of students receiving paid internships	4
% of students receiving grants	3
Average award package	$9,000
Average grant	$1,000
Average graduation debt	$10,000

ADMISSIONS

# of applications received	126
% applicants accepted	26
% acceptees attending	70
Average GMAT (range)	561 (510–600)
Minimum TOEFL	540
Average GPA (range)	3.40 (3.19–3.63)
Application fee (in/out-state)	$40/$40
Early decision program available	Yes
Regular application deadline	March 30
Regular notification	Rolling
Admission may be deferred?	Yes
Maximum length of deferment	1 year
Transfer students accepted?	Yes
Non-fall admission available?	No
Admissions process need-blind?	Yes

APPLICANTS ALSO LOOK AT

University of Colorado at Boulder, University of Texas at Austin, University of California—Berkeley, Dartmouth College, University of Georgia, University of Michigan Business School, University of Texas at Arlington, University of Virginia

EMPLOYMENT PROFILE

Placement rate (%)	71

YALE UNIVERSITY
Yale School of Management

ACADEMICS

The Yale School of Management calls its business degree a Master's in Public and Private Management (MPPM), which one student describes as "the true master's of management degree." Whatever the description, SOM's primary mission is to "educate global leaders for business and society." Yale was one of the first business schools to emphasize the interrelations of the public, private, and non-profit sectors. Given the historical interconnectedness of business and government, Yale considers its integrated, multi-sector approach to management simply more pragmatic than a strict MBA curriculum.

In addition to their sector studies, first-year students take an intensive group of core classes in the typical, functional areas of business; hence the description "MBA-plus." There is a strong emphasis on quantitative as well as on soft skills. Second-year students focus on a specialization and take up to seven electives. One outstanding department is finance. Overall, students describe a rigorous and intellectually challenging program that meets their academic expectations. "To excel here, it'll take everything you've got," wrote one student, "it's very intense, but you learn." The faculty garnered rave reviews. One student said, "The professors present the intuition, along with the analytics, that is important for explaining ideas." For academic support, review sessions and personal tutors are available free of charge. Despite all this, there are some weak spots, especially by an MBA's standards. A large number of students report that they feel only adequately prepared in operations management. All Yale business school students are now required to have their own lap top computers, which eliminates the complaints about crowded computer labs that students had in prior surveys. The school has recently instituted an optional computer training for incoming students to ensure basic computer proficiency.

A new source of satisfaction this year was the appointment of Dean Garten. Students praised his leadership and the effect it's had on the administration as a whole. Many agreed with the student who wrote "Dean Garten is providing a fresh, exciting environment. His positive impact is being felt every day."

PLACEMENT AND RECRUITING

In the past, students have expressed dissatisfaction with Yale's Career Development Office (CDO). Explained one student, "Our placement office has the daunting task of finding jobs for 200 people who have 200 different career goals. We are hurt by the fact that companies aren't going to come here and find a lot of people who fit their molds." The school has worked to remedy this situation, reportedly tripling the CDO's professional staff to meet the specialized needs of SOM students. A Professional Strategies Program pairs students and CDO staff to help students "plan and implement their career objectives." SOM has also added a new interviewing center.

These changes, according to the CDO, have led to an increase in the number of organizations visiting the campus; in recent years on-campus recruiting has increasd 84 percent. In terms of placement, a Yale degree seems to carry most weight in the world of finance; wrote one student, "Yale has had tremendous success in placing banking and finance people, due to the reputation of its faculty." Top recruiters include Mitchell Madison Group; UTC—Pratt & Whitney; McKinsey & Co.; Citibank/Citicorp; Hewlett-Packard; Merrill Lynch; Ernst & Young; Hoffman-

LaRoche; Lehman Brothers; NationsBank; and Booz-Allen. The CDO proudly reports that "100 percent of the Class of 1998 were placed in summer internships."

STUDENT/CAMPUS LIFE

According to our survey, the intelligence and diversity of the student body is the heart and soul of SOM's program. As one Yalie put it, "This is not a cookie-cutter school. Individuality is respected here. Hard-core finance types peacefully co-exist with nonprofit types. This range of backgrounds makes for interesting discussions and relationships." Agreed another, "There is no typical SOMer. Everyone has a different background and different goals." One student enthused, "SOM has been the best two years of my life. Never again will I have the opportunity to work with such intelligent and interesting people in the cooperative learning environment that SOM fosters."

Students report a demanding workload and spend an average of thirty-five to forty hours a week preparing for class. SOM's scale of grading (distinction, proficient, pass, and fail) de-emphasizes student-against-student competition. Some believe it is key to the whole SOM experience: "The forging of great community spirit begins with the noncompetitive grading system." Still, like many MBAs, Yale students report a fair amount of academic pressure, although students says this "varies because it's self-imposed." MBAs rave about the support they get from classmates: "These are the kind of people you want by your side when you are running a business." Students expect their ties to hold long after graduation has passed. Said one, "Classmates will be friends and assets for life."

Yale's hometown of New Haven got mixed reviews. But with the strides the city has made in crime reduction over the past five or so years, its not uncommon for students to rave: "The Yale community provides everything you could want: World-renowned speakers, theater, shopping, nightclubs . . . and if you need more, New York City is only ninety minutes away." The majority of students opt to live off-campus in apartments in the city's residential neighborhoods, inland or along the Long Island Sound. Students say off-campus housing is both attractive and reasonably priced. Wrote one student, "We don't rely on public transportation but on Yale University shuttles, which are very convenient, efficient, and free." One student boasted that Yale has the "best golf course of any b-school in the country." Beyond golf, students report an active and varied social life, though this doesn't include dating. Students tend to socialize and travel in packs. One student lamented this group mentality: "If you are slightly older and single or not part of the yuppie mainstream, it can be an isolating atmosphere."

ADMISSIONS

Applicants to Yale must have excellent GPAs and GMAT scores if they hope to attract the attention of the admissions committee. One student wrote, "Nearly everyone here is a genius! No one that I've compared backgrounds with has a GMAT below 700." Work experience, letters of recommendation, and a strong background in mathematics complete the list of admissions criteria. In fact, in recent years there has been a trend toward increasing numbers of applications from candidates with engineering or physical science backgrounds.

Yale admits students in a series of "rounds." According to Yale, the round you apply in "does not impact admissibility."

FINANCIAL FACTS

Tuition	$25,250
Fees	$16,625
Cost of books	$940
Room & Board (on/off-campus)	NR/$8,675
% of students receiving aid	65
% first-year students receiving aid	63
% of students receiving loans	55
% of students receiving grants	51
Average award package	$25,900
Average grant	$7,400
Average graduation debt	$35,000

ADMISSIONS

# of applications received	1,620
% applicants accepted	26
% acceptees attending	51
Average GMAT (range)	679 (640–720)
Minimum TOEFL	600
Average GPA (range)	3.38 (3.18–3.63)
Application fee (in/out-state)	$120/$120
Early decision program available	Yes
Early decision deadline	November 10
Regular application deadline	March 16
Regular notification	May 21
Admission may be deferred?	Yes
Maximum length of deferment	2 years
Transfer students accepted?	No
Non-fall admission available?	No
Admissions process need-blind?	Yes

APPLICANTS ALSO LOOK AT
University of Pennsylvania, Columbia University, Harvard University, Stanford University, New York University, Dartmouth College, University of Chicago, Duke University

EMPLOYMENT PROFILE

Placement rate (%)	99
# of companies recruiting on-campus	125
% grads employed immediately	86
% grads employed within six months	98
Average starting salary	$69,073

Grads employed by field (avg. salary):

Accounting	1% ($55,000)
Communications	2% ($63,750)
Consulting	30% ($76,210)
Entrepreneurship	2% ($7,667)
Finance	34% ($68,272)
General Management	5% ($65,000)
Marketing	5% ($68,244)
MIS	7% ($69,369)
Strategic Planning	2% ($93,333)
Venture Capital	1% ($80,000)
Other	

Alphabetical Index

LOCATION INDEX

ABOUT THE AUTHOR

Nedda Gilbert is a graduate of the University of Pennsylvania and holds a master's degree from Columbia University. She has worked for The Princeton Review since 1985. In 1987, she created The Princeton Review corporate test preparation service, which provides Wall Street firms and premier companies tailored educational programs for their employees. She currently resides in New Jersey.

NOTES

NOTES

NOTES

NOTES

NOTES

NOTES

NOTES

NOTES

NOTES

Expert Advice

www.review.com

Talk About It

www.review.com

Pop Surveys

Paying for it

www.review.com

www.review.com

THE
PRINCETON
REVIEW

Getting in

Word du Jour

www.review.com

Find-O-Rama School & Career Search

www.review.com

Finding it

Best Schools

www.review.com

FIND US...

International

Hong Kong
4/F Sun Hung Kai Centre
30 Harbour Road, Wan Chai,
Hong Kong
Tel: (011)85-2-517-3016

Japan
Fuji Building 40, 15-14
Sakuragaokacho, Shibuya Ku,
Tokyo 150, Japan
Tel: (011)81-3-3463-1343

Korea
Tae Young Bldg, 944-24,
Daechi- Dong, Kangnam-Ku
The Princeton Review- ANC
Seoul, Korea 135-280,
South Korea
Tel: (011)82-2-554-7763

Mexico City
PR Mex S De RL De Cv
Guanajuato 228 Col. Roma
06700 Mexico D.F., Mexico
Tel: 525-564-9468

Montreal
666 Sherbrooke St.
West, Suite 202
Montreal, QC H3A 1E7 Canada
Tel: (514) 499-0870

Pakistan
1 Bawa Park - 90 Upper Mall
Lahore, Pakistan
Tel: (011)92-42-571-2315

Spain
Pza. Castilla, 3 - 5° A, 28046
Madrid, Spain
Tel: (011)341-323-4212

Taiwan
155 Chung Hsiao East Road
Section 4 - 4th Floor,
Taipei R.O.C., Taiwan
Tel: (011)886-2-751-1243

Thailand
Building One, 99 Wireless Road
Bangkok, Thailand 10330
Tel: (662) 256-7080

Toronto
1240 Bay Street, Suite 300
Toronto M5R 2A7 Canada
Tel: (800) 495-7737
Tel: (716) 839-4391

Vancouver
4212 University Way NE,
Suite 204
Seattle, WA 98105
Tel: (206) 548-1100

National (U.S.)
We have over 60 offices around the U.S. and
run courses in over 400 sites. For courses and locations
within the U.S. call 1 (800) 2/Review and you will be
routed to the nearest office.